OXFORD ENGLISH MONOGRAPHS

General Editors

Shakespeare's
Unreformed Fictions

GILLIAN WOODS

OXFORD
UNIVERSITY PRESS

OXFORD
UNIVERSITY PRESS

Great Clarendon Street, Oxford, OX2 6DP,
United Kingdom

Oxford University Press is a department of the University of Oxford.
It furthers the University's objective of excellence in research, scholarship,
and education by publishing worldwide. Oxford is a registered trade mark of
Oxford University Press in the UK and in certain other countries

First Edition published in 2013

Impression: 3

British Library Cataloguing in Publication Data

Data available

ISBN 978–0–19–967126–7

Printed in Great Britain by the
CPI Group (UK) Ltd, Croydon, CR0 4YY

For John

Contents

Acknowledgements

This book began as a DPhil thesis at Oxford University, where I was very fortunate in being supervised by Laurie Maguire. She remains a constant source of inspiration and this book owes much to her enthusiasm and commitment. Many thanks are likewise due to Emma Smith, who has read and reread drafts with her typical grace, humour, and erudition. I am also very grateful for the encouragement and constructive comments of my DPhil examiners, Alison Shell and Tiffany Stern, and I would like to thank Alison for sharing her pre-publication work on Shakespeare and religion with me. Henry Woudhuysen and Richard Proudfoot offered instructive comments on sections of the book in its earliest incarnations, and I remain indebted to them for their advice. Kate Rumbold has provided wisdom and raised morale at key moments.

This book would not have been possible without the doctoral funding provided by the Oxford English Faculty and the Arts and Humanities Research Council. I am grateful too for a scholarship from the Drapers Society and travel grants from Hertford College. Helen Barr, Anne Hudson, and Janie Steen provided invaluable help in starting the project. The book began its post-doctoral life at Wadham College, Oxford, where I worked as a Lecturer and then a Tutor and Junior Research Fellow. Thanks to my friends and colleagues in English, Ankhi Mukherjee and Bernard O'Donoghue, and to the Senior Tutors, Jane Garnett, Caroline Mawson, and Nicola Cooper-Harvey. This book was finished during my time as a Lecturer at the University of Sheffield, where I benefited enormously from the help of incredibly supportive colleagues. I would particularly like to thank those in the Renaissance team who talked through parts of the book at various 'Brown Bag' research lunches, including Nicky Hallett, Emma Rhatigan, and especially Marcus Nevitt and Cathy Shrank, who both reread material and offered helpful comments. Thanks also to Madeleine Callaghan, Ranjan Sen, and Carmen Szabo. My future colleagues at Birkbeck showed interest in the project when it was most needed, for which I am very grateful.

Various sections of this book have been presented at Oxford University, Cambridge University, the Shakespeare Institute, and a number of Shakespeare Association of America meetings. I am grateful to auditors and seminar participants for their interest and input. The superb librarians at the British Library, the Bodleian, the Oxford English Faculty Library, and Senate House made the research possible, and a pleasure.

Particular thanks also to Jacqueline Baker, Jenny Townshend, and the anonymous readers at OUP, whose enabling suggestions have vastly improved the book.

While my debts to others are many, the faults are all my own.

A shorter and earlier version of Chapter 2 appears under the title, 'Catholicism and Conversion in *Love's Labour's Lost*', in *How to Do Things with Shakespeare*, ed. Laurie Maguire (Oxford: Blackwell, 2008). I would like to thank the editor and the press for their permission to reproduce this material here.

Most importantly, thanks to my family for all their support and patience. My parents' belief and love have made everything possible. And John has done more than can be put into words.

List of Abbreviations

EEBO	*Early English Books Online*
ELH	*English Literary History*
ELN	*English Language Notes*
ELR	*English Literary Renaissance*
HLQ	*Huntington Library Quarterly*
MLQ	*Modern Language Quarterly*
PQ	*Philological Quarterly*
RES	*Review of English Studies*
SEL	*Studies in English Literature, 1500–1900*
SQ	*Shakespeare Quarterly*
SS	*Shakespeare Survey*
SSt	*Shakespeare Studies*
STC	*Short Title Catalogue*, ed. A. W. Pollard and G. R. Redgrave, 2nd edition, rev. W. A. Jackson, F. S. Ferguson, and Katharine F. Pantzer (London: Bibliographical Society, 1976)
TLS	*Times Literary Supplement*

Editions Used

In chapters 1 to 5, references in the text to the plays that are the subject of those chapters are to the following editions:

King Henry VI Part 1, ed. Edward Burns (London: Arden Shakespeare, 2000)

Love's Labour's Lost, ed. Henry Woudhuysen (London: Arden Shakespeare, 1998)

Measure for Measure, ed. N. W. Bawcutt (Oxford: Oxford University Press, 1998)

All's Well that Ends Well, ed. Susan Snyder (Oxford: Oxford University Press, 1993)

King Lear: A Parallel Text Edition, 2nd edn, ed. René Weis (Edinburgh: Pearson Education Ltd, 2010) (Quarto text unless otherwise stated)

The Winter's Tale, ed. Stephen Orgel (Oxford: Oxford University Press, 1996)

Unless otherwise stated, other references to Shakespeare are to *The Oxford Shakespeare: The Complete Works*, 2nd edn, ed. John Jowett, William Montgomery, Gary Taylor, and Stanley Wells (Oxford: Oxford University Press, 2005). References to the Bible are to the 1560 Geneva Bible.

Introduction

Catholicism had an imaginative hold on early modern drama long after the Reformation had outlawed its practice. Friars had been banned from England in the 1530s, but they continued to populate the nation's plays; the 'wandering of pilgrimages' had been dismissed as 'idolatry and superstition', but palmers trekked across the stage regardless; dramatic dialogue was suffused with idioms and metaphors from the old faith, no matter how abhorrent their theological meaning was to orthodox thought.[1] Shakespeare's drama especially is pervaded with traces of a culture that was theoretically past, but which remained troublingly present: the ghost of Hamlet's father complains of purgatorial pains; Romeo woos Juliet as a saintly statue able to grant prayers; Olivia grieves for her dead brother in a chantry; Prospero closes his play bargaining with pardons and indulgences. Residual Catholicism haunts different aspects of the dramaturgy: in the words the characters utter and the costumes they wear, in the traditional stories and real-life events that haunt the plays, and in the settings that situate the drama as fiction. This book explores the creative function of such unreformed content. It argues that, dislocated from their theological context, these contested signs have significant dramatic value, but that reading them requires an understanding of their multi-faceted nature.

An expression as familiar as 'by the mass' helps to pinpoint the conflicted connotations of 'Catholic' meaning. Referring to an outlawed sacrament, the expletive has an obvious Catholic heritage. In his epigram *'Against Swearing'*, John Harington mischievously records the loss of the idiom's theological impact as part of a broader spiritual catastrophe. The 'ancient custome' of swearing 'in weighty matters by the Masse' is lost 'when the Masse went downe', and is gradually replaced by less doctrinally controversial terms until:

---

[1] 'Announcing Injunctions for Religion' (1559), in *Tudor Royal Proclamations*, ed. Paul L. Hughes and James F. Larkin, 3 vols, ii (New Haven, CT: Yale University Press, 1964–9), pp. 117–32.

Last, hauing sworne away all faith and troth,
Only God dam'n them is their common oath.
Thus custome kept *decorum* by gradation,
That losing Masse, Crosse, Faith, they find damnation.[2]

The irony of the joke communicates nostalgia while refusing to take responsibility for it.

Other commentators offer clear-cut condemnation in sectarian terms. The puritan preacher Stephen Jerome itemizes: 'Superstitious Oathes, as by the Masse, Rood, Crosse, by our Lady, and by Popish Saints'.[3] For hotter Protestants swearing 'by the mass' was a form of the same dangerous sin that was inherent in the mass itself: idolatry. In the hugely popular and influential *The Plaine Mans Path-Way to Heauen*, Arthur Dent explains: 'it is an hainous thing to sweare by idoles: as S. *Mary*, our Ladie, by the Masse, by the Rood, &c.'[4] John Boys (the dean of Canterbury) spells out the structure of the sin: 'An oath is an inuocating of God: he therefore that sweares by the light, makes light his God: hee that sweares by the Masse, doth make that Idoll his God.'[5] Swearing by anything other than God turns that thing into an idol; swearing by the idolatrous mass is idolatry doubled. Likewise, William Vaughan reasons: 'When they sweare by senseles blocks & stocks, by the *Masse*, by *Gog* or *magog*, they detract from *Gods* honour, in attributing his due to dumbe and deafe Idols.'[6] The staunchly anti-Catholic Calvinist Andrew Willet is similarly emphatic: swearing by God's name in a lawful oath is 'a peculiar parte of Gods worship', but those that swear 'by creatures, by Saints, nay by Idols, as by the Masse, by the Roode, and such lyke ... doe giue the honor due vnto God vnto others, and so commit idolatrie'.[7] These condemnations carefully avoid attributing to the mass any sacred significance,

[2] John Harington, *The Most Elegant and Witty Epigrams* (London, 1618), sigs. [K5v–K6r]. Harington described himself in equivocal terms as a 'protesting Catholicke Puritan'; as cited in Jason Scott-Warren, 'Harington, Sir John (*bap.* 1560, *d.* 1612)', *Oxford Dictionary of National Biography* (Oxford: Oxford University Press, 2004), online edn, May 2010 <http://www.oxforddnb.com.eresources.shef.ac.uk/view/article/12326?docPos=4, accessed 24 August 2012>.
[3] Stephen Jerome, *Seauen Helpes to Heauen* (London, 1614), p. 434.
[4] Arthur Dent, *The Plaine Mans Path-way to Heauen* (London, 1607), p. 144. [First published 1601.]
[5] John Boys, *An Exposition of al the Principal Scriptures Vsed in our English Liturgie* (London, 1610), sig. N2r.
[6] William Vaughan, *The Arraignment of Slander Periury Blasphemy* (London, 1630), sig. R2v.
[7] Andrew Willet, *A Fruitfull and Godly Sermon ... Vpon the 5. Chapter of the Prophesie of Zacharie, 1, 2, 3, 4 Verses* (London, 1592), sig. [D4r–v].

while also warning against its continuing menace. The very lack of divine meaning in the mass makes it an inappropriate term to swear by, and thus this profanity is as dangerous as taking God's name in vain, if differently so.

These interpretations of 'by the mass' as idolatrous are hardly representative views of the early modern public; such sensitivity to the word 'mass' is not too distant from the caricatured precision of those who refer to the 'nativity' as a means of avoiding 'Christ*mas*'. Even so, as a profanity, 'by the mass' was strong enough to have fallen under the prohibitions against staged swearing stipulated by the 'Acte to restraine Abuses of Players'. The Act itself does not detail the old expression. It forbids: 'any Stage play Intrerlude Shewe Maygame or Pageant [to] jestingly or p[ro]phanely speake or use the holy Name of God or of Christ Jesus, or of the Holy Ghoste or of the Trinitie'.[8] Yet in practice 'by the mass' was interpreted as belonging to this proscription against blasphemy. The expurgated folio text of *2 Henry IV* alters the quarto's 'by the masse' to 'Looke, looke' (2.2.62) and 'By the mas' to 'Then' (2.4.17); similarly, the folio *Hamlet* removes the quarto's 'By the masse' (2.1.50).[9] Such alterations mark out 'by the mass' as a stronger profanity than words such as 'heaven', attesting to its enduring meaningfulness.

Nevertheless puritanical railing and the need to restrain such abuse indicates that many people saw no harm in it, or at least, not enough to prevent them from using the term. The Church of England clergyman Nicholas Byfield protested at the irony that 'many will not forsweare that will sweare at euery worde, at least by lesse oathes, as by the masse, faith, troth, truth, &c.'[10] By 1628, John Earle (who would later become the Bishop of Salisbury) describes both 'by the Masse' and 'by our Ladie' as 'olde out of date innocent othes'.[11] These Catholic expletives characterize the idiom of a 'Blunt Man': as a pre-Reformation profanity in a post-Reformation context, 'by the mass' has the connotation but not the actual meaning of blasphemy.[12]

But decades earlier, the notion that the antiquated quality of the oath made it innocent infuriated the moderate puritan William Perkins. In 1591 he bemoans as an example of the 'great ignorance' prevalent in

---

[8] 3 Jac. I, *c.* 21: 27 May 1606; as quoted by Gary Taylor, ''Swounds Revisited: Theatrical, Editorial, and Literary Expurgation', in *Shakespeare Reshaped, 1606–1623*, ed. Gary Taylor and John Jowett (Oxford: Clarendon Press, 1993), pp. 51–106 (p. 51).

[9] Taylor, pp. 69–70, p. 74.

[10] Nicholas Byfield, *An Exposition Vpon the Epistle to the Colossians* (London, 1615), p. 104.

[11] John Earle, *Micro-cosmographie* (London, 1628), sig. G3v.

[12] Earle, sig. G3r.

England the belief: 'That a man may sweare by the Masse, because it is nothing now: and byr Ladie, because she is gone out of the country.'[13] This misapprehension is listed among other '*common opinions*' that suggest shades of theological indifference and casual nostalgia for pre-Reformation times:

> 13 That it is the safest, to doo in Religion as most doo....
> 19 That it was a good world when the old Religion was, because all things were cheap....
> 24 That if a man remember to say his praiers in the morning (thogh he neuer vndersta[n]d them) he hath blessed himselfe for all the day following....
> 26 That a man eats his maker in the Sacra[ment].[14]

Here, swearing 'by the mass' is part of a behavioural pattern of religious passivity (points 13 and 24), cultural reminiscence (point 19), and outright theological confusion (point 26). Perkins' Protestant enthusiasm makes him particularly sensitive to imperfectly reformed attitudes; but his complaint usefully isolates the way in which an apparently Catholic word could and did function in an unreformed manner, without denoting straightforwardly Catholic theology. For some the Catholic status of the idiom made it safe, precisely because Catholicism had (in their eyes) lost its meaning. The expression 'by the mass' thus exhibits something of the conflicted nature of Catholic meaning in post-Reformation England: alternatively dangerous and benign, spiritually Catholic and sinfully papist, idolatrously damnable and nostalgically 'nothing'. Part of the imaginative appeal of Catholicism on the post-Reformation stage derives from this very sense of its being 'safely' antiquated rather than theologically relevant. Just as the swearer can sound provocative without really blaspheming, dramatists can play with aesthetics that lack real meaning. The desire of commentators such as Perkins to cancel out the linguistic traces of the nation's Catholic heritage is an implicit acknowledgment that this semantic currency (however downgraded) meant continued survival. There are different registers of Catholicism that speak to different (if sometimes overlapping) attitudes to the religion. Understanding unreformed fiction depends upon recognizing this multiplicity.

In recent years literary critics have become more fluent in the religious dialects of the post-Reformation period, and have come to realize that the centrality of religion to early modern experience cannot be ignored. Groundbreaking work by scholars such as Debora Shuger has caused us to acknowledge the religiosity of post-Reformation religion and revise

---

[13] William Perkins, *The Foundation of Christian Religion* ([London?], 1591), sig. A3r.
[14] Perkins, sigs. A2v–A3r.

fashionable 1980s assumptions that reformed religion was simply secularism by a more palatable name.[15] Our understanding of the complexity of denominational difference has also deepened. Interdisciplinary engagement with revisionist historians including Eamon Duffy, Christopher Haigh, Peter Lake, and Michael Questier has provided us with an invaluably nuanced vocabulary and framework for understanding what one critic neatly terms 'hybrid faith': belief and practice as 'variegated'.[16] Now that theological context looks different, complexities within literary content have become newly available, provoking a surge in theologically sensitive scholarship. Religion has reached beyond its traditional critical limits of passing references to overtly Christian genres (sermons, religious verse) and allegorizing Christian readings of secular texts.[17] Brian Cummings' superbly erudite *The Literary Culture of the Reformation* reveals the close relationship between religious thought and grammar of linguistic expression in the period.[18] Most significant for Catholic studies in particular has been Alison Shell's *Catholicism, Controversy and the English Literary Imagination, 1558–1660*, which opened a new critical paradigm by articulating and explaining the importance of attending to both Catholic and anti-Catholic epistemologies.[19] Drawing on ideas of otherness and gender, work by Arthur F. Marotti and Frances Dolan has also insightfully suggested ways in which Catholicism differentially (and problematically) defined English national identity.[20] The perceived place of

---

[15] See, for example, Debora Shuger, *Habits of Thought in the English Renaissance: Religion, Politics, and the Dominant Culture* (Berkeley, CA: University of California Press, 1990); and *The Renaissance Bible: Scholarship, Sacrifice and Subjectivity* (Berkeley, CA: University of California Press, 1994).

[16] Jean-Christophe Mayer, *Shakespeare's Hybrid Faith: History, Religion, and the Stage* (Basingstoke: Palgrave Macmillan, 2006); Peter Lake, 'Religious Identities in Shakespeare's England', in *A Companion to Shakespeare*, ed. David Scott Kastan (Oxford: Blackwell, 1999), pp. 57–84 (p. 79). Important revisionist history includes: Eamon Duffy, *The Stripping of the Altars: Traditional Religion in England, c.1400–c.1580* (New Haven, CT: Yale University Press, 1992); Christopher Haigh (ed.), *The English Reformation Revised* (Cambridge: Cambridge University Press, 1987); and Christopher Haigh, *English Reformations: Religion, Politics, and Society Under the Tudors* (Oxford: Clarendon Press, 1993).

[17] In *Sermons at Court: Politics and Religion in Elizabethan and Jacobean Preaching* (Cambridge: Cambridge University Press, 1998), Peter E. McCullough inaugurated a new genre of criticism which recognizes the theological, political, and literary importance of the sermon.

[18] Brian Cummings, *The Literary Culture of the Reformation: Grammar and Grace* (Oxford: Oxford University Press, 2002).

[19] Alison Shell, *Catholicism, Controversy and the English Literary Imagination, 1558–1660* (Cambridge: Cambridge University Press, 1999).

[20] Arthur F. Marotti, *Religious Ideology and Cultural Fantasy: Catholic and Anti-Catholic Discourses in Early Modern England* (Notre Dame, IN: University of Notre Dame Press, 2005); Frances Dolan, *Whores of Babylon: Catholicism, Gender, and Seventeenth-Century Print Culture* (Ithaca, NY: Cornell University Press, 1999).

Catholicism in the margins of early modern culture has re-positioned it in the central ground of modern scholarship (along with Moors, Jews, homosexuals, and women).

But the question of how fiction translates theology into literary forms still lingers, even as it has become more urgent. Despite the increasing popularity of studies into 'Shakespeare and religion', the methods used to investigate connections between theology and drama remain in their relatively early stages. Within Shakespeare studies revisionism has primarily generated work focused on the question 'Was Shakespeare a Catholic?'[21] Much of this scholarship is deeply sensitive to the confessional complexities of the age. Stephen Greenblatt and Gary Taylor have, for example, provocatively theorized about a Shakespeare who negotiated the epistemological difficulties of dealing with a familial and perhaps personal allegiance to the outlawed Roman faith.[22] These readings remind us of tensions inherent in religious experience in the period and make us aware of Shakespeare's exposure to Catholic ideas (through his school teachers Simon Hunt and John Cottom, and Catholic relatives on his mother's side).[23] This biographical work may help to explain why Shakespeare has a knowledge of and an interest in Catholic material. But arguments for Shakespeare's personal Catholicism are sometimes predicated on reductively circular

[21] This is an old question. Famously, Richard Davies, a seventeenth-century archdeacon of Lichfield, claimed Shakespeare 'died a papist'. More recently, critics have associated Shakespeare with the 'William Shakeshafte' mentioned in the 1581 will of the Catholic gentleman Alexander Hoghton. Following E. K. Chambers, Oliver Baker, and Peter Milward, E. A. J. Honigmann gave this idea its first book-length exploration, suggesting that Shakespeare may have spent time in Hoghton's recusant household in the predominantly Catholic county of Lancashire; *Shakespeare: The 'Lost Years'*, 2nd edn (Manchester: Manchester University Press, 1998).

[22] Stephen Greenblatt, *Will in the World: How Shakespeare became Shakespeare* (London: Jonathan Cape, 2004); Gary Taylor, 'Forms of Opposition: Shakespeare and Middleton', *ELR* 24 (1994), 283–314; and 'The Cultural Politics of Maybe', in *Theatre and Religion: Lancastrian Shakespeare*, ed. Richard Dutton, Alison Findlay, and Richard Wilson (Manchester: Manchester University Press, 2003), pp. 242–58. Other biographies that entertain the possibility of a Catholic Shakespeare include Anthony Holden's *William Shakespeare* (London: Abacus, 2000); Ian Wilson's *Shakespeare: The Evidence* (London: Headline, 1993); and Michael Wood's *In Search of Shakespeare* (London: BBC, 2003). Park Honan's *Shakespeare: A Life* (Oxford: Oxford University Press, 1998) is persuaded by, but does not fully endorse, the theory, pp. 60–71. For a summary of the biographical debates about Shakespeare's religion, see David Bevington, *Shakespeare and Biography* (Oxford: Oxford University Press, 2010), pp. 74–98.

[23] A common focus for discussion about the religion of Shakespeare's family, especially of his father, is the 'Spiritual Testament': a recusant document supposedly signed by John Shakespeare. This testament was found at the Shakespeare family house in Henley Street by builders. Edmund Malone published the testament but later denounced it as a forgery. See William Shakespeare, *The Plays and Poems*, ed. Edmund Malone, 10 vols (London, 1790), I, Part II, pp. 161–6; and Edmund Malone, *An Inquiry into the Authenticity of*

logic: a lack of evidence is translated as evidence (the prudent Catholic Shakespeare necessarily hides his faith; his silence signals his commitment);[24] alternatively (or in addition) read in a particular way, decontextualized aspects of Shakespeare's texts supposedly yield biographical information that simultaneously corroborates that Catholic literary analysis. I am more persuaded by James Shapiro's cogent description of early modern religious identity in terms of palimpsest. He rejects biographical attempts to give Shakespeare and his family a confessional label:

> To argue that the Shakespeares were secretly Catholic or, alternatively, mainstream Protestants, misses the point that except for a small minority at one doctrinal extreme or other, those labels failed to capture the layered nature of what Elizabethans, from the Queen down, actually believed. The whitewashed chapel walls, on which perhaps an image or two were still faintly visible, are as good an emblem of Shakespeare's faith as we are likely to find.[25]

Certain Miscellaneous Papers and Legal Instruments (London, 1796), pp. 195–204. This document retains its disputed status in the twenty-first century: it was disregarded by Alastair Fowler during the course of a highly critical review of Stephen Greenblatt's *Will in the World*, but subsequently defended as authentic in a letter by Richard Wilson. See Alastair Fowler, 'Enter Speed', *TLS*, 4 February 2005, pp. 3–5; and Richard Wilson, Letter, *TLS*, 18 February 2005, p. 17. Peter Davidson and Thomas McCoog also dismissed the idea of Shakespeare's involvement in a 'Jesuit plot', pointing out the significant difference between nostalgia for Catholicism and active militancy, as well as the lack of evidence for Jesuit distribution of the 'Testament'. But Peter Milward objected to the broadness of the dismissal. See Thomas McCoog and Peter Davidson, 'Unreconciled: What Evidence Links Shakespeare and the Jesuits?', *TLS*, 16 March 2007, p. 12, and Peter Milward, Letter, *TLS*, 28 March 2007. Robert Bearman shows the evidentiary problems with claims for the identity of 'Shakeshafte', the Testament, and John Shakespeare's recusancy; '"Was William Shakespeare William Shakeshafte?" Revisited', *SQ* 53.1 (2002), 83–94; 'John Shakespeare's "Spiritual Testament": A Reappraisal', *SSt* 56 (2003), 184–202; 'John Shakespeare: A Papist or Just Penniless?', *SQ* 56.4 (2005), 411–33. Similarly, Thomas M. McCoog and Peter Davidson scrutinize the historical evidence on which 'Catholic Shakespeare' readings are predicated and criticize the standards of related scholarship; 'Edmund Campion and William Shakespeare: *Much Ado About Nothing?*', in *The Reckoned Expense: Edmund Campion and the Early English Jesuits*, 2nd edn, ed. Thomas McCoog (Rome: Institutum Historicum Societatis Iesu, 2007), pp. 165–85.

[24] This 'false syllogism' is pointed out in Michael Davies, 'On this Side Bardolatry: The Canonisation of the Catholic Shakespeare', *Cahiers Elisabéthains* 58 (2000), 31–47. In *That Man Shakespeare* (Hastings: Helm Information, 2005), David Ellis outlines the methodology employed by biographers of Shakespeare, and the academically irresponsible masking of its limitations that is sometimes practised. He responds to Greenblatt's book specifically in 'Biographical Uncertainty and Shakespeare', *Essays in Criticism* 55 (2005), 193–208. However, in the earlier *Hamlet in Purgatory* (Princeton, NJ: Princeton University Press, 2001), Greenblatt's speculations generate a nuanced reading of the tragedy that shows the potential of tempered, biographically inflected criticism.

[25] James Shapiro, *1599: A Year in the Life of William Shakespeare* (London: Faber and Faber, 2005), p. 167. For a related reading of 'whitewash', see Juliet Fleming, 'Whitewash and the Scene of Writing', *SSt* 28 (2000), 133–8.

Of course, that certain critical readings are undermined by syllogism does not invalidate all biographical lines of inquiry: knowledge of an author's faith (as it changes through time) can enhance our understanding of his or her work. But it seems to me that in the absence of stronger external evidence this is not the most helpful goal of literary criticism. Shakespeare could be a crypto-Catholic or an unenthusiastic Catholic, a writer intrigued by the cultural implications of religious problems or a professional who understands the value of denominational equivocation, or any or none of these at any given moment. (Given the way Shakespeare often reminds us of anti-Catholic meanings as well as Catholic ones, he is certainly very sensitive to the negative perceptions of the religion.) Even in less turbulent times, religion operates as a framework, whereas faith is interstitial: religion stipulates a set of principles about belief and practice to which individuals adhere in individual ways. Even if a startling document could emerge that proved some form of Catholic belief on the part of Shakespeare, it would be useful for our understanding of the man, but it wouldn't 'solve' the drama, and nor should we wish it to. Biographical criticism problematically implies that Catholic content in the plays is only significant if Shakespeare was Catholic, when for heterogeneous early modern audiences Catholic resonance could never be neutral. If the goal of criticism is to tell us what Shakespeare believed, we risk skipping over the theatrical impact of the plays themselves. The ambiguity of Shakespeare's engagement with religion self-evidently cannot tell us anything certain about his faith, but analysing this ambiguity can help us better understand the drama.

A related but different branch of criticism finds in Shakespearean drama a definite Catholic meaning and agenda.[26] This scholarship has done invaluable work in exposing the quantity of Catholic images and idioms in the drama. But reviewers frequently articulate frustration with the methodological limits of such interpretations. Sectarian messages are read into words or images that have a Catholic resonance. Commentators note a narrowness of focus on theological possibility to the near exclusion of its complicating literary shape and situation, and an unwillingness to take account of ambiguity. For example, David Daniell protests: 'Too often, Shakespeare's strategies are identified as doctrinaire and Catholic

---

[26] See, for example, Peter Milward, *Shakespeare's Religious Background* (London: Sidgwick & Jackson, 1973); Richard Wilson, *Secret Shakespeare* (Manchester: Manchester University Press, 2004); Clare Asquith, *Shadowplay: The Hidden Beliefs and Coded Politics of William Shakespeare* (New York: PublicAffairs, 2005); David N. Beauregard, *Catholic Theology in Shakespeare's Plays* (Newark, DE: University of Delaware Press, 2008); John Waterfield, *The Heart of his Mystery: Shakespeare and the Catholic Faith in England Under Elizabeth and James* (Bloomington, IN: iUniverse, 2009).

when we can say only that their intention was dramatic'.[27] Hannibal Hamlin thinks that being fixedly 'intent on establishing Shakespeare's Catholicism' produces 'reductive, or forced' readings of the plays.[28] Even work that is less doctrinally categorical in its literary and biographical claims has been seen to elide the representational equivocality of Shakespeare's Catholic signs. Anthony Low qualifies his praise of Maurice Hunt's rigorous and informative reading of *Shakespeare's Religious Allusiveness*: the 'detailed discussion is sometimes uneven because of the occasional failure to allow that, although Shakespeare does indeed constantly play with religious terms and concepts, he usually does so analogically, with further complications of context and speaker.'[29] The broader dynamics of the drama is often under-explored when Catholic meaning is at stake.

In the face of an absence of obvious Catholic plots, other critics have pushed deeper, finding Catholic meaning encoded in Shakespeare's secular action. Anne Barton criticizes a 'preference [for] misty allegorical readings...supposedly communicating to the Catholic faithful among the theater audience a shadowy other drama (often embarrassingly at odds with the one more straightforwardly—not to mention interestingly— being acted on the stage).'[30] Dympna Callaghan is uneasy with the way 'some strains of recent work on religion...compartmentalize issues so that they cannot take, say, sexuality and religion in the same breath'. Thus 'the new and potentially momentous issues around Shakespeare's religion are in danger of being addressed as if the past twenty years of literary study never happened.'[31] Thus while these studies of Catholicism and Shakespeare have been crucially instrumental in drawing attention to the post-Reformation contexts of the drama, they threaten to keep Catholic scholarship disconnected from literary appreciation of the plays, effectively consolidating the very marginalization they seek to remedy.

One problem with identifying Shakespeare's works as 'Catholic' is that the label overlooks the secular content of the drama and the theological function of Catholic discourse in the era. Even if Shakespeare did nurture an inner Catholic faith, his plays do not manifest such a faith in the way

[27] David Daniell, Review of Velma B. Richmond, *Shakespeare, Catholicism, and Romance*, *Modern Language Review* 97.2 (2002), 387–8 (388).

[28] Hannibal Hamlin, Review of David Beauregard, *Catholic Theology in Shakespeare's Plays*, *SQ* 59.4 (2008), 506–8.

[29] Anthony Low, Review of Maurice Hunt, *Shakespeare's Religious Allusiveness*, *SQ* 57.3 (2006), 359–61 (360–1).

[30] Anne Barton, 'The One and Only', *New York Review of Books*, 11 May 2006.

[31] Dympna Callaghan, 'Shakespeare and Religion', *Textual Practice* 15.1 (2001), 1–4 (2).

that contemporary Catholics deemed imperative. Any critic seeking to claim a 'Catholic Shakespeare' needs at the very least to register the significant differences between the Shakespearean canon and the relatively large body of extant Catholic writings from the period. A brief survey of the numerousness and variety of early modern Catholic texts disabuses us of the notion that Shakespeare's ambiguous writing was the only available means of Catholic expression. Allison and Rogers record the publication of 932 Catholic texts in this period. The inclusion of works in Latin or European languages takes the total up to 1,619.[32] This level of production made Catholic printed works a significant—though illicit—presence in the post-Reformation book trade.[33] Ceri Sullivan calculates that Catholic secret press production accounted for a tenth as much as the legal market in devotional texts. In the midst of Shakespeare's career, the numbers of Catholic texts were growing: in the years 1593–1603 production almost doubled on the previous decade.[34] In their aims and forms these writings are distinct from secular drama. Certainly the prohibited production and circulation of Catholic materials created a very different experience for consumers of such texts than for the publicly performed and legally printed Shakespearean plays. A healthy black market in Catholic books took a variety of forms: texts might be smuggled in from Europe or printed in secret presses in England, and then delivered by itinerant priests as they journeyed between households, or sold by merchants in shops, or by private individuals in their homes, or even under the counter at the public bookshops in St Paul's churchyard in London.[35] And of course an individual item could find multiple 'readers': texts might be read aloud to groups of the faithful, and were also lent, copied, and bequeathed in wills. Not only printed works but also manuscripts carried Catholic writings across the country.[36] However, the risks of supplying and obtaining such

---

[32] Antony Allison and D. M. Rogers, *The Contemporary Printed Literature of the English Counter-Reformation Between 1558 and 1640*, 2 vols (Aldershot: Scolar Press, 1989–94). This statistic is also recorded in Patrick Collinson, Arnold Hunt, and Alexander Walsham, 'Religious Publishing in England 1557–1640', in *The Cambridge History of the Book in Britain*, vol. IV: *1557–1695*, ed. John Barnard and D. F. McKenzie (Cambridge: Cambridge University Press, 2002), pp. 29–66 (p. 46).

[33] T. A. Birrell, 'English Counter-Reformation Book Culture', *Recusant History* 22 (1994), 113–22.

[34] Ceri Sullivan, *Dismembered Rhetoric: English Recusant Writing, 1580–1603* (London: Associated University Presses, 1995), pp. 36, 29.

[35] Lisa McClain, *Lest We Be Damned: Practical Innovation and Lived Experience Among Catholics in Protestant England, 1559–1642* (New York: Routledge, 2004), p. 53. For details about the locations of presses, see Collinson, Hunt, and Walsham, p. 45.

[36] Nancy Pollard Brown, 'Paperchase: The Dissemination of Catholic Texts in Elizabethan England', in *English Manuscript Studies 1100–1700*, ed. Peter Beal and Jeremy Griffiths (Oxford: Blackwell, 1989), pp. 120–43; David Shorney, *Protestant Nonconformity*

material were real: William Carter was imprisoned and subsequently executed for printing Catholic writing that was deemed treasonous.[37]

Readings of 'hidden' or 'encoded' Catholicism in Shakespeare's works adapt as a metaphor the concealed condition of certain Catholic writings. It is a beguiling metaphor, but the differences between the modes of discourse need to be identified and analysed. Where the case for Shakespeare's encrypted Catholic meaning is unverifiable, other writings manifest clear signs of concealment. In order to pass by state censors and speak to those who wouldn't knowingly pick up a 'papist' book, some Catholic writers adopted rhetorical disguise such as a deceptively anti-Catholic title or preface.[38] More regularly, texts bore the strains of necessary concealment as they were printed with false publishing or authorial information. These practices required special papal dispensation since the Tridentine *Decretum de editione et usu sacrorum librorum* stipulated that books should identify their authors.[39] Necessary shifts were also made in manuscripts as well as print. In his *Autobiography* (*c.*1609–10), the Jesuit John Gerard carefully details the means by which he disseminated secret messages to other Catholics while imprisoned. Single letters bore double messages: a spiritual one written in charcoal that was legible to the authorities as well as to the recipient, and a private instruction written in orange juice in 'the white spaces between the lines', that was only visible once heat was applied (Gerard preferred orange juice to lemon juice because it remains visible after it cools, so the receiver could see if the secret had been violated). Anne M. Myers argues convincingly that because communication was vital to covert recusant communities, writing technique and form take on a meaning as important as the literal message of the texts being disseminated. She contends that 'Gerard's interest in the methods of circulation surpasses his interest in what is actually being circulated'. In introductory letters between the priest and new communicants 'information itself is less important than the personal connection forged by its exchange', and in the *Autobiography* he recounts more about

---

and Roman Catholicism: A Guide to Sources in the Public Record Office (London: PRO Publications, 1996). Gerard Kilroy has done excellent work discovering and transcribing Catholic manuscripts from the period, though his discussion of the 'interior writing' is unhelpfully partial; *Edmund Campion: Memory and Transcription* (Aldershot: Ashgate, 2005), p. 37.

[37] Robert S. Miola, *Early Modern Catholicism: An Anthology of Primary Sources* (Oxford: Oxford University Press, 2007), p. 35. I discuss this case further in Chapter 2.

[38] Alexandra Walsham, '"Domme Preachers"?: Post-Reformation Catholicism and the Culture of Print', *Past and Present* 168 (2000), 72–123 (92).

[39] Collinson, Hunt, and Walsham, p. 46; Walsham, 83.

his methods than the content of his communication.[40] The secret bond of communication itself is the Catholic meaning; it is this which both sustains and proves the vitality of the English Catholic community. We might also note that Gerard's secret message—the Catholic shibboleth— is *not* here the theological part of his missive. Catholicism is more and less than its spiritual heart. In the circumstances of post-Reformation England, Catholicism adapts to its illicit status, and makes meaning through (and not just in despite of) straitened conditions.

However, Gerard's 'orange-juice writing' does not adequately explain the mechanisms of all Catholic writing in the period, and still less the dynamics of Shakespeare's secular plays. The strength of Myers' reading of Gerard lies in its specificity: she draws on clear evidence of secret messages, and pushes beyond the novelty (for modern readers) of coded writing to analyse the significance of such a mode. But Gerard's literally interstitial writing is different even from the camouflage of printed works adopting anti-Catholic disguise: the absence of individualized address (found in Gerard's invisible ink) and the more direct duplicity of false information (as opposed to hidden information) mean these texts generate different reading experiences. For all such devices may have helped bond some readers in a sense of righteous persecution (like the Christians of ancient Rome), one wonders how far the moral pragmatism of the form undermined the absoluteness of the message for others. Much work remains to be done into the relation of form and message across the diversity of Catholic literature.

Furthermore, not all Catholic discourse of the period is structured by secrecy and fostered sectarian difference. Protestant readers turned to devotional texts written by Catholics since Reformed writers were slow to develop the genre. Famously, Robert Persons' *Christian Directorie* proved extremely popular with a non-Catholic readership. The text went through six editions issued from the Catholic secret press; in 1584 Edmund Bunny published a 'Protestant' version that maintained ninety per cent of the original, and which would be reprinted more than thirty times.[41] Thus while religious discourse of the period pulled in denominationally different directions, there was also a good deal of overlap that sees writers of different faiths borrowing from as well as reacting against one another.

---

[40] Anne M. Myers, 'Father John Gerard's Object Lessons: Relics and Devotional Objects in *Autobiography of a Hunted Priest*', in *Catholic Culture in Early Modern England*, ed. Ronald Corthell, Frances E. Dolan, Christopher Highley, and Arthur F. Marotti (Notre Dame, IN: University of Notre Dame Press, 2007), pp. 216–35 (pp. 223–4).

[41] Collinson, Hunt, and Walsham, p. 53; Miola, p. 28; Sullivan, p. 27; and Walsham, 105.

(Had Shakespeare been particularly committed to expressing his religious beliefs through his writings, there was a space for a pious but confessionally ambiguous voice.) Revisionist scholarship has exposed the reductiveness of a taxonomy that puts Catholicism in straightforward opposition to English Protestantism. The critical challenge of reading Catholic writing lies in needing to understand its distinctive features *and* its integration into English discourse.

Catholic texts themselves differ in content as well as form; Robert S. Miola's recent anthology *Early Modern Catholicism* illustrates creative diversity and ideological differences. Rather than being cut off from the literary innovations of the age, Catholic writers adapted secular genres for devotional ends: Robert Chambers turned to allegory in *Palestina* (1600); Richard Verstegan wrote *Odes in Imitation of the Seaven Penitential Psalmes* (1601); and poets such as Southwell, Alabaster, and Constable translated the literary conventions of amour into piety. Far from all of the texts published were 'devotional' in nature. Works such as catechisms, hagiographies, and meditations accounted for only a third of the publications produced by the British Catholic secret press between 1580 and 1603; the remaining majority of works were political, reflecting the need to keep pace with controversy.[42] In these works Catholics disputed not only with Protestant adversaries, but also amongst themselves on issues such as the imperatives of religious resistance, the nature of political allegiance, and the structure of ecclesiastical hierarchy.[43]

Nevertheless what connects all such texts (political and pious) as Catholic is a shared attention to matters of the faith and a determined effort to change the reader's mind or spirit in some way. The numerous students at the English College in Rome who cite recusant books as a prompt to conversion testify to the persuasive power of Catholic discourse to activate transformation.[44] Even from the 1580s, when textual efforts may have been less directed to proselytizing and more towards sustaining the

---

[42] Sullivan, p. 37.

[43] For discussion of these inter- and intra-confessional controversies, see Thomas H. Clancy, *Papist Pamphleteers: The Allen–Persons Party and the Political Thought of the Counter-Reformation in England, 1572–1615* (Chicago, IL: Loyola University Press, 1964); Peter Holmes, *Resistance and Compromise: The Political Thought of the Elizabethan Catholics* (Cambridge: Cambridge University Press, 1982); Peter Milward, *Religious Controversies of the Elizabethan Age: A Survey of Printed Sources* (London: Scolar Press, 1977); Peter Milward, *Religious Controversies of the Jacobean Age: A Survey of Printed Sources* (London: Scolar Press, 1978). Central texts in these disputes are available in *Recusancy and Conformity in Early Modern England: Manuscript and Printed Sources in Translation*, ed. Peter Holmes, Ginerva Crosignani, Thomas M. McCoog, and Michael Questier (Rome: Institutum Historicum Societatis Iesu, 2010).

[44] Sullivan, pp. 21–2; Walsham, 103.

Catholic faithful, the point was to enable the reader to do battle against sin and fight the inevitable corrosion of Protestant influences.[45] Books performed an active role in the varied and besieged Catholic community, doing the work of outlawed priests who could no longer easily reach their flock. Thus Father Luis de Granada explained that his *Memoriall of a Christian Life* 'may serve thee for a preacher, to exhort thee unto good life... for an confessionall, to instructe thee, how thou oughtest to confesse thy sinnes, and to make due preparation, when thou intendest to communicate.'[46] From 1585 either being or harbouring a priest was an act of treason, a crime punishable by death.[47] Catholics require regular access to priests (who minister the sacraments) in order to practise their religion. But, as John Wilson—the director of the Saint Omer Press—astutely pointed out in 1616, 'books penetrate where the priests and religious cannot enter'.[48] In substituting for a 'preacher', books performed a crucial didactic and spiritual function. Manuals, primers, psalters, missals, breviaries, and prayer books provided English Catholics with clerical instruction and a means of focusing their faithful practice. For example, readers who could not access the sacrament of penance with any predictability could train themselves to make a regular and rigorous examination of conscience. While some works unrealistically maintained the imperative of confession to a priest, meditating on the stages of the sacrament and following instructions for penitential behaviour provided readers with a virtual alternative to confession. Other writers were explicit about how readers might pragmatically access some of the benefits of the sacraments without actually receiving them. Thus where English Catholics may 'want opportunitie' to receive the Eucharist, William Stanney counselled that 'by making due examination of their consciences, with like preparation, and feruent desire, to receaue spiritually their sweete Sauiour, in the holy Sacrament of the Altar, doe in this Spiritual receauing, sometimes gaine almost as much merit, by their contrition and charitie, as if they had receaued corporally.'[49] In this way books were both an intellectual apparatus that kept English Catholics schooled in religious regulations, and also integral to the activity of lived faith. Books affected a spiritual transformation in

---

[45] Walsham, 97.

[46] Luis de Granada, *A Memoriall of a Christian Life*, trans. R. Hopkins (Rouen, 1586), p. 19; as quoted in Sullivan, p. 13.

[47] For further details, see Patrick McGrath and Joy Rowe, 'The Elizabethan Priests: Their Harbourers and Helpers', *Recusant History* 19 (1989), 209–33.

[48] *Calendar of State Papers, Milan*, I, 654; as quoted in Walsham, 102.

[49] William Stanney, *A Treatise of Penance* (Douai, 1617; facs. edn, Menston: Scolar Press, 1972), p. 298.

the reader who no longer had ready access to sacramental grace.[50] Along with political works, these texts aim to shape the Catholic subject, and have at their heart the central importance of the Catholic faith.

In producing romantic comedies, martial histories, and political tragedies about kingship, Shakespeare wrote drama that neither contemporary Catholics nor official Protestant censors recognized as Catholic.[51] Acknowledging this is not the same as declaring Shakespeare Protestant, lapsed Catholic, or agnostic; it is simply a statement of early modern genre. Critics who identify a Catholic Shakespeare often argue that the ambiguity of his writing is a defence against the penalties associated with confessional revelation. But even so, artistic choice underpins the secular subject matter (if not the denominational ambiguity) of Shakespeare's works. Alison Shell points out that

> Metrical biblical translation would have been an acceptable generic choice for both Catholic and Protestant at any time in Reformation England; and for most of the latter part of Shakespeare's career, religious verse of a more imaginative kind would also have spanned the denominations and been relatively unproblematic to write.[52]

Shakespeare did not take the generic opportunities available to him to fashion an explicitly religious voice.

One of the most important Catholic literary theorists of the age, the Jesuit poet Robert Southwell, directly criticized writers who did not use their gifts to praise God: 'Poetes by abusing their talent, and making the follies and feyninges of love the customary subject of theire base endeavors, have so discredited this facultye that a Poett a lover and a lyer, are by many reckened but three wordes of one significacon.'[53] Where Philip Sidney famously celebrated the 'golden' world of fiction as dealing in deeper truths, defending it from accusations of fraud ('the poet, he nothing affirms, and therefore never lieth'), Southwell sees secular subject

---

[50] For further discussion, see McClain, pp. 47–50; and Sullivan, pp. 14–25.

[51] For a rigorous and measured argument on this point, see Alison Shell, 'Why Didn't Shakespeare Write Religious Verse?', in *Shakespeare, Marlowe, Jonson: New Directions in Biography*, ed. Takashi Kozuka and J. R. Mulryne (Aldershot: Ashgate, 2006), pp. 85–112.

[52] Shell (2006), p. 102.

[53] Robert Southwell, '[Epistle]' from 'The Sequence of Poems from the "Waldegrave" Manuscript (Stonyhurst MS A.v.27)', in *Collected Poems*, ed. Peter Davidson and Anne Sweeney (Manchester: Fyfield Books, 2007), p. 1; also quoted in, Shell (1999), p. 67. For more on Southwell's proselytizing discourse, see Shell (1999), pp. 63–77; and Nancy Pollard Brown, 'Robert Southwell: The Mission of the Written Word', in *The Reckoned Expense: Edmund Campion and the Early English Jesuits*, 2nd edn, ed. Thomas McCoog (Rome: Institutum Historicum Societatis Iesu, 2007), pp. 193–213.

matter as precluding truth.[54] An irony here is that many anti-Catholic writers not only condemned Catholics as outright liars, but also associated them with the production of 'idle' fictions. Roger Ascham, condemning the illiterate ignorance of the pre-Reformation past, claimed that no religious books were read, but only outlandish romances 'made in Monasteries, by idle Monkes, or wanton Chanons'. Still worse, in the post-Reformation present, the infection of Catholicism was spread through fiction rather than doctrinal works:

> Mo[re] Papistes be made, by your mery bookes of *Italie*, than by your earnest bookes of *Louain*... when the busie and open Papistes abroad, could not, by their contentious bookes, turne men in England fast enough, from troth and right iudgement in doctrine, than the sutle and secrete Papistes at home, procured bawdie bookes to be translated out of the *Italian* tonge, whereby ouer many yong willes and wittes allured to wantonnes, do now boldly contemne all seuere bookes that sounde to honestie and godlines.[55]

This kind of accusation (however fictional itself) sees Catholicism as invested not only in theological deceit but also in the pretences of fiction, putting the two on a continuum. False Catholic doctrine is exchanged for frivolous fiction, as a more effective assault on the Protestant Word. In fact people like Southwell would have disapproved of 'bawdie bookes' just as much as Ascham, but the association of Catholicism with fiction on the one hand and the Catholic rejection of fictional subject matter on the other marks one of the many complexities of textual culture in the period. Catholic writers certainly did make use of imaginative motifs in texts they promoted as true. Alison Shell describes a 'self-conscious interplay of fact and fiction' being deployed as a means of negotiating the intellectual difficulties of telling improbable miracle stories.[56] The spiritual truth inherent in the sacred subject matter meant that fictional embellishment enhanced rather than impeded the message. But fiction lost its unambiguously Catholic value when it became an end in itself.

Hence the use of the word 'unreformed' rather than 'Catholic' in my title. I consciously use an unconventional word to signal that I am

---

[54] Philip Sidney, *The Defence of Poesy*, in *Sir Philip Sidney: The Major Works*, ed. Katherine Duncan-Jones (Oxford: Oxford University Press, 2008), p. 235. Alison Shell discusses possible Catholic critiques of Shakespeare's secular writing in *Shakespeare and Religion* (London: Arden Shakespeare, 2010), pp. 79–119.

[55] Roger Ascham, *The Scholemaster* (London, 1570), sigs. I.iiv–I.iiir.

[56] Alison Shell, 'Divine Muses, Catholic Poets and Pilgrims to St Winifred's Well: Literary Communities in Francis Chetwinde's "New Hellicon" (1642)', in *Writing and Religion in England, 1558–1689*, ed. Roger D. Sell and Anthony W. Johnson (Aldershot: Ashgate, 2009), pp. 273–88 (p. 283).

discussing ideas and themes in Shakespeare that are not straightforwardly Catholic in doctrinal terms. However, in identifying ambiguously Catholic material as 'unreformed', I am not endorsing a prejudicial perspective that celebrates the Protestant Reformation (in reality not the united movement that term implies) as a necessary correction of the old faith, and which ignores the reformations within the sixteenth-century Catholic Church.[57] Rather, the term serves a practical purpose. With its negative prefix, 'unreformed' points to the way the 'Catholic' material under discussion refuses the orthodox narratives of the state Church without actively promoting an alternative theological agenda. The content studied in this book has a distinctively Catholic resonance, but it does not necessarily convey theologically or politically Catholic meaning. This material is sometimes broadly cultural or aesthetic rather than exclusively religious. That is not to say that culture and theology did not overlap, but rather to acknowledge that while sermons, polemics, and plays may have influenced one another, they had fundamentally different purposes. I deliberately avoid categorizing Shakespeare's fiction as 'Catholic' because although such material is semantically pervasive (present in idioms, metaphors, and even costumes), it is peripheral in terms of plot and subject. Indeed it is part of the argument of this book that Shakespeare makes imaginative rather than confessional use of Catholic aesthetics in his drama. Unlike Catholic texts, which didactically school readers in the ways of the faith, Shakespeare's plays heuristically frame dilemmas for audiences. Shakespeare encourages us to think with and about the problems attendant on unreformed content, but he does not tell us what to think.

Nevertheless it is impossible (and undesirable) to avoid the use of the term 'Catholic' in such a discussion. But I use the term recognizing that 'Catholic' (like 'Protestant') represents a rather nebulous category. The very words we use to distinguish different denominational affiliation (often providing both too much and too little specificity) have a peculiar habit of switching sides. Thus while 'Catholic' usually refers to the unreformed Christian faith, it was also a label occasionally appropriated for official descriptions of the Church of England's presumed universality.[58] Qualifying with the term 'Roman' provides a helpful but not necessarily accurate distinction, since the subjects so designated might adhere to the

---

[57] Miola rejects even the term 'Reformation' as 'prejudicial'; pp. 4–9.

[58] For further discussion of this and other taxonomic quirks, see Thomas H. Clancy, 'Papist–Protestant–Puritan: English Religious Taxonomy 1565–1665', *Recusant History* 13 (1975–6), 227–53.

old faith in spiritual matters but patriotically reject the absolute authority of Rome: not every 'papist' supported the pope. This literally broad category 'Catholic' encompasses 'recusants' (those who made an outward sign of their Catholicism by refusing to attend the mandatory Church of England services) and 'church papists' (who attended services but secretly rejected the teachings of the state Church).[59] Yet the term 'recusant' was also used to refer to people who openly or privately disputed the practices of the Church of England for not being reformed enough.[60] While I do not want to overstate the practical ambivalence of such terms it is instructive to bear in mind the way this linguistic flexibility reflects the permanent flux of the broader theological and cultural situation. Catholics themselves disagreed on what constituted Catholic behaviour: Robert Persons insisted that Catholics could not attend mandatory Church of England services, since doing so was 'a signe now in England distinctiue, betwixt religion, and religion';[61] Alban Langdale argued to the contrary that 'this is made *signum distinctivum* between a true subject and a rebel, and, therefore, if the bare going be but in his own nature a thing indifferent, let every wise man weigh his own case'.[62] Throughout this book I make pragmatic use of convenient terms like 'Catholic' and 'Protestant', 'papist', and 'puritan', but this usage is meant to signal shared characteristics within given groups rather than homogenous identity.

---

[59] A changing understanding of the nature of early modern Catholicism can be gleaned from a survey of Catholic histories over the last fifty years: John Bossy, 'The Character of Elizabethan Catholicism', *Past and Present* 21 (1962), 39–59; John Bossy, *The English Catholic Community, 1570–1850* (London: Darton, Longman and Todd, 1975); Caroline M. Hibbard, 'Early Stuart Catholicism: Revisions and Re-revisions', *Journal of Modern History* 52 (1980), 1–34; J. J. Scarisbrick, *The Reformation and the English People* (Oxford: Blackwell, 1984); Anthony Milton, *Catholic and Reformed: The Roman and Protestant Churches in English Protestant Thought, 1600–1640* (Cambridge: Cambridge University Press, 1995); Thomas McCoog (ed.), *The Reckoned Expense: Edmund Campion and the Early English Jesuits: Essays in Celebration of the First Centenary of Campion Hall, Oxford (1896–1996)*, 2nd edn (Rome: Institutum Historicum Societatis Iesu, 2007); Robert Bireley, *The Refashioning of Catholicism, 1450–1700* (Washington, DC: The Catholic University of America Press, 1999); John Coffey, *Persecution and Toleration in Protestant England, 1558–1689* (Harlow: Longman, 2000); Ethan Shagan (ed.), *Catholics and the 'Protestant Nation': Religious Politics and Identity in Early Modern England* (Manchester: Manchester University Press, 2005); Michael C. Questier, *Catholicism and Community in Early Modern England: Politics, Aristocratic Patronage, and Religion, c.1550–1640* (Cambridge: Cambridge University Press, 2006).

[60] Alexandra Walsham, *Church Papists: Catholicism, Conformity and Confessional Polemic in Early Modern England* (Woodbridge: Boydell Press for the Royal Historical Society, 1993), pp. 1–21; Shell (1999), pp. 14–15; Lake (1999), pp. 71–2.

[61] [Robert Persons], *A Brief Discours Contayning Certayne Reasons Why Catholiques Refuse to goe to Church* (Douai, 1580), 15v.

[62] As reprinted in Miola, p. 74.

Catholic significance is particularly fluid in this period. The state religion had changed repeatedly between 1534 and 1559, but as Peter Lake stresses, even during a lengthy period of relative stability the official Church was somewhat hybridized: 'the religious scene of Elizabeth's reign is best seen as a number of attempts, conducted at very different levels of theoretical self-consciousness and coherence, at creative bricolage, mixing and matching, as a variety of cases or pitches were made for popular support.'[63] The Elizabethan Settlement patched a vernacular and scriptural religion with residual elements of the old faith (such as the use of the sign of the cross in baptism). Nevertheless, the 'Catholicism' that remained was very different from the medieval Catholicism that had been openly celebrated as the national religion. And the 'creative bricolage' was underpinned by a network of legal and polemical distinctions that aimed at dichotomy, rather than blurred differences. Regardless of the complexity of both the Settlement and of spiritual conscience, anti-Catholic laws and polemic re-coded previously sanctified signifiers to express sectarian divide.[64] Rather than reproducing such binaries ourselves by assuming that good Protestant subjects accepted them unquestioningly, it is helpful to note the cultural availability of sectarian ideas that were lent the weight of orthodoxy. The critical challenge this historical situation presents is the need to be sensitive both to fluid boundaries and binary distinctions.

However, the aims of this book are not primarily historical: it is not a cultural survey that uses literature to answer questions about history, nor is Shakespeare here being used as a pretext for the study of Catholic discourse (Shakespeare would be an anomalous starting point for such work); rather this is an irreducibly literary project that seeks to illuminate the drama of the plays through an awareness of the cultures of post-Reformation Catholicism. Its questions are not primarily biographical, historical, or theological, but rather creative: what is the imaginative function of the Catholicism in Shakespeare's drama? This perspective marks a deliberate attempt to refocus some of the debates that have surrounded the 'turn to religion' in recent years. In the magisterial *The Antichrist's Lewd Hat*, Peter Lake draws the final chapter on *Measure for Measure* to a close with a conclusion entitled 'The Historian's Excuse'.[65] In it he indicates that his

---

[63] Lake (1999), p. 79.

[64] Peter Lake, 'Anti-Popery: The Structure of a Prejudice', in *Conflict in Early Stuart England: Studies in Religion and Politics, 1603–1642*, ed. Richard Cust and Ann Hughes (London: Longman, 1989), pp. 72–106.

[65] Peter Lake with Michael Questier, *The Antichrist's Lewd Hat: Protestants, Papists and Players in Post-Reformation England* (New Haven, CT: Yale University Press, 2002), pp. 689–700.

analysis aims not to 'enhance anybody's aesthetic or literary appreciation of the play' and offers a compelling argument for the use of drama as a historical 'source', since fiction represents 'sites on which contemporaries could imagine, play with, act out and question the ideological and cultural contradictions and concerns of the day with rather greater freedom, or at least with less overt constraint, than they tended to show in other more "serious" or ostensibly "reality"-based genres'.[66] This statement sensitively identifies the political possibilities of fiction. And such work has unquestionably enriched our understanding of the contexts which dramatists both drew upon and shaped. But for interdisciplinarity to remain useful it is helpful to maintain some sense of distinction between disciplines. This book is by no means a territorial attempt to re-establish critical boundaries, but it does make an appeal for literary critics to cultivate our particular strengths, even as we explore other fields. Readings driven primarily by historicist motivations are less sensitive to the mechanisms of literary genres: just three pages after acknowledging that 'we are dealing here, after all, with a play, not a piece of polemic', Lake asserts 'it seems clear that whatever else the play is, it is a piece of anti-puritan satire or polemic'.[67] By returning to some of its aesthetic and formal principles, literary criticism might help rather than hinder interdisciplinary debate.

My methods and my motivations are primarily literary. I concentrate on what I term Shakespeare's 'fiction'. Obviously, this is a word which we tend to associate with prose narratives. But in its broadest sense 'fiction' usefully foregrounds the imaginative status of Shakespeare's works, which are primarily stories rather than polemics. The fact that the texts under consideration are theatrical is nevertheless crucial: this study analyses a range of dramaturgical features. However, I stress the fictitious quality of the drama partly because the double-edged meaning of the word 'fiction' foregrounds the moral anxieties attendant on literary allusion. In 1604 Robert Cawdrey defined 'fiction' as 'a lie, or tale fained', and in 1598 John Florio translates the Italian '*Fittione*' as 'a fiction, a dissembling, faining or inuention'.[68] Thus 'fiction' could mean something immorally deceitful or amorally entertaining. As we have already seen in relation to the Catholic Southwell and the Protestant Ascham, religious arguments sometimes collapsed these senses. But still more importantly, thinking about 'fiction' (as well as drama) is critically enabling, since the term highlights a funda-

---

[66] Lake (2002), pp. 689, 693.
[67] Lake (2002), pp. 696, 699.
[68] Robert Cawdrey, *A Table Alphabeticall* (London, 1604), sig. Ev; John Florio, *A Worlde of Wordes* (London, 1598), p. 133.

mental difference (sometimes overlooked in discussions about drama) between these creative works and theological or political writings. This book recognizes that transformations in meaning necessarily occur when religious content is placed in a fictional context. The word 'saint' registers differently in Catholic hagiography, puritan polemic, Church of England sermon, anti-Catholic propaganda, Petrarchan verse, and staged romantic comedy. Focusing exclusively on the Catholic theology behind such a term not only misrepresents the secular action of the drama, but also misses the point that the *Catholic* significance of such material is only properly understood once its ambiguity and fictional application is confronted. I seek to explore the ludic quality of Shakespeare's unreformed fiction, attending to the way word-play pitches multiple and even competing connotations rather than fixing doctrinal meanings. By interrogating the ways in which unreformed material operates in the context of a particular plot and genre, I aim to reconnect a historical understanding of post-Reformation culture to the aesthetic and theatrical experience of the plays.

The 'unreformed content' under investigation is purposefully eclectic: I explore, amongst other things, metaphors, allusions, bodies, character names, costumes, and icons. This diversity captures something of the variety of the unreformed forms that appear in Shakespeare's plays. Acknowledging this range gives a clearer sense of the complexity of Shakespeare's engagement with ideas of post-Reformation Catholicism. Furthermore, as we have already seen, attitudes to Catholicism in this period are fraught with complication: it represented a past domestic heritage and a present international threat; nostalgia for a Catholic 'merry' world coexisted with fear of papist corruption; Protestant writers adapted Catholic texts that were also banned and condemned. But this very messiness seems to have been a key part of Catholicism's imaginative appeal for Shakespeare, who makes dramatic use of the contradictions, not least as a means of exploring the boundaries between self and other.

Shakespeare wrote multivalent plays for heterogeneous audiences that would have included Catholics and Protestants of varying kinds (not to mention differing ages, rank, and gender). Thus, like the religious words already discussed, the uniform sounding 'audience' is potentially misleading. However, in using this necessary shorthand I am not claiming that Shakespeare's plays produced a unified audience response. People react differently to plays for a range of reasons. Nevertheless I aim to show how the drama speaks to a contemporary context that early modern audiences shared, albeit in different ways. Catholics would be aware of the anti-Catholic conventions of the period, in the same way that Protestants would have some knowledge of nostalgia, tolerance, or proselytizing arguments for Catholicism. In pointing out how Shakespeare manipulates such familiar ideas, I make no assumptions about the convictions of the individual audience members who watched them. Instead I am interested in showing how Shakespeare's scripts play with the orthodox and unorthodox theological narratives of his age.

Furthermore, in focusing on 'unreformed' material I am not implying that Shakespeare's plays do not engage with the various strands of Protestant thought. Recent work by Huston Diehl, Beatrice Groves, Jeffrey Knapp, and Adrian Streete, to name but a few, indicates how deeply the drama is influenced by Reformed theology and culture.[69] I concentrate on unreformed content because the fraught status of Catholicism gives it a particular connection with the pleasures and problems of fiction. Shakespeare's plays are particularly sensitive to the alternative ways in which Catholicism is implicated in different modes of fiction. Broadly speaking, two main trends can be observed when Catholicism appears on the post-Reformation stage: a nostalgic Catholic aesthetic announces itself as safely past when supernumerary friars and the occasional hermit situate plays in the realm of 'once upon a time'; while elsewhere politically and theologically engaged anti-papistry characterizes scheming Machiavels and identifies fiction as fraud. But where other dramatists polarize, Shakespeare is playful. His use of unreformed content is deeply syncretic: he puns on the multiple associations of Catholic aesthetics, and in so doing puts fiction in conversation with the real, and sets fraud against creativity. Shakespeare enlists the tensions inherent in unreformed content as part of a broader interrogation of the ethics of fiction. My eclectic approach takes its cues from the nature of Shakespeare's dramaturgy.

The on-going Reformation brought with it a representational crisis, as not just the meaning of signs, but also the way they signified, was put in question; for Shakespeare unreformed material often provides a means of examining the representational limits of his theatre. Each of the following chapters focuses on a particular representational problem, but takes a different generic perspective. Again, this diverse focus is part of a deliberate attempt to confront the range of unreformed fiction in the canon. Attending to the contingencies of different genres enables a detailed and

---

[69] Huston Diehl, *Staging Reform, Reforming the Stage: Protestantism and Popular Theater in Early Modern England* (Ithaca, NY: Cornell University Press, 1997); Beatrice Groves, *Texts and Traditions: Religion in Shakespeare, 1592–1604* (Oxford: Clarendon Press, 2007); Jeffrey Knapp, *Shakespeare's Tribe: Church, Nation, and Theater in Renaissance England* (Chicago, IL: University of Chicago Press, 2002); and Adrian Streete, *Protestantism and Drama in Early Modern England* (Cambridge: Cambridge University Press, 2009). Groves's work demonstrates that Shakespeare's drama is informed by both Catholic and Protestant traditions; Knapp suggests Shakespearean drama is underpinned by Erasmian inclusivity.

comparative investigation of the way religious words, images, and ideas are translated into fiction.

Chapter 1 asks how a history play remembers the pre-Reformation past. It focuses on *1 Henry VI*, a drama that interrogates its own historicity; its characters (like its dramatists) continually confront the problem of what's gone before. Remembering the past had become particularly problematic in the post-Reformation era, when the nation's stories about itself had to be retold in order to cope with the major redraft of the Reformation. *1 Henry VI* organizes the past in anachronistically denominational terms, but it simultaneously complicates this same epistemological order. Opposing the French 'papist' Joan la Pucelle with the English proto-Protestant Talbot, the play explores the phenomenological differences that emerge through sectarian division, differences that also problematize the mechanics of theatre. Most likely the product of authorial collaboration, this major Elizabethan hit thus raises representational problems that Shakespeare will continue to wrestle with throughout his career.

Moving from history to comedy, Chapter 2 considers how Catholic content functions in a less politically upfront genre. Focusing on *Love's Labour's Lost*, it questions why the male romantic leads should be oddly encumbered with real names, famous from the bloody sectarianism of the French wars of religion. Here we see the diversity of Shakespeare's 'Catholic' material, which is not only residual and rooted in a pre-Reformation past, but is also contemporary and political. The pun saturated drama explores the social implications of linguistic mutability, whereby the meaning of words seems endlessly adaptable. Converting the name of the famous apostate Henri of Navarre to a comic role that lacks historical specificity, Shakespeare puts this problem on a representational level, and connects it to the real-life problem of mutable meaning. The generic breakdown at the play's close, when the happy ending is postponed, implies that these tensions cannot be resolved and that in the final estimation they cannot be comedic.

Chapter 3 tackles 'problem' comedy to investigate how unreformed material does get resolved into the structurally happy (if tonally ambiguous) endings of *Measure for Measure* and *All's Well that Ends Well*. Although these plays lack real-life character names, they notoriously test comedic ideals against more grimly realistic pragmatism. Here the representational problem is one of visual seeming: the Catholic costumes of the pilgrim's, friar's, and nun's habits are at once highly legible and awkwardly polysemous. *Measure for Measure* plays with the conflicting connotations of religious habits, and in interrogating the relation between the inner self and the fashioned self, it goes on to debate the limits of selfhood and the nature of otherness. An open rejection of comedy's social and sexual values, Isabella's status as a novice nun helps Shakespeare to spot-light the ethical demands the genre and Christianity make on the self. By contrast, Helen readily adapts to the generic strictures of *All's Well*: the multiple associations of her pilgrim's garb give her a representational flex-ibility that both enables her to win a happy ending and also puts a ques-tion mark over it.

Chapter 4 assesses the denominationally charged question of selfhood and otherness from a tragic perspective. This chapter re-examines Shake-speare's use of Samuel Harsnett's *Declaration of Egregious Popish Impostures* in *King Lear*. Harsnett's polemical satire functions as a piece of genre criti-cism that redefines Catholic exorcisms as sometimes ironically tragic and more frequently bawdily comic; Shakespeare's tragic treatment of demo-niac material pointedly un-reforms Harsnett's taxonomies and rehabili-tates the affect of possession. The chapter looks closely at the language and behaviour of Edgar in his 'assumed' role as the possessed Poor Tom. This performance sees Edgar speak from multiple grammatical positions and in various phenomenological forms, thus taking on the representa-tional disorderliness exhibited by Joan la Pucelle and the flexibility used by Helen. Still more radically than in *Measure for Measure*, self and other are collapsed, as Edgar speaks as beggar, demon, and Catholic contro-versy. The tragedy's formal interest in the individual, all the more pro-nounced due to its hero's solipsism, again takes on an ethical dimension that explores relationships with others. With defiantly explicit references to performance and fairytale, Shakespeare reclaims fiction as an authentic space to establish such bonds.

But it is in *The Winter's Tale* that the boldest experiment with unre-formed content takes place. Chapter 5 explores the irrationality of a ro-mance that is bizarre in plot, geography, and chronology. In this play Shakespeare confronts the ideological awkwardness of fiction, drawing attention not only to the drama's fantastical status, but also associating it with papist 'superstition'. Where in earlier plays characters such as Joan and Helen were unable to sustain the representational agility of their un-reformed roles, Hermione's statue brings the past into the present and the 'deceased' back to life. Directly asking the audience to 'awake [their] faith', and associating reconciliation with a pointedly superstitious plot device, *The Winter's Tale* celebrates the ethical capacity of fiction to help audi-ences transcend the divisions between self and other.

1

Incorporating the Past in *1 Henry VI*

> How would it haue ioyed braue *Talbot* (the terror of the French) to thinke that after he had lyne two hundred yeares in his Tombe, hee should triumphe againe on the Stage, and haue his bones newe embalmed with the teares of ten thousand spectators at least, (at seuerall times) who in the Tragedian that represents his person, imagine they behold him fresh bleeding.[1]
>
> Henry is dead, and never shall revive[.] (*1 Henry VI* 1.1.18)

Remembrance in *1 Henry VI* (1592) takes the form of a desire for re-membering. Opening with the funeral of Henry V, the play's first scene centres on the presence of a body that now signifies absence. Bedford's mourning invocation to the 'ghost' of the dead king to 'Prosper this realm' (1.1.52–3) is interrupted with news 'Of loss, of slaughter and discomfiture' in France (1.1.59), immediately belying any notions of the practical vitality of the mythical 'scarce-cold conqueror | That ever-living man of memory' (4.3.50–1). Bedford fantasizes that the French losses 'Will make [Henry] burst his lead and rise from death' (1.1.64), only for his metaphor to be bathetically extended by Gloucester: 'If Henry were recalled to life again | These news would cause him once more yield the ghost' (1.1.66–7). But the discord of the nobles' uncomprehending hyperbole and unseemly recriminations emphasizes that Henry's death severs the present from previous glory. Bedford calls for 'Comets, importing change of times and states' (1.1.2) but is instead faced with information about the rapidly changing state of the times; the passing of Henry's body inaugurates a sense of the past. In this emphatically embodied history the sensations of physicality and of things passing are meaningfully connected. Where tragedies traditionally end with death, this chronicle play opens with history figured as corpse.

---

[1] Thomas Nashe, *Pierce Penilesse his Supplication to the Diuell* (London, 1592), sig. F3r.

1 Henry VI stages characters who are faced with the challenge of recognizing what has passed as the past.[2] The historical figures are thus shown as engaged in a process similar to that which concerns the writers of the history play. Of course, remembering the pre-Reformation past presents an ideological problem in post-Reformation England. How could the emergent Protestant nation state incorporate its Catholic heritage into its sense of self? How could the good repute of ancestors be reconciled with the newly recognized damnability of their faith? How might real historical and spiritual authority be differentiated from mere ritual and tradition? John Foxe, and others working to a similar apocalyptic script, made sense of God's plot by revealing Catholic history to be a corrupting innovation: reformation returned the church to its true heritage. Where necessary, historical figures were re-characterized according to anachronistic denominational categories. For example, King John, one-time resister of the pope and villain of medieval history, was redefined as a Proto-Protestant, a type of the later hero Henry VIII and his reformed resistance. *1 Henry VI* makes similar manoeuvres to impose interpretative organization on the history of the end of the Hundred Years' War. The English fight the French, and this fundamental national difference is extended and explicated through a related set of binaries: Proto-Protestant/Catholic, masculine/feminine, saint/demon, aristocratic/common, honour/pragmatism, romance/realism. Denominational difference is integral to the play's tone and elucidates the past and the present simultaneously: history is familiarized in contemporary terms, while current struggles are endowed with (fictional) historical depth. The assertion of anachronistic binaries thus ostensibly creates ideological order in the face of awkward historical difference.

However, the Reformation involved phenomenological as well as ideological change. With the denial of 'real' Eucharistic presence and of post-scriptural miracles Protestant theology severed physical connections between the divine and mortal realms. The physics of Catholic and Reformed faiths were, at key points, fundamentally different. *1 Henry VI* registers this disjunction dramaturgically in the staging of the opposing French and English figureheads, Joan la Pucelle and Talbot. In these two characters we encounter not only a familiar ideological polarity but also

---

[2] John W. Blanpied also recognizes that 'the past is peculiarly the subject of this play'; ' "Art and Baleful Sorcery": The Counterconsciousness of *Henry VI, Part 1*', *SEL* 15 (1975), 213–27 (213). Phyllis Rackin explores the play's different conceptions of history in gendered terms, in 'Anti-Historians: Women's Roles in Shakespeare's Histories', *Theatre Journal* 37 (1985), 329–44; and Brian Walsh explores the relationship between the play's self-conscious historicizing and its metatheatricality in, ' "Unkind Division": The Double Absence of Performing History in *1 Henry VI*', *SQ* 55 (2004), 119–47.

alternative representational and presentational modes that key into different understandings of presence (divine and mortal, spiritual and somatic,
performed and actual). This early history play takes us to the technical
crux of what is at stake in staging reformed and unreformed content. A
new critical commonplace teaches us that the abolition of purgatory, and
the prayers for the dead it had necessitated, made the act of remembrance
particularly problematic in post-Reformation England.[3] However, the
mechanics of staged remembrance also illuminate the interactions between theatre and theology, and the tensions of reformed memorial
(which is not to say that the drama preaches on these themes). The link
between theatrical re-membering and remembering is not merely linguistic, but is a functional fact of the dramatic medium. The status of the
body on stage is vexed by the iconoclastic pressures of reformation.
Michael O'Connell discerns an affective difference between pre- and
post-Reformation drama. In medieval Catholic theatre, the incarnational
mode of the art-form consolidates a play's theological significance: dramas
of Christ's suffering take their force from the palpable proximity between
God and man, actor and audience. But once reformed iconoclasm out-
laws such drama as blasphemous (emphasizing the uniqueness of Christ's
divinity rather than the affinity of his human physicality), early modern
theatre sheds this numinous functionality and (mostly) avoids biblical
plots.[4] O'Connell's narrative provides a useful general overview of theatrical transition. However, *1 Henry VI* stages reformed and unreformed representational phenomena within the bounds of the same story, flirting
with the pleasures and threats of recent unorthodoxy.

Thomas Nashe's frequently quoted celebration of *1 Henry VI* (assuming
that this play's Talbot—only extant here—is the one to whom Nashe
refers), participates in a similar rhetoric of moribund resuscitation to that
of the mourners in the first scene.[5] He argues that the subject of plays

> borrowed out of our English Chronicles, wherein our forefathers valiant acts
> (that haue line long buried in rustie brasse, and worme-eaten bookes) are
> reuiued, and they themselues raised from the Graue of Obliuion, and

[3] Famous critical examples include Stephen Greenblatt, *Hamlet in Purgatory* (Princeton, NJ: Princeton University Press, 2001); and Michael Neill, *Issues of Death: Mortality and Identity in English Renaissance Tragedy* (Oxford: Clarendon Press, 1997). For a different view, see Lorna Hutson, 'From Penitent to Suspect: Law, Purgatory, and Renaissance Drama', *HLQ* 65 (2002), 295–319.

[4] Michael O'Connell, *The Idolatrous Eye: Iconoclasm and Theater in Early-Modern England* (New York: Oxford University Press, 2000).

[5] It has been argued that Nashe himself wrote act 1. See Brian Vickers, 'Incomplete Shakespeare: or, Denying Coauthorship in *1 Henry VI*', *SQ* 58 (2007), 311–52.

brought to pleade their aged Honours in open presence: than which, what can be a sharper reproofe to these degenerate effeminate dayes of ours.⁶

Drama resurrects history from the sepulchral text: collapsing the substitutive process of representation, Nashe instead bears witness to a presentation of real agency ('they themselues raised…brought to pleade their aged Honours') in a tantalizingly immediate and embodied 'open presence'. Nashe claims that this dramatic revivification has exemplary value for its 'degenerate effeminate' audience; the characters come to recognize that such a process is only a fantasy, since they grieve the loss of a forefather who 'never shall revive' (1.1.18). But then the ambiguity of Nashe's description reflects the representational complexity of the dramaturgy. Talbot's reported 'triumphe' is predicated on the immediacy of a 'freshly bleeding' body, as if the warrior's presence is confirmed by the immanence of his absence. The exhumation is paradoxically in the service of re-interment: the action provokes tears that 'newe embalm' the 'bones' of the dead man. There is no shortage of other decaying, departing male bodies in this play: the first royal funeral is echoed by the corpses of Salisbury (2.2), Mortimer (2.5), and Bedford (3.2) being carried offstage (the last two having been brought on in a state of seated decrepitude), not to mention the extinction of Talbot's line as he and his son die in the same battle, doomed by the demands of patrilineal expression (4.4). Mortimer's wasted body blazons forth not only the decline of English chivalry but also the play's sense of a present tainted by a burgeoning past that is somehow pervasive and elusive:

> These eyes, like lamps whose wasting oil is spent,
> Wax dim, as drawing to their exigent;
> Weak shoulders, overborne with burdening grief,
> And pithless arms, like to a withered vine
> That droops his sapless branches to the ground.
> Yet are these feet, whose strengthless stay is numb,
> Unable to support this lump of clay,
> Swift-winged with desire to get a grave,
> As witting I no other comfort have. (2.5.8–16)

Loss is both recuperated and reaffirmed on the body. Drawing attention to the actor's body (as *1 Henry VI* does with explicit intensity) exposes the dramatic process itself, and blurs the boundaries between representation and presentation. After all, unlike the symbols employed by other art forms, the staged body is no mere arbitrary sign, and is closer to metonymy than metaphor. As Max Harris argues, 'the theatre is irredeemably

---

⁶ Nashe, sig. F3r.

fleshy, incapable of loosing its link entirely with the world of flesh and blood in which we live'.[7]

This chapter investigates the theologically charged significance of the insistently corporeal remembrance in *1 Henry VI*.[8] The retrospective narrative is dramatized through spectacular physical action. In addition to numerous decaying bodies, we witness a phenomenal amount of bodily combat (at least five 'skirmishes', four 'fights', one 'strikes', one 'beat out', and one 'beaten back', not to mention one 'rush', one 'shot', three 'retreats', two 'flights', one 'leap over', and no less than fourteen 'alarums'). Charles Edelman suggests that the violence is technically innovative, since this is the first play to involve principal characters in staged swordplay (compare, for example, the absence of onstage battles in the rhetorically visceral *Tamburlaine* plays).[9] Both the action of violence and the inaction of death advertise the presence of human bodies, offering a variety of instances that, to use Carol Rutter's term, 'interrupt intellect'.[10] Our awareness of the actors' bodiliness temporarily unfixes their representational status. Joan and Talbot, in significantly different ways, explicitly draw attention to their physicality and the division between representation and presentation that it troubles. And they do so at moments when the binary nature of their opposed characterization is particularly strong. The actor's body becomes a site where fantasies of essential difference are both inscribed and confounded; it is a site which manifests the ideologically fraught difficulties and possibilities of histrionic history.

---

[7] Max Harris, *Theatre and Incarnation* (London: Macmillan, 1990), p. 37.

[8] In the background of this discussion is the substantial collection of criticism on the early modern body, especially, Jonathan Sawday, *The Body Emblazoned: Dissection and the Human Body in Renaissance Culture* (London: Routledge, 1995); Keir Elam, '"In What Chapter of His Bosom?": Reading Shakespeare's Bodies', in *Alternative Shakespeares Vol. 2*, ed. Terence Hawkes (London: Routledge, 1996), pp.140–63; *The Body in Parts: Fantasies of Corporeality in Early Modern Europe*, ed. David Hillman and Carla Mazzio (New York: Routledge, 1997); Susanne Scholz, *Body Narratives: Writing the Nation and Fashioning the Subject* (Basingstoke: Palgrave Macmillan, 2000); Margaret E. Owens, *Stages of Dismemberment: The Fragmented Body in Late Medieval and Early Modern Drama* (Newark, DE: University of Delaware Press, 2005); and the articles in *Shakespeare Studies: Body Work*, ed. Bruce R. Smith (2001). For alternative readings of 'embodiment' in *1 Henry VI* that do not explore the theological shadows of the theme, see Lisa Dickson, 'No Rainbow Without the Sun: Visibility and Embodiment in *1 Henry VI*', *Modern Language Studies* 30 (2000), 137–56; and Michael Harrawood, 'High-Stomached Lords: Imagination, Force and the Body in Shakespeare's *Henry VI* Plays', *Journal for Early Modern Cultural Studies* 7 (2007), 78–95.

[9] Charles Edelman, *Brawl Ridiculous: Swordfighting in Shakespeare's Plays* (Manchester: Manchester University Press, 1992), p. 52.

[10] This phrase is used to describe moments when actors' bodies generated meanings that 'exceeded' the script; Carol Chillington Rutter, *Enter the Body: Women and Representation on Shakespeare's Stage* (London: Routledge, 2001), p. xii.

1 Henry VI 'incorporates' the past in various senses. As a history play rather than a history book, it enacts memory in flesh (and frequently draws attention to this process). Its narrative focuses on the problem of how to consolidate a nation that incorporates a factious France and a factional nobility. Taking Nashe at his word, at least a possible impact of the story, 'reuiued' in this way, is the wider incorporation of the viewing audience, recreated from present degeneracy into a body politic united across time. Such incorporation is enforced by the crude, even bigoted, oppositions that provide the thematic structure of the play, and operate according to a logic of 'us/them'. Joan's and Talbot's different ontological conditions as theatrical characters (presentational and representational) are bound up with their strategies for consolidating national success.[11]

JOAN'S INFUSED FLESH

The most problematic body in *1 Henry VI* is not the child king himself (absent from his own play until act 3), but Joan la Pucelle. Even her name is problematic. Arden 3 editor Edward Burns opts for Joan 'Puzel', a variant form of the name in the Folio text. The historical character who named herself 'Jeanne la Pucelle' took a title that meant both 'virginity and incipient sexuality'.[12] In English 'Pucelle' (much like 'nun') could also be used against its literal meaning as the insult 'whore'. Burns uses 'Puzel' as the early modern English phonetic translation of the term, arguing that its 'puzzling' connotations emphasize for modern readers the instability of name and character, also hinting at a pun on 'pizzle' (penis): 'The woman in man's clothes wielding a sword is a pucelle with a pizzle, and therefore a puzzle'.[13] Testifying to the disorder engendered by Joan, the general editors of the Arden series disagree with this decision, because 'it deprives the French characters of an intelligible French epithet for their saviour, Joan

---

[11] The play may also be the product of 'incorporate' (i.e. collaborative) authorship. See Vickers, and Gary Taylor, 'Shakespeare and Others: The Authorship of *Henry the Sixth, Part One*', *Medieval and Renaissance Drama in England* 7 (1995), 145–205. Recent editors of the play are divided on the issue of authorship. Michael Hattaway insists the play is the product of Shakespeare alone (Cambridge: Cambridge University Press, 1990), as does Michael Taylor (Oxford: Oxford University Press, 2003). Edward Burns cautions against the unreliability of scholarly methods of ascription (p. 82); however, he agrees 'It makes sense to me to see this play as a commissioned piece...written by a group of writers, among whom Shakespeare took a major part' (p. 83). I suggest that at this early point in his career, Shakespeare worked on a play that opened out the representational difficulties of religious content. Shakespeare returns to these difficulties later in the canon, and treats them idiosyncratically.

[12] Burns, p. 25.   [13] Burns, p. 26.

"the Maid"; and it further imposes on them the necessity of adopting a derogatory English alternative', since 'Puzel' is an insult.[14] While recognizing the puzzle usefully stressed by Burns, I regard its signification to be better marked through the ambiguity of 'Pucelle', and this is how I shall refer to Joan.

The larger critical puzzles of Joan la Pucelle are usually focused on her gender. Scholars have seen in Joan an expression of masculine anxiety that pinpoints 'threatening' aspects of femininity. Some time ago, David Bevington recognized that the play 'invented and greatly elaborated the theme of sexual domineering' from the historical sources.[15] Nina Levine reads Joan as the focal point for a topical tension: 'Serving up a pastiche of Elizabethan court "romance"' that 'lays bare the threat that female rule posed to relations of rank and gender within the patriarchal nation-state'.[16] Kathryn Schwarz defines a more expansive danger: 'Joan disrupts the rhetoric that connects men to men'.[17] Gender difference has also been recognized as explicitly troubling to the play's formal order. Detecting 'a pattern of masculine history-writing and feminine subversion' across Shakespeare's history plays, Phyllis Rackin finds its 'clearest' expression in *1 Henry VI*, so that Joan disrupts generic as well as social order.[18] Nevertheless, Nancy Gutierrez concludes that 'the moral worth assigned to "masculine" and "feminine" categories in the play is compromised...because the play depicts a grey, ironic world, in which such black and white categories are obvious and fragile fictions of a human mind attempting to find order and meaning.'[19] These accounts reasonably look upon gender difference as the thematic linchpin of the play. But the concerns expressed by the characters themselves stretch beyond the social essentials so usefully analysed in feminist criticism. Joan's 'threat' is spiritual as well as sexual; it has not just political but also divine implications. This is not to minimize the discomfort provoked by Joan's confusion of gender categories. Political, religious, and gendered orders are interrelated in the early

---

[14] Burns, pp. 294–5.

[15] David Bevington, 'The Domineering Female in *1 Henry VI*', *SSt* 2 (1966), 51–8 (51).

[16] Nina Levine, *Women's Matters: Politics, Gender, and Nation in Shakespeare's Early History Plays* (Newark, DE: University of Delaware Press, 1998), p. 35.

[17] Kathryn Schwarz, 'Fearful Simile: Stealing the Breech in Shakespeare's Chronicle Plays', *SQ* 49 (1998), 140–67 (147).

[18] Phyllis Rackin, 'Anti-Historians: Women's Roles in Shakespeare's Histories', *Theatre Journal* 37 (1985), 329–44 (330).

[19] Nancy A. Gutierrez, 'Gender and Value in "1 Henry VI"', *Theatre Journal* 42 (1990), 183–93 (193). I disagree with Gutierrez's earlier insistence that Joan 'has no power to influence the audience, because she is trapped in the paradigmatic configuration of the female/passive object of the male/active gaze' (192). I read Joan's role and relationship with the audience in more fluid terms.

modern period, when social and sexual hierarchies were thought to have been sanctioned by God. In specifically sectarian discourse, gender metaphors were used to explicate denominational difference as an unnatural corruption of God-given order. Thus at its most vitriolic extremes, Protestant polemic typed the Roman Church as the Whore of Babylon (Rev. 17:9), so that Catholic practice (aesthetically dazzling) was akin to a corrosive, sexual deception that feminized all who fell prone to its allure. Joan's 'negative' attributes—French, female, Papist, cunning, demonic—are part of a familiar semantic network.[20] Exploring the spiritual and theological aspects of Joan therefore complements and necessarily enlarges earlier gender-focused readings.

Joan's main antagonist, Talbot, first learns of her (from an *English* source) as 'A holy prophetess, new risen up' (1.4.101). This announcement is presaged not just by military '*alarum*', but also thunder and lightning that leaves Talbot asking: 'What tumult's in the heavens?' (1.4.97). The elemental rupture is felt at an epistemological level. After his first fight with Joan, Talbot exclaims: 'Heavens, can you suffer hell so to prevail?' (1.5.9). While these words clearly damn Joan as demonic, the question implies a deeper, contrary fear than the one that the hellish French might win: the French might not be so hellish after all. The adversarial dialogue of the French and the English elevates the significance of Joan's identification to a providential pitch. As an enemy and untowardly martial female, Joan's successes are only comprehensible to the English in demonic terms: 'Devil, or devil's dam...thou art a witch' (1.5.5–6); 'A witch' (1.5.21); 'that witch, that damned sorceress, | Hath wrought this hellish mischief unawares' (3.2.37–8); 'vile fiend and shameless courtesan' (3.2.44); 'Foul fiend of France and hag of all despite' (3.2.51); 'that railing Hecate' (3.2.63); 'ugly witch' (5.2.55); 'Fell banning hag, enchantress' (5.2.63); 'sorceress' (5.3.1); and Charles is therefore said to 'join with witches and the help of hell' (2.1.18) and 'converse with spirits' (2.1.25). This rhetorical reaction is not all that unusual in an age when socially 'wayward' women were often categorized as 'wyrd'. But Joan's own claims, and those of the French for whom she fights, widen the spiritual angle. Joan declares: 'Assigned am I to be the English scourge' (1.2.129) and the French promise to canonize her (1.5.68; 3.3.15) and meanwhile bless her

---

[20] For discussion of the gendered representation of the Catholic Church in early modern England, see Frances E. Dolan, *Whores of Babylon: Catholicism, Gender, and Seventeenth-Century Print Culture* (Ithaca, NY: Cornell University Press, 1999). Patrick Ryan applies the Protestant deployment of this biblical trope to *1 Henry VI* in 'Shakespeare's Joan and the Great Whore of Babylon', *Renaissance and Reformation* 28 (2004), 55–82. However, this reading is limited by its maintenance of binaries that the play itself undoes.

as a 'holy maid' (1.2.51) who is 'Ordained' (1.2.53), the 'Divinest creature' (1.5.43) and a 'glorious prophetess' (1.5.47).[21]

Joan's difference from the English is given a sectarian colour, since the
playwrights repeatedly cast her 'holiness' in Catholic terms. For example,
celebrating the rescue of Orleans, Charles declares that a pointedly Cath-
olic clergy, 'all the priests and friars in my realm | Shall in procession sing
[Joan's] endless praise' (1.5.58–9); and in encouraging Joan to 'turn' Burgundy to the French side, Alençon offers the bribe of monumental sanctity rejected by iconoclastic reformers: 'We'll set thy statue in some holy
place | And have thee reverenced like a blessed saint' (the casual 'some'
and analogizing 'like' perhaps implying the diminished spirituality
alleged by Protestants (3.3.14–15)). More importantly, Joan herself regards her mission and success as rooted in a holy visitation from the
Virgin Mary that, as we shall see, rests on decidedly unreformed epistemologies of the relationship between the human body and the divine. As
important as the social threats usually addressed by critics is the spiritual
controversy figured in Joan, particularly since the two are interconnected
in a play where enemies claim God's favour. Joan's opposition to English
chivalric, sexual, and theological values must necessarily be damnable,
otherwise English understanding of the divine order is perilously askew.
Talbot insists: 'God is our fortress' (2.1.26); should God seem contrarily
to prefer Joan, English taxonomies of righteousness would be shaken to
their faithful core.

But these declarations of divine significance are felt to be in excess of
the chaotic, repetitive story. Joan poses an 'either/or' interpretative polarity to the audience which validates one side only. But the reversibility of
binaries renders them unstable, an anxiety that seems to underpin Reigni-
er's response to the Bastard's contention that 'this Talbot be a fiend of
hell': 'If not of hell, the heavens sure favour him' (2.1.46–7). The limitations of mortal perception create a disturbing equivalence, and this is
sustained in the structure of the drama through the frequent 'switchback
reversals' that blur the distinction between the French and the English,
and between success and defeat.[22] If the characterization of Joan exposes

[21] For witchcraft in *1 Henry VI*, see Frances K. Barasch, 'Folk Magic in *Henry VI, Parts
1* and *2*: Two Scenes of Embedding', in *Henry VI: Critical Essays*, ed. Thomas A. Pendleton
(London: Routledge, 2001), pp. 113–25; Jean-Christophe Mayer, *Shakespeare's Hybrid
Faith: History, Religion, and the Stage* (Basingstoke: Palgrave Macmillan, 2006), pp. 14–
39; and Deborah Willis, 'Shakespeare and the English Witch-Hunts', in *Enclosure Acts*,
ed. John Michael Archer and Richard Burt (Ithaca, NY: Cornell University Press, 1994),
pp. 96–120.
[22] Roger Warren, ' "Contrarieties Agree": An Aspect of Dramatic Technique in "Henry
VI" ', *SS* 37 (1984), 75–83 (83).

the ideological fault-lines of the gender relations that help organize society, so too does it reveal post-Reformation tensions running through the understanding of both the microcosmic human body and God's macrocosmic universe.

Joan describes her prophetic and athletic powers as a gift bestowed on her during a heavenly visitation, so that her political cause, 'masculine' behaviour, and spiritual condition are coalescent. She speaks of a fundamentally physical experience:

> Heaven and Our Lady gracious hath it pleased
> To shine on my contemptible estate.
> Lo, whilst I waited on my tender lambs
> And to sun's parching heat displayed my cheeks,
> God's mother deigned to appear to me
> And, in a vision full of majesty,
> Willed me to leave my base vocation
> And free my country from calamity:
> Her aid she promised and assured success.
> In complete glory she revealed herself.
> And, whereas I was black and swart before,
> With those clear rays which she infused on me,
> That beauty am I blest with, which you may see. (1.2.74–86)

There is something curiously active in the description of Joan's exposure to the sun in the course of her shepherd's work ('I... displayed my cheeks'), as if the sacrificial showing of her humble skin is answered by Mary's manifestation ('In complete glory she revealed herself'). Joan's self-conscious physicality primarily sets up an evidentiary miracle. The environmental is merged with the divine: the 'shine' of 'Heaven and Our Lady gracious' and the 'clear rays' emitted by the 'glory' of 'God's mother' are on the same rhetorical and experiential continuum as 'the sun's parching heat', but miraculously rework its effects, so that Joan's 'black and swart' appearance is transformed to 'beauty'.[23] Joan's body is a manifest miracle.

In the post-Reformation period, to be miraculous was to be controversial. True miracles were understood by all Christians to be demonstrations of God's power. The 'seales and testimonials of Euangelicall Faith', miracles were a gift given to the apostles that 'increased the number of

---

[23] Joan's transfigured flesh alleges a divine extension of a less controversial humoural physiology, which understood the body as 'porous and thus able to be influenced by the immediate environment'; Gail Kern Paster, *The Body Embarrassed: Drama and the Disciplines of Shame in Early Modern England* (Ithaca, NY: Cornell University Press, 1993), p. 9.

the faithfull'.[24] But for reformers, that age had 'fully seast'.[25] Polemicists reviled Catholic claims of ongoing miracles as 'lothsome stuffe': the 'perfect' nature of reformed religion 'requireth no fabulous miracles to confirme it', but in the Catholic Church 'where vanitie is worke-mistris, then all thynges are confirmed with shadowes'.[26] Indeed miracles did continue to function discursively in Catholic literature: miracles were proselytizing phenomena unfettered by learned textuality, but nevertheless repeatable in proselytizing texts. According to the Catholic priest Robert Chambers, miracles even offered 'more euident proofes of a true religion the[n] eare the Scripture[s], especially consider[i]ng how Scriptures are so subiect to falce misconstruing, & deuil[i]sh bad interpretation'.[27] Rather optimistically, Chambers suggested that while 'the impugners of the Catholick Church' might draw all other Catholic arguments 'into their books, sermons, and disputations, at miracles al parties must make a stand, and be silent; there, God himself alone must speak, and shewe himself'.[28] In this view a miracle is a manifestation of God's Word, an axiomatic repudiation of wordy controversy: phenomenon as eloquence. Miracles were wrought by God 'for the producing and maintenance of vnitie in faith', a unification that divided correct and incorrect religions.[29] As another Catholic writer stipulated, 'onelie Gods religion can be confirmed with true miracles'.[30] The miraculous reports translated by Robert Chambers issue from Brabant, at a town on 'the frontiers of those that are enemyes & rebelles'.[31] Sectarian and political violence (as in *1 Henry VI*) give urgency to the evidentiary meaning of miracles as signs 'that God is wel pleased' with a particular group.[32] And indeed miracles operated as proof at the discursive 'frontiers' of Catholicism and Protestantism too, but what was proved varied according to the view from either side: either substantive, supernatural works communicating God's favour, or insubstantial tricks betraying Antichristian corruption. The miraculous work of Joan's flesh likewise divisively consolidates the

---

[24] Fernando Texeda, *Miracles Vnmasked* (London, 1625), sig. B2v.

[25] R. P., *The Iesuits Miracles* (London, 1607), sig. Cr.

[26] R. P., sig. Cr; Barnabe Rich, *The True Report of a Late Practise Enterprized by a Papist* (London, 1582), sig. E.iij.v.

[27] Philippe Numan, *Miracles Lately Wrought by the Intercession of the Glorious Virgin Marie*, trans. Robert Chambers (Antwerp, 1606; facs. edn, Menston: Scolar Press, 1975), sig. [B7v].

[28] Chambers (Dedication), sig. A4r.

[29] Chambers (trans.), sig. [B8v].

[30] Richard Smith, *The Prudentiall Ballance Of Religion* (n.p., 1609; facs. edn, Menston: Scolar Press, 1975), sig. [ā6r].

[31] Chambers (trans.), sig. G3r.

[32] Chambers (Dedication), sig. A4r.

French force against the English, drawing an epistemological boundary between the two sides.

The emphasis on the Virgin Mary's role in empowering Joan confirms the confessional alignment of the depiction. Responding to the intensity of Marian devotion, scandalized reformers said Catholics took 'the blessed Virgine, as they say, our Ladie' for 'the Sauiour of mankinde...as wee do Christ'.[33] Intercession to Mary was an idolatrous redundancy: God alone deserved and answered prayer. Protestant reverence for the Virgin had its proper place: 'We for our parts only, will euer call *blessed and happie, that blessed Virgin* who reigneth and euer shall reigne with her Sonne in euerlasting glory, not their *Loretto* or *Sichem* Ladies'.[34] The kind of visitation Joan describes was impossible to reformed theology and physics. In contrast, Catholicism celebrated an enduringly 'puissant' Mary, who was, after all, the very site and means of incarnation. Her repetition of God's first creating '*Fiat*' made 'farre greater & more important matters' than even the original, 'seeing that by means of this *Fiat*, the same God made him-self man, and man was made God'.[35] The Virgin's indubitable miraculous power was of a piece with a violent aggression against Satan that is surprising to modern sensibilities:

> Great is the force vndoubtedly of the mother of God; who not onely was, and is able to combate with the deuil, but to crush him, & domineere ouer him, as ouer a poor worme whose head is brused and squised to durt. Therfore it is no meruail if miracles are atchiued by her meanes, who was able to bring vnder her foot that feendish *Leuiathan*.[36]

In *1 Henry VI*, Joan's body bears contentious witness to Mary's forceful intervention into providential history (Joan is charged to 'free my country') and physical creation. Joan's description of having heavenly rays 'infused on' her fuses the physical and the metaphysical. As the grammar of the sentence suggests, infusing could be an act of pouring into or, as here, onto something. But the 'innerness' of the prefix is emphasized in the verb's figurative applications in early modern writing, where infusing frequently signals a spiritual rather than a physical change. The word often referred to God's imparting of grace. Thus Henoch Clapham pleaded: 'Heauenly Father, infuse thy sanctifying grace into the hartes of all thy

[33] Thomas Rogers, *An Historical Dialogue Touching Antichrist and Poperie* (London, 1589), sig. Cv.

[34] Richard Sheldon, *A Survey of the Miracles of the Church of Rome* (London, 1616), sig. D2v.

[35] Gaspare Loarte, *Instructions and Advertisements How to Meditate vpon the Misteries of the Rosarie of the most Holy Virgin Mary* (Rouen, 1613; facs. edn, Menston: Scolar Press, 1970), sig. B6v.

[36] Chambers (trans.), sig. C4r.

Children'; and Nicholas Breton prayed: 'Thou deepest Searcher of each secret thought, | Infuse in me thy all-affecting grace'.[37] In discussion of the Sacrament of the Lord's Supper, the word also occasionally differentiated between substantive and spiritual change. The Protestant convert Thomas Bell argued that, instead of Catholic transubstantiation: 'the alteration is vnspeakeable, when the diuine power of Christ doth infuse it selfe into the hearts of the faithful by the visible sacrament, as by his ordinarie organ and instrument, and then and there worketh the diuine effectes signified by the sacrament'; and the Warden of Winchester College, Thomas Bilson quoted Cyprian saying: '*and as in the person of Christ, his humanitie was seene, his diuinitie was hidde and secret: so in the visible sacrament the diuine essence doth infuse it selfe, after an vnspeakeable manner*'.[38] While such religious infusions are transformative, the change is spiritual and hidden rather than somatic and visible.

However, the infusion 'on' Joan's body is both an outward drenching that remakes her appearance (a fair complexion, golden hair?), and an inward spiritual possession that 'worketh the diuine effects'. David Bevington glosses this scene as a 'blasphemous type of incarnation', usefully hinting at the jointly physical and spiritual significance of what is said to have happened.[39] The nature of the 'blasphemy' is key to the threat (and possibility) represented in Joan. Essentially, Joan's very body re-members a Catholic conception of an ongoing physical connectedness between the heavenly and the mortal realm. As previously noted, Michael O'Connell has demonstrated the somatic preoccupations of medieval theatre, where an actor's dramatization of the suffering Christ before the sentient audience relates the mystery of the incarnation to the incarnational mode of theatre: 'God and man share a body'. Such drama flourished at a time when the evidence of stigmatics such as St Francis attested to the 'sense of the transformative character of the body and the phenomenal world'.[40] Catholics preserved this connection between the spiritual and the physical into the post-Reformation period. The numerous miracles that took place at the behest of the Virgin or of particular saints, at shrines or before holy images, usually took the form of the curing of disease or deformity. Such events were celebrated as awesome, but their multiplication emphasized the everyday possibility of divine intervention (in properly Catholic conditions): for example, a pamphlet outlining St Ignatius's intercessory

---

[37] Henoch Clapham, *A Tract of Prayer* (London, 1602), sig. Bv; Nicholas Breton, *The Passion of a Discontented Minde* (London, 1601), sig. [A2v].
[38] Thomas Bell, *The Suruey of Popery* (London, 1596), sig. Ii4r; Thomas Bilson, *The True Difference Betweene Christian Subiection and Vnchristian Rebellion* (Oxford, 1585), p. 811.
[39] Bevington, 52.   [40] O'Connell, pp. 88, 73.

care of his pilgrims details at least twenty-one cures in nineteen pages.[41] The physical action of these miracles was often carefully elaborated. Thus, while praying to St Ignatius a woman with a paralysed arm feels 'a great conuulsion of the bones and synewes, and presently after found her selfe well, and her arme perfectly recouered'.[42] A nun with a deformed leg that was six inches shorter than the other was healed at stages of Catholic ritual, 'feeling a marckable stretching and plucking within her hip, and throughout all her left leg' once she had made a pilgrimage, and then at the solemn mass said in thanksgiving 'her leg much me[n]ded, waxed greater, & increaced in strength: insomuch as the bunch before me[n] tio[n]ed became altogether eue[n] & equal, her leg turned right, & her heel stretched to the due proportion'.[43] These descriptions testify to a palpable involvement of the divine in the corporeal world. They are moments of intensified wonder in a faith that experiences Christ's physical presence at every Eucharist. Special individuals (often very lowly members of their society) were blessed with still more remarkable sensations of incarnate divinity. For example, a 'little hogardesse' called Agnes is visited by the Virgin Mary while tending animals (like Joan la Pucelle).[44] Joan's beautiful transformation puts her in a pious company of saintly figures who were not merely restored to regular physical health and appearance, but bore abnormal marks of sanctity, such as stigmatic wounds or transfigured brightness. (Joan's namesake, Joan of the Cross, was said to have shown physiological traces of visitations: 'her face was very bright...a sweet sauour proceeded from it...She was most beautifull and shining in these rapts'.)[45] In the Catholic faith the human body is a ready medium for spiritual communion, a communion that remakes created flesh in an assertion of presence.

But to reformers, tales of 'presence' betokened fraudulent emptiness. 'Unmasking' these miracles, Fernando Texeda reveals how the apparent stigmata of a female religious had been 'painted' on and her shining brightness achieved by setting burning coals before a mirror, causing 'beames' to 'reflect vpon her face'.[46] Numinous metamorphosis was in reality material manipulation. The miracles Protestants claimed in their own cause were momentous signs of providential favour or disfavour, not localized presence in holy places or transformations of individual human

---

[41] *S. Ignatius his Triumph*, printed with *The Theater of Iaponia's Constancy*, trans. William Lee ([St Omer, 1624]; facs. edn, Menston: Scolar Press, 1972).

[42] *S. Ignatius his Triumph*, sig. [D4r].

[43] Chambers (trans.), sigs. [O7r–O8r].

[44] Antonio Daza, *The Historie, Life and Miracles, Extasies and Revelations of the Blessed Virgin, Sister Ioane, of the Crosse*, trans. James Bell (St Omer, 1625), sigs. A2v–[A6v].

[45] Daza, sigs. [C6r–v].   [46] Texeda, sig. E2v.

forms. (One polemicist bragged that the preservation of Elizabeth and the exposure of Catholic treasons were miracles that 'doth farre surpasse, | Those idle tales that papists cast at vs'.)[47] The human body had a different significance—or at least a different potential—for Protestants and Catholics. Reformed (especially Calvinist) theology stressed the corrupted nature of fallen humanity, with the fleshly body the inevitable site of sin. Thus William Perkins described sin residing 'In euerie part both of bodie and soule, like as a Leprosie that runneth from the crowne of the head, to the sole of the foote', the dignity of the homonymic associations of 'crowne' and 'sole' here serving only to measure out the completeness of humanity's depravity.[48] Such attitudes did not constitute a complete moral rejection of God's physical creation. Linda Gregerson outlines reformed ambivalence: 'The self that properly sees the self as a sign reads in the self a double image: at once the likeness of God and the sin that has rendered that likeness obscure.'[49] Calvin regarded the human body as a work of divine art by which 'the maker of it may worthily be judged wonderfull'.[50] And the value of embodiment as the 'defining form of God's involvement in creation and in the ordering of human society' is, as Alison Jasper argues, attested by the enduring metaphor of the body of the Church.[51] Still more intensely physical metaphors to describe the purging effects of repentance—akin to the sick body taking medicine—were common to both Catholic and Protestant writings. Bodily sensations even remained a part of Christian worship. The affective physical re-enactment of Christ's passion in the mystery plays may have been rejected by the reformed church, but the ministry of the Word ideally provoked manifest *feeling* in the bodies of the congregation (an affect rather than a transfiguration).[52]

Nevertheless, denominational differences over the physicality of human and divine relations were significant, and were most fully evident in disputes over the Eucharist (as we shall see more fully in the next section). William Reynoldes' insistence that Christ '*truly conioyned* his body with

---

[47] R.P., sig. E3r.

[48] William Perkins, *The Foundation of Christian Religion* ([London?], 1591), sig. [A8r].

[49] Linda Gregerson, *The Reformation of the Subject* (Cambridge: Cambridge University Press, 1995), p. 66; as quoted by Adrian Streete, 'Reforming Signs: Semiotics, Calvinism and Clothing in Sixteenth-Century England', *Literature and History* 12 (2003), 1–18 (5).

[50] John Calvin, *Institutes of Christian Religion*, trans. Thomas Norton (London, 1562), 1.5.2; 2.6.1. For discussion of reformers' attitudes to the body, see David Tripp, 'The Image of the Body in the Formative Phases of the Protestant Reformation', in *Religion and the Body*, ed. Sarah Coakley (Cambridge: Cambridge University Press, 1997), pp. 131–52.

[51] Alison Jasper, 'Body and Word', in *The Oxford Handbook of English Literature and Theology*, ed. Andrew Hass, David Jasper, and Elisabeth Jay (Oxford: Oxford University Press, 2007), pp. 776–92 (p. 777).

[52] See Katharine A. Craik, *Reading Sensations in Early Modern England* (Basingstoke: Palgrave Macmillan, 2007), pp. 28–33.

the holy sacrament' so that to it one may 'looke for helpe to our body and sowle' was grotesquely literalistic to reformers, and diminished the true spiritual importance of the Lord's Supper with false physics and idolatrous celebration of mere matter.[53] Andrew Willet regarded Eucharistic belief as a distinguishing marker of confession, with faith in 'the diuelish canon of the Masse' the appropriately carnal heart of Catholic error: 'it is an epitome and abridgement of Papistrie, the marrow, sinewes, and bones of their idolatrous profession: yea the very darling of the popish Church: it is the very proper badge and marke of a papist'.[54] Thus, while the body remained a post-Reformation sign of God's creation and a useful rhetorical and practical vehicle for spiritual infusion, a tangible and transformative relationship had been broken.

This connection is, in both a disputative and restorative sense, reclaimed on Joan's body. Joan's success in the trial by combat against Charles and her sustained martial ability (until act 5) threaten to corroborate the claim that her physical agency was transformed by the glorious rays 'infused on' her body; her metamorphosed flesh (if accepted as such) marks a continuing real presence of the divine in the world. But her appearance is more immediately indicative. Holy 'rays' remake into 'beauty' what had once been 'black and swart' (1.2.84–6). This assertion of sanctified beauty is appended with a conditional sense of perspective: 'which you may see' (1.2.86). Even if we read 'may' at its most positively infinitive, Joan directs the eyes of the on- and off-stage audience to her body, demanding interpretation of whether or not it is legibly divine. We are asked to assess a claim of infused presence. At this moment the boy actor pushes the limits of representation. While one could easily imagine a Joan whose fraudulence is manifest in obviously dyed hair or a poorly fitting blonde wig, less pantomimic costuming (as encouraged by the ambiguity of Joan's characterization) would present a more engaging complexity. Awareness of the representational quality of (aspects of) the boy actor's feminine beauty bleeds into the possibly deceptive spiritual beauty of Joan: is the wig being worn by the character or the actor? English Chronicles disagreed on the issue of Joan's looks: Hall maintained that she had a 'foule face' whereas Holinshed's *Chronicles* recorded that 'Of favour she was counted likesome'.[55] *1 Henry VI* dramatizes both points of view, with the English damning Joan as 'ugly' (5.2.55) and the French burning with

---

[53] William Reynoldes, *A Treatise Conteyning the True Catholike and Apostolike Faith of the Holy Sacrifice and Sacrament Ordeyned by Christ at his last Supper* (Antwerp, [1593]), p. 168.

[54] Andrew Willet, *Synopsis Papismi* (London, 1592), p. 493.

[55] *Narrative and Dramatic Sources of Shakespeare*, ed. Geoffrey Bullough, 8 vols, iii (London: Routledge, 1964), p. 56, p. 75.

'desire' for her (1.2.108). Combined with the repetitive structure of the plot (that fails to confirm or deny Joan's status as 'the English scourge' (1.2.129)) this ambivalence leaves Joan's body open to the heuristic perspective of the audience.

The phenomenology of the theatre simultaneously upholds and refutes Joan's affirmations. The character is, after all, essentially theatrical; the art-form literalizes Protestant accusations of Catholic trickery. But, on the other hand, if Joan's character feels theatrical, why should we not, as is usual, look past the necessary representational fiction to recognize a represented truth? Joan's miraculous body raises an either/or dilemma, but produces an impact that oscillates between both.[56] It is up to the audience to determine representational value: is this an actor playing a deceptive 'actress of miracles',[57] or is this an actor playing a miraculous character? Where the 'truth' of some early modern characters seems to reside in their inaccessible interiority, Joan's truth is located in the histrionic surface of her flesh. An individual's response to Joan's (lack of) attraction complicates ideologically charged representational and presentational boundaries, boundaries that this character repeatedly challenges.

Richard F. Hardin argues that Joan 'inhabits a mimetic drama as a symbolic, mythic character, the sort who transcends mimesis'.[58] This thesis is useful to a point, though, as is true with virtually any label one tries to apply to Joan, 'symbol' and 'myth' refuse to stick. These terms are too abstract to capture the physicality of Joan's presence and too static for her fluid relationship with the audience. Joan straddles different representational modes, moving between history and the present, romance and realism, the worldly and the other-worldly, locus and platea, here and there. Characterized by the polarized views of those who confront her, she herself seems to occupy a conceptual space between, or perhaps beyond, these categories. She knowingly exploits her ambivalent potential with innuendos that playfully acknowledge the baffled male response to her female bellicosity, but somehow chastely translate it into linguistic power: 'And while I live I'll ne'er fly from a man' (1.2.103); 'Are ye so hot, sir?' (3.2.57). Unlike the cross-dressing heroines of Shakespeare's romantic comedies (or even the equally martial Britomart of Spenser's *Faerie Queene*), the armoured Joan does not adopt a male costume that

---

[56] Focusing on Joan's gendered significance, Schwarz similarly observes that her 'iconographic effect is a result of being at once neither and both' (149).

[57] This term is taken from Texeda, sig. E2r.

[58] Richard F. Hardin, 'Chronicles and Mythmaking in Shakespeare's Joan of Arc', *SS* 42 (1990), 25–35 (35).

protectively disguises her female body, but rather lays claim to an an-drogyny that asserts *both* masculinity and femininity.

Joan's body, then, is a site at which interpretative binaries are both es-tablished and deconstructed. The male characters pointedly find Joan be-wildering: 'A maid? And be so martial?' (2.1.21). (Compare the lack of concern in *Alphonsus, King of Aragon*, where the titular hero at first runs from battling Iphigina, specifically not because 'it be a shame | For knights to combat with the female sect', but because he has been 'benumbed' by love; he is quickly restored to violent capability when Iphigina refuses him: 'Alphonsus *and* Iphigina *fight*'.)[59] Furthermore, the storyline Joan brings with her seems to belong generically as much to romance as it does to history.[60] She is a peasant girl who passes various tests set by a royal male (her correct identification of the Dauphin and success in the trial by combat in 1.2), she adopts disguise, and is associated with magic.[61] Of course, magic, witchcraft, and demonology were not inevitably 'fantasti-cal', performing, as they sometimes did, an explicatory function in both early modern historiography and 'news' reportage. For example, the meta-phoric slips into the literal when the writer of one French news pamphlet expostulates at recalcitrant Parisians: 'Are you so depriued of common sence & all knowledge of God, that you cannot perceiue them to be wicked spirites among you, and angels of darknesse seducing you? spirites of warre and discord, leading you into the way of perdition'.[62] At this time, God's providential hold over history was still detected, even as Machiavellian man was recognized as plotting his own narrative. And Joan exists at the edge of the plausible, between the medieval and the modern. Her allusive papistry is over-determined, as she is both 'Catho-lic' in her older spiritualized physicality and in her newer scheming. The martial ability she first claims as miraculous is later realized in the form of the more artful sounding 'shift' (2.1.75) and 'policy' (3.2.2), which Charles nevertheless reads faithfully: 'Saint Denis bless this happy strata-gem' (3.2.17).

Joan's representational equivocality holds in tandem various ideologi-cal, phenomenological, and generic possibilities. Hardin's 'mythic' reading

[59] Robert Greene, *The Comicall Histoire of Alphonsus, King of Aragon* (London, 1599), sigs. Hr–v.

[60] Paul Dean, 'Shakespeare's *Henry VI* Trilogy and Elizabethan "Romance" Histories: The Origins of a Genre', *SQ* 33 (1982), 34–48.

[61] Joan also has a literary aspect: she is read as a parodic Tamburlaine figure in John D. Cox, 'Devils and Power in Marlowe and Shakespeare', *Yearbook of English Studies* 23 (1993), 46–64 (57); and David Riggs, *Shakespeare's Heroical Histories* (Cambridge, MA: Harvard University Press, 1971), pp. 22, 105.

[62] *The Discouerer of France to the Parisians, and all other the French Nation*, trans. E[dward] A[ggas] ([London], 1590), sig. [B3v].

is readily seen in Joan's claims about her 'ordained' role as 'scourge', but she also regularly punctures myth. We see this in her cynical debunking of English honour, as when she pragmatically refuses the chivalric call to 'come forth and meet us in the field' (3.2.60) after the English lose Rouen: 'Belike your lordship takes us then for fools, | To try if that our own be ours or no' (3.2.61–2); or when she derides Lucy's eulogistic twelve-line list of Talbot's titles with the brutally blunt: 'Here's a silly stately title indeed' (4.4.184). Joan pits herself against English values of old-fashioned prestige and patrilineage, her humour exposing the weakness of those ideals, even if it is a French mouth that does so. Joan is partly an uncomfortably attractive stage villain, a descendent of the medieval Vice. Except that unlike, for example, *Titus Andronicus*'s Aaron, she does not wear her villainy on her sleeve. And unlike Marlowe's Guise (another French figure who dispatches the audience's coreligionists in violence interlaced with jokes), she is not a two-faced Machiavel. Joan does not, like the Guise, whisper to the audience in the privacy of soliloquy that 'My policy hath fram'd religion', or that with 'aspiring wings' she aims at 'A royal seat, a sceptre, and a crown'.[63] Even when she conjures up the demons that would seem to contradict the heavenly motivation she has claimed, her desire is 'that France may get the field' (5.2.33), not personal glory. Her cunning is villainous in that it is practically and ideologically anti-English, but as a characteristic it reveals little about the make-up of her character (is she a knowing fraud whose divine pretensions are merely crafty pretence?—is her strategic skill divinely infused?—is she simply self-deluded?).

Joan's varying ideological tempos—mythic and mundane—see her stepping in and out of the representational world of the play. The process of winning Burgundy over to the French side is described in magical terms: Charles exhorts her to 'enchant him with thy words' (3.3.40) and Burgundy wonders if 'she hath bewitched me' (3.3.58).[64] Yet Joan also uses the more secular sounding 'secret policies' (3.3.12) referred to by the Bastard, and Burgundy muses alternatively whether patriotic 'nature makes me suddenly relent' (3.3.59). Female thaumaturgy had clear-cut narrative significance in earlier romantic histories: in *Orlando Furioso* Melissa charms the deranged Orlando with potion and wand, restoring him to his senses with visions; in *Alphonsus, King of Aragon* Medea's provision of dream visions contribute to both catastrophe and the final happy

---

[63] Christopher Marlowe, *The Massacre at Paris*, in *The Complete Plays and Poems*, ed. E. D. Pendry (London: Everyman, 1976), 2.65; 2.46; 2.105.

[64] Historically, the already captured Joan was not responsible for Burgundy's change of allegiance.

ending. Joan's 'enchantment' is not so unambiguously magic, but neither is it simply a secular rebranding of sorcery as statecraft, since she does not soliloquize a newly rational 'cunning' to us. Her manipulation ends on the incantatory plea: 'Come, come, return; return, thou wandering lord' (3.3.76). But her 'magic' rhetorically manipulates emotion and politics, so that after depicting a vulnerably embodied France (with its 'woeful breast' and bleeding 'bosom' (3.3.51, 54)) Joan then needles at Burgundy's jealousies (Henry will be 'lord' of France instead of him; the English have freed, without ransom, his 'foe' (3.3.66, 69)). At the climax of her success, Joan steps out of history, dramatic locus, and her national allegiance, mocking: 'Done like a Frenchman: turn and turn again' (3.3.85). The ability to 'descry' 'What's past and what's to come' (1.2.57) now extends from medieval providential history to the Machiavellian Elizabethan present: the aside seems to wink at what the English chose to view as Henri of Navarre's 'temporizing' switch from defender of the Protestant faith to Catholic convert (discussed further in Chapter 2).[65] Even if the specific topicality of this remark is uncertain, Joan here speaks out of her patriotic role to the English audience. Richard Hillman sees in this a similarity with Richard III, 'whose triumphant comments on his wooing speeches stake out a position beyond discourse itself'.[66] However, Joan is unlike Richard in her representational inconsistency: where Richard brags about his malevolent deception, Joan remains mystified. It is not so much that she does not wear a mask, as that there is nothing hidden beneath her masks. Like a clown, Joan peers through representation, momentarily dismantling illusion, while at the same time retaining the characteristic (i.e. representational) cynicism that she elsewhere directs less surprisingly at English nobles.[67] To laugh with Joan is to unsettle the neatly jingoistic English/French distinction between audience and character, even as it seems to be precisely her French slipperiness that is unsettling.[68] Instead of being granted epistemological purchase we are faced with epistemological collapse. And it is this instability that gives Joan, for a good proportion of the play at least, real theatrical presence. Joan is threatening

---

[65] See Richard Hillman, *Shakespeare, Marlowe and the Politics of France* (Basingstoke: Palgrave Macmillan, 2002), p. 131; Hillman points out that the 'widespread anticipation' of Navarre's conversion means that 'such a reference would not necessarily date the text at 1593 or later'; n. 25, p. 218.

[66] Hillman, p. 131.

[67] For a discussion of the way clowning takes place at the 'frontier of representation', see Robert Weimann and Douglas Bruster, *Shakespeare and the Power of Performance* (Cambridge: Cambridge University Press, 2008).

[68] Joan's echoes of Elizabeth (e.g. her androgyny, the epithet of 'Astraea's daughter' (1.5.43)) also problematize national distinctions. See Leah S. Marcus, *Puzzling Shakespeare* (Berkeley, CA: University of California Press, 1988), p. 88.

because she is equivocally beguiling, offering a physical incorporation of the human and the divine, and a presentational incorporation of the past with the present. Frequently referring to herself in the third person, the 'relentlessly self-referential' Joan gazes back at those who would try to contain her, but always displays herself to view.[69]

TALBOT'S SUBSTANCE

Of all the play's characters, Talbot is the most eager to destroy the danger inherent in Joan:

> My breast I'll burst with straining of my courage
> And from my shoulders crack my arms asunder,
> But I will chastise this high-minded strumpet. (1.5.10–12)

In his ready chivalric sacrifice Talbot defines himself against Joan to the point of self-destruction. As personal and thematic rivals they necessarily fight, but neither can seem to outlive the other (Joan's powers mysteriously dissipate after Talbot's death). The pair share dramatic significance: both command theatrical attention as protagonists, despite failing to make a lasting narrative impression on the *Henry VI* series. But Joan unfixes the values that constitute Talbot's identity. The English warrior reels in confusion once the scornful Joan has left the stage after their first fight: 'My thoughts are whirled like a potter's wheel, | I know not where I am nor what I do' (1.5.19–20). And indeed Joan presents not just an ideological challenge to Talbot, but a phenomenological alternative. The re-membering of the historical Talbot throws into relief the over-determined presence offered by Joan. Phyllis Rackin argues that Joan and Talbot embody and disembody the past differently: 'His language reifies glory, while hers is the language of physical objects; and the play defines their conflict as a contest between English words and French things, between the historical record that Talbot wishes to preserve and the physical reality that Joan invokes to discredit it.'[70] But the opposition is not only a gendered distinction between physical immediacy and historical referentiality; it is also a more radically spiritual difference of ontology. Joan draws attention to a *doubled* presence that incorporates the divine in her physical form (and challenges reformed 'reality'). Talbot is otherwise empowered.

---

[69] M. L. Stapleton, ' "Shine it like a Comet of Revenge": Seneca, John Studley, and Shakespeare's Joan la Pucelle', *Comparative Literature Studies* 31 (1994), 229–50 (244).
[70] Rackin, 331.

Talbot's understanding of his own substance is most famously articulated not in confrontation with Joan herself, but with a female character linked to her (through her gender, nationality, adversarial qualities, craft, and stress on physical presence).[71] When the Countess of Auvergne sues to receive and behold 'the man | Whose glory fills the world with loud report' (2.2.42–3), Burgundy jests:

> Nay, then I see our wars
> Will turn unto a peaceful comic sport,
> When ladies crave to be encountered with. (2.2.44–6)

The subsequent scene thus marks a generic (and gendered) interruption in the business of history. The 'stubbornly gratuitous' nature of 2.3, which refers to no historical 'source' and is of no narrative 'consequence', has been condemned as a 'pointless excrescence'.[72] However, it is this very supplementarity and disruption which constitutes the scene's meaning. The Countess tries to trap Talbot in a courtly love narrative.[73] Having long held Talbot's 'shadow' (his picture) in 'thrall' (2.3.35), she now plans to imprison his 'substance' (2.3.37): 'I will chain these legs and arms of thine' (2.3.38). Talbot outwits the Countess with a bizarrely militaristic lesson in neo-Platonism. Insisting that 'I am but shadow of myself: | You are deceived, my substance is not here' (2.3.49–50), he blows his horn, calling forth the soldiers he identifies as his 'substance, sinews, arms and strength' (2.3.62). Talbot's self-possession is thus markedly different from that of Joan, whose bodily presence and infused flesh testify to her uniquely 'ordained' role. By contrast, Talbot disembodies himself by means of a masculine blazon ('substance, sinews, arms and strength') that bespeaks not the partition normally fundamental to that form, but rather a fantasy of fraternal integrity. Orchestrating a dynamic spectacle (and thus outdoing the Countess's 'picture' (2.3.36)) he redirects the gaze from his own 'smallest part | And least proportion of humanity' (2.3.51–2) to his comitatus.

The opposition between 'shadow' and 'substance' was conventional enough in early modern dramatic literature. The Countess's distinction between *picture* (shadow) and *person* (substance) is common, as when in *The Two Gentlemen of Verona* Proteus begs Sylvia for her 'picture' (4.2.118): 'For since the substance of your perfect self | Is else devoted,

---

[71] Rackin, 332; Bevington, 51; Gabriele Bernhard Jackson, 'Topical Ideology: Witches, Amazons, and Shakespeare's Joan of Arc', *ELR* 18 (1988), 40–65 (48).

[72] Blanpied, 217, 218; M. Mincoff, 'The Composition of *Henry VI, Part I*', *SQ* 16 (1965), 279–87 (279).

[73] For the scene's affinity with the genre of romance, see Dean, 36.

I am but a shadow, | And to your shadow will I make true love'
(4.2.120–2). More generally, 'substance' referred to a reality only betokened by a potentially misleading shadowy sign. Hence in *The True
Tragedie of Richard the Third* the rumour that Buckingham is up in
arms to fight for the crown is dismissed as 'a shadow without a substance, and a feare without a cause'.[74] However, in its emphasis on
spatial paradox, the scene in *1 Henry VI* also alludes to the ongoing
Reformation dispute about Eucharistic substance and accident. The
baffled Countess emphasizes the oddity of Talbot's claim that 'my substance is not here' (2.3.50):

> This is a riddling merchant, for the nonce.
> He will be here, and yet he is not here:
> How can these contrarieties agree? (2.3.56–8)

Physical location was a major sticking point in the Eucharistic disagree-
ment between Calvinist Protestants (including Church of England members) and Catholics.[75] Clergyman Andrew Willet explained that one of
the 'difficulties or impossibilities, which doe hinder the reall presence of
Christs bodie in the Sacrament' is the mockery it makes of the laws of
physics: 'it would follow, that a natural bodie, such as Christs is, might
be in two places at once: for [Catholics] say, that it is in heauen, and in
the Eucharist all at once'.[76] Robert Bruce (a Church of Scotland minister)
insisted: 'All true humane bodie, is in a certaine place: Christ Iesus bodie
is a true humane bodie: therefore it is in a certaine place… quherever the
bodie be, of necessitie, it is limitat within that place, and quhill it is there,
it cannot be els quhere.'[77] Since Christ's body had ascended to heaven, it
could not be present simultaneously in the Eucharist on earth. The 'presence' of Christ in the reformed Sacrament of the Lord's Supper was not
'any natural or local presence, but a spiritual presence that conveyed the
"efficacy and power" of the body of Christ'.[78] However, Catholic belief in
the real presence of Christ in the Eucharist amounted to an ubiquitarian
acceptance that Christ's body could be in heaven and numerous Eucharis-

---

[74] *The True Tragedie of Richard the Third* (London, 1594), sig. Cv.
[75] Lutherans, however, rejected the Catholic theory of transubstantiation, but re-
tained Catholic belief in the 'real presence'; Jaroslav Pelikan, *The Christian Tradition: A
History of the Development of Doctrine*, 5 vols, iv (Chicago: University of Chicago Press,
1984), pp. 200–1. For a concise description of the various denominational strands that
made up the text of the Church of England's 'Black Rubric', see Tripp, p. 143.
[76] Willet, p. 452.
[77] Robert Bruce, *Sermons vpon the Sacrament of the Lords Supper* (Edinburgh, [1591]),
sig. 3r [n.b. the signatures are irregular in this text; the quotation appears in image 78 of
the EEBO facsimile].
[78] Pelikan, p. 201.

tic hosts at the same time. Indeed this was part of what made the sacrament so wonderful. The Jesuit poet Robert Southwell rhapsodizes:

> Whole may his body be in smallest breadd
> Whole in the whole, yea whole in every crumme…
> God present is at once in everye place
> Yett god in every place is ever one[.][79]

Repetition emphasizes the complete transformative communion of God in the physical world: an indivisible presence that is miraculously multiplied.

When the figure on stage announces that only 'Talbot's shadow' (2.3.45) is present, that 'my substance is not here' (2.3.50), on one level the actor speaks through the character, admitting to the lack of historical substance. Emrys Jones long ago pointed out in reference to this scene that 'shadow' was a familiar Elizabethan term for 'actor'.[80] The metatheatrical statement and the Eucharistic allusion work in tandem: the actor makes a declaration of representation, highlighting the absence of the 'real presence' of Talbot. In his account of 'the double absence of performing history' in *1 Henry VI*, Brian Walsh describes the operational similarity of drama and history: 'Conceptually, history and theater share a reliance on referring, and in each the referent is dubious and unstable'. Performance in the theatre is 'Ruled by a tense logic of substitution and replacement'.[81] Calvinist (as opposed to Catholic) understanding of the Eucharist also fits into this substitutive pattern. And the Eucharistic substitution marks, like history, a passage of time. The Protestant Sacrament of the Lord's Supper was a divinely instituted memorial ('do this in the reme[m]brance of me' Luke 22:19), not a repeated sacrifice like the Catholic Mass.

Clearly, the play does not encode a Eucharistic allegory, but understanding the sacramental debates about presence illuminates its representational attitude. Scene 2.3 is fundamentally about power. Talbot mocks the Countess's conviction that she could constrain his 'substance':

[79] Robert Southwell, 'Of the Blessed Sacrament of the Aulter', in *Collected Poems*, ed. Peter Davidson and Anne R. Sweeney (Manchester, Fyfield Books, 2007), pp. 23–5 (p. 25).

[80] Emrys Jones, *The Origins of Shakespeare* (Oxford: Clarendon Press, 1977), p. 146. Rackin reads gendered significance into the metatheatrical exposure: 'The masculine authority of history is thus sustained against the feminine challenge of physical presence as the play is revealed as a representation' (334). For a reading of the dramaturgical transition between Catholic mystery drama and early Protestant history plays as reflecting this sacramental shift, see Benjamin Griffin, 'The Birth of the History Play: Saint, Sacrifice and Reformation', *SEL* 39 (1999), 217–37.

[81] Walsh, 123.

> I tell you, madam, were the whole frame here,
> It is of such a spacious lofty pitch
> Your roof were not sufficient to contain't. (2.3.53–5)

Again, this chimes with an argument that saw confessants of different Eucharistic theologies accusing each other of diminishing Christ's omniscience. Catholics, such as William Reynoldes, made a case for Christ's ubiquitous capability, exhorting '*Bind not Christs body*'.[82] To claim that Christ could not be in heaven and in the host simultaneously was to delimit God's power. However, Protestants contrarily regarded the Catholic Mass as a ludicrous diminution: Robert Bruce was incredulous that anyone should believe Christ's body could be present 'in sa narrowe ane compas' as the communion bread.[83] Andrew Willet elaborated:

> Christ is almightie, and yet can doe nothing against his owne will, his word, or glorie: as to dishonor his glorious bodie, and to bring it within the compasse of a piece of bread, that it may be deuoured of cats, dogges, rats, mice, or which is worse, to be eaten of wicked men the members of the diuell.[84]

The proto-Protestant Talbot insists on the absence of substance that cannot be contained in the narrow confines of the French woman's house and literalistic imagination. For Willet, the Protestant representational alternative demonstrates 'not a wa[n]t of power, but a signe of greater power in God'.[85] Similarly, both Talbot-the-character and the actor-as-Talbot find their strength *through* a referential system: Talbot is not the mere 'weak and writhled shrimp' (2.3.22) the Countess perceives, but is metonymically enlarged as the greater comitatus myth of Talbot. (Early in the scene he implies absence constitutes more meaningful proof than mere presence, honourably departing at the Countess's incredulous insults about his disappointing physique: 'I go to certify her Talbot's here' (2.3.31).)

In drawing his band of soldiers to him, Talbot triumphs through incorporation: his men are incorporated under the unified idea of 'the Talbot', making up a corporeal force that proves Talbot's own 'incorporate' (i.e. without material substance) status. As the term 'communion' might suggest, both Catholic and Protestant Eucharistic practices were understood to unify faithful 'members' as one Christian 'body'. Similarly, the 'body' of Talbot's 'substance' depends on a community fostered by fraternal fidelity. Talbot's victory over the Countess is, in a proto-Protestant fashion, a successful assertion of faith in an absent substance. Ewan Fernie

---

[82] Reynoldes, sig. Y5v.   [83] Bruce, sig. 2v [EEBO, image 78].
[84] Willet, p. 453.   [85] Willet, p. 454.

briefly describes the 'spacious lofty pitch' (2.3.54) of this substance as Talbot's 'colossally elevated spiritual subjectivity', a new critical category of 'alternative identity'.[86] Talbot's enlarged identity, only metonymically located in the actor and even the character, operates as a Protestant ideal: essence exceeds the flesh and binds members of the national body to one another. As nationalistic as Talbot, Joan, on the other hand, asserts a unique presence: she is a chosen individual whose body is divinely em-powered 'to be the English scourge' (1.2.129) and is the sole force 'by whom the day is won' (1.5.56).[87] However, to argue that Talbot displays the triumph of 'the truest sort of masculinity—not man's body but his mind and soul—over the trammels of the flesh' is to elide the irony of Talbot's (temporary) victory.[88] Talbot's power may not be limited to his own fleshly presence, but it certainly depends on a show of physical force. The moment is one of pure theatrical spectacle: '*Winds his horn. Drums strike up. A peal of ordnance. Enter soldiers*' (2.3.59.1–2). It is this emphati-cally physical presence that confounds the Countess's tamer attempt to overwhelm. The soldiers do not refer to any specific historical event (the instance is not derived from a source) and they do not even speak; thus in spite of the representational properties insisted upon by the Talbot-actor, the drama is here also a presentational demonstration of athletic force. The dramatized history has been comedically interrupted by the Coun-tess, whose plot is metatheatrically interrupted by Talbot, with a disrup-tively visceral set piece. *1 Henry VI* realizes and dissolves binaries. Talbot proves his English, masculine superiority through a show of physical force that simultaneously manages to disclaim reliance on the body.[89] It is a feat that proves unsustainable.

---

[86] Ewan Fernie, 'Introduction', in *Spiritual Shakespeares*, ed. Ewan Fernie (London: Routledge: 2005), pp. 1–27 (p. 3).

[87] The dramaturgical difference between the characters may have been the product of (at least) two authors. But this does not make the characterological distinctions any less signifi-cant: the dramatists have responded tellingly to the challenges of depicting a French vision-ary and a medieval English noble.

[88] Bevington, 55.

[89] Theologians likewise failed to maintain rigid distinctions between representation and presentation. Pelikan explains that when Calvin and his followers: 'declared that there was a "true communication" of the body of Christ to believing communicants, this proved that they were not speaking only of "a bare and empty sign," and they were prepared to oppose any effort to reduce the Supper to this. The bread and wine were, rather, "visible signs, which represent the body and the blood to us and to which the name and title of the body and blood is attributed." Even "represent" was not an adequate term; it would be more accurate to say that they "present" the body and the blood' (p. 192). B. A. Gerrish also points out that Calvin himself is rather confusing in his use of the term 'substance', and seems to have altered his application of the term over time; *Grace and Gratitude: The Eu-charistic Theology of John Calvin* (Edinburgh: T&T Clark, 1993), pp. 178–9.

Absent substance is not very useful if it remains absent. Talbot is finally defeated not by the French but by the betrayal of the English, who leave him impossibly outnumbered in a brutal reversal of his minor triumph over the Countess. Lucy explicitly condemns Somerset and York, since their rivalry means aid has been withheld: 'The fraud of England, not the force of France, | Hath now entrapped the noble-minded Talbot' (4.3.89–90).[90] Talbot dies for want of physical presence, the bonds of faith that bind him to his national brothers having failed. The circumstances of his death fit into a pattern of breached faith throughout the play: for example, Sir John Fastolfe's selfish cowardice (1.1.131–4; 3.2.102–7); Burgundy's 'turn' to the French side (3.3); Henry's breaking of his engagement to the daughter of the Earl of Armagnac in favour of Margaret.[91] And the system of referentiality (through which his identity has such unified power) is elsewhere shown to have a divisive as much as a cohesive force in this play. Immediately after Talbot enforces the referential meaning of 'Talbot' over the immediate meaning of his body in the scene with the Countess, the Temple Garden scene stages the manufacture of referents of difference to enable and produce factional discord. Warwick announces himself able to judge between pairs of 'hawks', 'dogs', 'blades', 'horses', and 'girls', but unable to arbitrate between the (unspecified) 'quillets of the law' that puts Somerset and Richard (later York) in disagreement (2.4.11–17). Arbitrary signifiers of undetermined difference are used to galvanize division. Richard suggests: 'Since you are tongue-tied and so loath to speak, | In dumb significants proclaim your thoughts' (2.4.25–6), with his supporters picking white roses and those of Somerset red roses, sowing the seeds of civil war.

At his death, Talbot's incorporate subjectivity causes his utter extinction, when he dies alongside the son who would have referentially perpetuated the 'Talbot' identity. Dishonourable flight might save the life of the individuals named Talbot, but it would destroy the essential meaning of 'Talbot': 'Is my name Talbot? And am I your son? | And shall I fly?' (4.4.12–13). To be Talbot is to privilege a subjectivity that extends beyond one body: 'No more can I be severed from your side | Than can yourself yourself in twain divide' (4.4.48–9). Father and son sacrifice their bodies for an incorporate ideal that is lost because they so faithfully preserve it. And in death the limitations of Talbot's absent substance are

[90] Dominique Goy-Blanquet, *Shakespeare's Early History Plays* (Oxford: Oxford University Press, 2003), p. 38; Levine, p. 27; Riggs, p. 111.

[91] Jerome Mazzaro, 'Shakespeare's "Books of Memory": *1* and *2 Henry VI*', *Comparative Drama* 35 (2001–2), 393–414 (400–1); Faye L. Kelly, 'Oaths in Shakespeare's *Henry VI* Plays', *SQ* 24 (1973), 357–71 (362).

immediately apparent. As noted earlier, Joan swiftly deflates as 'a silly stately style' (4.4.184) Lucy's attempts to sustain the Talbot myth with the long list of his titles; Joan points out: 'Him that thou magnifiest with all these titles | Stinking and fly-blown lies here at our feet' (4.4.187–8). Talbot is finally *only* a putrid body. Lucy may claim that Talbot's ashes are regenerative, and will rear 'A phoenix that shall make all France afeared' (4.4.205), but this prophecy is not realized within the cycle, and Talbot himself is not mentioned in either the second or third parts of *Henry VI*, his military endeavours having made no lasting narrative impact on the plot of *Part 1*.

JOAN'S REFUSED FLESH

With the passing of Talbot, Joan's power seems weirdly to wane.[92] It is as if her role as individualized, physically immediate scourge is taken from her. Ironically, the English force temporarily reunifies itself without its incorporate hero:

> The English army, that divided was
> Into two parties, is now conjoined in one
> And means to give you battle presently. (5.2.11–13)

Joan's ambivalent characterization narrows in focus to something more demonic in this late scene: she appears onstage alone and desperately conjures up fiends that embody the hellishness that was previously a mere English insult. Frances K. Barasch claims that the physical appearance of the fiends '"argues proof" for the first time and forces the reader/viewer to readjust earlier receptions of Joan's character.'[93] But Michael Hattaway argues to the contrary that since the scene appears so late in the play, it 'cannot be taken as an unequivocal manifestation of the diabolic power of Joan. She turns to witchcraft only in despair, and there is no evidence earlier in the text to support the English view that her victories were won through supernatural agency.'[94] Indeed the ambivalence of the characterization still obtains. Joan's words certainly do create Barasch's air of 'proof': Joan explicitly calls not on God, or the Virgin Mary (the sources from whom she earlier claimed to derive her power), but on Satan's minions: 'speedy helpers, that are substitutes | Under the lordly monarch of the north' (5.2.26–7). Her remark at the entrance of the devils has the tone of rather clumsy exposition: 'This speedy and quick appearance argues

---

[92] Historically, Talbot actually died 20 years after Joan was executed.
[93] Barasch, p. 118.   [94] Hattaway, p. 24.

proof | Of your accustomed diligence to me' (5.2.29–30). She details a familiar (in both senses) acquaintance with the fiends whereby she 'was wont to feed you with my blood' (5.2.35) and now entreats the 'wonted [i.e. usual] furtherance' (5.2.42). The sound of '*Thunder*' (5.2.25) that accompanies her witchcraft echoes the earlier storm that introduced her to Talbot, perhaps confirming his diabolic interpretation of it. But Hattaway is right to maintain that the scene is far from unequivocal. These oddly taciturn demons are choreographed to emphasize not only their *lack* of intervention in Joan's plight, but also their refusal (or inability) to explicate the situation: '*They walk, and speak not*' (5.2.33.1), '*They hang their heads*' (5.2.38.1), '*They shake their heads*' (5.2.40.1), '*They depart*' (5.2.44). Demons offered spectacular theatrical capital, often appearing amidst a blaze of thunder, lightning, and fireworks.[95] In *1 Henry VI* the thunder promises the long awaited fiendish pay-off for the play's equivocal diabolical suggestiveness, only to stage devils who resolutely refuse to perform. The theatrical anticlimax short-circuits the potential ideological clarification. With a paradox typical of the characterization of Joan, a climactic scene feels marginal, and revelation remains occulted.[96] Joan's nature is apparently disambiguated without really being made any more legible. We are offered new 'insight' into Joan, not through a soliloquy in which she articulates her interiority, or even a confession of her deeds to other characters, but rather through a reappraisal of her body. Her once (possibly) divinely empowered flesh is now redefined as meat for demons: 'I'll lop a member off and give it you' (5.2.36), 'My body shall | Pay recompense' (5.2.39–40), 'Cannot my body nor blood sacrifice | Entreat you' (5.2.41–2), 'take my soul—my body, soul, and all' (5.2.43). Joan's fleshly presence, just like Talbot's spiritual substance, finally fails. Her assertion of transfigured beauty has degenerated into an offer of mutilation, and even that is refused. The appearance of demons does not discredit Joan as superstitious, or at least if it does, the audience, witnesses to demonic presence, are also implicated in the error. To stage demons but not demonic assistance is to keep the play located in the realm of phenomenological possibility, where contact between the mortal and immortal realms remains a possible uncertainty.

Once the demons leave the stage, Joan's defeat is sealed by her capture by York and the English forces. Yet Joan continues to elude epistemological confines. The accusations of witchcraft may now seem to carry more

[95] See Alexander Leggatt, *Jacobean Public Theatre* (London: Routledge, 1992), pp. 67–70.
[96] Cox writes that the devils appear only in 'the margins of *1 Henry VI*'; 61.

weight, but even at this point, Joan refuses the definition. She is, she claims:

> Virtuous and holy, chosen from above
> By inspiration of celestial grace
> To work exceeding miracles on earth.
> I never had to do with wicked spirits[.] (5.3.39–42)

Of course, such a declaration might seem risible in relation to the previous demonic scene, but inconsistency is Joan's abiding characteristic. At this point Joan rejects kinship with the Shepherd who claims to be her father: 'Not me begotten of a shepherd swain' (5.3.37). Yet when she had first appeared she spoke of a pastoral heritage that lent an almost biblical resonance to her miraculous tale: 'I am by birth a shepherd's daughter' (1.2.72).[97] From one point of view, Joan is here a fraudulent villain, but her vehemence lacks the knowing irony that usually enriches such characterizations.[98] Instead, her warning that her 'maiden-blood, thus rigorously effused, | Will cry for vengeance at the gates of heaven' (5.3.52–3), in the context of the jeering brutality of her English captors has a ring of integrity. Yet there is no sense that her body hosts a subjective continuity.

Joan's physical claims are now more mundanely mortal: the indwelling presence she speaks of is not of being with God but 'with child' (5.3.62). Her frantic suggestions of various fathers (''Twas neither Charles, nor yet the Duke I named, | But Reignier, King of Naples, that prevailed' (5.3.77–8)) have been read alternatively as an admission of the promiscuity the English have long accused her of, or as the despairing lies of a terrified woman trying to avoid death. Revelation or mere desperation, the change of claims from a divinely porous body to one which is whorishly open has an anti-Catholic predictability. York's taunt articulates this: 'Now heaven forfend, the holy maid with child?' (5.3.65). The numinous possibility of Joan's paradoxical nature is rationally exposed as impossibility; her affinity with the Virgin Mary is a conventional joke that denigrates chastity as hypocritical lechery. Within the represented world this is the interpretation that finally has practical force: Joan's troublesome body is to be burnt away, her slipperiness purged from the history cycle. However, given the cruel eagerness with which these nobles are (unhistorically) willing to kill

---

[97] Such discrepancy is possibly the product of joint authorship, though we should not assume that collaboration inevitably generated incoherence, well-rehearsed in the practice as dramatists were. In any case, potentially unintentional inconsistencies appropriately accentuate a thoroughly (and deliberately) paradoxical characterization.

[98] The rejection of a father also extends the thematic opposition with Talbot, whose patriarchal identity had proved tragically fatal.

a pregnant woman, this purge does not purify.[99] And while Joan's claims to divine ontology have been overwritten by the demonic interlude, the representational difficulties that her inconsistency raises are not put in order. She is dragged off cursing, defeated but not resolved.

INCORPORATE PEACE?

Even before Joan has been removed from the play (perhaps underscoring the imbalance between her dramatic and narrative importance), the wheels are in motion to secure a 'knot of amity' (5.1.16) between the English and the French. Henry readily accedes to this vision of incorporate peace recommended by the pope, emperor, and Earl of Armagnac. Ironically eliding the anachronistic differences established by the play, the naive King laments:

> I always thought
> It was both impious and unnatural
> That such immanity and bloody strife
> Should reign among professors of one faith. (5.1.11–14)

Similar pity was also felt in sectarian 'Christendom'. Sealing up a peace between England and France, the conclusion superficially reconciles difference. With both Joan and Talbot erased from the historical script that carries forth to *2* and *3 Henry VI*, it is almost as if the play's differences finally do not matter. But then, just as neither character could secure a fully (re)presentational role, the play more generally reveals binaries to be unsustainable. The interpretative order offered by the association of the play's French fighters with papistry and English nobles with reformed rationality is disrupted by the anachronism of the distinction. The English may offer no intercessory prayers and Talbot may favour Old Testament allusions over stories of extra-scriptural visits from the Virgin Mary, but the historical Catholicism of medieval England leaks out. Sectarianism animates the language of attack, and so just as anti-Catholicism

---

[99] Hardin (following Waugh) indicates that the story of Joan claiming to be pregnant was invented in the fifteenth century, perhaps 'to account for the long period between her capture and execution'; 28. Stowe records that Joan 'fained her selfe to be with child' but specifies that she was 'condemned & brent' only 'when the contrarie was known'; as quoted by Hardin, 27. The 1587 edition of Holinshed's *Chronicles* also records that Joan pretended to be pregnant and was accordingly given a nine-month stay of execution. Since this account suggests it was shameful for Joan to pretend she was not a virgin, Hardin argues that Shakespeare 'goes out of his way to invent the most unpleasant part of his portrayal of Joan, the scene where she debases herself into a camp whore (5.6)'; 30. But in sending a possibly pregnant woman to her death, the dramatist also blackens the English characters.

allusively undergirds York's taunting of the French and supposedly pregnant 'holy maid' Joan (5.3.65), Gloucester uses a related rhetoric to berate
his fellow Englishman Winchester as a 'scarlet hypocrite' (1.3.56). Moreover, 'real life' messiness undermines the ideological distinctions it requires. The crisis of the drama is, as Rowland Cotterill points out,
paradoxical: 'England is England-with-France. But England is also at war
with France'.[100] The English nobles oppose France in order to assert affiliation between the two nations, finally achieving only English division.
Such unstable identifications are further complicated by the circumstances of the early 1590s, which saw England battling against and on the
side of France, when Elizabeth sent troops into the French Wars of Religion to support Henri of Navarre's Protestant claim to the throne. In the
play, a repetitive structure loosens the thematic binaries: battle after battle
reverses gain and loss with a frequency that indicates the futility of asserting difference between the two sides.[101]

But if differences bleed into one another, the force of opposition in *1
Henry VI* remains emphatic, and renders the incorporate peace dissatisfac-
tory. York bristles at the 'effeminate peace' which renders wasteful the
death of 'So many captains, gentlemen and soldiers' (5.3.104), and he
predicts 'The utter loss of all the realm of France' (5.3.112). Charles ac-
cepts the truce only after advice to 'break it, when your pleasure serves'
(5.3.164). Even Henry reneges on his role in the peace-making, breaking
off his engagement to the daughter of the Earl of Armagnac that was to
'surer bind' (5.1.16) the knot of amity. Instead he prefers a love for Margaret (whom he has not yet met) that he experiences as 'sharp dissension'
(5.4.84). England is already fractured by the factionalism that will soon
overspill into the total division of civil war. The play's differences have been
imperfect but unstoppable. Neither Talbot's fraternally incorporate absent
substance nor Joan's divinely incorporate presence successfully consolidates
victory. The play's final words are left to a character who looks set to repeat
the past, without properly remembering its consequences:

> Thus Suffolk hath prevailed, and thus he goes,
> As did the youthful Paris once to Greece,
> With hope to find the like event in love—
> But prosper better than the Trojan did.
> Margaret shall now be queen, and rule the King:
> But I will rule both her, the King and realm. (5.4.103–8)

---

[100] Rowland Cotterill, 'The Structural Role of France in Shakespeare's First and Second
Historical Tetralogies', *Renaissance Studies* 9 (1995), 460–76 (468).

[101] See also Wayne L. Billings, 'Ironic Lapses: Plotting in *Henry VI*', *Studies in the Literary Imagination* 5 (1972), 27–49.

Residual Catholicism is nowhere so representationally challenging in Shakespeare's history plays as it is here in the characterization of Joan. And even *1 Henry VI* finally cancels out Joan and her riskiness. The play's rhetoric of political providentialism means too much is at stake for Joan (and her claims of God's favour) not to be obliterated. While the dramatists have manipulated their historical sources in various details,[102] they take care to stage and emphasize the fatal end of Joan's story. The dramatic equivocality of her characterization is delimited by the shape of the plot. The paradoxes of her (re)presentation are not rationalized, but simply removed. More thoroughly fictional dramatic spaces offer greater ideological room to explore such tensions. Critics of *1 Henry VI* often note that the gendered threat embodied by Joan is resurrected in the subsequent plays of the tetralogy through the figure of Margaret. But Shakespeare, as we shall see in later chapters, also returns to the particular paradoxes of Catholic femininity in plays that are more safely distanced (though not removed) from political sectarianism. For example, in *All's Well that Ends Well* the contradiction of 'the holy maid with child' is not a joke but a comic ending in which a chaste pilgrim is pregnant with adulterous offspring; and in *The Winter's Tale* a painted statue comes to life in a radical dramatic experiment in 'reuiued' memorial. Catholic aesthetics problematize the mechanics of representation, but that representation (of Catholicism) is also contingent on genre.

The next chapter analyses this nexus by looking at *Love's Labour's Lost*. This play self-consciously turns, to use Burgundy's description, 'wars...unto a peaceful comic sport' (2.2.44–5). Its protagonists are oddly named after figures famous from the French wars of religion, so that theological resonance again creates a metatheatrical awareness of the disjunction between fiction and reality, character and actor. The 'what' and 'how' of representation are partly conditioned by confessional differences and their tendency to unsettle stable meaning, not least because this play alludes to the 'Frenchman' who did 'turn and turn again' (3.3.85). Where *1 Henry VI* is brutally physical, *Love's Labour's Lost* revels in a relentless display of verbal pyrotechnics, and concerns itself with semantic rather than phenomenological variation. As a comedy, *Love's Labour's Lost* is generically committed to reconciliation in a way that history is not. Why then, does this prove to be a labour lost?

[102] See Burns, pp. 24–5.

2

Converting Names in *Love's Labour's Lost*

Love's Labour's Lost (1595–6) takes the name of a Catholic convert and converts it to comic use. Navarre is both a romantic lead and a man who for a short period prior to 1593 was 'the most famous and beloved non-English person of the time.'[1] Henri IV of France, King of Navarre had been fighting the Protestant cause in the French religious wars, to great acclaim in England. However, in July 1593 'Navarre' gained new Catholic significance when Henri abjured Protestantism and converted to Catholicism in a move which, if not spiritually insincere, was certainly politically expedient. Unlike most Catholic signifiers, the name 'Navarre' thus peculiarly has a Protestant history. Shakespeare's Navarre is a representation that apparently does little to represent its topical referent, and is a character who has few individuating characteristics.

For the English populace throughout the 1590s, anxiety about Protestant Navarre's martial success and Catholic Navarre's spiritual health was felt in a range of different ways. Morning and evening prayers featured petitions to God for the success of the Protestant King in winning his country from the Catholic League,[2] the English Government sent money to assist the military operation, and families sent loved ones as soldiers to protect the Protestant faith generally and England specifically.[3] The proximity of France rendered it a potential station for invasion should the Catholic League defeat Navarre. Furthermore, English Protestants could respond emotionally and spiritually to a martial hero whose endeavours looked set to confirm their view that the rest of the world would join England in a providential and reformed future. In order to secure victory in Paris the man who was once famed for his Protestantism converted to the infamous Roman Catholic religion. No wonder Gabriel Harvey cited

[1] Paul Voss, *Elizabethan News Pamphlets: Shakespeare, Spenser, Marlowe and the Birth of Journalism* (Pittsburgh, PA: Duquesne University Press, 2001), p. 103.

[2] *Liturgical Services of the Reign of Queen Elizabeth*, ed. W. K. Clay (Cambridge: Cambridge University Press, 1847), pp. 647–51.

[3] Elizabethan subjects were also prohibited from assisting the French King's enemies; see *Tudor Royal Proclamations*, ed. Paul L. Hughes and James F. Larkin, 3 vols, iii (New Haven, CT: Yale University Press, 1964–9), pp. 77–9.

'Nauarre *wooes* Roome' as an example of how 1593 was a 'wonderfull' (i.e. astonishing) year.[4]

In calling his king Navarre, Shakespeare points to an awkward piece of reality from his highly stylized fictional world. And in case we miss the point, the contemporary frame of reference is highlighted and widened by the presence of Berowne (alluding to Armand de Gontant, Marshall Biron, a loyal adherent of Navarre), Longaville (Henry of Orleans, the Duke of Longueville, a loyalist Catholic who came to fight against the League with Navarre),[5] Dumaine (Charles of Lorraine, the Duke of Mayenne, a well-known Catholic opponent until 1595),[6] and Boyet (Boyset, leader of the Huguenot forces). Networked in this way, the topicality of the play's onomastics is beyond doubt, and connotes a brutal sectarian conflict from which the romantic plot is entirely dislocated.[7]

Throughout the play's critical history, scholars baffled by the play's prioritization of artifice over plot have detected various allegorical 'solutions' that direct us away from the drama itself. The few who have paid attention to the open topicality of the dramatis personae also tend, as Mary Ellen Lamb puts it, to 'locate the primary "meaning" or focus of the play outside the play in the historical counterparts themselves, thereby diverting the critic from more central concerns, such as the play's quality'.[8] Paul Voss's subsequent brilliant work on Elizabethan news pamphlets demonstrated the inescapability of the topical resonance of *Love's Labour's Lost*, most likely more familiar to contemporary audiences than the classical and chronicle sources to other plays, and establishes a connection between

---

[4] Gabriel Harvey, *A New Letter of Notable Contents with A Straunge Sonet, Intituled Gorgon, or The Wonderfull Yeare* (London, 1593), sig. D3r.

[5] See Voss, p. 135.

[6] Known as the 'Duke de Maine' and as Navarre's enemy in a great number of texts. See, for example, *The Mutable and Wauering Estate of France* (London, 1597), sig. M3v; *An Excellent Ditty made vpon the Great Victory, which the French King Obtayned against the Duke de Maine, and the Romish Rebels in his Kingdome* (London, 1590); and *A Briefe Declaration of the Yeelding vp of Saint Denis to the French King the 29. of Iune, 1590* (London, 1590), sig. B2v. For an alternative reading of the contemporary literary significance of the Marcade–Mercury–Boyet nexus, see Frederick W. Clayton and Margaret Tudeau-Clayton, 'Mercury, Boy Yet and the "Harsh" Words of *Love's Labour's Lost*', *SS* 57 (2004), 209–24.

[7] Even Moth and Marcade have their topical counterparts (the French governor of Gravelines, la Mothe and the Catholic Duke of Mercoeur respectively). See Voss, p. 125; and Henry Woudhuysen, 'Introduction', in William Shakespeare, *Love's Labour's Lost* (London: Arden Shakespeare, 1998), pp. 67–8, 344–5.

[8] Mary Ellen Lamb, 'The Nature of Topicality in "Love's Labour's Lost"', *SS* 38 (1985), 49–59 (54). See Clare Asquith, 'Oxford University and *Love's Labour's Lost*', in *Shakespeare and the Culture of Christianity*, ed. Dennis Taylor and David Beauregard (New York: Fordham University Press, 2003), pp. 80–102; Hugh Richmond, 'Shakespeare's Navarre', *HLQ* 42 (1978–9), 193–216; and Albert H. Tricomi, 'The Witty Idealization of the French Court in *Love's Labor's Lost*', *SSt* 12 (1979), 25–33.

the fictional Navarre's perjury and the historical Navarre's conversion.[9] However, he does not explore the literary, representational, or linguistic implications of the topical intrusion, that is, the impact of these names in *this* play as opposed to any other romantic comedy. Furthermore Voss speculates that the 'newly corrected and augmented' extant text has been supplemented by an oath-breaking story missing from an original play written prior to Henri of Navarre's 1593 denominational change.[10] It seems incredible to him that Shakespeare, writing before 1593, could co-incidentally anticipate an act of oath-breaking, but thinks it equally un-likely that the playwright would choose to write a play with a central character called Navarre after the topical counterpart's maligned conver-sion.[11] Given the centrality of the theatrical Navarre's oath-breaking to an otherwise plotless play I am unconvinced by this argument. I suggest that the topical constellation of names is introduced precisely *because* of the anxiety generated by the conversion and that it both connects to and il-luminates the play's linguistic themes and generic structure.

Shakespeare sets his audience an awkward interpretive problem: there is a disconcerting gap between the horrific wars of religion (deliberately evoked by the dramatis personae) and the light comic tone of the play (created by its language and action). This chapter explores why a group of feckless romantic leads have been saddled with names particular to a bloody sectarian conflict. Why the names without the characterization? The play produces open tension between what is present on stage (topi-cal names) and what is absent from the plot (the topical events they connote). The point is not that Shakespeare encodes a religio-political allegory here. Rather, he seems to be reflecting on what produces and constitutes meaning. How secure is the connection between names and their referents, or between words and things? Interpretation is always perilously careening in different directions in this pun-heavy play. Wordplay relentlessly distorts meaning. By the drama's end, the lords have to be taught that they need a better understanding of the relation-ship between sign and referent (having, for example, wrongly 'wooed but the sign of she' (5.2.469)); their own (disjunctive) names are an

---

[9] Voss, pp. 129–30.

[10] *Love's Labour's Lost*, title page to 1598 quarto. Arthur Freeman and Paul Grinke have discovered documentary evidence for an earlier quarto of *Love's Labour's Lost*: a catalogue of Viscount Conway's books lists 'Loves Labours Lost by W: Sha: 1597' (an edition which would have been lost with the rest of Conway's books in a fire of 1641); 'Four New Shake-speare Quartos', *TLS*, 5 April 2002, pp. 17–18 (p. 18). (Though note that the number of 'discovered' lost plays was reduced to three in their letter to *TLS*, 14 June 2002, p. 17.) Since even this earlier edition post-dates Navarre's conversion it remains unlikely that the oath-breaking story formed part of the later quarto's 'augmentations'.

[11] Voss, p. 138.

illustrative aspect of the semantic misalignment of the drama. Furthermore, these are odd names for an oddly formed comedy. The inappropriately sectarian associations of the dramatis personae take part in the
disruptive intrusion of the real into the comedic world that loses us our
happy ending.

IRONIC ONOMASTICS

The representation of characters who share names with famous living
people in *Love's Labour's Lost* is unique in the Shakespeare canon and unusual in other Renaissance drama. Of course sixteenth-century produc-
tions, like twenty-first-century drama, often carried contemporary
allusions. Plays might hide contemporary references beneath a character
name, but they simultaneously lampooned real people with devastatingly
accurate representations. (Middleton famously got into trouble with the
Privy Council for the similarity between the former Spanish Ambassador,
Gondomar, and the character of the Black Knight in *A Game at Chess*.)
Love's Labour's Lost inverts this analogical process. The names of the chief
male protagonists are glaringly topical to a 1590s audience and yet their
contemporary associations with sectarian warfare and conversion are
transmuted into romantic comedy's battle of the sexes and the failure to
keep an over-the-top oath of scholarly asceticism. Shakespeare uses specifically famous names only to avoid historical detail. Instead of engaging
in character assassinations, he represents his four lords as markedly similar, though their real-life counterparts differed in age, religion, and political opinion.[12] It is not so much that 'Th'allusion holds in the exchange'
(4.2.42), but rather, as in Dull's malapropism, 'the pollution holds in the
exchange' (4.2.46). This is allusion polluted by an exchange of poetry for
politics, wit for war, and romance for religion.

In the mid 1590s French politics was the kind of exciting topic allusion
hunters would detect at the slightest hint. Prefacing *Christs Teares Over
Jerusalem* (1594), Thomas Nashe complains about the 'busie wits' who
had read topical meaning into his *Unfortunate Traveller*:

> Let one but name bread, they will interpret it to be the town of Bredan in
> the low countreyes; if of beere he talkes, then straight he mocks the Countie
> Beroune in France. If of foule weather or a shower of raine, he hath relation
> to some that shall raigne next. Infinite number of these phanatical strange
> hieroglifhicks haue these new decipherers framed to them selues, & stretcht

---

[12] Voss, p. 135.

words on the tenter hooks so miserably, that a man were as good considering euerie circu[m]sta[n]ce, write on cheuerell as on paper.[13]

Whereas Nashe's overly 'busie' readers create topicality out of strained paronomasia, satirically ludicrous in the incongruous association of 'bread' and 'Bredan', 'beere' and 'Beroune', and a 'shower of raine' and monarchical 'raigne', viewers of Shakespeare's play are conversely faced with explicitly named topicality (including Berowne) that incongruously refers to uncontroversial material. Nevertheless, Shakespeare is concerned with the process that sees 'stretcht words on the tenter hooks' and any one of his characters might cry out in exasperation with Navarre: 'Construe my speeches better' (5.2.341). The homonymic process Nashe detects in wrong-headed topical readings is fundamentally linguistic, a consequence of the 'cheuerell' quality of language to metamorphose in interpretation. It is this linguistic dynamic that Shakespeare's characters so frequently exploit; and it is within this dynamic that we might best understand their 'converted' names.

Clearly, *Love's Labour's Lost* is not 'about' Henri IV of France, King of Navarre and his followers. Indeed, Shakespeare's Navarre is a Ferdinand, not an Henri. 'Ferdinand' (and the abbreviations 'Ferd.' and 'Fer.') appear in both quarto and folio texts, in the opening stage direction and in the speech prefixes of the first scene (with two further appearances in the speech prefixes of what we now designate 2.1 in the quarto). However, the name never sounds in the play's dialogue, unlike 'Navarre', which we hear on nine occasions.[14] The ghost name has been alternatively interpreted as an afterthought to tone down the dangerous topicality of 'Navarre', and as the character's original name which gave way to a controversial revision.[15] Whatever the order or motivation, the presence of 'Ferdinand' makes it clear that Shakespeare did not characterize the historical Henri of Navarre in the same way that Marlowe did in his recent-history play, *The Massacre at Paris*. Rather, the controversial associations of the inescapably specific name Navarre cling to the character much like unfortunate connotations punningly attaching themselves to a word.[16]

[13] Thomas Nashe, *Christs Teares Over Ierusalem* (London, 1594), sigs. **v–**ijr. I am grateful to Beatrice Groves for this reference to 'the Countie Beroune'.

[14] The most regular designation for the character in the speech prefixes of both the quarto and folio texts is 'King' and the abbreviation 'Kin.' 'Nauar' and 'Nau' emerge briefly in the stage directions and speech prefixes of 2.1 in quarto and folio.

[15] Richmond, 197; Alfred Harbage, '*Love's Labour's Lost* and the Early Shakespeare', *PQ* 41 (1962), 18–36 (27).

[16] For a different reading of the allusive 'shadows' of dramatic names, see Peter Holland, 'Theseus' Shadows in *A Midsummer Night's Dream*', *SS* 47 (1994), 139–52.

But why should Shakespeare impose such a bizarre incongruity on his characterizations, and how does it work within a play bedevilled by practical (in the misdirected letters), semantic, and generic dislocation? Straightforwardly political interpretations of the onomastics do little justice to the experience of the play itself. For all that some Elizabethan audiences might have found it satisfying to see the apostate soldier king and notorious womanizer reduced to a foolish lover who is repeatedly humiliated, the play instead invites its viewers to delight in his mistakes. (Audiences were, of course, mixed in their confessional and religious allegiances, but the public were nevertheless subject to strategies of acculturation, and Navarre's heroic status in news quartos had noticeably diminished after 1593.) Albert H. Tricomi suggests that Shakespeare's representation of the lords is an 'idealization' of the grim reality of the French civil war that 'charmingly refuses to acknowledge [contemporary sectarian issues] in any but a metaphoric way'.[17] Such a reading 'reforms' the sectarian meaning of the names, much as old signs were purged of Catholic meaning (for example, in the re-forming of papist holy water stoups as secular wash troughs, and the hanging of sanctus and sacring bells on sheep and cows).[18] But this seems like a remarkably unsatisfactory way of making people feel better about bloodshed. And in any case the play itself, with its postponed happy ending, seems unable to endorse even generic idealization, never mind the more difficult political task.

The particularities of French sectarianism are obviously absent from *Love's Labour's Lost*. Even so, the dialogue flirts with the unrepresented associations of the topical names. Martial imagery is used to describe the lords' attempts at scholarly exclusion and romance, and the ladies' defence against courtship:

> Therefore, brave conquerors—for so you are,
> That war against your own affections
> And the huge army of the world's desires—
> Our late edict shall strongly stand in force. (1.1.8–11)

> *King* And, soldiers, to the field!
> *Berowne* Advance your standards and upon them, lords!
> Pell-mell, down with them! But be first advised
> In conflict that you get the sun of them. (4.3.340–3)

> Prepare, madam, prepare!
> Arm, wenches, arm! Encounters mounted are
> Against your peace. Love doth approach disguised,

---

[17] Tricomi, 31.
[18] See Eamon Duffy, *The Stripping of the Altars: Traditional Religion in England, c.1400–c.1580* (New Haven, CT: Yale University Press, 1992), p. 586.

> Armed in arguments: you'll be surprised.
> Muster your wits, stand in your own defence,
> Or hide your heads like cowards and fly hence. (5.2.81–6)[19]

To engage such topically named characters in metaphorical warfare is to emphasize their literary distance from reality, but keep that reality ominously in view.

Indeed two more of the dramatis personae help maintain this disjunction. 'Armado', a popular variant of *Armada*, again nominally insinuates sectarian violence into the comedy.[20] One over-exerted rhyme limped, the Spanish:

> in a bravado,
> Spent many a Crusado,
> In setting forth an Armado
> England to invado.[21]

Since the 'Duke of Maine' had 'brought' Spaniards into the French war (supporting the Catholic League against Henri), Armado's name extends the divided nature of the play's topical onomastics headed by Navarre.[22] Pamphlets attempting to rationalize (for readers on both sides of the Channel) the unlikely alliance of the old enemies England and France stressed a common political and even racial antipathy for Spain: the English and French descended from 'the selfe same extraction' unlike the hot-blooded Spanish tyrant.[23] French Catholics were not to trust apparent Catholic bonds with 'this newe vpstart, this new come Christian, whom not yet long since we haue drawen from the Alcoran, and from Paganisme' and was thus a 'Saracin Castillian, or Castillian Saracin'.[24] Such discourse also pinpointed the Spaniard's linguistic crimes: their 'doughtiest deedes are bragges and boastinges' and their 'vaine and foolish bragging' bespeaks only 'imaginatiue greatnesse'.[25] But while Shakespeare's Armado is a Braggart in quarto and folio speech prefixes, his 'imaginatiue greatnesse' is in linguistic skill (or its lack), not in exaggerated tales of martial prowess. This 'Most military sir' (5.1.34) seeks to 'command' love rather than nations, transposing 'Veni, vidi, vici' from military to amatory

---

[19] Other military language is found at 2.1.86, 2.1.225, 3.1.61–2, and 3.1.78.

[20] *OED*, s.v. 'Armada'.

[21] *A Skeltonicall Salutation* (London, 1589), sig. [Ar].

[22] *A Discourse of All Such Fights* (London, [1590]), sig. C2r.

[23] *A Comparison of the English and Spanish Nation*, trans. R[obert] A[shley] (London, 1589), sig. Cr.

[24] Antoine Arnauld and Michel Hurault, *The Coppie of the Anti-Spaniard*, trans. Anthony Munday (London, 1590), pp. 21–2.

[25] *Comparison*, sigs. A3r, F2r–v.

'victory' (4.1.68–79). Topicality thus oddly encumbers even the light relief in this fundamentally light play.[26]

Similarly, Holofernes is onomastically haunted by violence since his biblical counterpart was decapitated. Generically, at least, his name is less unconventional than the others, given that writers including Rabelais styled pedagogical despots after the Old Testament tyrant.[27] However, the name was also exploited for sectarian purposes. Reformers likened Elizabeth to Judith, 'who cutt off the heade of proud Holifernes'.[28] In such analogies the 'Romish *Holofernes*' might stand for generalized Catholic menace or specific Romish plots: 'our Iudith' was said to have 'foiled' domestic treason and Robert Greene described the Armada as a 'proud *Holofernes* [that came] into our seas' while the reformed '*Iudith*' sat 'peaceably in her royall seat' letting God do the work of destruction.[29] But on the other hand Catholics were blamed for appropriating the story to promote regicide (Elizabeth now starring as Holofernes). Rejecting Catholic protestations to the contrary, Thomas Morton quotes alleged incitement to typological murder: 'Your Reinolds: *Reuenge and roote out as Iudith did Holofernes*: violence'.[30] Robert Persons countered with the explanation that Judith merely exemplified lawful 'strategeme'.[31] But the Catholic William Carter paid the ultimate price for the controversial value of the names: he was executed in 1584 for printing Gregory Martin's *A Treatise of Schisme*. This book featured a passage extolling Judith:

[26] Lynne Magnussen makes a convincing case for a glancing reference to Don Antonio de Pérez, 'a charismatic and oddball political refugee' who appeared in England as an emissary from Navarre in 1593–4; 'To "Gase So Much at the Fine Stranger": Armado and the Politics of English in *Love's Labour's Lost*', in *Shakespeare and the Cultures of Performance*, ed. Paul Yachnin and Patricia Badir (Aldershot: Ashgate, 2008), pp. 53–68 (p. 57). This identification extends the multivalence of the characterizations in *Love's Labour's Lost*.

[27] Ursula Potter, 'The Naming of Holofernes in *Love's Labour's Lost*', *ELN* 38.2 (2000), 11–24.

[28] Leonard Wright, *The Hunting of Antichrist* (London, 1589), sig. C4r. See also Clay, p. 596.

[29] Lodowick Lloyd, *Certaine Englishe Verses* (London, 1586), sig. A2.r; George North in Henri Estienne, *The Stage of Popish Toyes* ([London], 1581), p. 90; Robert Greene, *The Spanish Masquerado* (London, 1589), sig. D3r.

[30] Thomas Morton, *A Full Satisfaction Concerning a Double Romish Iniquitie* (London, 1606), sig. Ir.

[31] P. R. [i.e. Robert Persons], *A Treatise Tending to Mitigation towardes Catholicke-Subiectes in England* ([St Omer], 1607), pp. 160, 292. Some Protestants objected to Judith's sexual deception and the apocryphal nature of her story. See, for example, the discussion of George Abbot (an evangelical Calvinist who would later become Archbishop of Canterbury) in *The Reasons which Doctour Hill hath Brought, for the Upholding of Papistry… Unmasked* (Oxford, 1604), esp. pp. 318–19. But Eamon Duffy indicates that the reading of her story (along with that of Susannah) was prescribed during September and October in the Elizabethan *Book of Common Prayer*; 'Was Shakespeare a Catholic?', *The Tablet*, 27 April 1996, pp. 536–8.

'whose godlye and constant wisedome if our Catholike gentlewomen woulde folowe, they might destroye Holofernes, the master heretike, and amase al his retinew, and neuer defile their religion by communicating with them in anye smal point'.[32] William Allen objected that the authorities had stretched the topical meaning of the names beyond their contextual function:

> no worde was found against the state, the quarel onelie most vniustlie being made, vpon a certaine clause, which by no likelie honest construction could apperteine to the Q. person: *viz.* that the Catholike religion should once haue the vpperhand of heresie, and *Iudith* cutt of the head of *Holophernes*: which they in their extreame ielousie and feare of all thinges wold needes wreast against her Maiestie.[33]

Certainly, one clear purpose of Martin's analogy is to recommend Judith's religious scruples to passive Catholics tempted to communicate in the Church of England: 'she woulde not yeelde so muche as to eate of his meates', setting an example to her serving women, 'And surely one constant Iudith shal easily make many like seruants, a thing much to be wished, for the Catholike bringing vp of yonge gentlewomen, who otherwise are in daunger of Holofernes, and his vngratious ministers'.[34] Nevertheless, the definitive violence of Judith's story inevitably but uneasily complicates Martin's recommendations for ritual, even if it is not his intention. Cyndia Susan Clegg points out that the text, which 'had been around for some time' became problematic in 1584, in the context of the Throckmorton Plot.[35]

Onomastic meaning can be reshaped by writer, reader, period, and place. Holofernes was a name that travelled and had particularly fatal currency in France. The pamphlet *Martine Mar-Sixtus* reprinted and condemned Pope Sixtus V's celebratory comparison of Henri III's assassin (a friar) with Judith.[36] Jesuits were long accused of having encouraged the murder by calling Henri III 'the names of *Tyrant, Holofernes, Moab, Nero,* & such like'.[37] In 1594 the continued use of such allusions apparently threatened Henri IV, in spite of his Catholic conversion.

---

[32] Gregory Martin, *A Treatise of Schisme* (Duaci [i.e. London], 1578), sig. D.ij.r.

[33] William Allen, *A True, Sincere and Modest Defence, of English Catholiques that Suffer for their Faith both at Home and Abrode* ([Rouen], 1584), sig. [A5v].

[34] Martin, sigs. D.ij.r–v. For a discussion of the 'bogus' nature of the state's prosecution, see A. C. Southern, *English Recusant Prose 1559–1582* (London: Sands, 1950), pp. 352–3.

[35] Cyndia Susan Clegg, *Press Censorship in Elizabethan England* (Cambridge: Cambridge University Press, 1997), p. 94.

[36] R. W., *Martine Mar-Sixtus* (London, 1591), sigs. D2r–D3v.

[37] *Le Franc Discours*, trans. William Watson ([London], 1602), sig. C3v.

Combined with the Spanish presence in Paris, the use of the same nominal insults ('*Holofernes, Moab,* and *Nero*') against the current king was invoked as ominous.[38] And indeed after Henri's eventual murder in 1610, the 'SECRET AND hidden Mysterie' whereby Jesuits allegedly prepared the assassin included the ritualistic invocation of motivating names with the presentation of the knife: 'Goe thou forth like *Iephtah*; the sword of *Sampson*; the sword wherby *Dauid* did cut off the head of *Goliah*; the sword of *Gedeon*; the sword wherewith *Iudith* did cut off the head of *Holofernes*'.[39] Politically adaptable, the name Holofernes works in concert with the topical names of the romantic lords (including one to whom associations with biblical tyranny was very troubling) and shrinks potential controversy to a comic format while maintaining a prominent topical give.

The play's onomastic structure thus bristles with an irony that flickers between the contemporary and the comic; its representational structure repeatedly jokes about the disjunction between the character and the role played. When the lords reveal their oath-breaking love in supposed privacy, three different levels of metatheatrical awareness emerge as each lord only sees and hears the lords who enter after him, addressing the audience accordingly. Revelling in a mutual transformation (4.3.79) that puts them 'much out o'th' way' (4.3.73) of their (scholarly) roles, the lords tantalizingly move from the represented world without ever leaving it. Berowne's gloating revelation—'O me, with what strict patience have I sat, | To see a king transformed to a gnat!' (4.3.162–3)—articulates the theatrical diminution of the real-life king to comic character. But the joke is also on Berowne, primarily because his own metamorphosis into love-struck sonneteer is soon revealed, but also because this would-be 'demi-god' (4.3.76) is unaware of the full extent of the transformation: from famed military leaders to 'affection's men-at-arms' (4.3.286).

Where Talbot announces the absence of his real referent, Berowne (like his friends) is unaware of what might be present. The representational structure of *Love's Labour's Lost* elaborates the play's point about language. As misnamed theatrical signs, the lords reproduce the violence their characters do to linguistic signs. Berowne is a pragmatic nominalist. Sensibly pointing out the philosophical pitfalls of the scholarly oath, he outlines a practical theory of knowledge that is also comically convenient to one seeking to avoid 'strict observances' (1.1.36):

---

[38] Antoine Arnauld, *The Arrainment of the Whole Society of Iesuits In France* (London, 1594), sig. C.ij.r.

[39] Pierre Coton, *The Hellish and Horribble Councell,* trans. Anon. (London, 1610), sig. [A4v].

> These earthly godfathers of heaven's lights,
> That give a name to every fixed star,
> Have no more profit of their shining nights
> Than those that walk and wot not what they are.
> Too much to know is to know naught but fame,
> And every godfather can give a name. (1.1.88–93)

Astronomers are 'earthly godfathers' because they name stars, an act as common and unremarkable as that performed by 'every' domestic 'godfather'. In describing knowledge as 'fame' Berowne rejects scholarship as vanity and further suggests that knowledge is merely the knowledge of the names things have been given rather than of the things themselves. This belief in the arbitrary relationship between *verbum* and *res* later allows him to 'gloze' his way out of the oath. To Berowne there are no true correspondences between the signifier and the signified and so there is no need to be limited by traditional semantic relationships. However, while words may not be the things themselves, *Love's Labour's Lost* reveals the social function of the meaning that is located in words and names, the 'fame' of the communal understanding of a thing. Ironically, these male characters go about their theatrical existence and 'wot not what they are', blissfully unaware of the topical suggestiveness of their names. Words are not the things themselves, the actors are not French lords, and these characters are not French military leaders, but nevertheless, the play does not release the lords from the associations of their names (embedded as they are in a whole network of onomastic contemporary allusions, military metaphors, and a plot that constantly refers back to oath-breaking).

Recovering from the semiotic lesson taught them by the mistaking of mis-tokened ladies, the irony of the lords' unknowing disjunctiveness is intensified when they cruelly mock the actors of the Nine Worthies as inappropriate signs. They now refuse theatrically acceptable semiotic relationships as too loose: Costard cannot play Pompey simply because it is a 'lie', he is 'not he' (5.2.543), the shape of Nathaniel's nose 'says no' to his Alexander (5.2.561), and the 'clean-timbered' Armado 'cannot be Hector' because 'His leg is too big' (5.2.633–7). Most ironically, the taunting of Holofernes for attempting to represent Judas Maccabaeus even though there is another (in)famous Judas who haunts that name rebounds on characters who are similarly onomastically afflicted. The sectarian connotations of their names make these romantic lords even more representationally inadequate than the players of the pageant. The awkward misfit between sectarian name and comic character seems neither idealizing nor idealistic, particularly since avoiding real life (either in an oath repressing natural desires, or in a rejection of the oath that ignores the real meaning it communicates) brings only disappointment to the lords.

In *1 Henry VI* denominational and phenomenological difference helped to separate antagonists in an (imperfect) organizational epistemology. *Love's Labour's Lost* is less interested in the nature of difference (the details of sectarianism) than in its consequences: the troubling of epistemological co-ordinates. The conversion of a convert's name to a comic role sets up (paradoxically) a chain of dislocations. The topical names inescapably remind its Elizabethan audience of the fact of difference and the condition of semiotic fluidity it produces, and this becomes part of the drama's interrogative experimentation in language and genre that looks to the consequences of this 'play'.

FAITH AND THE WORD

In redefining topical names as comic characterization, the play repeats a linguistic manoeuvre attempted by the lords themselves. Seeking to avoid the tightly expressed strictures of their own oath, Navarre and Longaville ask Berowne to 'prove | Our loving lawful and our faith not torn' (4.3.280–1) by 'Some tricks, some quillets how to cheat the devil' (4.3.284). Berowne obliges by reclassifying 'women's eyes' as 'the books, the arts, the academes, | That show, contain and nourish all the world' (4.3.324–7). This is a central act of linguistic manipulation in a play where language is endlessly multiplied in synonyms, sense repeatedly metamorphosed in puns, and meaning twisted from its original sense by both speakers and auditors. In the first scene, Navarre-the-anxious-humanist has endeavoured to pin down a legal meaning with no linguistic loopholes; Costard tries in vain to wriggle out of the proclamation against association with women through a list of alternative words (wench, damsel, virgin, maid) that, it turns out, have already been specified by the careful king (1.1.269–83). But Navarre and his friends subsequently prove more audacious in their 'cheating' language. The play as a whole registers an early modern ambivalence between delight in verbal *copia* that creatively enables more precise expression and a fear of linguistic hyperinflation, whereby real meaning disappears between innumerable synonyms that are themselves multivalent. The joke that sees real-life names played without characterological meaning is perhaps part of the drama's threatened dissolution of significance. But the nature of the topicality of 'Navarre' in the mid 1590s also has a specific resonance for the world of semantic flux.

Henri of Navarre's conversion to Catholicism in 1593 enacted a particularly disruptive change. All religious conversion destabilized meaning. While it may have been something of a fiction, Elizabethans were taught that Roman Catholicism and Protestantism were distinct and oppositional confessional categories, but the reality of confessants switching back and forth between the two undermined the denominational boundary even as it was supposedly reasserted.[40] Elizabethans had seen Navarre as almost definitively Protestant, one whose confessional allegiance was witnessed in his martial opposition to Catholicism.[41] One news pamphlet declared that: 'The Lord...hath preserued this most worthy Prince, for the better enlarging of his Gospell, to be a worthy follower of our most famous King, King Henry the eight, in [the] pulling down of Papistry, and all their diuelish deuises.'[42] This pamphlet's representation of the 'worthy Prince' elides national and temporal boundaries: at one with the past anti-Catholic victories of 'our...King Henry the eight', Navarre's current martial struggles work to bring about the reformed future ordained by 'The Lord'. The epistemological glue that seals this typological image is Navarre's active Protestantism. Reformed Elizabethans had equated Navarre's religion with fidelity itself. In 1590, a pamphlet containing *The Oration and Declaration of the French King* celebrated Navarre's fidelity to his faith in the face of temptations to recant and keep the support of the Catholic nobles.[43] His constancy and his Protestantism are shown to be symbiotic. He asserted that 'neyther this Crowne, nor the Empire of all the whole earth were able to make me chaunge the Religion wherein I haue bene brought uppe' and that 'I am resolued...not to varie nor chaunge in any wise my religion'.[44] But change and vary he does, and it is in these terms that he comes to be understood. Navarre's conversion marks the climactic conclusion of a work that sets out to illustrate what a 'slipperie and vncertaine estate' the realm of France is:

> Thus this noble and renowned Monarke, the hope (as it were) of al that fauored Gods truth, whom God had beautified with so many excellent graces and notable vertues, as courage, wisdom, zeale, and constancy in so many apparant dangers...and to the admiration and wonderment of all

[40] See Michael C. Questier, *Conversion, Politics and Religion in England, 1580–1625* (Cambridge: Cambridge University Press, 1996); and Molly Murray, *The Poetics of Conversion in Early Modern English Literature: Verse and Change from Donne to Dryden* (Cambridge: Cambridge University Press, 2009).

[41] Navarre's early temporary conversion to Catholicism after the St Bartholomew's Day Massacre was glossed over as enforced. Marlowe does not include it in *The Massacre at Paris*.

[42] *A Briefe Declaration of the Yeelding vp Of Saint Denis to the French King the 29. Iune, 1590* (London, 1590), sig. B2v.

[43] This pamphlet was published by Shakespeare's Stratford contemporary, Richard Field, so it is possible that Shakespeare had easy access to such material. Field printed *Venus and Adonis* (1593) and *The Rape of Lucrece* (1594), and is alluded to in *Cymbeline* as 'Richard du Champ' (4.2.379).

[44] *The Oration and Declaration of the French King, Henrie the Fourth of that Name and by the Grace of God, King of Nauarre* (London, 1590), sigs. AIIIr and AIIv.

men continually protected him in despight of all those who sought his ruine and ouerthrow, is another argument of the mutabilitie and interchangeable estate of all things in the world.[45]

In this assessment 'Navarre' represented a person who had changed and a person who was change itself. His conversion to Catholicism undid the meaning of his previous representation and identification in pamphlets printed in England.

After 1593 Elizabethan news quartos simply stop being printed about Navarre. While a work detailing the fraught history of France might utilize Navarre's conversion to make a broader point about mutability, there are apparently no works that focus on Navarre's conversion to a religion that in orthodox terms has to be regarded as 'false and superstitious'.[46] This does not suggest that the conversion was unremarkable in the sense of being unworthy of mention, but rather that it was difficult for the news pamphlet writers to pass remark on such an event because it caused representational crisis. While it would of course have been politically dangerous to criticize a king who continued to receive military aid from Elizabeth, the fact that we do not find post-1593 pamphlets that celebrate Navarre's wartime exploits but which simply avoid religious themes indicates the structural role played by sectarianism in such representation and identification.

It is significant, then, that Shakespeare should put his fractured and ironic representation of the un-represented convert in a play where language and signs constantly mislead. *Love's Labour's Lost* is influenced by sectarian reversal and the semiotic difficulty it produces. As the play opens the audience are pointedly made aware of the lords' topical names: the scene centres on their subscribing their names to an oath already 'passed' (1.1.19, 49). As Katharine Maus points out, this focus on oaths and contracts means that the play opens with 'performative' language: 'This kind of language is not referential; it performs actions rather than describe or point to an extralinguistic reality. As such, performative utterances seem to close the gap between signifier and signified, *verba* and *res*, word and world.'[47] Navarre looks on his and his lords' names as epistemological anchors:

---

[45] *Mutable*, sig. [N3v]. The English conventionally regarded the whole French nation as mutable; see Andrew M. Kirk, 'Marlowe and the Disordered Face of French History', *SEL* 35.2 (1995), 193–213. But Navarre's change was more acutely distressing for the English.

[46] *Mutable*, sig. [N3v].

[47] Katharine Eisaman Maus, 'Transfer of Title in *Love's Labor's Lost*: Language, Individualism, Gender', in *Shakespeare Left and Right*, ed. Ivo Kamps (New York: Routledge, 1991), pp. 205–23 (p. 209).

> Your oaths are passed, and now subscribe your names,
> That his own hand may strike his honour down
> That violates the smallest branch herein. (1.1.19–21)

Prior to his conversion not only was Henri reputed to be 'a true fulfiller of his word and promise' in general terms,[48] but his reformed faith was also figured in terms of an 'oath' and a 'promise'. The Huguenot Du Bartas celebrated Henri's Protestant allegiance thus:

> [The world d]id neuer' see a prince religiouslie more loath
> To shake in any sort his honnor-binding oath.
>   Offer vnto my Lord the crowne of *Germanie*
> The diadem of *Spaine*, the Turks *Grand-Signorie*:
> Yea make him *Monarch* of the world (by guile)
> Hee'l spurne al sceptres, fore his faith defile.[49]

Even some French Catholics, who prayed for a heartfelt conversion on the part of their king, understood his Protestantism as 'the expresse commandement that his mother the Q. of Nauarre at her decease gaue and lefte vnto him, as it were a testamentarie legacie' and cautioned against an expedient conversion using language which related religion to promises: 'Banish the ceremonies of our vows in matters of greatest co[n]science, as religion, and ye shall ere ye be aware banish a great part of all religions'.[50] That a post-1593 Navarre should continue to view names as a guarantor of an oath would have been ironic to an Elizabethan audience disabused of faith in Henri's 'constancie'.[51] Navarre's own name, rather than sealing the deal, breaks it, and supplements the comic expectation that the oath will be broken.

Words relating to oath-breaking saturate the play: forms of the verb *forswear* appear twenty times and forms of *perjury* appear thirteen times. Yet such words are in concert with the antithetical word *faith* which (with its cognates) appears seventeen times in the text. 'Faith' is popular as an exclamation in *Love's Labour's Lost* (4.3.8; 4.3.22; 5.2.280; 5.2.577; 5.2.671); its meaning is poised liminally between interjection (an almost meaningless verbal tic) and asseveration (an emphatically meaningful assertion).[52] The word is repeatedly used to describe the lords' original oath of scholarly asceticism:

---

[48] *The Coppie of a Letter Sent into England* (London, 1590), sig. Bv.

[49] Guillaume de Salluste Du Bartas, *A Canticle of the Victorie Obteined by the French King, Henrie the Fourth*, trans. Joshua Sylvester (London, 1590), sig. [B2v].

[50] *An Answeare to the Supplication Against Him, Who Seeming to Giue the King Counsel to Become a Catholike*, trans. Edward Aggas (London, 1591), sigs. B3r, B3v.

[51] *Oration*, sig. AIIv; *A Discourse Vppon a Question of the Estate of this Time*, trans. Edward Aggas (London, 1591), sig. A4v.

[52] For examples of faith as romantic love, see 5.2.50, 5.2.279–80, 5.2.454, and 5.2.822.

If I break faith, this word shall speak for me:
I am forsworn 'on mere necessity'. (1.1.151–2)

Ah, never faith could hold, if not to beauty vowed.
Though to myself forsworn, to thee I'll faithful prove. (4.2.106–7)

You would for paradise break faith and troth;
And Jove for your love would infringe an oath.
What will Berowne say when that he shall hear
Faith infringed which such zeal did swear? (4.3.140–3)

good Berowne, now prove
Our loving lawful and our faith not torn. (4.3.280–1)

In each instance faith is thought of as either broken or potentially broken. As well as referring to a linguistic act (a promise), 'faith' also has obvious religious connotations so that the historical Navarre's switching (and breaking) of his celebrated Protestant faith is kept in the audience's minds.

Prior to his conversion, Henri's faith (in both senses) was celebrated as absolute: 'For what Prince was there euer more carefull of his faith then the King?'[53] Even Catholics who hoped for the day when their king would share their faith were concerned that a sudden conversion would be 'very vnseemely' to Navarre's reputation of 'inuiolable faith . . . to his constancie'.[54] Perhaps the insistence on superlative faith covers a contrary fear. Gabriel Harvey annotated his copy of Du Bartas's *A Canticle of Victorie* (cited earlier) which acclaims Henri's heroism and steadfast Protestant allegiance:

> *An vnquam fides Heroica frigeat? Quicquid non est ex fide, est peccatum. Nisi quatenus Sol interdum latet; aut etiam patitur Eclypsin.*[55] What if heroic virtue cools? Whatever is not of faith is a sin, lest the sun hide or even suffer eclipse.[56]

Navarre's conversion marks a loss of absolute value that had been rhetorically (if not actually) available before. The cross-confessional incredulity about the sincerity of Navarre's new-found faith saw the king suspected of being a 'counterfeit Catholic'.[57] The writer of *The Mutable and Waurering Estate of France* describes 'continual *practising* to draw the king to the

---

[53] *Discourse*, sig. B3v.   [54] *Discourse*, sig. A4v.

[55] As cited in, Eleanor Relle, 'Some New Marginalia and Poems of Gabriel Harvey', *RES* 23 (1972), 401–16 (414).

[56] As translated by Anne Lake Prescott, 'Foreign Policy in Fairyland: Henri IV and Spenser's Burbon', *Spenser Studies* 14 (2001), 189–214 (206).

[57] *Calendar of State Papers, Domestic, 1575–1625*, ed. M. A. E. Green et al, 12 vols, v (London: Longman, Brown, Green, Longmans & Roberts, 1856-72), 28 April/8 May 1599, p. 189.

liking of Poperie: wherein there was such paines taken, and so farre humane *pollicie* preuailed' resulting in '*apparant* inclination to Poperie' (my emphasis).[58] Elizabeth herself cautioned Navarre that 'it is dangerous to do evil to make good out of it'.[59] It suited the Catholic League to suggest that Navarre's conversion was insincere and thus claim that they had 'undertaken the war upon a just cause'.[60] The Pope feared that the abjuration was 'a ruse suggested to him by the Queen of England'.[61] Constancy had been replaced not by straightforward conversion to another constant, but to uncertainty.

In Book 5 of *The Faerie Queene*, where Navarre is allegorized as Burbon, Spenser articulates contemporary attitudes when he describes the knight's forsaking of his shield (read 'conversion') as a self-confessed act of 'temporiz[ing]' (*FQ* 5.11.56.3).[62] Artegall berates Burbon for 'forgerie', and declares it wrong 'Vnder one hood to shadow faces twaine. | Knights ought be true, and truth is one in all' (*FQ* 5.11.56.6–8). Burbon's unethical behaviour is figured as the loss of the unitary quality of the sign, a 'truth' that is 'one in all'. This semiotic integrity is something Spenser's own post-lapsarian (and post-Reformation) text is incapable of achieving: allegorical meaning frequently evades allegorical signs (as, to take a famous example, when errors perpetuate after Redcrosse has defeated Errour). At this moment, the point is political: Artegall, like Elizabeth, continues to offer aid to a flawed Burbon.[63] The loss of absolute semantic and ethical value is critically symbiotic.

Love's Labour's Lost eschews the political for the linguistic, in a plot where perjury is quadrupled and thus de-particularized. But language is

[58] *Mutable*, sigs. N3r–N3v.

[59] Elizabeth I, *Collected Works*, ed. Leah S. Marcus, Janel Mueller, and Mary-Beth Rose (Chicago, IL: University of Chicago Press, 2000), p. 371.

[60] *Calendar of State Papers, Venetian*, ed. Rawdon Brown et al, 39 vols, ix (London: Longman, Green, Longman, Roberts & Green, 1864–1947), No. 232, 6 November 1593, p. 113.

[61] *CSP Venetian*, No. 130, 30 January 1593, pp. 57–8; see also No. 215, 11 September 1593, p. 106.

[62] Edmund Spenser, *The Faerie Queene*, ed. A. C. Hamilton, Hiroshi Yamashita, and Toshiyuki Suzuki (London: Longman, 2001); all references to *The Faerie Queene* in the text are to this edition.

[63] Elizabeth's pragmatic support was premised on the belief that the dominance of a Catholic Navarre was preferable to the dominance of the Catholic League. Her religious indignation may have been emphasized because of her political displeasure with Navarre's organization of the war; N. M. Sutherland, *Henry IV of France and the Politics of Religion, 1572–1596*, 2 vols, i (Bristol: Elm Bank, 2002), pp. 521–4. For further discussion of Spenser's treatment of the issue, see Lowell Gallagher, *Medusa's Gaze: Casuistry and Conscience in the Renaissance* (Stanford, CA: Stanford University Press, 1991); Tobias Gregory, 'Shadowing Intervention: On the Politics of *The Faerie Queene* Book 5 Cantos 10–12', *ELH* 67 (2000), 365–97; and Prescott.

shown to have social significance. The moral pragmatism that Longaville identifies was widely registered in the historical Navarre's famous (but probably apocryphal) declaration: 'Paris is worth a mass'. It is not that the oath-breaking in *Love's Labour's Lost* allegorizes Navarre's apostasy, but rather that the inescapable allusion (or 'pollution') emphasizes the reach of social and spiritual implications of adapting meaning to fit circumstance more comfortably. The epistemological tensions created by a context of religious division and apostasy enlarge the drama's broader linguistic concerns about the slipperiness of meaning. The redefinitions of the Reformation, the semiotic disputes of a sectarian age, and the relativizing impact of multiple conversions (even at a national scale in the Tudor period) all meant meaning had been unfixed. *Love's Labour's Lost* points at these problems in its vision of semantic flux.

Triumphantly concluding his semantic evasion of perjury, Berowne declares:

> It is religion to be thus forsworn,
> For charity itself fulfils the law,
> And who can sever love from charity? (4.3.337–9)

The paradoxical identification of perjury (being 'forsworn') with 'religion' hints at Henri of Navarre's apostasy through a skilful piece of specious rhetoric. The final demonstration takes on biblical righteousness in allusions to Romans 13:10 ('Charitie woorketh no ill to his neyghbour, therefore the fulfilling of the lawe is charitie' [Bishops' Bible]) and Romans 13:8 ('he that loueth another, hathe fulfilled the Law).[64] Berowne counters Longaville's earlier accusation that Dumaine's '[erotic] love is far from [Christian] charity' (4.3.124), by claiming that a generative romantic love binds 'wisdom', 'men', and 'women' (4.3.331–4) and thus enables the lords to keep the commandment (i.e. the 'lawe') to 'loue your neighbour as yourself'.

However, the unthinkable severing of 'love from charity' has a controversial linguistic reality. William Tyndale's rendering of the Greek *agape* as 'love' instead of 'charity' (as in the Vulgate's Latin *caritas*) throughout his English *New Testament* was labelled heresy by Thomas More. One of

---

[64] Naseeb Shaheen, *Biblical References in Shakespeare's Plays* (Newark, DE: University of Delaware Press, 1999), p. 134. The Bishops' Bible is unique among Renaissance bibles in speaking of 'charitie' at Romans 13:10. For example, the Geneva Bible has 'Loue doeth not euil to his neighbour: therefore is loue [the] fulfilling of the Law'. The larger controversy about the choice of 'charity' or 'love' in scriptural translation is discussed in the present chapter. Adrian Streete detects the (non-partisan) influence of *Calvin's Sermons…on the Epistle of S. Paule to Timothie and Titus* (1579); 'Charity and Law in *Love's Labour's Lost*', *Notes and Queries* 49 (2002), 224–5.

More's key problems with this translation was that the English *love*, unlike the Vulgate's Latin *caritas*, was too polysemous: 'For though charity be always love, yet is not, ye wot well, love always charity.' More makes it clear that erotic connotations are called to mind as he deadpans references to St Francis's comic thanks to God for 'charity' when he sees a 'young man kiss a girl', and the contrasting 'mistrust' of a man who 'but find[s]' his wife 'in bed with a poor friar'.[65] Tyndale rejected *charity* as too semantically narrow and grammatically inflexible, and contended that the correct sense of *love* is evident to good readers: 'though we saye a man ought to loue hys neyboures wife and his doughter/ a christen man doeth not vnderstonde/ that he ys commaunded to defyle hys neyboures wife or hys doughter.'[66] The lords can hardly be accused of a lecherous love (unacceptable to both Catholics and Protestants), but Berowne's theological-linguistic footwork is explicitly described as 'flattery' for the 'evil' of perjury (4.3.282) and 'glozes' that are distinct from 'plain dealing' (4.3.344). The rhetoric ultimately fails to move beyond the self-interest of *eros* to produce *agape*'s communal force, since it is this very trickery that makes the ladies distrust the lords and postpone marriage. Berowne's compression of erotic and charitable love (carefully parsed by More and Tyndale) is a comic punch-line that uneasily testifies to the dissolution of absolute meaning that translation and religious controversy ostensibly aimed to prevent but actually enabled. Competing polemicists split God's Word into disputed words.[67]

A generic world away from *Love's Labour's Lost*, Marlowe's Navarre play, *The Massacre at Paris*, stages the semiotic opposition in sectarian difference. Where topical-religious hints in *Love's Labour's Lost* participate in an exploration of what happens when language and significance are endlessly manipulated, in *The Massacre at Paris* religious violence is manifested as a

---

[65] Thomas More, *A Dialogue Concerning Heresies*, in *Early Modern Catholicism: An Anthology of Primary Sources*, ed. Robert S. Miola (Oxford: Oxford University Press, 2007), p. 51. See also Thomas More, *The Co[n]futacyon of Tyndales Answer* (London, 1532), p. clii.

[66] William Tyndale, *An Answere vnto Sir Thomas Mores Dialoge*, ed. Anne M. O'Donnell and Jared Wicks (Washington, DC: The Catholic University of America Press, 2000), p. 20.

[67] Charlotte Scott also recognizes an allusion to 'a seminal point in the history of the churches in the relationship between translation and interpretation, symbol and meaning'. But she regards Berowne as following Tyndale's technique of transposing 'the traditional language of response by "sensing" the text and "explaining" the spirit'; *Shakespeare and the Idea of the Book* (Oxford: Oxford University Press, 2007), pp. 97–8. This useful suggestion does not account for the lords' explicit moral pragmatism that complicates 'spiritual' integrity. R. Chris Hassel sees a joke on the 'notoriously uncharitable' nature of sectarian debate, and an indication that the lack of 'indwelling spirit' in the lords' labours means they will never win 'the Catholic ladies of France'; *Shakespeare's Religious Language: A Dictionary* (London: Continuum, 2005), p. 57.

brutal insistence on one (sectarian) meaning. Marlowe dramatizes recent French history (the marriage of Navarre to Margaret up to the murder of Henri III) as a revenge tragedy, replete with the blood and irony that became conventional to that genre. The Protestant deaths in the massacre itself are delivered with jokes that play on denominational difference: 'Then pray unto our Lady; kiss this cross. *Stab him*' (6.29); 'Dearly beloved brother, thus 'tis written. *He stabs him*' (7.8).[68] Violence asserts the significance of the division between Catholic and Protestant as puns between words ('cross', 'written') and actions (the weapons stabbing) close down difference. Before the killing of the Huguenot philosopher Ramus, the Guise explains his murderous dislike:

> He that will be a flat dichotomist,
> And seen in nothing but epitomes,
> Is in your judgement thought a learned man;
> And he, forsooth, must go and preach in Germany,
> Excepting against doctors' axioms,
> And *ipse dixi* with this quiddity,
> *Argumentum testimonii est inartificiale.*
> To contradict which, I say; Ramus shall die.
> How answer you that? Your *nego argumentum*
> Cannot serve, sirrah. Kill him. (9.29–38)

This Machiavellian Catholic (concerned with Catholic power rather than Catholic faith) objects to both the splitting open of the sign by a 'flat dichotomist' and the notion that authority does not authorize meaning ('*Argumentum testimonii est inartificiale*': Argument by authority is not of its own nature conclusive). Not for the Guise the innumerable quibbles of *Love's Labour's Lost* (in contrast to Shakespeare's Navarre, whose words are believed by neither the Princess nor Costard, the Guise's 'oaths are seldom spent in vain' (17.31)). Killing Ramus unites word and referent and asserts the power of authority to determine meaning (though Ramus, unlike the other victims of the massacre, is afforded a few lines of philosophical defence before death, for what good they do him).[69] The Guise ultimately falls prey to the dichotomy he would eradicate. The fatal opposition between Catholic and Protestant is translated into mere analogy by the structure of the play, which exchanges Catholic violence for Protestant

---

[68] Christopher Marlowe, *The Massacre at Paris*, in *The Complete Plays and Poems*, ed. E. D. Pendry (London: Everyman, 1976); all references to *The Massacre at Paris* in the text are to this edition.

[69] For an excellent discussion of the denial of speech in *The Massacre at Paris*, see Kristen Elizabeth Poole, 'Garbled Martyrdom in Christopher Marlowe's *The Massacre at Paris*', *Comparative Drama* 32.1 (1998), 1–25.

violence. Marlowe's Navarre mouths an allegiance to 'truth' and the 'holy word' (13.50–1) that Shakespeare's Navarre so comically fails to respect, but his conclusive oath of vengeance against Catholics would have rung hollow for a good proportion of the play's early modern theatrical life, which extended well into the post-1593 period.[70]

In *Love's Labour's Lost* the literalization of sectarian meaning adumbrates social relationships rather than tragic violence. The Princess extorts a compliment out of a Forester unused to courtly flattery by misappropriating his reference to the 'fairest shoot' (the best situation from which to hunt) as praise of her beauty. She then pays him money:

PRINCESS Fair payment for foul words is more than due.
FORESTER Nothing but fair is that which you inherit.
PRINCESS See, see, my beauty will be saved by merit!
          O heresy in fair, fit for these days! (4.1.19–22)

Like the Guise, the Princess controls meaning through authority.[71] Being 'saved by merit' alludes to the Catholic doctrine of participating in one's salvation through good works (or by literal or metaphorical monetary purchase, as the reformers understood this dogma).[72] That this suggestion is 'heresy...fit for these days' has resonance both specific (the newly Catholic court of Navarre) and general (heresy can exist wherever there is orthodoxy). At a small scale, the Princess's revaluing of the Forester's words with puns and actual remuneration serves to devalue both the speaker (not allowed to own his meaning) and the theology of merit (merely money). But it is this very unfixing of meaning (and thus of lines of social communication) to which the Princess and her ladies object in the lords.

In *Love's Labour's Lost* words are themselves violent: 'Bruise me with scorn, confound me with a flout, | Thrust thy sharp wit quite through my ignorance, | Cut me to pieces with thy keen conceit' (5.2.397–9). In the

---

[70] In rebuttal of Sir Ralph Winwood's objections to the staging of *l'Histoire Angloise contre la Roine d'Angleterre* in Paris in 1602, it was pointed out that 'the Massacre of St Bartholomews hath ben publickly acted, and this King represented upon the stage'. Winwood won the prohibition but the French counter-argument implies discomfort with the representation of not just the massacre but also Navarre. Marlowe's Navarre is ostensibly heroic, but immediately after 1593 the nature of this heroism was (for different reasons) uncomfortably anachronistic on both sides of the Channel. See E. K. Chambers, *The Elizabethan Stage*, 4 vols, i (Oxford: Clarendon Press, 1923), p. 323.

[71] See also Lynne Magnusson, 'Scoff Power in *Love's Labour's Lost* and the Inns of Court: Language in Context', *SS* 57 (2004), 196–208.

[72] Catholic theologians carefully stressed the crucial role of God's grace and '*merit* of Christ' (emphasis mine) in salvation. See Peter Canisius, *A Summe of Christian Doctrine*, trans. Henry Garnet ([London?, *c*.1592]), esp. p. 483.

play's lengthy final scene Berowne has finally realized the divisive consequences of irresponsible language. This is no gory tragedy like Marlowe's
drama, but the wordplay of *Love's Labour's Lost* proves to be a losing game.
The ladies' exchange of love tokens that fools suitors into wooing 'but the
sign of she' (5.2.469) exposes the dangers of shifting signs at will, a lesson
the lords have yet fully to comprehend. Uncomfortably, the comic force
of language (its generative polysemy) is found to prevent a comedic
ending (its generative union). The failure of generic reconciliation is partly
conditioned by the disjunctive intrusions of topicality; but that topicality
makes the lack of happy ending all the more serious.

MAKING THE SPORT A COMEDY

The generic structure of *Love's Labour's Lost* imposes an epistemological
expectation on the play: comic realms are fundamentally social places, finally bounded by harmony and continuity (represented in marriage). The
denial of generically promised happiness is all the more striking in a wider
theatrical context. In addition to Marlowe's would-be revenger, Navarre is
also found in the pseudo-historical romance, *The Trial of Chivalry*. This
play is set in an unspecified past where knights are prepared to devote
their lives to the memory of their friends, and hermits have magic potions
to cure faces poisoned by spurned lovers. On one hand the names used in
this play simply connote 'historicity': there is a 'Lewes, *King of France*', a
King of 'Nauar', and a Duke 'Burbon' (A2r).[73] However, these onomastics
intriguingly reproduce the recent French civil wars (and are alterations of
the story's source, Sidney's *Arcadia*).[74] The play opens with Navarre and
France about to go to war, the English Pembrooke supporting Navarre.
The temporary peace initially agreed upon is broken down, in part because
of the machinations of the topically named Burbon. The elderly Catholic

---

[73] *The Trial of Chivalry* (London, 1605; facs. edn, [London]: Tudor Facsimile Texts,
1912); all references to *The Trial of Chivalry* in the text are to this edition. The toponymous
names had different referents in different periods. For example, the play's union between
the French prince Philip and the Navarrese princess Bellamira was historically enacted in
1286 when the princess of Navarre (Joan rather than Bellamira) married the French heir
who would become Philip IV of France.

[74] The story of Philip, Bellamira, and Burbon (in which Bellamira's face is poisoned by
her spurned lover Burbon but her true love Philip remains faithful) is taken from that of
Argalus, Parthenia, and Demagorus in Book 1, Chapters 5–7 of the *New Arcadia/Countess
of Pembroke's Arcadia*, and the part of the plot concerning Ferdinand, Katharina, and Pembrooke (where Katharina falls for Pembrooke who woos her on behalf of his friend) uses
material from the story of Philoxenus, Helen of Corinth, and Amphialus in Book 1, Chapters 10–11. See also C. R. Baskervill, 'Sidney's "Arcadia" and "The Tryall of Chevalry"',
Modern Philology 10 (1912), 197–201.

Cardinal Charles de Bourbon (Henri of Navarre's uncle) had been the Catholic League's preferred successor to the French throne, prior to his death in 1590.[75] While the play's French King is called Lewes and is referred to as such in the speech prefixes, when Navarre engages in war against him for the second time, he is most frequently called 'Fraunce' (see, for example, Fv, F2r, and Ir).[76] The two kings are symmetrical characters: they each have a daughter and a son (who is in love with the other king's daughter), a parallel situation that is underlined by the use of repeated lines between the two factions (as in most of the first scene where they enter from opposite sides of the stage and then again when war breaks out again at Fv). In this way the religious difference that kept the actual French civil wars raging for so long is here effaced by theatrical stylization. *The Trial of Chivalry* is closer to the idealization some critics have read in *Love's Labour's Lost*. This Navarre is no oath-breaker (he may have been conceived before the 'wonderfull yeare' 1593), but more importantly the topically resonant 'ciuill butchery' (I4r) is pacified only once the younger generation successfully work through a romance narrative, and the daughters and sons of the two kings are secure in their love for one another. Military strategy enables Pembrooke to stop the fighting, but it is the comedic-political bond of marriage which secures long-term peace:

> ...and now Nauar and Fraunce,
> Here end your strife, and let all hatred fall,
> And turne this warre to Hymens festiuall. ([K2r])

This ending stands in telling contradistinction to that other highly patterned play featuring a king called Navarre.

But then marriage is not an inevitably happy option in the Navarre story. Marlowe's *Massacre at Paris* shows the cross-faith marriage between the Protestant Navarre and the Catholic Margaret of Valois resulting in the devastation of the St Bartholomew's Day Massacre, and the revenge cycle of civil wars that followed. This 'funerall wedding' stayed in the public memory long after the French wars had ended.[77] Closer to home, Protestant Elizabethans had been relieved when marriage negotiations between their Queen and the French Catholic François Hercule, Duc

---

[75] Spenser's 'Burbon' obviously represents Navarre as the first Bourbon king, but perhaps there is also an onomastic underlining of the way that the apostatizing Henri becomes the very threat he had fought against.

[76] Perhaps coincidentally, the young prince of Navarre is named Ferdinand, like Shakespeare's king in the opening stage direction and speech prefixes of *Love's Labour's Lost*.

[77] Vignolle, *Abridgement of the Life of Henry the Great, the Fourth of that Name*, trans. Anon. (London, 1637), p. 3.

d'Alençon (suggested at 2.1.61 and 2.1.194 of *Love's Labour's Lost*) had failed in the 1580s.[78] By contrast, *The Trial of Chivalry* dissolves differences and shows marriage to be a salve for violence, uniting opposing sides. Key to the new unity is the answer marriage provides to the problem of succession: 'What matter ist who weares both Diadems, | When the Succession liues in eythers heyre?' (A3r). The lack of this politically happy 'ending' was also troubling in both France and England. Problematic succession could lead to civil war, as is evident in a brief allusion in *The Comedy of Errors*, where Dromio of Syracuse's parodic topography of Nell's body includes a reference to France, which is to be found 'In her forehead, armed and reverted, making war against her heir' (3.2.126–7). The pun on *hair/heir* (orthographically present in the Folio's 'heire') defines the French civil wars as Navarre's difficulty in securing his succession to the throne in the face of the Catholic League's 'armed' opposition.

Indeed the French wars were a constant reminder to the English of what could go wrong when there was no immediate heir to succeed to the throne. That there was a persistent anxiety about civil war throughout the early modern period up to the country's final descent into violence is witnessed by the number of literary works focusing on that theme.[79] In the 1590s this anxiety was specifically related to concern about who would succeed the aging Queen, particularly since the number of candidates for the job made it seem unlikely that the matter would proceed straightforwardly. James VI of Scotland, Lady Arabella Stuart, Catherine Grey, and the Spanish Infanta, to name but a few, all had claims to the English throne.[80] Indeed in the 1590s James was making it clear that he would not let the matter go without a very literal fight.[81] Wishing to preserve her own safety and that of any potential successor, Elizabeth forbade the publication of any such claims, and her need to do so suggests what an

---

[78] See Richard Corum, '"The Catastrophe Is a Nuptial": *Love's Labor's Lost*, Tactics, Everyday Life', in *Renaissance Culture and the Everyday*, ed. Patricia Fumerton and Simon Hunt (Philadelphia, PA: University of Pennsylvania Press, 1999), pp. 271–98 (p. 284), for the view that both *Love's Labour's Lost* and Elizabeth avoid the bloodshed of the historical and theatrical *Massacre at Paris*.

[79] See, for example, Thomas Lodge, *The Wounds of Ciuill War* (London, 1594); William Fulbecke, *An Historicall Collection of the Continuall Factions* [...] *of the Romans and Italians* (London, 1601); Samuel Daniel, *The Civil Wars* (London, 1595); Michael Drayton, *Mortimeriados* (London, 1596). For a discussion of civil war images in England and France, see Lisa Ferraro Parmelee, *Good Newes From Fraunce: French Anti-League Propaganda in Late Elizabethan England* (Rochester, NY: University of Rochester Press, 1996), pp. 53–73.

[80] Joel Hurstfield, 'The Succession Struggle in Late Elizabethan England', in *Elizabethan Government and Society*, ed. S. T. Bindoff, Joel Hurstfield, and C. H. Williams (London: Athlone Press, 1961), pp. 369–96 (pp. 372–3).

[81] Hurstfield, p. 393.

attractive topic it made. In 1593 Peter Wentworth was sent to the Tower for his *Pithie Exhortation* on the subject.[82]

In 1594 the Jesuit Robert Persons (under the pseudonym R. Doleman) published *A Conference About the Next Succession to the Crowne of Ingland* (Antwerp) for it to be smuggled into England in 1595. This lengthy debate favoured (unsurprisingly given Persons' Jesuitism) the Spanish Infanta's claims as well as facetiously stirring up political trouble with a dedication to the Earl of Essex.[83] This book made manifest in print the concerns about the uncertainty of the country's future:

> were the tymes neuer so quiet, and religion neuer so vniforme: yet are ther great doubtes in many mens heades, about the lawfulnes of diuers preten-tions of the famylies before named: but if you adde vnto this, the said won-derfull diuersity in matters of religio[n] also, which this tyme yealdeth: you shal finde the euent much more doubtfull.[84]

A Conference prompted a number of rebukes which served to keep the debate alive and to indicate how Persons was correct in his claim that sectarian difference made the event 'more doubtfull'.[85]

Thus the years when *Love's Labour's Lost* was probably written (1594–5) were years when concerns about succession and civil war were both acute and intimately related. The incongruous onomastic allusions to figures from the French civil war not only widen the play's linguistic perspective, but also give its generic structure a political inflection. It is significant that these particular characters (rather than their less topical comedic compan-ions in the canon) fail to secure marriage at the end of the play. The loss of comedic marriage is the loss of a bond which *The Trial of Chivalry* ex-plicitly states is procreative. As the obstetric pun in the title suggests, in *Love's Labour's Lost* we lose the promise of a labour to bring forth a child who would perpetuate inheritance cycles and lineage.[86] (Instead, Jaquenetta

---

[82] Hurstfield, p. 372.

[83] See Peter Holmes, 'The Authorship and Early Reception of a *Conference about the Next Succession to the Crown of England*', *The Historical Journal* 23 (1980), 415–29.

[84] R. Doleman [i.e. Robert Persons], *A Conference About the Next Succession to the Crowne of Ingland* (1594; facs. edn, Menston: Scolar Press, 1972), sig. B3v.

[85] Replies to Persons' book included Henry Constable's *A Discouerye of a Counterfecte Conference* (Paris, 1600); and John Hayward's *An Answer to the First Part of a Certaine Conference* (London, 1603).

[86] Mark Thornton Burnett sees the ending of the play in terms of gift exchange and Elizabeth's failure to offer her people an heir to the throne; 'Giving and Receiving: *Love's Labour's Lost* and the Politics of Exchange', *ELR* 23 (1993), 287–313 (310). In 1594 Henri of Navarre's mistress gave birth to a much longed-for son, but since Pope Gregory XIII refused to annul Navarre's marriage to Marguerite this potential heir was a labour lost to the realm. See Katherine B. Crawford, 'The Politics of Promiscuity: Masculinity and Heroic Representation at the Court of Henry IV', *French Historical Studies* 26 (2003), 225–52.

is pregnant with an illegitimate child and will be 'cast away' if Armado refuses to accept paternity (5.2.672).) The lords' very names bespeak inheritance. Maus points out that the aristocratic proper name 'is normally an inherited name; moreover, it is the name of *what* is inherited, the piece of property that guarantees its owner income and status'.[87] In a manner contrary to other comic Shakespearean characters, the lords' names raise the question of succession and lineage both by their topical connotations of a war about succession, and in a more general indication of onomastic inheritance that is denied other comic roles. Anne Barton observes that speaking characters in Shakespeare's comedies tend not to have surnames.[88] The lords' topical names expand their nominal definition beyond a first name (as noted earlier, Navarre is a *Ferdinand* only to the text's readers). It is as if they have stumbled into the wrong genre. They are nominally incompatible with the more comedically appropriate 'Rosaline', 'Maria', and 'Katherine'. However, it is the ladies' inherited names that concern Dumaine and Longaville:

DUMAINE   Sir, I pray you a word. What lady is that same?
BOYET   The heir of Alençon, Katherine her name. (2.1.193–4)

LONGAVILLE   Pray you, sir, whose daughter?
BOYET   Her mother's, I have heard.
LONGAVILLE   God's blessing on your beard!
BOYET   Good sir, be not offended.
              She is an heir of Falconbridge.
LONGAVILLE   Nay, my choler is ended.
              She is a most sweet lady. (2.1.200–6)

Longaville departs without even learning Maria's first name: he is more interested in her lineage and what kind of inheritance she could share with him.[89] The Princess is known only by a positional name which simultaneously nominates her a neutral fairytale type and marks her out in accordance to her position to her father, the French king, on whose business she comes to the Court of Navarre. At the very moment that the Princess becomes Queen, the moment when succession is in action as royal title passes from deceased father to living daughter, she refuses a move that would secure succession for the generations after her. Like England's contemporary queen she prevaricates when it comes to the subject of marriage.

[87] Maus, p. 210.
[88] Anne Barton, *The Names of Comedy* (Oxford: Clarendon Press, 1990), p. 36.
[89] For further references to inheritance and 'issue', see 1.1.7, 1.1.73, 2.1.5, 2.1.40–3, 2.1.194, 2.1.247–8, 4.1.20, 4.1.81–2, 4.3.342–3, 5.2.172, and 5.2.668–73.

If the onomastic allusions to wars of succession render this ending particularly troubling, then in some ways the play's onomastic structure also explains the open-ended finish. In plot terms it is the shocking intrusion of 'real' mortality (the French king's death) that obstructs the comedic direction of the conclusion. The 'real-life' names and their associations deepen the generic violation. Shakespeare seems to be testing the epistemological limits of comedy. The expression of theatrical failure makes it clear that we have reached breaking point:

> The *scene* begins to cloud. (5.2.716, my emphasis)

> Our wooing doth not end like an *old play*:
> Jack hath not Jill. These ladies' courtesy
> Might well have made our sport a *comedy*. (5.2.862–4, my emphasis)

> That's too long for a *play*. (5.2.866, my emphasis)

Comedy has proved unable to meet the demands placed on it by the material of *Love's Labour's Lost*. The play's linguistic mutability has infected the action and plot structure. Irresolution dominates the final scene, since we do not know if the lords will finally be able to keep their promises. The topical concerns raised by many of the names make this irresolution all the more troubling; but it is precisely because historical processes do not have endings that the play cannot round things off and say what will happen tomorrow (whereas tragedy can show us the certain end of the individual, death). Both real life political figures and historical stagings of 'real life' looked to marriage to do the comedic work of forward-looking reconciliation. Shakespeare's history plays frequently exposed the flaws in such unions: for example, in *1 Henry VI* Henry's unhappy marriage to Margaret only nourishes the factions of wars in which Margaret will herself participate; the comic ending that sees Henry V kiss 'Kate' is undercut by an epilogue reminding the audience that the marriage's issue 'lost France and made his England bleed' (Epilogue 12); and in *King John* Blanche's marriage to Louis fails to stop war that means 'Whoever wins, on that side shall I lose' (3.1.261). The 'real' perspective afforded by *Love's Labour's Lost*'s allusiveness shows comedic vision to be merely illusory.

The Trial of Chivalry manages its topical hints differently, by thoroughly transforming them into literary historicity. Like other romance texts that bear a 'temporal signature' and are 'pervaded by [a] spirit of "pastness"',[90] *The Trial of Chivalry* is deliberately old-fashioned in style (even if it was written and performed a number of years prior to its publication in

---

[90] Alex Davis, *Chivalry and Romance in the English Renaissance* (Cambridge: D. S. Brewer, 2003), p. 3.

1605).[91] As in *Love's Labour's Lost*, religion does not feature in the plot, but unlike Shakespeare's play the text is full of residual Catholicism that helps to fictionalize the conflict. For example, Katharina takes Bellamira to 'an Hermit' (G2r) for a cure for her poisoned face (translating into a more Catholic register the 'Phisition' to whom Helen of Corinth sends Parthenia in the *Arcadia* (Lib. 1, ch. 7, p. 50)).[92] Katharina also forms romantic attachments to images in an idolatry that reformed audiences were taught to associate with Catholicism. The 'Homilie Agaynst Perill of Idolatry' described the sin as spiritual 'fornication' (an unfaithful worship of something non-divine).[93] Katharina might not worship Catholic icons but her attention to images of her beloved(s) is unreformed. Both her misdirected love for Pembrooke and her politically appropriate love for Ferdinand are channelled through images. After Pembrooke's rejection she consoles herself with an 'Image far more kind, | Then is the substance' and she holds the picture 'within mine armes' (B4r–B4v).[94] Then, reversing Renaissance practice whereby some (including royalty in the *Arcadia* and real life) fall in love with a person *before* meeting them, Katharina rejects the flesh and blood Ferdinand but then *later* falls for him after contemplating his image. Looking on Ferdinand's picture she idolatrously blurs the distinction between image and thing, fantasizing that:

> I claspe my Ferdinand betweene mine armes:
> So long as I behold this liuely forme,
> So long am I refreshed by his smiles:
> So long, me thinks, I heare him speake to me. (Gr)

Ferdinand and Pembrooke simply work with this iconophilia, by having Ferdinand present himself as his own statue. When Katharina subsequently

---

[91] For a consideration of a possible date of composition for *The Trial of Chivalry* and the contemporary circumstances of its 1605 publication, see Gillian Woods, 'The Contexts of *The Trial of Chivalry*', *Notes and Queries* 252.3 (2007), 313–18.

[92] Philip Sidney, *The Countesse of Pembrokes Arcadia*, ed. Albert Feuillerat (Cambridge: Cambridge University Press, 1912).

[93] *Certaine Sermons appoynted by the Quenes Maiesty* (London, 1563), sig. Ii(iiii)r.

[94] Katharina's iconophilia exceeds that of her Sidnean counterpart, Helen of Corinth. Helen finds the sight of a picture or 'Idol' of Amphialus distracting (Lib. 1, ch. 11, p. 67), but unlike Katharina, she has not commissioned this picture and is painfully aware that the image is a poor substitute for Amphialus's substance (Lib. 1, ch. 11, pp. 68, 73). Ferdinand's source character, Philoxenus, is killed and there is no equivalent of the scenes in which Katharina's love is redirected from Pembrooke to Ferdinand by means of a picture and a statue. For a discussion of the *Arcadia* and idolatry, see Blair Worden, *The Sound of Virtue* (New Haven, CT: Yale University Press, 1996), esp. pp. 305, 303. For a nuanced interpretation of Sidney's understanding of images, see Claire Preston, 'Sidney's Arcadian Poetics: A Medicine of Cherries and the Philosophy of Cavaliers', in *English Renaissance: Prose History, Language, and Politics*, ed. Neil Rhodes (Tempe, AZ: Medieval and Renaissance Texts and Studies, 1997), pp. 91–108.

speaks to the 'statue' as if it were Ferdinand himself, she is rewarded with the living and breathing prince. Katharina's unreformed feelings are thus managed by a theatrical trick, and the fictional world quickly absorbs an ideologically risky wonder, as only eight lines pass before Pembrooke urges the couple to keep pace with the plot: 'Of that no more: now let vs haste from hence, | To quiet the dissension lately sprung' (H2r). (Obviously, this contrasts with the enlarged spiritual potential of the more mysterious statue scene in *The Winter's Tale*, to be discussed in Chapter 5.) Earlier, Pembrooke's attempt to play the romance protagonist, by guarding a tomb honouring his 'dead' friend's memory, is carefully undermined: his first encounters are with women not battle-hungry knights and the memorial is but an 'empty Monument' (F3r).

Such vestigial Catholicism is historical in the sense of belonging to the past realm of 'once upon a time'. Ironically, the effect is partly achieved through instances of anachronism: for example, Bowyer asseverates 'and I lye, call me a Iebuzite' (Cv) and later the Clowne (entering the stage immediately after Katharina's raptures over the picture of Ferdinand) compares Bellamira's disfigured appearance to 'a tortur'de Image made of playster worke' (Gv).[95] Allusions to Jesuits and iconoclastic ruins enable these comic characters to wink at the audience from the fictional past on the stage, to remind them that what they watch is temporally, ideologically, and theatrically circumscribed *as* fiction. Elizabeth Mazzola has shown that 'abandoned symbols' persist in occupying space in the mental landscape of each generation.[96] Clearly, Catholic symbols continue to exist even after the Reformation ostensibly empties them of their sacred significance and categorizes them as false. Of such outmoded ideas and symbols Mazzola says:

> they fail to describe reality, while ignoring other cultural requirements for meaning, power or guidance. Rather than actively continuing to shape texts or readers, these ideas constitute a secret record of the imagination's failures or an arrangement of its lies. In the same way that Latin becomes a dead language, *these dead or dying symbols become poetry* [my emphasis].[97]

Catholic symbols are a fiction (a papist lie) and can be used to give a sense of the fictional (something more neutrally distant from the everyday). The residual Catholicism of *The Trial of Chivalry* contributes to the

---

[95] 'Jebusite' was a biblical name for one of the tribes of Canaanites dispossessed of Jerusalem by David, but in the seventeenth century it was also a nickname for Roman Catholics, especially Jesuits. See *OED*, s.v. 'Jebusite'.

[96] Elizabeth Mazzola, *The Pathology of the English Renaissance: Sacred Remains and Holy Ghosts* (Leiden: Brill, 1998), p. 1.

[97] Mazzola, p. 4.

fantastic nature of the romance genre, at the same time that the context of the romance genre neutralizes the Catholic elements as merely fiction. In pseudo-histories, political thought is provoked by the juxtaposition of different reality states: a non-real space is created where the contemporary problems suggested by the play's onomastics are resolved and absolved by fiction, in part, because the Catholic meaning present is *only* fiction (fantastic statues and fairytale hermits). It is not so much that the sectarian is idealized in *The Trial of Chivalry* as that it is made distant, and importantly, reaches happy closure.

In *Love's Labour's Lost*, instead of being pushed to the past, the onomastic sectarianism is of 'these days' (4.1.22). The play is not populated with (nearly) 'abandoned symbols' that implicitly acknowledge a Catholic-to-Protestant narrative order: as a newly minted symbol of Catholicism, 'Navarre' preposterously has a Protestant history. An apostate (one who 'falleth from true Religion') was considered to be a backslider,[98] and so Navarre's name is appropriate to a play that, as Patricia Parker argues, puts 'relentless emphasis on the inversion of order and sequence, on the reversal of beginning and end, front and back, prior and "posterior"'.[99] Such motion prevents the safe distancing of Catholic connotations.

But if this material proves resistant to comedic closure neither does Shakespeare give us satirical purchase on it. One (pre-conversion) pamphlet puts the French civil war in a wider sectarian context through a mocking recreation of denominational difference. The 'merry' author, an English man who fights with 'the inuincible *Henry*', briskly passes over the military exploits that usually constitute 'news' from France to recount the 'cometragicall historie' of two friars in the company of 'the dastard traytor *de Mayn*'.[100] Operating by a standard anti-Catholic logic, the story tells of a sexual love triangle between two friars and a young nun: Friar Francis usurps Friar Donnet's place at 'shrift betwixt the sheets' with the nineteen-year-old by deceiving his elder that Henry has been captured and presented to De Mayn, and suggesting the first to tell the Pope will be well rewarded. Nevertheless the lovesick nun forces Francis to follow Donnet. Rome rejoices at Donnet's news with the inevitable holy water, bonfires, procession, and mass. However, a despairing letter from De

---

[98] Henry Cockeram, *The English Dictionarie* (London, 1623), sig. [B5v]; see definitions in Edmund Coote, *The English Schoole-Maister* (London, 1596), sig. L2r; and Robert Cawdrey, *A Table Alphabeticall* (London, 1604), sig. [B5r]. Protestant polemicists saw Catholicism as 'plaine apostacie from the true faith'; Francis Bunny, *A Suruey of the Popes Supremacie* (London, 1595), p. 203.

[99] Patricia Parker, 'Preposterous Reversals: *Love's Labor's Lost*', *MLQ* 54 (1993), 435–82 (443–4).

[100] L. R., *A Subtill Practise* (London, 1590), sigs. A2r, [A4r], A2r.

Mayn (who has fled battle in disguise) forces Donnet and Francis to admit their deceptions to the furious Pope. As penance, the friars walk barefoot through Rome, whipping each other into a state that is both horrific and humorous (and reminiscent of the graphic passages of Nashe's *The Unfortunate Traveller*): 'rawbond ridges shewed in all pointes so like a redde lattice, that if a tincker had seene them he would vndoubtedly haue mistooke him for an alehouse'.[101] The comic ending punishes Catholic sexual hypocrisy with suitably Catholic penitential excess. It may not offer the delight of reconciliation, but the alternative assertion of difference affords reformed readers a comforting laugh at their moral inferiors and also consolidates confidence in the military victories that provide the tale's framework. More tellingly, the fictional quality of the story—its anecdotal unreality—only serves to confirm the fundamental falseness of the Catholic subject (rather than of the writer who makes it up). The merry teller states openly that 'the substance of it is true, although it faile in some circu[m]stance': glancing at Eucharistic controversy, the literary lack of literal truth is substantially Catholic.[102]

But it seems to be the reality of 'Catholicism' that confounds conclusion in *Love's Labour's Lost*. The last-minute appropriation of a fictional and distanced unreformed aesthetic creates a generic switch that masks a failure to contain the immediate problems. The tasks imposed on Navarre and his lords register and open out uncertainty, rather than marking a definitive Catholic penitence.[103] Not trusting the perjured Navarre's romantic fidelity, the new queen sets him the year's task of enduring 'frosts and fasts, hard lodging and thin weeds' (5.2.795) in some 'forlorn and naked hermitage' (5.2.789), while she shuts herself up in a 'mourning house' (5.2.802). The preposterous commencement of a romance tale where a comedy should end also looks temporally backwards, to a pre-Reformation time of hermits and mourning houses. Structurally this mirrors Henri of Navarre's 'backsliding' to a world of Catholic ritual, but it is the 'Catholicism' of romance rather than early modern reality.[104] The fairytale duration of 'twelvemonth and a day' (5.2.815) is disruptive as well as distancing, since it breaks the limits of the play. We do not know if the lords will come good this time, but with the denial of the comic

---

[101] L. R., sig. [A4r].　　　　[102] L. R., sig. [A4r].

[103] Even Armado's claim to 'go woolward for penance' is undercut by Moth's exposure of financial necessity: 'True, and it was enjoined him in Rome for want of linen' (5.2.705–8).

[104] Catholic-League enemies of Henri IV pointed out his failure to perform the penitential acts which traditionally attested to sincere conversion; see Michael Wolfe, *The Conversion of Henri IV: Politics, Power and Religious Belief in Early Modern France* (Cambridge, MA: Harvard University Press, 1993), p. 161.

expectation for reconciliation and union, we really feel the 'loss' advertised in the drama's title. The comedy has proved unable to deal with the semantic flux and contingency to which the sectarianism alluded to by the play's onomastics has given a very serious inflection. It is left to Berowne to continue the more general generic experiment and see if the comic spirit can survive the fact of mortality: 'To move wild laughter in the throat of death' (5.2.843). We end on a rather melancholy division— 'You that way, we this way' (5.2.919)—maintaining a split either between oath-breaking lords and heirless ladies, or between one 'happy' couple (Armado and Jaquenetta) and four not so happy 'couples', or even between a fictional realm and the real world, where 'civil war' is far deadlier than the figurative war of 'wits' presented by the play (2.1.225).

Catholicism, or rather the fact of religious difference, intrudes in *Love's Labour's Lost* as an additional principle of semantic mutability that intensifies the need for resolution even as it makes it more difficult. The play refuses the conclusive defeat of Talbot and Joan found in *1 Henry VI*, but it shares the history's inability to resolve the epistemological tensions unleashed by sectarianism. In the later 'problem' comedies *All's Well that Ends Well* and *Measure for Measure*, where the commitment to real-life contingency is deepened, Shakespeare exploits Catholic 'material' so pointedly absent from *Love's Labour's Lost*. In these plays Catholicism is kept before the audience's eyes as a visual aesthetic in the form of religious costumes. The next chapter explores the fictional function of this Catholicism in plays that maintain a comic structure whereby love's labour is ostensibly won.

3

Seeming Difference in *Measure for Measure* and *All's Well that Ends Well*

In post-Reformation theatre Catholicism had a visibility that was prohibited in 'real life'. Hermits', nuns', and especially friars' habits were a staple part of early modern costume collections. At least 32 plays from the period 1500–1660 feature one or more hermits; 21 cast nuns and 64 starred friars.[1] Rosary beads and crucifixes also appeared as props signalling a Catholic aesthetic.[2] But what was visible on stage was practically invisible in reality. Since the dissolution of the monasteries in the 1530s, friars and nuns were not seen in public. Rare exceptions were found at times of execution or imprisonment. For example, in 1601 Mark Barkworth 'chose to be drawn to Tyburn in the Benedictine habit', and in 1600, when being sent to Wisbech Castle, a *'Franciscan* of the Order of Capuchins...wore his friar's weed all the way he went'.[3] Non-Catholic early moderns were more likely to see Catholic clothes as theatrical costumes than actual vestments. Rosary beads and crucifixes were contraband: signs of Catholic faith to be kept secret because of that very significance. Indeed the stage's simulations of Catholics were performed for audiences who had no means of readily recognizing Catholics in everyday life.

The question of what Catholics looked like formed a major part of the epistemological anxiety they caused in post-Reformation England. Physically speaking, Catholicism is illegible. Unlike other early modern

---

[1] Statistics gathered using *An Index of Characters in Early Modern English Drama: Printed Plays, 1500–1660*, ed. Thomas L. Berger, William C. Bradford, and Sidney L. Sondergard (Cambridge: Cambridge University Press, 1998). Only one of these plays, John Heywood's *The Pardoner and the Friar*, predates the dissolution of the monasteries in 1539.

[2] See Elizabeth Williamson, *The Materiality of Early Modern English Drama* (Farnham: Ashgate, 2009). Williamson explores a spectrum of visual meaning in which Catholic objects connote papism and also less ideologically risky tradition.

[3] Richard Challoner, rev. John Hungerford Pollen, *Memoirs of Missionary Priests as well Secular as Regular and of other Catholics of Both Sexes, that have Suffered Death in England on Religious Accounts from the Year of Our Lord, 1577 to 1684* (1924; repr. Farnborough: Gregg, 1969), pp. 255, 251.

'others', native Catholics were racially indistinct. This similarity was particularly problematic because it was embedded in post-Reformation culture's most significant difference. 'The contrast between Catholics and Protestants was', as Frances Dolan contends, 'central to the definition of identity and difference in the seventeenth century'; English national identity emerged differentially as not (Roman) Catholic. But at the same time 'Undermining Englishness and Protestantism by not being different enough, English Catholics unsettled the nation's relation to its own past and, with their allegiances divided between England's sovereign and Rome's pope, blurred the distinction between the English and foreigners, loyal subjects and traitors, us and them.'[4] This indistinctness was most (un)clear at the level of the body. Proclamations against Catholics promoted the Protestant national order of the day as emphatically 'natural' (an adjective repeatedly linked with the nouns 'prince', 'country', 'duty', 'subject', and 'sovereign').[5] The disobedient papist's opposition to such order is thus monstrously unnatural. However, the strained emphasis of this rhetoric also implicitly contained the troubling truth that there was no 'natural' distinction that could make evident the all-important difference between English Protestants and English Catholics.

Compounding the problem of somatic similarity, Catholic representation was thought to be inherently duplicitous. Fundamentally, Catholics and Catholic icons were not what they seemed. The significance of Catholic signs was the opposite of what they apparently signified. Thus apocalyptic anti-Catholic writing exposed the repellent and sinful interiors hidden beneath glittering and holy Catholic surfaces.[6] Dazzling displays produced moral and semantic corruption as gullible viewers were drawn to papist hypocrisy. In hotter Protestant writings, such as the work of J. Baxter, Catholics were found to be as deceptive as their iconography: 'If a window were framed in the brests of these discontented catholikes . . . then I know full well that many false hearts would be found lurking vnder painted hoodes, and cakes of foule cancred malice, vnder meale mouthed protestations'.[7] Baxter's fantasy marks an extreme position in the reformed

---

[4] Frances Dolan, *Whores of Babylon: Catholicism, Gender, and Seventeenth-Century Print Culture* (Ithaca, NY: Cornell University Press, 1999), pp. 1, 5.

[5] See, for example, *Tudor Royal Proclamations*, ed. Paul L. Hughes and James F. Larkin, 3 vols (New Haven, CT: Yale University Press, 1964–9): 'Declaring Jesuits and Non-Returning Seminarians Traitors' (1582), ii, pp. 488–91; and 'Ordering Martial Law Against Possessors of Papal Bulls, Books, Pamphlets' (1588), iii, pp. 13–17.

[6] Alison Shell, *Catholicism, Controversy and the English Literary Imagination, 1558–1660* (Cambridge: Cambridge University Press, 1999), pp. 23–55.

[7] J. Baxter, *A Toile for Two-Legged Foxes* (London, 1600), sig. Iv.

perspective and his metaphor of transparency pointedly yearns for the 'window' in which the Elizabethan state disclaimed interest.

Nevertheless, while Baxter's certainty and vitriol might be extreme, he exaggerates a discomfort felt by Elizabethans more widely, including members of the Government. While William Cecil, for example, distinguishes between missionary priests (whose 'secrecy' evidences villainy) and beloved subjects (whose private faith could be tolerated as conscience), he nevertheless fears contact between priests and subjects (who would become 'discontented').[8] The state fostered the very Catholic secrecy it railed against as treachery: outward conformity to the Church of England was officially regarded as a sufficient mark of obedience and there was (ostensibly) no making of windows into men's souls.[9] By its very nature, secrecy confounded interpretation: who could say whether a Catholic subject hid papist treason along with their Catholic faith?

But it was missionary priests who symbolized all that was to be most feared and despised in Catholicism: 'natural' subjects that were unnaturally Romish, these foreign-educated priests returned home, disguising their identities and purpose and allegedly spreading treachery alongside superstitious religion. For the most vociferously anti-Catholic polemicists these figures represented the depraved semiotic condition of papistry. In his *Anatomie of Abuses* Philip Stubbes describes the emphatic obscurity of 'papists':

> These sedicious Vipers, and *Pythonicall Hydraes*, eyther lurke secretly in corners, seducing her Maiesties suiectes, and withdrawing their heartes from their Soueraignes obedience, or els walke openly, obseruing an outward *decorum*, and an order as others do, and the[n] may no man say blacke is their eye, but they are good protestantes.[10]

There is an utter absence of visual markers that would separate these treasonous 'Vipers' from 'good protestantes'. Catholicism is a state of continual concealment: not only do Catholics 'lurke secretly' but, more worryingly, their alternative openness is itself a manifestation of being hidden from view. Similar appearance really denotes frightening difference. John Gee's description of 'How to know a Priest' in *Foot Out of the*

---

[8] William Cecil, *The Execution of Justice in England* (London, 1583), sigs. A.iii.v–[A4r], [E4r].

[9] For a discussion of these contradictions, see Ronald J. Corthell, '"The Secrecy of Man": Recusant Discourse and the Elizabethan Subject', *ELR* 19 (1989), 272–90; and Gillian Woods, '"Strange Discourse": The Controversial Subject of *Sir Thomas More*', *Renaissance Drama* 39 (2011), 3–35.

[10] Philip Stubbes, *The Anatomie of Abuses*, ed. M. J. Kidnie (Tempe, AZ: Arizona Center for Medieval and Renaissance Studies in conjunction with Renaissance English Text Society, 2002), p.186.

Snare likewise emphasizes the counter-intuition necessary to decode Catholic appearance:

> If, about *Bloomesbury* or *Holborne*, thou meet a good smug Fellow in a gold-laced suit, a cloke lined thorow with velvet, one that hath good store of coin in his purse, Rings on his fingers, a Watch in his pocket, which hee will valew at above twentie pounds, a very broad-laced Band, a Stiletto by his side,... then take heed of a Jesuite, of the prouder sort of Priests. This man hath vowed *poverty*.[11]

Paradoxically, a Catholic priest is identifiable as such because he does not look like a Catholic priest. Anxiety at the visual indeterminacy of Catholics is turned to polemical advantage as Gee emphasizes priestly hypocrisy by suggesting secular enjoyment of the gentleman disguise which Jesuits tended to adopt in England. The Catholic is inevitably opulent even in a disguise creating an 'everyday' appearance. Thus disguise tells the hypocritical truth about its wearer in its very falseness (both its moral corruption and its semiotic deceit).

Catholics themselves were conscious of the moral difficulties of pragmatic dissimulation. Priests protested reluctance at adopting such sumptuous, secular dress. The Jesuit John Gerard told his captors: 'I did not like wearing lay clothes... I would have much preferred my proper dress.'[12] He insisted the disguise of 'a gentleman of moderate means' was chosen for practical reasons, not from vanity:

> It was thus that I used to go about before I became a Jesuit and I was therefore more at ease in these clothes than I would have been if I had assumed a role that was strange and unfamiliar to me. Besides, I had to move in public and meet many Protestant gentlemen, and I could never have mixed with them and brought them slowly back to a love of the faith and a virtuous life had I dressed in any other way.[13]

Priestly disguise was justifiable in a heretical realm: it protected the Catholic identity of an individual and helped to advance the Catholic faith.

Not only defending but also regulating this practice was imperative. In the desperate circumstances of post-Reformation England, different Catholics loosened representational morality in different ways. Catholic authorities developed a complex moral system that governed what constituted acceptable and unacceptable feigning. Henry Garnet reported that

---

[11] *John Gee's Foot Out of the Snare 1624*, ed. T. H. B. M. Harmsen (Nijmegen: Cicero Press, 1992), p. 127.
[12] John Gerard, *The Autobiography of an Elizabethan*, trans. Philip Caraman (London: Longmans, Green, 1951), p. 94.
[13] Gerard, pp. 17–18.

a person 'may omitte the signe of his owne religion, [only] when it is not instituted for a protestation of religion'.[14] Thus 'Preistes among heretickes' might wear 'lay apparrell' without being 'reprehended by any deuoute conscience, for lying or dissembling'; however, those Catholics who believed they could conceal their faith and attend Church of England services as conformists were condemned.[15] Priests could adopt benignly misleading dress because there was a greater truth at stake. But some signs were incontrovertibly significant: attendance of Protestant services was to Garnet: 'a distinctiue signe and manifest note, wherby heretickes and schismatickes are discerned from trew Catholickes.'[16] The schismatic's sin left no room for differentiation between external action and inner belief: 'Schisme requireth nothing but a consent of the will to a diuision from the Church: and therfore euery outward Schismaticke, is also an inward Schismaticke'.[17] Many English Catholics disagreed, organizing their theological belief and political loyalty as contrary inward faith and outward conformity. For the Reformers' part, the state's own rather dubious definitions of the meaning of Church attendance (an insincere religious action read in terms of political fidelity) upset the more scrupulous and was rejected by hotter Protestants who, like some Catholics, recused themselves from Church of England services. Early modern England was peopled with subjects playing by different semiotic rules, and these differences did not fall into neat sectarian divisions. At a time when cultural otherness became more significant, its nature was not as easy to pinpoint as the polemic attempted to suggest. Parties from different confessional viewpoints changed their argument depending on circumstance and the people involved: false seeming *both* protected the integrity of the self *and* manifested inner corruption. How individuals seemed mattered; but how seeming mattered and what seeming meant was under dispute.[18]

From a Protestant perspective, 'Papists' were both troublingly invisible and overly visual. The anti-Catholic rhetoric that identified them condemned a representational system wholly fraudulent in meaning and mode. Thus even when Catholic clerics identified themselves through vestments, the piety signalled was thought to be a way of concealing an

---

[14] Henry Garnet, *An Apology Against the Defence of Schisme* (?1593; facs. edn, Menston: Scolar Press, 1973), sig. [I7v].

[15] Garnet, sig. [I8r].

[16] Garnet, sig. [I6r].

[17] Garnet, sigs. [G6v–G7r].

[18] This sectarian problem was part of a larger epistemological concern in the period. See especially, Katharine Eisaman Maus, *Inwardness and Theater in the English Renaissance* (Chicago, IL: University of Chicago Press, 1995).

exactly contrary sinful reality. Catholic writers explained that religious habits had a symbolic, mnemonic function:

> Although it is not the Habite which maketh a religious person, but their Profession, and due obseruation, of their aprooued order, yet not withstanding, for as much as the religious habit doth truely admonish them, of a holier and purer life, aboue the common people; all Religious persons, doe weare a distinct habite.[19]

But such vestments were, in Protestant polemical judgments, as much a disguise as the secular garb worn by missionary priests adopting false identities. And even the intended representational function of Catholic vestments was anathema to reformed thought. The detailed sartorial rules that differentiated between various Catholic religious orders were ridiculed as meaningless. Andrew Willet listed some of the 'great variety of their habits' as evidence of the Catholic Church's blasphemous preoccupation with 'humane traditions'. These vestments could not signify anything spiritual because they were not (it was argued) signs instituted by God, but were rather redundant man-made signs that signalled only their own worldliness.[20] More puritanical accounts stressed the materiality of Catholicism as excessive. Philip Stubbes provides lengthy itemizations of the rich fabrics (hypocritically) used in Catholic vestments, and gives examples of bishops wearing '14. sundry sortes of garments upo[n] their backes at once'.[21] While the Catholic body lacks meaningful markers of difference, the material signifiers of Catholicism lack meaning in their proliferation. Instead of conveying semiotic density the numerousness of the signifiers (the vestments) has one meaning: fraud. The focus on the materiality of Catholic identity keeps denominational difference importantly non-essential. Catholicism itself, with its insignificant signs, is a mere pretence of a religion and profoundly lacking in meaning. The notion that Catholicism might be located in (variously deceptive) sartorial layers is entirely appropriate to a reformist understanding of Catholicism as semiotically aberrant, as essentially 'anti-essential', fraudulent, and corrupt.

Thus Reformers frequently asserted a different understanding not just of what signs represented, but also of how they functioned. Nevertheless this difference should not be overstated. Protestants certainly made a point of refusing to place any kind of sanctified meaning on clothing.

---

[19] William Stanney, *A Treatise of Penance* (Douai, 1617; facs. edn, Menston: Scolar Press, 1972), p. 233.

[20] Andrew Willet, *Synopsis Papismi* (London, 1592), pp. 259–60.

[21] Philip Stubbes, *The Pope's Monarchy* (London, 1585), sig. E1r. For a related discussion of iconographic criticism, see Shell, p. 33.

Divine significance could not be found in human representation; worldly signs were necessarily imperfect and could not convey absolute meaning. Papists distanced themselves further from God with (among other things) their layers of intricately symbolic vestments. Defending the need for sumptuary 'decorum', Philip Stubbes carefully distinguished his position from Catholic practice: 'I put no religion in going, or not going in the like simple attire of our parents *Adam* and *Eua* (as the Sorbonicall Papists doe, placing all their religion in heathen garments and Romish ragges) so that we obserue a meane, and exceed not in pride.'[22] The word 'ragges' captures the way in which an idolatrous overvaluation of signifiers paradoxically voids them of significance. However, Stubbes attempts to assert that clothes should make manifest a God-given order while also denying sartorial signifiers any divine meaning. This creates a rhetorical awkwardness that reveals the logical contradiction in such thinking.

As Adrian Streete shows, this tension was part of a broader philosophical difficulty within Protestant thought: despite the 'iconoclastic impulse to distance *res* from *verba*' reformers felt uncomfortable with the absolute claim 'that the divine could not have a visible locus on earth.'[23] Thus, even though they argued conceptual difference, reformers could not always maintain a complete theoretical distinction from Catholic tradition. What emerges is a sense of the vexed significance of seeming in the post-Reformation period. Reading the difference between Catholicism and Protestantism was, in multiple senses, a problem of seeming: what made denominational difference apparent?—was that difference what it seemed?—how does seeming relate to being?—how *should* it relate to being?

The representational nature of the theatre makes it a particularly significant venue for the exploration of such dilemmas. As noted earlier, Catholicism frequently 'appears' on stage in a way that it couldn't in real life. Friars, monks, nuns, hermits, and pilgrims were free to wander the stage but not the realm. Sometimes such 'habited' characters are visually useful: they establish the verisimilitude of the past or a foreign location, and mark the space off from the reality of early modern England. This open and strikingly visual presence works in intriguing contrast to a culture in which Catholicism was concealed. Perhaps this explains a well-worn theatrical convention whereby characters used Catholic vestments as disguise. In Chapman's *May Day* Angelo objects to the suggestion that he puts a friar's habit to such use: 'Out vppon't, that disguise is worne

[22] Stubbes, *Anatomie*, pp. 92, 76.
[23] Adrian Streete, 'Reforming Signs: Semiotics, Calvinism and Clothing in Sixteenth-Century England', *Literature and History* 12 (2003), 1–18 (14).

thread bare vpon euery stage, and so much villany committed vnder that habit, that 'tis growne as suspicious as the vilest' (2.4.146–8).[24] The remark makes a theological and a theatrical point: the pious Catholic habit conceals villainy; the staging of Catholic clothes as nefarious disguise has become passé. The popularity of such disguise is instructive: it not only rehearses the (overly) familiar concept of Catholic hypocrisy, but it also makes this hypocrisy comfortingly legible for an audience taught to fear hidden Catholic traitors. The convention that exploited Catholic habits as disguises made visible the link between Catholicism and deception, and readily identified deceivers whose difference in reality was invisible. Stephen Greenblatt argues by a related logic that the reformation of attitudes to Catholic vestments was partly achieved by their use on stage. Recycling holy vestments as theatrical costumes helped convert faith into bad faith.[25]

However, 'seeming' is, almost by definition, a slippery concept. The production of 'bad faith' is clearly a major aspect of Catholic aesthetics on the post-Reformation stage. Yet there are also other perspectives, particularly in Shakespeare's drama. Theatrical fiction, as Greenblatt's earlier arguments highlighted, is an illusion, even a deception, and this certainly has a bearing on the meaning of the Catholicism used to help make theatre. But fiction is not therefore an inevitably contaminating space, tarring all its content with the associations of deceit. Released from some of the rules that govern reality (or at least subject to different ones), dramatic fiction can enable explorations of ethics and spirituality that consider ideals as well as frauds. To state the obvious, it is as much a creative as a deceptive space. And both these competing positive and negative possibilities illuminate the problem of Catholic seeming in Shakespeare.

This chapter studies the impact of visually Catholic characters in *Measure for Measure* (1604) and *All's Well that Ends Well* (1604–5). In these plays the 'putting on' (in both senses) of Catholic costumes complicates as much as it characterizes the wearer. In Shakespeare, as in other Renaissance drama, Catholic costumes can connote a degree of hypocrisy. But Shakespeare idiosyncratically uncovers other meanings also invested in the habits (worn by the Duke, Isabella, and Helen), and makes them

[24] George Chapman, *May Day*, ed. R. F. Welsh, in *The Plays of George Chapman*, gen. ed. A. Holaday (Urbana, IL: University of Illinois Press, 1970).

[25] Stephen Greenblatt, *Shakespearean Negotiations: The Circulation of Social Energy in Renaissance England* (Berkeley, CA: University of California Press, 1988), p. 6; see also Ann Rosalind Jones and Peter Stallybrass, *Renaissance Clothing and the Materials of Memory* (Cambridge: Cambridge University Press, 2000), p. 192. Williamson explores the recycling of religious materials as theatrical properties and moves beyond the 'emptying out' reading; see esp. pp. 1–31.

interact with one another. He attends to the theological and theatrical implications of the costumes in plays that explore the boundaries between fiction and reality, and the social values underpinning both. Catholic costumes are highly legible, but problematically multivalent. Characters attempt to self-fashion themselves with these habits, but must also contend with the worn-out meanings that others read into them. Catholic clothes help draw attention to the problem of the comedic self: an individual defined socially. Indeed seeming is a generic problem in these plays, which don't quite feel like the comedies they appear to be. The presence of Catholic aesthetics highlights the moral crux central to fiction (golden world or fraud) and the challenging nature of the relationship between the self and other(s). How should we read the other, and how do we live with him or her once we have recognized difference?

THE SEEMING SELF AND THE SEEMING OTHER: IS THIS HER FAULT OR MINE?

Measure for Measure, the only text in the Shakespeare canon with a biblical title, is also the play in which Catholicism is most visible and significant to the plot itself.[26] But the significance is ambiguous rather than clear-cut: we meet a woman who would like to be—but is not yet—a nun and a Duke who does not want to 'stage' himself as a Duke but instead disguises himself as a friar (1.1.69). Recent critical attention has focused on the Duke's religio-political correction of Angelo's puritanical rule, and the play's apparent attention to modes of monarchy.[27] This chapter looks instead at the Catholic habits that complicate characters' roles and invite us to consider the individual as well as society at large.

---

[26] Perhaps only *King John* (and, more obliquely, *Henry VIII*) also put Catholicism at the heart of the plot. In both these instances history determines the subject matter; *Measure for Measure*, by contrast, pitches Catholic and fictional (especially comedic) values against one another.

[27] See, for example, Sarah Beckwith, 'Medieval Penance, Reformation Repentance and *Measure for Measure*', in *Reading the Medieval in Early Modern England*, ed. Gordon Mc-Mullan and David Matthews (Cambridge: Cambridge University Press, 2007), pp. 193–204; Beatrice Groves, *Texts and Traditions: Religion in Shakespeare, 1592–1604* (Oxford: Clarendon Press, 2007), pp. 154–83; Thomas Healy, 'Selves, States, and Sectarianism in Early Modern England', *English* 44 (1995), 193–213; Peter Lake with Michael Questier, *The Antichrist's Lewd Hat: Protestants, Papists and Players in Post-Reformation England* (New Haven, CT: Yale University Press, 2002), pp. 621–700; Stacy Magedanz, 'Public Justice and Private Mercy in *Measure for Measure*', *SEL* 44.2 (2004), 317–32; Debora K. Shuger, *Political Theologies in Shakespeare's England: The Sacred and the State in Measure for Measure* (Basingstoke: Palgrave, 2001).

The play is generally concerned with the difficulties of seeming, whether it be the outrage of hypocrisy (Isabella exclaims 'Seeming, seeming!' when Angelo speaks his lust (2.4.151); the Duke moralizes wistfully: 'That we were all, as some would seem to be, | Free from our faults, as faults from seeming free!' (3.1.305–6)) or a wider epistemology (the Duke, in particular, wants to know the hearts of his subjects). The notoriously shifty Catholic aesthetic draws attention to and complicates the play's moral problems. It is a drama in which comedic structure is under real threat. The romantic coupling that usually bonds comedic communities has been replaced by a spectrum of sexual behaviour that testifies to social breakdown: prostitution devalues sexual relations as financial transactions; procreation becomes contamination, as diseases wreck bodies and pregnancy is defined as sin (new life punishable by the father's death); and at the heart of the plot sex functions as a bribe and a trap. Small wonder, then, that the play's female lead should want to withdraw from her genre's social and romantic pressures and live in the alternative Catholic sisterhood of the convent. In following the Duke's initial desire to investigate 'what our seemers be' (1.3.54), *Measure for Measure* explores the integrity of the comedic individual and the nature of his or her (generically necessary) relations with others.

Reluctant to participate in the comedic world, Isabella differentiates herself from the rest of the cast. As a would-be nun, it is possible that she looked distinctive. The text of *Measure for Measure* provides no instruction on Isabella's costume. The folio stage direction featuring her first appearance reads: '*Enter Isabell and Francisca a Nun*' (1.4.0.1). The specification that Francisca is a nun perhaps suggests that Isabella should not look like one. Costume-expert Jean MacIntyre asserts that since Isabella is a novice she should not wear a nun's habit, claiming that early modern novices did not wear full religious dress.[28] However, the Council of Trent stipulated that novices had to be 'clothed' for at least a year prior to their profession.[29] And the novice's clothes were closer to those of a nun than to secular attire. The Rule of the Order of Saint Clare (the sorority Isabella seeks to join) stipulated that even girls who were received into the convent before they came of age should 'haue their hayre cut of, and their secular habit taken away, and be cloathed with such cloth as the Religious, according to the discretio[n] of the Abbesse'.[30] 'No Nouice' was to 'weare

---

[28] Jean MacIntyre, *Costumes and Scripts in the Elizabethan Theatres* (Edmonton: University of Alberta Press, 1992), pp. 275–7; p 340, n. 16.

[29] Mary Laven, *Virgins of Venice: Enclosed Lives and Broken Vows in the Renaissance Convent* (London: Viking, 2002), p. 27.

[30] *The Rule of the Holy Virgin S. Clare* (n.p., 1621; facs. edn, Menston: Scolar Press, 1975), pp. 13–14.

the blacke veile, before she haue expressly made her profession', but sartorial distinction was made with 'the white kercher decently put on, according to the appointment of the Abbesse, & as it hath byn alwayes vnto this time accustomed'. Nevertheless, it was noted that any woman presenting herself 'to vndertake this Religion' should first hear 'the most hard and difficult points' of it 'before she change her secular habit and receaue the habit of Religion'.[31] Audiences meet Isabella in the midst of such a debriefing, and so strictly speaking the would-be novice should not yet have changed out of her ordinary clothes.

But different rules apply in theatre. Another early modern play explicitly costumes an uninitiated novice in a nun's habit. In *Friar Bacon and Friar Bungay* (1594), when Margaret makes her way to enter a convent she is already '*in nun's apparel*' (14.0). Attention is drawn to her religious dress as she sighs 'Adieu to dainty robes; this base attire | Better befits an humble mind to God' (14.31–2), and when she snatches at the alternative of marriage to the man who has tested her love she punningly declares 'Off goes the habit of a maiden's heart' (14.89).[32] In this instance the nun's costume is used for dramatic effect rather than theological or cultural accuracy. But then that is the point of costume. In making Isabella a novice Shakespeare consciously changes his source material: none of Isabella's earlier counterparts in the 'monstrous ransom' tradition share her religious way of life. It makes sense to register the deliberate literary choice through a costume that keeps it at the forefront of the audience's minds (the dialogue, including the apparent pun on biological/religious sister at 2.4.18 and 3.1.156 marking Isabella's conflict of loyalties, also achieves this linguistically). For these reasons I assume that early modern Isabellas would have been costumed in religious dress, but my argument (which takes in the sartorial and material metaphors in the play's dialogue) does not rely on this being the case.

Real nuns had not been visible in England since the dissolution of religious houses some 70 years previous. The remarkable Isobel Whitehead (d. 1587), who remained an English nun, found herself anomalously in the world, and necessarily wandered under a false identity and in disguise.[33] Between 1597 and 1642 around 300 young women were sent to English convents on the continent, but they too had to keep their Catholic

---

[31] St Colette, *The Declarations and Ordinances made vpon the Rule of our Holy Mother, S. Clare* (n.p., 1622; facs. edn, Menston: Scolar Press, 1975), sigs. C2v, B2r.

[32] Robert Greene, *Friar Bacon and Friar Bungay*, ed. J. A. Lavin (London: Benn, 1969).

[33] Roland Connelly, *The Women of the Catholic Resistance in England: 1540–1680* (Edinburgh: Pentland Press, 1997), p. 55.

profession hidden as they left their country.[34] The convents that emerged in London and Yorkshire were covert, and when Mary Ward attempted her English mission in the early 1620s her sisters wore lay dress.[35]

But while actual nuns may have disappeared from everyday life, they lingered on in the nation's cultural imagination. The literal meaning of 'nun' remained 'religious sister', but the word's colloquial associations registered the post-Reformation reading of Catholic virtue as its opposite: 'nun' was also slang for 'prostitute'. Early modern theatre likewise manifests this double-edged significance of the nun as a symbol of holy chastity on the one hand and of hypocritical lechery on the other.[36] For example, in *The Troublesome Reign of King John*, a kind of proto-dissolution scene in which a monastery is ransacked sees the exposure of a naked nun, concealed in a monk's trunk.[37] This moment of offhanded farce literalizes the hidden sordid reality of Catholic 'chastity' in a play with an emphatically Protestant political message. But less derisory representations still appeared, even alongside critical ones. *The Death of Robert Earl of Huntington* (1601) shows the elasticity of the symbolic value of the nun. Here the report of Doncaster's rape of a nun emphasizes the depths of his criminality: it is a specifically 'sacrilegious deede' victimizing a pious figure. But later in the play the Abbess with whom Matilda seeks shelter is stereotypically bawdy. The denigrated Catholic practice of exorcism facilitates sex between the Abbess and a monk.[38] Neither meaning contradicts (or even comments on) the other, as the nuns merely help contextualize the action.

Extant stage directions indicate that nuns often performed 'small or supernumerary roles' in early modern drama.[39] When not providing anti-Catholic ribald laughs, nunneries rather blandly signified a past (and past-it) piety, convenient locations to which awkward elements of the plot could be tidied. Hence Richardetto sends Philotis (grieving for her

<hr/>

[34] Marie B. Rowlands, 'Recusant Women, 1560–1640', in *Women in English Society, 1500–1800*, ed. Mary Prior (London: Methuen, 1985), pp. 149–80 (p. 167), Connelly, p. 208.

[35] J. C. H. Aveling, *The Handle and the Axe: The Catholic Recusants in England from Reformation to Emancipation* (London: Blond and Briggs, 1976), p. 89; Connelly, pp. 156–7.

[36] One polemicist claims 'It is no great miracle for a whore to become a Nunne; nor for a Nunne to become a whore'; Thomas Robinson, *The Anatomy of the English Nunnery at Lisbon in Portugall* (London, 1622), sig. [B4r] (marginal note).

[37] *The Troublesome Raigne of Iohn King of England* (London, 1591), sigs. [E4v]–Fr.

[38] Anthony Munday, *The Death of Robert, Earle of Huntington* (London: Oxford University Press for the Malone Society, 1965), sigs. C2v, Kv.

[39] Alan C. Dessen and Leslie Thomson, *A Dictionary of Stage Directions in English Drama, 1580–1642* (Cambridge: Cambridge University Press, 1999), pp. 151–2.

murdered fiancé) to a convent, away from the messy revenge society of
'Tis Pity She's a Whore. Friar Lawrence rather wishfully tries to remove
Juliet from the disastrously tragic climax of his plot: 'I'll dispose of thee |
Among a sisterhood of holy nuns' (5.3.156–7). Elsewhere the decision to
take up religious sisterhood works as a part of the protagonist's romantic
choice (or lack of it). Heroines demonstrate their fidelity to their earthly
beloved as much as their heavenly Lord by retreating to the convent when
death of the beloved or other obstacles interrupt the love story. But romance usually trumps religion, and characters such as the aforementioned
Margaret in *Friar Bacon and Friar Bungay* eagerly reject the habit for marriage. Such plots implicitly reform nuns, rejecting the Catholic overvaluation of virginity in favour of a more sociable chastity (i.e. married
fidelity). The flat polarity of the nun's alternatively virginal or whorish
meaning lent itself to verisimilar functions, or comic interludes, or convenient plot devices, but rarely constituted the heart of the dramatic dilemma itself. Shakespeare's Isabella—whose desire to join a convent
provides an ongoing, meaningful complication to the play's action—is
not only an innovation in terms of her story's immediate sources, but is
also unusual in the context of Renaissance drama.

On the post-Reformation stage the nun's highly legible Catholic costume frequently signifies against itself as sexual: either in the exposure of
comically bawdy scenes, or in the reformation of comedic romantic plots.
Shakespeare's Isabella wants to act against her dramatic type. Her desire to
be a nun is one of the ways the play pitches its generic problem about the
tensions between individuality and community. Isabella wishes to with-
draw from society but its various members (Claudio, Lucio, Angelo, the
Duke) try to pull her back in. The habit has been described as the nun's
'primary mediation of her carefully constructed identity to the world'.[40]
But Isabella's expression of herself as socially (and sexually) removed from
the world is repeatedly read by other characters and modern critics in
sexual terms. Her resistantly Catholic self-representation helps expose the
social pressures comedy places on the individual.

Even if Isabella is not costumed in a nun's habit, she expresses her
Catholic selfhood in material terms. When Angelo asks, hypothetically,
what she would do if she could save her brother by laying down the

---

[40] Rebecca Sullivan, 'Breaking Habits: Gender, Class, and the Sacred in the Dress of
Women Religious', in *Consuming Fashion: Adorning the Transnational Body*, ed. Anne
Brydon and Sandra Niessen (Oxford: Berg, 1998), pp. 109–28 (p. 109).

'treasures' (2.4.96) of her body to a man able to save him, she develops the image and translates its meaning:

> The impression of keen whips I'd wear as rubies,
> And strip myself to death as to a bed
> That longing have been sick for, ere I'd yield
> My body up to shame. (2.4.101–4)

Demonstrating a ready rhetorical skill Isabella transforms Angelo's masculine poetic trope (whereby the female body is both desirable and possessible) into a Catholic celebration of the virginal body. Following a traditional hagiographical manoeuvre she translates the torturer's fiction of power over the would-be saint's body ('The impression of keen whips') into a triumphant display of Christian fidelity and endurance ('rubies'). This is of a piece with the recommendations of Catholic devotional literature to recognize the salvific benefits of afflictions, which should be conserved as metaphorical 'pearles Iewells and pretious stones'.[41] Isabella is paradoxically able to embody a prosthetic identity (asserting a self that can choose and shape its own identity). In using the verb 'wear' Isabella identifies herself as active (she becomes the grammatical subject rather than the tortured object) and passive (she is adorned). In drawing attention to imagined marks on her skin that are both penetrating wounds and lapidary ornament, she shows an indifference to and a celebration of physical pain, locating her subjectivity in and beyond her body. Hers is an intra-subjectivity: she is essentially shaped by a torturer to whom she claims indifference. Isabella therefore identifies herself in terms that preserve an individual integrity against and through the definitions of another.

But such self-assertion is ignored by Angelo, or perhaps rather, it intensifies his desire to violate her. When he addresses Isabella he focuses on her gendered rather than her spiritual difference, reducing her fetishistically to the sum of her sexual parts:

> Be that you are,
> That is, a woman; if you be more, you're none.
> If you be one, as you are well expressed
> By all external warrants, show it now
> By putting on the destined livery. (2.4.135–9)

---

[41] Luke Wadding, rev. Francis Hendricq, *The History of the Angelicall Virgin Glorious S. Clare*, trans. Magdalen Augustine (Douai, 1635; facs. edn, Menston: Scolar Press, 1973), sig. Cc3r.

Appropriately for someone 'Dressed in a little brief authority' (2.2.120), Angelo, also, describes Isabella's identity in essential and non-essential terms: she is to be what she already is ('Be that you are'); she is only potentially what her body proves her to be ('If you be one, as you are well expressed | By all external warrants'); what her body already reveals she must show ('show it now') with clothing that is both detachable and preordained ('putting on the destined livery').[42] While such contradictions might index Angelo's subjective guilt ('O place, O form, | How often dost thou with thy case, thy habit, | Wrench awe from fools and tie the wiser souls | To thy false seeming!' (2.4.12–15)), they also make clear the threat that Isabella might, for all practical purposes, be constituted by a sexual interpretation of her body that not only takes place apart from her, but which entirely rejects her own preferred meaning of herself. The apparent pun on 'none'/nun reduces to nothingness her claimed identity.

It is entirely typical for the precise Angelo to expect the would-be nun to be sexually willing. Isabella's own language in the dialogue cited earlier ('strip'; 'longing') and from the moment she enters the scene ('I am come to know your pleasure' (2.4.31)) would seem to acknowledge the anti-Catholic stereotype of the sexed female papist, while at the same time pointedly rejecting it.[43] Metaphorically decking herself in 'rubies', Isabella takes on the glittering allure of Catholic icons decorated with precious materials. The 'sick jewel' motif found throughout Renaissance drama suggests that such sensual appeal dangerously concealed and created moral depravity.[44] For example, in Thomas Dekker's *The Whore of Babylon* (1607) the eponymous femme fatale contaminates her followers with a pox that is manifested as 'carbuncles and rich stones' (4.1.65): a lexicon that conflates desire with disease, material wealth with the venereal fruits of the sexual corruption enticed by such a display.[45] However, Isabella is metaphorically self-stripping rather than apocalyptically exposed, and the plot of *Measure for Measure* is predicated on this novice's theatrically unconventional refusal of sex. Indeed, even Angelo's sexual response to Isa-

---

[42] For information on early modern livery, see Jones and Stallybrass, pp. 20, 269–77.

[43] Jean MacIntyre's conviction that Isabella would be attired in secular dress stems from a discomfort with the sexual innuendos lurking in such dialogue, innuendos which she thinks would be wrongly confirmed by the bawdy associations of the nun's costume; p. 276. However, I do not agree that the language needs saving from itself, and suggest that this dialogue (and most likely a nun's costume) make ambivalence key to Isabella's characterization.

[44] Shell, p. 34.

[45] Thomas Dekker, *The Whore of Babylon*, in *The Dramatic Works of Thomas Dekker*, ed. Fredson Bowers, 4 vols, ii (Cambridge: Cambridge University Press, 1953–61); Sarah Scott, 'The Empress of Babylon's "Carbuncles and Rich Stones"', *Early Theatre* 7 (2004), 67–95.

bella reworks anti-Catholic tradition. He remarks that the devil breaks with the polemically exposed practice of seduction via *seeming* goodness:

> O cunning enemy, that to catch a saint
> With saints dost bait thy hook!...
> Never could the strumpet
> With all her double vigour, art and nature,
> Once stir my temper, but this virtuous maid
> Subdues me quite. (2.2.183–9)

Angelo is turned on by Isabella's essential virtue; when he later asks her to 'Be that you are' he wants her to be the papist strumpet who will submit to his desires and also the virtuous maid who inspires them through refusal.

Angelo, at least (and here Shakespeare brings depth to the anti-puritan stereotype of the hypocritical precisian), is guiltily aware that his insistence that Isabella is sexually available is at odds with his arousal by a certainty that she is not. However, there is a critical tendency to read Isabella's rejection of Angelo's sex-bribe as evidence of pathological sexual repression.[46] Thus the introduction to one widely-used edition of the play reads: 'Beneath the habit of the nun there is a narrow-minded but passionate girl afflicted with an irrational terror of sex which she has never admitted to herself.'[47] Such readings imply that women should always desire sex, even when the situation is abusive. The notion that Isabella is pathologically repressed because she does not want to have sex with a corrupt official who has sentenced her brother to death seems to me misguided. The fuller accusation that Isabella's wish to be a nun already marks out this repression reads Catholic identity as but a material fabrication, a self-deceit.

---

[46] See, for example, Barbara J. Baines, 'Assaying the Power of Chastity in *Measure for Measure*', *SEL* 30 (1990), 283–301; Carolyn E. Brown, 'Erotic Flagellation and Shakespeare's *Measure for Measure*', *ELR* 16 (1986), 139–65; Anthony B. Dawson, *Indirections: Shakespeare and the Art of Illusion* (Toronto: University of Toronto Press, 1978), pp. 109–28; Lisa Jardine, *Still Harping on Daughters: Women and Drama in the Age of Shakespeare* (Brighton: Harvester, 1983), pp. 190–1; Arthur Kirsch, *Shakespeare and the Experience of Love* (Cambridge: Cambridge University Press, 1981), pp. 71–107; G. Wilson Knight, *The Wheel of Fire* (London: Oxford University Press, 1930), p. 92; Vivian Thomas, *The Moral Universe of Shakespeare's Problem Plays* (London: Croom Helm, 1987), p. 177; and Robert N. Watson, 'False Immortality in *Measure for Measure*: Comic Means, Tragic Ends', *SQ* 41.4 (1990), 411–32. A minority of critics reject this commonplace reading, including Anna Kamaralli, 'Writing About Motive: Isabella, the Duke and Moral Authority', *SS* 58 (2005), 48–59 (51); and Jessica Slights and Michael Morgan Holmes, 'Isabella's Order: Religious Acts and Personal Desires in *Measure for Measure*', *Studies in Philology*, 95 (1998), 263–92 (285).

[47] Anne Barton, 'Introduction: *Measure for Measure*', in William Shakespeare, *The Riverside Shakespeare*, 2nd edn, ed. G. Blakemore Evans and J. J. M. Tobin (Boston, MA: Houghton Mifflin Company, 1997), pp. 579–83 (p. 580).

It is as if the misreadings of Catholic identity that Shakespeare interrogates in his post-Reformation play (whereby nuns are either sexually wayward figures or fair romantic game) are simply accepted in modern critical discourse. Refusing sex is not a valid decision, but rather a perversion of unacknowledged desire.

The rhetoric that supposedly identifies Isabella's sexual repression is in fact rather tame in the context of Catholic devotional practice and literature. Isabella may hypothesize a situation in which she is whipped, but early modern Catholic laywomen actually practised the 'discipline' and sisters of the Order of Saint Clare were required to use it three times a week during Advent and Lent, and twice a week during the rest of the year.[48] Reformers viewed this flagellation as 'cruel and inhumane'; most importantly it was 'vnlawful' because not found anywhere 'in all the scriptures'.[49] The practice was also an easy target for dirty jokes (see, for example, the description of an inn-sign in the second part of Heywood's *If You Know Not Me You Know Nobody* (or, *Queene Elizabeths Troubles*): 'the Fryer whipping the Nuns arse').[50] Like modern Freudians, early modern anti-Catholics often read Catholic discipline as sexual deviancy. And of course there may, on occasion, have been some truth in this accusation.

But self-affliction was more properly used as a means of policing the body's sexual urges. An account of Joan of the Cross details her 'stripping herselfe naked' and lying in a 'thornie bed' in the garden to ward off 'sensuall desires' sent by 'diuells'.[51] It is too simplistic to write off this feature of Catholic practice as straightforward repression and a perverted realization of human lust. In another part of the hagiographical report of Joan of the Cross the heroine is described:

> desiring to please her beloued espouse, and remembring with how great crueltie he was whippt at a pillar, desiring to imitate him in that point, asking first leaue for it of his diuine maiestie, she shut her selfe vp in a chamber, very close and secret, where shee was wont to do her mortifications and penances, and naked, she tyed her selfe to a pillar, which she had there for these mortifications: then fastning herself with cordes, first her feet, and after her body, leauing her armes free, shee whipped her selfe all ouer with a

---

[48] Rowlands, p. 163; St Colette, sig. [C7v].

[49] Willet, p. 258.

[50] Thomas Heywood, *The Second Part of Queene Elizabeths Troubles* (London, 1606), sig. D3r. See also Malcolm Jones, 'The English Print, *c*.1550–*c*.1650', in *A Companion to English Renaissance Literature and Culture*, ed. Michael Hattaway (Oxford: Blackwell, 2000), pp. 352–66 (p. 362).

[51] Antonio Daza, *The Historie, Life, Miracles, and Extasies and Revelations of the Blessed Virgin, Sister Joane, of the Cross*, trans. James Bell (St Omer, 1625), sig. Dr.

chayne of iron; and that the chayne might the better discharge its office, she hu[n]g at the end of it a ball of iron round and massiue, and taking it in her hand, she strook her selfe with the ends of the chayne ouer all the body, vntill she shed bloud.[52]

Flagellation in all its brutal violence against the 'naked' flesh is here a 'desiring' act of love for the 'beloued espouse', but not simply in the self-deluding mode of repression. The indication that this process took place in a 'very close and secret' chamber may offer some readers voyeuristic pleasure, but it primarily stresses that Joan is no exhibitionist. Instead of directing our attention to her naked flesh, successive clauses detail the mechanics of how she used the 'chayne of iron' to maximize mortification. The physical impact is expressed in a blandly informative four-word conclusion: 'vntill she shed bloud'. This mortification of the self also works as an enlarging *imitatio Christi*: the female penitent gets to merge her flesh with the divine by 'remembring' Christ's passion and imitating his suffering.[53]

The sensuality of religious rhetoric and practice, even when pain is involved, might be seen as an alternative form of sexual expression, significantly removed from the realm of human relationships. Caroline Walker Bynum contends that 'sexual feelings were . . . not so much translated into another medium as simply set free'.[54] We see something of this, for example, in St Bernard's *A Rule of Good Life*, which encouraged its 'virgin readers' in pointedly sensuous descriptions of their relationship with Christ: 'You truly lie sick and languishing for the loue of Christ, in the bed of internal loue and sweetnes'[55] (c.f. Isabella's words at 2.4.102–3, cited earlier). In such devotional literature sensuality is a conscious rather than an unconscious part of the affect. This yearning for a kind of contact with the other (i.e. the divine) represents something more complex than repression's deviant desires.

This reading does not claim for Isabella a passionate piety entirely free of the repressive cruelty countless critics have detected. After all, her response to her brother's desperate pleas for her to save his life ('O you beast! | O faithless coward, O dishonest wretch!' (3.1.139–40); 'I'll pray a thousand prayers for thy death, | No word to save thee' (3.1.149–50)) is horrifyingly unmerciful, even if it indexes her terror or need to quash her

---

[52] Daza, sig. [C8v].

[53] For a related discussion, see Caroline Walker Bynum, *Holy Feast and Holy Fast: The Religious Significance of Food to Medieval Women* (Berkeley, CA: University of California Press, 1987), p. 246.

[54] Bynum, p. 248.

[55] St Bernard, *A Rule of Good Life*, trans. Antonie Batt (Douai, 1633; facs. edn, Menston: Scolar Press, 1971), p. 96.

own doubts. Her characterization is emotionally complex. But criticizing Isabella as self-evidently wrong for not submitting to Angelo elides the dilemma Shakespeare has taken the trouble to create by significantly altering his sources. The monstrous ransom story has a long heritage: the antecedent wives of imprisoned husbands (and in Cinthio's adaptation of the story, sister of a rapist brother) had all yielded to the demands of corrupt officials.[56] Their submission is merely a plot development that drives the narrative to a conclusion in which issues of justice can be interrogated (what is the right punishment for the official?). Isabella breaks with textual tradition in refusing Angelo, highlighting the previously underexplored moral difficulty of the situation. In focusing new attention on the monstrous ransom itself, Shakespeare widens the story's concern for authority and justice to the moral dilemma of the individual. And in doing so he sets a theatrical precedent. Robert Davenport's *The City Night Cap* (1624) structurally and ideologically reforms Shakespeare's play. Here the rejection of the ransom is moved to the drama's climax where Abstemia's refusal to 'buy' her husband's 'life with baseness' (2397) and thereby give her 'soul a wound' (2402) is the conclusive mark of her exemplary chastity. After testing her resolve, her husband rejoices that they 'will dye the martyrs | Of marriage' (2413–14) (though they are in the event spared this fate).[57] However, this decision is carefully purged of any Catholic motivations: Abstemia is a wife not a nun, and she stands in pointed contrast to the parallel character Dorothea, whose adultery is given papist colouring (it is facilitated by twice-weekly shrift). Davenport's reworking of the story clarifies the unreformed complications of Shakespeare's plot; but it nevertheless reveals that the refusal of the monstrous ransom is not obviously immoral.

Shakespeare poses a dilemma critics have too often foreclosed: should Isabella risk her own soul to save the life of another? This is, for Shakespeare, an untypically theological problem. It extends the exploration of biblical ethics opened out by the play's titular allusion to Matthew 7:2. Here Jesus warns: 'For with what iudgement ye iudge, ye shal be iudged, and with what measure ye mette, it shal be measured to you againe.' The verse remakes the regulation of communal interactions: the Old Testament permits local, human retribution (Exodus 21:23–4: 'But if death

---

[56] For a survey of monstrous ransom stories, see 'Introduction', in William Shakespeare, *Measure for Measure*, ed. N. W. Bawcutt (Oxford: Oxford University Press, 1998), pp. 12–22.

[57] Robert Davenport, *A Critical Edition of Robert Davenport's The City-Night-Cap*, ed. Willis J. Monie (New York: Garland Publishing, 1979); all references to *The City Night Cap* in the text are to this edition.

followe, the[n] thou shalt paye life for life, Eie for eie, tothe for tothe'); the New Testament asks for reconciliation and cautions that larger-scale retribution makes treatment of the other effectively self-directed. The force of the New Testament warning depends on the recognition that all guilt is eventually communal since everyone sins. The problem faced by Isabella invites us to consider the moral implications of a Christian understanding that self and other are not different but rather share culpability. Two chapters earlier, Jesus explicitly rejects the retributive justice of 'eye for an eye' (Matthew 5:38–9) and demands: 'Giue to him that asketh, and from him [that] wolde borow of thee, turne not away' (Matthew 5:42). Shakespeare asks if there is or should be a limit to this charity. These theological concerns are also part of the play's unflinching interrogation of comedic values. The question of whether one's own soul should be prized above those of others relates to the comedic insistence that characters are not finally individuals, but members of a community. How much responsibility does the self ultimately owe to others?

Furthermore, the situation invites us to speculate about the integrity of the self. In addition to asking whether Isabella *should* risk her soul, we necessarily ask if she *would* be risking it in this bargain. Does any essential value reside in the body? What does the violation of the body do to the soul? As a good Catholic, Isabella dutifully rejects fornication (extramarital sex). St Bernard lays the matter out unambiguously:

> Fornication is a grieuous sinne, fornication doth surpasse all euills fornication is worse then death it selfe. It is better to die then to commit fornication, it is better to die, then to be defiled with a sinne so filthie: it is better to die then by fornication to destroy both soule and bodie.[58]

Of course Protestants as well as Catholics regarded fornication as sinful, hence the severity of Angelo's enforcement policy. However, it is not exactly fornication that Isabella rejects here. There is no such familiar moral instruction for the situation before us, which is closer to rape: Angelo seeks to coerce an unwilling woman to have sex with him. Rape did not defile the soul like fornication. Augustine had famously censured Lucrece for what the Romans had hailed as a noble act of self-slaughter to cancel out the body's violation: 'if she is acquitted of murder she is convicted of adultery; and if she is acquitted of adultery, then she is convicted of murder'. The logic ran that Lucrece should only feel shamed if she had secretly 'consented, seduced by her own lust' (and even then repentance not suicide should follow); otherwise she made herself responsible for

---

[58] St Bernard, p. 175.

murdering 'the innocent and chaste Lucretia'.[59] This argument was predicated on an understanding of chastity as not merely or even primarily physical. Augustine explained that no individual 'has power to control what is done to the flesh'.[60] Matters of the soul (virtues and sins) were necessarily characterized by an individual's capacity for consent or refusal. Behind the distinction between the related categories of flesh and spirit is an insistence on an inviolable but culpable self. As the true essence of the individual, the soul could not be damaged by any other, only the self. Thus lust 'will not defile, if it is another's; if it defiles it is not another's'.[61]

A seventeenth-century reader of Heywood's *The Rape of Lucrece* puts a denominational slant on this argument, annotating the copy of the text now held by the British Library:

> But though some men commend this Act Lucretian
> She shewd her self in't (for all that) no good Christian
> Nay eu'n those men yt seem to make ye best ont
> Call her a Papish good, no good Protestant.[62]

Lucrece's perceived inability to differentiate between violation of the body and of the soul is identified as a 'Papish' overestimation of the significance of the physical. (In fact, Catholics also maintained a sense of hierarchical difference between body and soul, though usually from the opposite perspective of warning that it is not enough to be 'virgins in bodie, and not in mind'.)[63] Isabella's pointedly Catholic status invites post-Reformation audiences to engage with this problem. Her desire to be a nun draws attention to the difficulty of working out what physical virtue says about the virtue of the self. It makes her rejection of Angelo's terms both self-evidently understandable (she is a novice ready to pledge life-long virginity) and all the more culpable (reformers see in such a pledge an overvaluation of virginity: it is so theologically unnecessary as to be almost superstitious and is, in any case, virtually impossible).[64] The moral problem of the monstrous ransom has been deepened in a way that forces us

---

[59] Augustine, *The City of God against the Pagans*, ed. R. W. Dyson (Cambridge: Cambridge University Press, 1998), Bk. 1, ch. 19, pp. 30–1.

[60] Augustine, Bk. 1, ch. 18, p. 27.

[61] Augustine, Bk. 1, ch. 18, p. 27.

[62] The note is signed: 'Of this opinion Grendon John was the Nine and fiftieth of June one-thousand six hundred thirty three'; Thomas Heywood, *The Rape of Lucrece* (London, 1608), sig. Kv.

[63] St Bernard, p. 162.

[64] See Willet, p. 236.

to think about the boundaries of the essential self and the relationship between will and action.

If what Angelo proposes is not exactly fornication, neither is it straightforwardly rape. He asks Isabella paradoxically to consent to coercion.[65] He reasons that 'Our *compelled* sins | Stand more for number than for account' (2.4.57–8, my emphasis) but also demands 'Fit thy *consent* to my sharp appetite' (2.4.162, my emphasis). Augustine (and early modern theologians) regarded withheld consent as the distinction between the violated body and the violated soul, and between the sin of the self and the sin of the other. Here consent would conflate charity and sin, and risk collapsing body and soul, self and other.

The 'pattern of substitution' Alexander Leggatt famously identified in the play (whereby Angelo stands in for the Duke, Isabella is asked to suffer for Claudio, Mariana performs Isabella's part in the bed-trick, Barnadine refuses to provide a corpse for Claudio, Ragozine supplies Barnadine's role, Isabella pleads for Angelo on Mariana's behalf, and so on) here has a metaphysical as well as a physical aspect.[66] After having been called out of the cloister into the comedic community, Isabella is asked to take a social responsibility for sin. Saving her brother means potentially sharing in Julietta's sin ('to redeem him, | Give up your body to such sweet uncleanness | As she that he hath stained' (2.4.53–5)) and Angelo's lust. But Isabella notoriously calculates that it is 'cheaper' (2.4.106) for her brother to die:

> Better it were that a brother died at once
> Than that a sister by redeeming him
> Should die for ever. (2.4.107–9)[67]

She prioritizes her essential self (that she feels to be in peril) over her brother's physical self: 'More than our brother is our chastity' (2.4.186). Yet this axiomatic logic contains hints of its post-Reformation weakness. The use of plural pronouns (together with double inverted commas at the

---

[65] Some years ago, Darryl J. Gless gave a more sensitive account of the difficult moral situation facing Isabella than has been recognized by most recent critics: 'Isabella must *choose* sin'. However, Gless did not probe at the questions this uncomfortable proposition provokes, but assumed that the post-Reformation culture of anti-monasticism clarifies Isabella's religious order as 'needless and trivial regulation' to be shaken off in an act of oddly sinful charity; *Measure for Measure, the Law, and the Convent* (Princeton, NJ: Princeton University Press, 1979), pp. 127, 101.

[66] Alexander Leggatt, 'Substitution in *Measure for Measure*', *SQ* 39 (1988), 342–59 (342).

[67] Alison Findlay suggests that Isabella's willingness to sacrifice her brother is an 'imitation of the Virgin's own maternal sacrifice'; *A Feminist Perspective on Renaissance Drama* (Oxford: Blackwell, 1999), p. 41.

beginning of the line in the Folio text) makes Isabella's assertion of self-will a deferral to a different set of (Catholic?) communal values which many would have regarded as suspicious. Indeed her self-preservation makes in turn a demand on another. She may have declared her readiness for martyrdom, but it is Claudio who would have to enact it on her behalf:

> had he twenty heads to tender down
> On twenty bloody blocks, he'd yield them up
> Before his sister should her body stoop
> To such abhorred pollution. (2.4.181–4)

This comedy asks a brutal price of its characters.

Self-fashioned (perhaps literally) as a novice nun, Isabella stands at the crux of the play's various generic and social pressures. Angelo (falsely) promises a happy ending in which death is prevented if Isabella will only play the comedic character (who recognizes her fundamentally social obligations) and stereotypically sexed nun. But Isabella reads her role rather differently, defining herself as a pious sister.[68] Her novice status has contradictory implications that are here brought into play in a way that involves the audience in a dilemma about the place of the self in a comedic vision: Isabella rightly privileges (her) soul over (her brother's) body; Isabella wrongly regards (her) body as being as significant as (her) soul; Isabella demonstrates extraordinary spirit (i.e. self-will and spirituality) in refusing the values of Vienna; Isabella's papist preservation of the self threatens her society. The multivalence of the Catholic nun draws attention to the structure of and pressures on the comedic role.

For Isabella, seeming like a nun is a means of wilful self-preservation, but it also leaves her open to a variety of (mis)interpretations. While Angelo is aroused by the paradox of the nun in post-Reformation language (maiden/whore), the Duke sees the novice Isabella as a character in a romantic comedy, and at the play's conclusion he repeatedly proposes marriage (5.1.495–6; 5.1.537–40). But Isabella, unlike Greene's Margaret, does not exclaim her eagerness to shed 'the habit of a maiden's heart', instead remaining silent. This silence signifies Isabella's subjection in a system that refuses to permit the self-identification she has spent the play battling to maintain and also her self-assertion since it is appropriate to a nun of the order of St Clare. The costuming possibilities mean that the scene could be staged as a bawdy anti-Catholic sketch of a romance be-

---

[68] Julia Reinhard Lupton reads a different generic tension, between hagiography and novella; *Afterlives of Saints: Hagiography, Typology, and Renaissance Literature* (Stanford, CA: Stanford University Press, 1996), pp. 110–40.

tween a friar and a nun, or a reformation of inappropriate Catholic celibacy, or a traditional comic pairing of characters.

But there is little space for a central character's chaste piety in a traditional comic ending. This is also evident in a later play, Philip Massinger's *The Maid of Honour* (written *c.*1621/2). Here, the titular heroine Camiola successfully reclaims her unfaithful fiancé only to shock her on and offstage audience by becoming a nun. In doing so Camiola renounces the various distorted modes of honour explored by the play. What is happy here is a refusal to let go of ideals after the dramatization of so much moral pragmatism, infidelity, and downright duplicity. But the social, procreative communion symbolized by marriage is absent. The decision to become a nun is figured as formally tragicomic: Camiola describes her vocation as both marriage ('When I am married (as this day I will be)' [L3r]; 'This is the marriage! this the port! to which | My vowes must steere me' [L4r]) and death ('I am dead to the world' [L4r]).[69] Deciding to become a nun, Camiola also takes over the theatrical and political business of arranging the play's ending, dictating what other characters must do. The symbolic value of 'sisterhood' here gives Camiola the moral authority to produce resolution. In *Measure for Measure*, by contrast, the fraught meanings of 'nun' have been exploited in a way that resists final closure. The would-be nun represents a critique of comedic values, even as the comedy exposes her flaws.

CATHOLIC DISGUISE

Where Isabella is reluctant to participate in comedic society, the Duke is busily active. Yet his mode of seeming is still more of a retreat than that of the novice. By contrast with Isabella the Duke adopts a costume that hides his real self. In the very first scene of the play he states his troubled attitude to the public reception of his self-image:

> I love the people,
> But do not like to stage me to their eyes.
> Though it do well, I do not relish well
> Their loud applause and aves vehement,
> Nor do I think the man of safe discretion
> That does affect it. (1.1.68–73)

[69] Philip Massinger, *The Maid of Honour* (London, 1632).

It is as if being viewed risks destroying the integrity of the self. His solution is to adopt disguise, that is to stage himself to be seen without being seen. However, disguise does not so much protect the self as double it, thus problematizing notions of its wholeness. Lloyd Davis contends that disguise 'reproduces the dialectic between essentialist and non-essentialist selfhood.'[70] On the one hand the self is 'the authentic and determinant origin of disguise', but on the other, the revealed identity 'would seem to fall short of a personal telos and appear instead to be marked by its concealment of and difference from the identity it "transcends"'.[71] If the Duke seems more intimidatingly Duke-like when he emerges from beneath his friar's disguise at the conclusion, it is notable that his authoritative knowledge that structures the 'happy ending' was won not because he concealed the tiresome trappings of being a Duke, but because he usurped the sacramental privileges of *being* a friar: 'Love her, Angelo; | I have confessed her, and I know her virtue' (5.1.529–30). He treats the habit as both a disguise and (in a manner still more morally problematic) a guise. Thus he refers to his appearance to guarantee his integrity, using his friar's habit as a kind of material promise or contract by telling the Provost 'My mind promises with my habit no loss shall touch her by my company' (3.1.180–1). But when he is later surprised that 'neither my coat, integrity, nor persuasion' (4.2.186–7) are enough to convince the Provost to do his will, he is forced to supplement the one identity with 'the hand and seal of the Duke' (4.2.189); he needs both personae. The particulars of Lucio's defamation of 'the Duke' may be false rumour, but his cynical condemnation of this fake friar is apt: '*Cucullus non facit monachum.* Honest in nothing but in his clothes' (5.1.264–5). The Duke's costume keeps his character located in sartorial surfaces, at the level of prosthetic. But what a resonant costume this is.

'Habit' refers to apparel put *on* the body; the bearing, demeanour, deportment, or behaviour *of* the body; and the mental qualities *within* the body. It signifies behavioural patterns as well as sartorial identification.[72] It is appropriate, then, that when the Duke puts on the friar's habit he also takes on the conventional practices associated with it; he is in fact shaped by the very disguise that he thinks he controls. Concerned throughout with deflecting slander, the Duke acts out the kind of behaviour associated with friars in anti-fraternal and later anti-Catholic traditions. Stories like that of Friar Francis and Friar Donnet (see chapter 2) emphasize the

[70] Lloyd Davis, *Guise and Disguise: Rhetoric and Characterization in the English Renaissance* (Toronto: University of Toronto Press, 1993), p. 10.

[71] Davis, pp. 10, 6–7.

[72] *OED*, s.v. 'habit'.

fictional potential of friars (ready-made fabliau figures) to discredit their religious significance. Representative of this mode is the tale of Friar Pedro Ragazoni in Dekker's *The Ravens Almanacke* (1609). Ragazoni impregnates fifteen nuns 'vnder the color of auricular confession' only to suffer (along with other friars who would emulate him) a brutal 'pennance' at the hands of the Abbess: the friars must 'geld' themselves to avoid being burnt to death.[73] The satire makes a serious ideological attack through an easygoing bawdiness, sensationally reformed through graphic violence. In the real world friars made headlines as political plotters and regicides: for example, Henry III of France was assassinated by the Dominican Friar Jacques Clément. As mentioned earlier, on the post-Reformation stage the friar's costume could signify a generally nefarious nature (as when Faustus tells Mephostophilis to 'return an old Franciscan friar, | That holy shape becomes a devil best' (1.3.25–6)).[74] Even though friars (like nuns) did sometimes benignly help create a fairytale past, there was a strong tradition of hypocritically sexed lechers and Machiavellian political schemers. The Duke's disguised character is entangled with this familiar stage practice.

However, Shakespeare typically ambiguates conventions and in *Measure for Measure* makes this play key to the dramatic action. For example, in *Romeo and Juliet* Friar Lawrence inhabits and redirects the stereotypes of the lecherous and politically motivated friar; but the stakes are raised in the Duke('s) plot. Friar Lawrence (however imperfectly) acts in the interests of the young lovers who have the audience's emotional support; the comic landscape of *Measure for Measure* is rather more problematic. Where Friar Lawrence arranges marriage between two people who love one another, the Friar–Duke arranges sex between a desperately loving woman and a duped man who has already rejected her (marriage follows as a necessary retrospective legitimization). Where Friar Lawrence meddles in civic affairs between important citizens, the Friar–Duke plots against the city's acting ruler (albeit an official he himself appointed). The friar's habit gives the audience pause when watching action that is related to but different from stereotypically bad behaviour.

For this reason (among others) I find it hard to agree with readings of the Duke as primarily symbolic of divine intervention. Certainly, his authority and explicit concern for souls as well as citizens put this possibility

---

[73] Thomas Dekker, *The Ravens Almanacke* (London, 1609), sigs. [D4r]–Fr.
[74] Christopher Marlowe, *Doctor Faustus*, in *The Complete Plays and Poems*, ed. E. D. Pendry (London: Everyman, 1976). See also Paul Voss, 'The Antifraternal Tradition in English Renaissance Drama', *Cithara* 33 (1993), 3–16.

in play. But the anti-fraternal associations of the habit (made available by his rather flawed conduct) seem to invite the audience to question the character rather than view him as an unequivocal force for good.[75] Shakespeare avoids the conclusions of anti-fraternal polemic, but uses their connotations to focus his audience on the moral problems of the play. It is hard to see through the Duke's performance as friar to what he really is (the 'self' beneath the disguise). He voices no lengthy soliloquies that explain his inner motivations, but rather speaks his plots in axiomatic rhyming tetrameters. His disguise helps him to deflect all questions of his own inner being as he pries into that of others (indicating that characterological interiority is a concern in this play) by playing the part of Catholic confessor.

The Catholic sacrament of penance, practised through auricular confession, was much maligned by reformers: it was regarded as both a theological error (it had no basis in scripture; the repetition of every misdemeanour was unnecessary and counterproductive; the confessor blasphemously usurped Christ's power of forgiveness) and a political threat (the secrecy of confessional conversation could facilitate treasonous intrigues).[76] The dangers of confession were dramatized from early in the post-Reformation era. John Bale's *King Johan* presents a confessional scene in which Sedicyon directs Nobylyte:

> whyll I have yow here underneth *benedicite*,
> In the Popes be halfe I must move other thynges to ye
> ... to do the best ye canne
> To [King Johan's] subduying. (1166–72)[77]

One year after *Measure for Measure* was staged at court the details about the Gunpowder Plotters' alleged confessional communications with Henry Garnet would have seemed to confirm such long-held suspicions.

However, Shakespeare's Friar–Duke undertakes an odd inversion: instead of a religious figure using confession to meddle in political matters, *Measure for Measure* stages a political leader using the sacrament for reli-

---

[75] Here I differ from Shuger, who argues that if Shakespeare had wanted us to view the friar's disguise as 'wildly improper, the play would have raised the possibility'. This view underestimates the ideological disapproval felt for friars in post-Reformation England; p. 5.

[76] See John Bossy, 'The Social History of Confession in the Age of Reformation', *Transactions of the Royal Historical Society* 25 (1975), 21–38; Thomas N. Tentler, *Sin and Confession on the Eve of the Reformation* (Princeton, NJ: Princeton University Press, 1977); and Gillian Woods, 'The Confessional Identities of *'Tis Pity She's a Whore*', in *'Tis Pity She's a Whore*, ed. Lisa Hopkins (London: Continuum, 2009), pp. 114–35.

[77] John Bale, *King Johan*, in *The Complete Plays of John Bale*, ed. Peter Happé, 2 vols, i (Cambridge: D. S. Brewer, 1985).

gious ends. Thus the Duke takes on (or perhaps puts on) the confessor's role of examining consciences: he teaches Julietta how to 'arraign your conscience | And try your penitence' (2.3.21–2) and a similar assumed authority underlies conversations with Claudio, Isabella, and Mariana. He even appropriates sacramental power: while he ostensibly professes the importance of Barnardine's pre-execution sacramental 'shrift' (4.2.203), both before and after his failed attempt at bringing Barnardine to penitence he thinks that he should be the one to 'Persuade this rude wretch willingly to die' (4.3.78).[78] Confession affords the Duke a unique opportunity to know 'what our seemers be' (1.3.54) and act on this knowledge. In plotting a happy ending and social reconciliation, the Duke needs his citizens to publicize their inner selves to him, as if there were no space for privacy in his comedic vision. Except that the Duke himself remains a private being. Furthermore, as one who only seems to be a friar, he uncomfortably usurps the authority of the confessor in hearing secrets and forgiving sins.

Perhaps surprisingly, the Jesuit Henry Garnet declared a friar disguise lawful: 'a lay man may weare a religious mans ordinary apparell, or a man a woman's gowne for a good end, or for necessity, and yet not make any lye at all in the outward shew: but vsing that [which] hath an other end besides the signification; permitt the beholders to thinke him, to be either a freer or a woman, which in deed he is not.'[79] He makes the point to distinguish between Church Papistry and legitimate disguise in times of necessity, arguing that the friar's habit was not an exclusively religious sign and therefore not a damnable disguise: 'a Freers weed, although it signifie a Freer' is not 'so religiouse as a Surplesse, Cope, Tunicle, or such like, whose principall and onely end is religion'.[80] However, the Duke does draw on and enact the religious meaning of the habit. If his meddling has a vaguely papist shape it also seriously offends Catholic rules. The production of the happy ending is predicated on violation of the individual.

Davenport's aforementioned *The City Night Cap* reforms the Catholic sacrament and simplifies Shakespeare's treatment of it. In this play Lodovico disguises himself as a friar to hear the confession of his wife (Dorothea) and thereby learns of her adultery. Dorothea's papist piety (she goes to confession 'twice a week' (939)) is of a piece with her rampant infidelity. However, Lodovico reforms both Dorothea and confession through the imposition of a penance that makes the traditional Catholic tasks of 'prayer'

---

[78] Ultimately, however, he gets to forgive Barnardine's sins in only a legal capacity as Duke (5.1.485–8); spiritual authority is handed over to the real Friar (5.1.488–9).

[79] Garnet, sig. [I7v].   [80] Garnet, sig. [I8v].

and 'zealous pilgrimage' seem as nothing (1430): she is to repeat her confession during a public feast hosted by her husband, out of the protected
Catholic confessional space. Dorothea cannily fulfils this obligation in the
context of reporting a dream. But the fake friar can impose justice in a way
that a real (and ritually silenced) friar cannot: Lodovico returns in disguise
and breaks the confessional seal, the exposure of his disguise as he is un-
robed only serving to authorize his attacks on Dorothea. He banishes his
wife to a Catholic convent but has undone the Catholic sacrament. Davenport thus carefully reconciles the fabliau pleasures of papist plots with a
reformed structure that uncovers their hypocrisies; the convent provides
poetic justice that feels safely distant from reality.

But the fiction of *Measure for Measure* fits far more awkwardly with the
'real' implications of the action. The Duke seems to want to be a fairytale
friar who benevolently helps the plot to a happy conclusion, but he takes
his role too far: the other characters seem to object to the translation of
confession into a plot device and being treated as mere characters who
must conform to a comedic structure. The Duke does not manage theatricality particularly well, committing gaffes that make his plot seem uncomfortably real rather than consummately performed. He nearly fluffs
his first line in costume by betraying more knowledge than his part allows:
'Hail to you, Provost—so I think you are' (2.3.1). This is not slick theatre.
His plot-writing skills also have their limitations. The conclusion to the
play may mark his technical success but this denouement is the result of
Plan B; the Duke's rhyming summation of events in act 4 (answering the
chorus-like rhyme that set up his plot at 3.1.515–36) indicates his anticipation of a much earlier conclusion:

> This is his pardon, purchased by such sin
> For which the pardoner himself is in.
> Hence hath offence his quick celerity,
> When it is borne in high authority.
> When vice makes mercy, mercy's so extended
> That for the fault's love is the offender friended. (4.2.108–13)

The bed-trick fails in its immediate purpose of securing a pardon for
Claudio; furthermore, the subsequent attempt to substitute Barnardine
for Claudio is also unsuccessful because Barnardine refuses his part in the
Duke's plot. And in the scene before the conclusion Isabella expresses
disquiet at the notion and nature of the production:

> To speak so indirectly I am loath.
> I would say the truth, but to accuse him so,
> That is your part. Yet I am advised to do it,
> He says, to veil full purpose. (4.6.1–4)

Though he controls the basic structure of the conclusion, the Duke's stage-management is clumsy. Needing to leave the stage to change costume he cannot devise a motivated exit: 'I for a while | Will leave you' (5.1.258–9). When he is required to tie up the loose ends of the plot he struggles with the timing of his proposal to Isabella: 'Give me your hand and say you will be mine, | He is my brother too—but fitter time for that' (5.1.495–6). He does not even reveal his identity on his own terms: he is exposed as Duke because Lucio strips him of his friar's costume.[81]

The Duke's flawed plotting continues to demand that characters take on the roles of others. Not only does Mariana substitute for Isabella in the bed trick, but the ploy also puts Angelo in the place of Claudio (having sex with his betrothed) and in the situation he intended for Isabella (consenting to non-consensual sex). Both sin and salvation are communal phenomena in this play, as characters are forced to partake in the desires and mistakes of others. The Duke requires Isabella to make a false confession, trusting that simulation of another will secure communal order. But when it comes to the conventional manner of formalizing the social bonds that comedy celebrates, through marriage, the relationships seem to have been overstrained. This is not for want of potential couples: Claudio and Juliet, Angelo and Mariana, Lucio and the 'punk', and even, potentially, the Duke and Isabella are paired off. But as Katherine Eisaman Maus observes, most of these characters refuse to speak their cooperation in the Duke's wedding-planning.[82] With most of the cast retreating into taciturnity (with the exception of Lucio, who is explicitly unhappy), the Duke's climactic discovery feels like a re-covering. These characters wrest back their individual innerness and essential otherness, even as they find themselves scripted into particular social positions. The continuing silence of the key players in *Measure for Measure* is suggestive of the superficiality (or at least imperfection) of the social reconciliation. The comedy has sacrificed individuals for a communal ending that is only formally happy, that only 'seems'. The Catholic aesthetics of the play have helped focus attention on the dilemmas of the genre and the Catholic habits (sartorial and behavioural) have created representational cruxes that highlight the difficulties of managing individuality and otherness. *Measure for Measure* implies, rather troublingly, that society may not be such a happy place for the individual.

---

[81] Huston Diehl reads this scene more positively as making the audience aware of the need for divine grace; '"Infinite Space": Representation and Reformation in *Measure for Measure*', *SQ* 49 (1998), 393–410 (410).

[82] Maus, p. 180.

ALL SEEMS WELL

Exchanging *Measure for Measure*'s biblical title for a proverbial one, *All's Well that Ends Well* is still more self-reflexively concerned with the merits and failings of fiction and uses the slippery meanings of Catholic clothing as a means of highlighting those concerns. It is a play that, as Susan Snyder has described, works like a deconstructed fairytale, by testing fantasy against reality. Thus the clever wench who miraculously cures a king and wins a husband of her choosing is in love with a 'prince' who is not so charming; class prejudice spoils the dream of social elevation; and the plot weaves its way around a particularly unheroic war.[83] The play thus exposes the awkward acts of social engineering that happy endings usually elide, showing up both the limitations of comedic values and the inadequacies of the real world. It reveals the seams of seemingly wonderful fiction, so that, for example, the heroine triumphs not only through wit and worth, but by paying her accomplices. Yet this drama also mystifies even as it demystifies: we know that Helen's healing of the King is motivated by self-interest, but we don't know precisely how this cure is effected; we know that reports of her death are greatly exaggerated but the circumstances of the manipulation are occluded. The play explicitly resists the rational (and reformed) idea that 'miracles are past' (2.3.1). As such the theatrical fiction is pitched between an idealistic golden world and a self-consciously illusory realm.

In the middle of the action the central character adopts a pilgrim's habit, identifying herself with a practice that was outlawed in post-Reformation England and categorized as one of those old errors 'tending to idolatry and superstition'.[84] The Catholic Church regarded pilgrimages to holy places as meritorious, a way of piously working to the salvation Christ had enabled.[85] By contrast, reformers scoffed at the notion that one earthly place could be holier than another, dismissed as idolatrous the intercession of saints usually invoked at shrines, and abhorred the idea that Christ's gift of salvation needed supplementing. But *All's Well* is not about theology. Like the rest of the text, the pilgrim's habit is threaded with fictional and 'real' meaning; the varied signifying potential of

---

[83] 'Introduction', in William Shakespeare, *All's Well that Ends Well*, ed. Susan Snyder (Oxford: Oxford University Press, 1993), pp. 5–6.

[84] 'Announcing Injunctions for Religion' (1559), in Hughes and Larkin, ii, pp. 117–32. A minority of English Protestants continued to follow European pilgrimage routes, motivated by either anthropological or spiritual interest.

[85] See, for example, Henry Garnet's supplementary discussion of the practice in Peter Canisius, *A Summe of Christian Doctrine*, trans. Henry Garnet ([London?, c.1592]), pp. 505–61.

Catholicism in post-Reformation England is brought into play. The pilgrim's costume participates in the drama's interrogation of the relation-ship between fiction and reality, and the crux between fiction-as-ideal and fiction-as-fraud.

The wearer of the habit is herself problematic, and attending to how her characterization engages an audience helps clarify the function of her Catholic costume change. In the very first scene the silent, weeping appearance of Helen, discussed by the Countess and Lafeu, suddenly provokes unease:

> *Countess* Go to, no more, lest it be rather thought you affect a sorrow than to have—
> *Helen* I do affect a sorrow indeed, but I have it too. (1.1.52–4)

The Countess suggests that to express extreme grief can give the impres-sion of mere performance; Helen separates performance (affect) from sin-cere feeling while also indicating that the two are linked. As in *Hamlet*, her insistence on 'that within which passes show' (1.2.85) implicitly admits to the risk that the display of emotion of inner meaning might in some way invalidate it. But Helen's 'affect' turns out to be a kind of deceit after all. Once left alone she reveals that she cries out of hopeless love for Bertram rather than grief for her father:

> I think not on my father,
> And these great tears grace his remembrance more
> Than those I shed for him. What was he like?
> I have forgot him. My imagination
> Carries no favour in't but Bertram's. (1.1.81–5)

But her discussion is grammatically ambiguous: does 'his' refer to the same person as the first 'him'? Together with the abruptness with which she re-jects the demands of memory this may imply a continuing grief in which Bertram substitutes for her father. Indeed Helen rejects the past by looking like it. The means by which she first pursues Bertram allows her to re-member her father: she uses the prescriptions which he bade her 'store up as a triple eye, | Safer than mine own two' (2.1.106–7) when she cures the King. It is not that Helen's romantic pursuit of Bertram is shown as an un-equivocal displacement of a grief for her father that she cannot acknowl-edge,[86] but rather that even when Helen provides the audience with a full explanation of how the way she appears relates to how she feels, Shakespeare creates a sense that there is more that 'passes show'. Performance is either

---

[86] For a psychoanalytical reading that makes this argument, see Lynne M. Simpson, 'The Failure to Mourn in *All's Well that Ends Well*', *SSt* 22 (1994), 172–88.

the sincere enactment or the mere acting of deeds and emotions, or some-how both at once. Truth and deceit slip out of their binary relationship.

In the first scene and throughout the play characters pass comment on Helen, interpreting her appearance, performance, motivation, and virtue. The Countess learns of Helen's love for Bertram because the Steward has overheard Helen talking to herself, as if he were an audience listening to her soliloquy: 'Alone she was, and did communicate to herself, her own words to her own ears' (1.3.107–9). Placing an almost tautological stress on the privacy he has invaded, the Steward indicates the need to look beyond Helen's public persona. Elsewhere she is represented (and repeat-edly represents herself) in textual terms. When trying to convince the King to let her attempt his cure she ventures 'A strumpet's boldness, a divulgèd shame; | Traduced by odious ballads' (2.1.169–70), but after the successful cure she is instead related to celebratory broadside ballads: '*A Showing of a Heavenly Effect in an Earthly Actor*' (2.3.23–4). Crucial mo-ments in the development of her story take the form of rhyming couplets that provide a fairytale-like linguistic structure: when she convinces the King to let her try to heal him (2.1.128–208); when she gives a riddling explanation of the bed-trick (3.7.44–7); and when the King, thinking her dead, decides Helen must have been but a minor character, merely to be forgotten (5.3.61–4, 69–70). These textual figurations encourage us to try to read Helen; but rather than providing her any unequivocal mean-ing she is opened out to interpretation.

Even when we are given assistance in interpreting Helen's textuality in the early scenes of the play, we are reminded that interpretation is inevitably shaky. Our access to her plans and emotions through solilo-quies gives us knowledge about her motivations but also provokes fur-ther questions and uncertainty. Helen's onstage audience faces a similar task. The Countess confidently articulates a reading of Helen's body as revealing love for Bertram: she notes that Helen 'start[s]' (1.3.142) and cries (1.3.150–2) at the word 'mother', and she claims that Helen's body tells tales on her, so that her 'cheeks | Confess' and her 'eyes...speak' (1.3.176–9). Nevertheless, the Countess needs Helen to validate this reading: she asks her to 'Speak' (1.3.181) and, with an adverb register-ing suspicious uncertainty, 'tell me truly' (1.3.185). Having been forced to reveal her love for Bertram Helen retreats behind rhyming textual complication:

> O then give pity
> To her whose state is such that cannot choose
> But lend and give where she is sure to lose;
> That seeks not to find that her search implies,
> But riddle-like lives sweetly where she dies. (1.3.213–17)

Through the simile of the riddle Helen ostensibly reveals herself (a riddle has an answer) and also resists self-exposure (the answer is not provided). The paradoxes at once announce her emotional turmoil (she cannot pursue what her heart looks for; she endures a living death) and equivocally conceal planned action (she cannot hope for what she will nevertheless actively pursue). But at this point in the play ambiguity is cleared up by the Countess's sharp interrogation: 'Had you not lately an intent— speak truly— | To go to Paris?' (1.3.218–19); 'Wherefore? Tell true' (1.3.219); 'This was your motive for Paris, was it? Speak' (1.3.231). These questions insist that Helen's motivations are both important and not easily accessible.

So before Helen puts on her pilgrim's habit we have been taught to engage with the nature of what she 'performs'. The Catholic resonance of the habit further emphasizes and problematizes the signifying structure of her characterization. Details of the plot complicate our ability to read Helen's wearing of the habit. When she first meets the Widow in Florence she claims that she is on her way '*To* Saint Jacques le Grand' (3.5.34, my emphasis), yet when the First Lord gives news of her ostensible death he reports that he has his (false) information from the 'rector' of the shrine (4.3.58), lending credence to the belief that she had 'accomplished' her pilgrimage (4.3.50). Her journey is not necessarily geographically erratic since there are other pilgrims in Florence (3.5.91).[87] Is she on her way to a pilgrimage?—does she ever complete a pilgrimage?—did she ever intend to go on a pilgrimage? Perhaps the contradictions are a compositional confusion or perhaps the Lord has been entirely deceived, but the play has elsewhere taught us to care about and question Helen's motivations and intentions and it here remains notably silent.

The problem of whether Helen wears a pilgrim's costume as a disguise is raised because Shakespeare disguises her motivations.[88] In the source, 'Giletta of Narbonne', William Painter makes it clear that Giletta uses the appearance of a pilgrimage to track her beloved: 'arriving by fortune at a poor widow's house, she contented herself with the state of a poor pilgrim, desirous to hear news of her lord'.[89] However, when Helen puts on the pilgrim's habit she becomes more symbolic and, paradoxically, all the more difficult to interpret. Whereas her earlier motivations had been care-

[87] See Russell Fraser's introduction to his edition of the play; William Shakespeare, *All's Well that Ends Well* (Cambridge: Cambridge University Press, 1985), p. 6.

[88] Rowe expanded the folio stage direction 'Enter Hellen' (3.5.29.1) to include the description 'disguised like a pilgrim'; *The Works of Mr. William Shakespear*, ed. Nicholas Rowe, 6 vols, ii (London, 1709). Recent editors have preferred the more neutral terms 'dressed' (Oxford) and 'habited' (Riverside).

[89] 'Giletta of Narbonne', as reprinted in Snyder (1993), pp. 225–32 (p. 228).

fully examined in soliloquy or through the Countess's cross-examinations, her intentions are now obscured. In the soliloquy at the end of 3.2 Helen announces that she plans to leave so that Bertram may return home and avoid the dangers of war, but she makes no reference to pilgrimage. We learn about the spiritual nature of the journey at several removes in 3.4 when the Steward reads a letter (that takes the form of a sonnet) in which Helen declares herself to be 'Saint Jacques' pilgrim' seeking 'With sainted vow' to amend her 'faults' while also leaving Bertram 'free' to return home in her absence (3.4.4–17). Now that Helen is absent the Countess can only study a literal text. Helen's voice, displaced through the Steward's, is doubly textual: both the tangible stage prop of a letter and also a sonnet. Not surprising then that her use of a pilgrim's costume should feel fictional.[90]

There is, after all, something almost blandly verisimilar about the pilgrim's costume. In post-Reformation drama a pilgrim's habit might mark a valid expression of historicized spirituality or simply operate as a harmless pretence appropriate to and conventional in fiction. For example, in *King Leir* the 'good' King of Gallia adopts a pilgrim's disguise without picking up nefarious behaviour and Cordella's virtue is articulated via a willingness to 'hold thy Palmers staffe within my hand, | And thinke it is the Scepter of a Queene'.[91] In such instances the costume is benignly fictional rather than negatively ideological; it is part of the play's fairytale aesthetic.

But in *All's Well* an alternative mode of fiction is also brought into play. The First Lord refers to Helen's pilgrimage as 'pretence' (4.3.48), a word that, like 'perform', conflates the acting out of a deed with acting, but also emphasizes the possibility of fraudulence.[92] The wearing of religious dress to conceal non-religious action seems more intensely deceitful than simply wearing alternative professional dress.[93] Thus in *The Duchess of Malfi* Cariola objects to Bosola's recommendation that the Duchess should escape to her husband by 'feign[ing] a pilgrimage': 'I do not like this jesting with

---

[90] The text does not describe Helen's costume, but since the Widow immediately identifies her as a 'pilgrim' (3.5.30) her clothes are clearly distinctive. A '*hatte, staffe and Pilgrimes gowne*' (32) is detailed in *The Weakest Goeth to the Wall*, ed. W. W. Greg (London: Oxford University Press for the Malone Society, 1912).

[91] *The True Chronicle History of King Leir* (London: Oxford University Press for the Malone Society, 1907), 698–9.

[92] Susan Snyder also notes the ambiguity of this word; *Shakespeare: A Wayward Journey* (Newark, DE: University of Delaware Press, 2002), p. 110.

[93] The pilgrim's habit allowed wearers to 'copy religious functionaries who displayed their special status through their dress'; Simon Coleman and John Elsner, *Pilgrimage: Past and Present in the World Religions* (London: British Museum Press, 1995), p. 110.

religion, | This feigned pilgrimage'. Webster plots ideological coordinates in his revenge landscape that direct us how to interpret this pretence. The Duchess rejects Cariola's qualms as those of 'a superstitious fool' and thus her pragmatic pilgrimage bears a (reformed) indifference to Catholic symbolism as she attempts to flee the tyranny of her (markedly papist) brothers.[94]

In contrast, not only do we not know if Helen's pilgrimage is sincere or feigned, but we are also given mixed messages about how to read the habit itself. Pilgrimage cropped up metaphorically in amorous sonnets throughout the post-Reformation period (its conceptual familiarity evident in titles such as that of the love-poetry anthology, *The Passionate Pilgrim* (1599)). In having Helen announce her pilgrimage through the medium of a sonnet, Shakespeare raises the possibility that she is something of a Petrarchan stalker, tracking her unwilling husband across Europe. But the Countess's reading is more spiritual. Where once she had been suspicious of Helen's motives, when she hears of the pilgrimage she exclaims:

> What angel shall
> Bless this unworthy husband? He cannot thrive
> Unless her prayers, whom heaven delights to hear
> And loves to grant, reprieve him from the wrath
> Of greatest justice. (3.4.25–9)

This is praise couched in Catholic terms: the pilgrim Helen has intercessory power.[95] The clash of generic codes makes it difficult to know how to assess the action: is Helen, as the sonnet form might suggest, a pilgrim in the non-sectarian, Petrarchan sense; or is she an 'angel' to Bertram's Everyman in a medieval morality play; or somehow both at once; or something different in addition?

The pilgrimage is almost onomastically inevitable since Helen's saintly namesake was famous for her successful search for the True Cross. In the long term this discovery helped foster the relic industry so important to the Catholic world's pilgrimage network. Indeed the Catholic poem *Iesus praefigured* offered 'English Queenes' the example of Helen, who undertook 'holy journey for deuotion sake' and performed 'Iust honours to...Reliques'.[96] Similarly, E. W. argued that his translation of *The Pilgrime of Loreto* should not be 'excluded for the only name of Pilgrime;

---

[94] John Webster, *The Duchess of Malfi*, ed. Brian Gibbons (London: A. & C. Black, 2001), 3.2.303–14.

[95] For a reading of Helen in 'Marian' terms, see Alison Findlay, ' "One that's Dead is Quick": Virgin Re-Birth in *All's Well that Ends Well*', in *Marian Moments in Early Modern British Drama*, ed. Regina Buccola and Lisa Hopkins (Aldershot: Ashgate, 2007), pp. 35–46.

[96] John Abbot, *Iesus Praefigured* ([Antwerp], 1623), p. 34.

which Name (though now strange) hath heertofore beene so vsuall, and esteemed in our Court, and Country, as Kinges and Queenes haue not only vndertaken it, but gloried therein'; the marginal note clarified: 'S Helene'.[97] And defending the visitation of and worship at shrines, Henry Garnet claimed 'for that cause was Saint HELEN commended'.[98] By contrast, quoting St Ambrose, the reformed writer of the 'Homilie Agaynst Perill of Idolatry' tried to use the biography of St Helen as a way of distinguishing idolatrous practice:

> Helene founde the crosse and the tytle on it. She worshipped the king, and not the wood surely (for that is an ethnyshe errour, and the vanitie of the wycked) but she worshypped hym that hanged on the crosse, and whose name was written in the title, and so forth.[99]

Yet making St Helen a point of difference between idolatrous and non-idolatrous behaviour also admits to her position on an ideological boundary. And again this ambivalence is realized and extended in the characterization of the Shakespearean Helen. In the first scene she bemoans Bertram's departure saying 'But now he's gone, and my idolatrous fancy | Must sanctify his relics' (1.1.99–100). Her pilgrimage embodies this Catholic respect for 'relics' and performs a romantic appropriation of such concepts that knowingly admits to idolatry.[100]

Just as the saintly pilgrim Helen kept a foothold in the reformed Church, pilgrimage itself remained conceptually important even though the physical practice was outlawed. William Fennor explained: 'it is not the use of the word [pilgrimage] that makes it odious before God, and good Christians: But the use and abuse of the matter meant by the word'.[101] The importance of pilgrimage as a spiritual metaphor is widely evident (hence the existence of devotional works such as William Webster's *The Plaine Mans Pilgrimage* (1613) and Leonard Wright's *The Pilgrimage to Paradise* (1591)). Yet even metaphorically, its papist associations kept the semantic potential of pilgrimage double-edged. In his emblem book *Minerva Britanna* (1612), Henry Peacham illustrated the 'Hypo-

[97] Louis Richeome, *The Pilgrime of Loreto*, trans. E. W. (Paris [i.e. St Omer], 1629; facs. edn, Menston: Scolar Press, 1976), sig. *2r.

[98] Garnet in Canisius, p. 558.

[99] *Certaine Sermons Appoynted by the Quenes Maiesty* (London, 1563), sig. Dd(iiii) v–[Dd5r].

[100] When first determining to pursue Bertram she exclaims 'Who ever strove | To show her merit that did miss her love?' (1.1.228–9). This suggestion that she can earn the love of Bertram chimes with the Catholic understanding of good works as helping one access redemption. Even before she wears the habit, her pursuit of Bertram is allusively associated with 'meritorious' pilgrimage.

[101] William Fennor, *Pluto his Trauailes* (London, 1612), p. 2.

crite' with a picture of a pilgrim, replete with habit, staff, wide-brimmed bonnet, shell and rosary beads, explaining:

> The Hypocrite, that doth pretend in show,
> A feigned Zeale of Sanctitie within,
> Eschew betime, nor haue with such to doe,
> Whose hoodes are but the harbour of their sinne,
> And humblest habits, but a false disguise,
> To cloke their hate, or hidden villanies.[102]

The use of this sectarian emblem to illustrate a broader point about the internal/external dichotomy of hypocrisy takes for granted that the putting on a Catholic habit is inevitably a put-on.[103] And in keeping with this representational flexibility it is never certain if Helen is wearing a guise or a disguise.

But the wider connotations of pilgrimage comment on the action of the plot. While metaphorical pilgrimages could be romantic, actual papist pilgrimages were often reviled as mere excuses for lechery. These erotic associations pre-dated the Reformation (as Chaucer's *Canterbury Tales* testify), but as late as 1612 Fennor complained that 'There are too many of those dissembling Pilgrimes now a daies' (the black letter type perhaps registering the anachronistic aspect of the subject matter).[104] His pamphlet recounts stories of bawdily false pilgrims: in 1603 one young man is said to have disguised himself as a 'she Pilgrime' to accompany his love when she is sent to a convent; once there, his questionable religious faith is matched by sexual infidelity as he impregnates not just his original companion but also two other 'sisters'. As in *All's Well*, travel 'in deuotion to Saint Jaques' has an erotic tone, but unlike *All's Well* no ambiguity of motivation: in a historical example, the (already betrothed) sister of Edward III 'trauailed to Spaine for the sight of a Spanish Lord'. Finner's ideological framework firmly exposes the moral fraud of these accounts but he also capitalizes on their fictive energies. Stern glosses warning that 'this kind of dissimulation was euill' append, without fully upending, tales that do not end unhappily (the Duchess is 'freed from death, and shame' and eventually marries her Spanish Lord and the passionate 'she Pilgrime' is 'wealthily married to the Burgomaisters daughter' of Amsterdam). Nevertheless, the com-

---

[102] Henry Peacham, *Minerva Britanna* (London, 1612), sig. Eeir.
[103] As *All's Well* itself makes clear, it was not just Catholics who were sartorially associated with hypocrisy: 'Though honesty be no puritan, yet it will do no hurt: it will wear the surplice of humility over the black gown of a big heart' (1.3.93–5).
[104] Fennor, p. 10.

bination of moral deceit and narrative disbelief squeeze out any spiritual idealism.

Helen is hardly lecherous, but the play does question her sexual scruples.[105] On the one hand, her active desire for physical intimacy with her husband is legitimate and liberating; but on the other, she repeatedly removes Bertram's power of consent. She traps Bertram into her happy ending through a bed trick: a moral paradox she herself describes as a 'wicked meaning in a lawful deed' (3.7.45). Of course the 'wicked meaning' is partly Bertram's, since he intends adultery; but the riddling rhetoric also implicates Helen, who lawfully has sex with her husband somewhat wickedly against his will. The bed-trick encapsulates the ambivalence of the play as a whole.

The fairytale structure and grimly realistic content of *All's Well* expose the contradictory demands faced by romantic heroines, who must be both virtuous (i.e. passively chaste) while enabling a patriarchal future through active sexuality.[106] Helen's adept adaptation to these drastically different roles polarized earlier critical viewpoints accordingly, as scholars found her to be either a conniving deceiver or a paragon of saintly virtue. But the text gives both these sides (and more) to Helen's character, and presents related critical problems by having her break gender codes: she chooses her own husband, is sexually proactive, travels independently, and even provides another woman with a dowry. Perhaps what is most troublesome is that Helen does not have the conventional grace to do all of this under cover of male disguise. While the representation of a cross-dressed boy actor as a transvestite character may have some frisson, male disguise presents female agency as a temporary usurpation of masculine behaviour, located in a tangible fabrication. Helen's use of a Catholic habit means that her 'masculine' action is neither validated by nor reduced to a sartorial explanation. The pilgrim's costume has its practical uses, affording both fictional and real travellers of continental Europe a protected status.[107] But Helen also exploits the representational slipperi-

---

[105] The classical connotations of her name might complicate the allusions to the pilgrim St Helen. Helen of Troy was infamously desirable and damnable, and the Shakespearean Helen in some ways inverts her namesake's myth: Bertram is repulsed rather than enticed and Helen is a pursuer rather than a subject of *raptus*. But the mythical Helen's reputation for sexual looseness provides a sub-textual commentary on the Shakespearean Helen's sexual assertiveness. See Laurie Maguire, *Shakespeare's Names* (Oxford: Oxford University Press, 2007), pp. 74–119; and Snyder (2002), pp. 106–11.

[106] For a feminist account of these tensions, see Kathryn Schwarz, '"My Intents are Fix'd": Constant Will in *All's Well that Ends Well*', *SQ* 58 (2007), 200–27.

[107] The Spanish Infanta encouraged the English Catholic Mary Ward to protect herself while travelling by donning the pilgrim's garb; Mary Catherine E. Chambers, *The Life of Mary Ward (1585–1645)*, 2 vols, i (London: Burns and Oates, 1882–5), p. 484. However,

ness of the habit. Where Isabella struggled to assert her meaning of 'novice' against the sexualized (mis)readings of the cast, Helen uses the conflicted meanings of the pilgrim's costume to adapt to impossible ideological demands. Her habit signifies disguise and devotion, romantic fidelity and scheming obsession. In Helen Catholic and papist connotations are compounded: she is meritorious and devious, miraculous and cunning. The costume thus punningly holds in tandem the conflicting post-Reformation connotations of the pilgrimage, dilating a conceptual space. Generally speaking, the reformation of the idea of pilgrimage interiorized a Protestant spiritual journey (though of course such metaphors were not denominationally exclusive).[108] However, here, it is the papist costume that outlines characterological interiority.

All's Well emphasizes and questions the magic that underpins the social reconciliation achieved by comedy. The pretence inherent in fictionality has given Helen space to 'be' the self she desires to be. When she first reads Bertram's post-wedding letter she understands it as a straightforward rejection: 'This is a dreadful sentence' (3.2.60–1); ''Tis bitter' (3.2.75). She subsequently rereads this grimly realistic rejection as a fairytale imposition of tasks that will ultimately allow Helen to write herself as Bertram's wife proper. The theological–fictive multivalence of 'pilgrim' helps Helen to adapt to the ideological demands required for the play to end well. The simultaneously erotic, pious and cunning impulses perform the impossible ideal of the actively sexual and passively chaste woman who secures the patriarchal future in her womb. Helen's own statements about her role testify to fluidity (if not contradiction): she announces 'Our remedies oft in ourselves do lie | Which we ascribe to heaven' (1.1.218–19), while also laying claim to an 'Inspirèd merit' (2.1.146) which collapses a Catholic doctrine of 'meritorious works' (whereby one could supplement God-given saving grace with good deeds such as penitential pilgrimages), with a Reformed understanding of Redemption as possible only through God's freely-given

---

the riskiness of female travel remained a concern. An account of St Clare praises Clare's mother for showing 'manly courage and magnanimous spirit' in undertaking pilgrimages, but cautioned that it was a practice 'more admirable than imitable in the Feminine sex'; Wadding, sig. L3v. Intrepid Protestants such as Fynes Moryson used the pilgrim's habit as a disguise to gain access to Catholic sites in Europe; Clare M. Howard, *English Travellers of the Renaissance* (London: John Lane, 1914), p. 91.

[108] Grace Tiffany usefully traces the Protestant figuration of the pilgrimage as an inner journey made by the soul to God. However, I see Helen's pilgrimage as more multivalent than Tiffany's secularized erotic reading of *All's Well* allows; *Love's Pilgrimage: The Holy Journey in English Renaissance Literature* (Cranbury, NJ: University of Delaware Press, 2006), pp. 87–109.

grace.[109] Elsewhere she assures the Widow 'Doubt not but heaven | Hath brought me up to be your daughter's dower' (4.4.18–19), conflating a heavenly narrative with the material means behind it. Whether Helen is autonomous or providentially directed remains occulted: we are shown possibilities but it is for us to judge the means and the ends of this play. For Kiernan Ryan the play's religious discourse is 'figurative rather than factual' so that Shakespeare 'declutches it from dogma'.[110] Certainly, Shakespeare does not proselytize a Catholic (or Protestant) belief through this play. But the figurative quality of the drama nonetheless uses competing theological and non-theological pilgrimage, neither defining it as mere pretence, nor promoting it as real meritorious piety. Rather he has made these different possibilities spark off one another to engage the audience spiritually, emotionally, and socially with the ethical problems of the comedy.

But in utilizing multivalence, Helen has to pay the price of continuing ambiguity. She enters the play's conclusion as a pregnant pilgrim, apparently returned from the dead and announced as a riddle: 'Dead though she be, she feels her young one kick. | So there's my riddle: one that's dead is quick' (5.3.302–3).[111] This riddle echoes and answers the riddle in which she first hinted at her plans in 1.3: the paradoxical extremes are now given emotional reality as her earlier metaphorical living-death is dramatized as pregnant resurrection from reported death. Small wonder the King should ask 'Is't real that I see?' (5.3.306). Reality is the miracle Helen now most desires, wanting to escape the fluctuations of polysemy and close the gap between signifier and signified: ''Tis but the shadow of a wife you see, | The name and not the thing' (5.3.307–8). Agreeing to unite word and referent (though with a doubly dualistic 'Both, both' (5.3.308)) Bertram takes on the rhyming linguistics of fairytale, as prompted by Helen:

---

[109] For more 'theological' readings of the play that make claims for the thematic importance of these lines, see Maurice Hunt, *Shakespeare's Religious Allusiveness* (Aldershot: Ashgate, 2004), pp. 47–72; and David N. Beauregard, *Catholic Theology in Shakespeare's Plays* (Newark, DE: University of Delaware Press, 2008), pp. 40–56. Cynthia Lewis also discusses Shakespeare's unresolved allusions to theological controversy in '"Derived Honesty and Achieved Goodness": Doctrines of Grace in *All's Well that Ends Well*', *Renaissance and Reformation* 14 (1990), 147–70.

[110] Kiernan Ryan, '"Where Hope is Coldest": *All's Well That Ends Well*', in *Spiritual Shakespeares*, ed. Ewan Fernie (London: Routledge, 2005), pp. 28–49 (p. 38).

[111] Since actors changed costume as infrequently as possible it is likely that Helen returns in her pilgrim's costume. The source specifies that Helen's counterpart remains 'in her pilgrim's weed' when she confronts her husband, emphasizing that 'she passed through the people without change of apparel'; as reprinted in Snyder (1993), pp. 231–2.

> *Helen* This is done.
> Will you be mine, now you are doubly won?
> *Bertram* If she, my liege, can make me know this clearly,
> I'll love her dearly, ever, ever dearly. (5.3.313–16)

But fiction is fundamentally about illusion, and this play retains its equivocal mode until the very end. Famously, Bertram's agreement is conditional, and instead of answering Helen directly he speaks to the man who had originally forced him to marry Helen against his will. Helen's last speech does not celebrate her new position as wife, but rather agrees to a condition and maintains the possibility of separation which she figures as fatal:

> If it appear not plain, and prove untrue,
> Deadly divorce step between me and you.
> —O my dear mother, do I see you living? (5.3.317–19)

She breaks out of rhyme to exclaim happily the word that had previously caused her so much angst: finally, she can call the Countess 'mother'. The King's last words are undercut with the same concerns with which the drama began: 'All yet seems well, and if it end so meet, | The bitter past, more welcome is the sweet' (5.3.333–4).

The pregnant Helen finally remains poised between the fecundity of fictional seeming and a darker reality which can *only* seem well. Where *1 Henry VI* drew to a close with jokes about the impossibility of a 'holy maid with child' (5.3.65), Helen has managed to produce that very paradox, even as we know it is no miracle. Comedy ideally promotes bonds between people. In this play, ostensible reconciliation has been achieved in part through the manipulation of the slippery multivalence of Catholic fictionality that enables Helen to be a paradoxically pious plotter. Helen tries to bring Bertram into a fictional golden world: a realm released from insurmountable class distinctions and which pertains to an alternative form of 'truth'. But the illusory nature of fiction is also felt to be inescapable: this is a mode that can only ever 'seem' and is founded on pretence. The meritorious saint has tricked her husband with a papist fraud. On first seeing Helen at her return, the King asks 'Is there no exorcist |Beguiles the truer office of mine eyes?' (5.3.304–5). The teleological title of the play implicitly poses the question 'do the ends justify the means?' and the King's reference to a beguiling 'exorcist' reminds us that this comic reunion might be the production of a papist trickster. The habit makes material the epistemological complexity that renders each subject different and unknowable. It advertises Helen's otherness, which is not only Catholic but more generally ethical. And herein lies the challenge of comedy's reconciliation. Both Helen and Bertram need to forgive one another, to make an imaginative leap of faith. The Catholic aesthetic extends the scope of the play's ambivalent ending, which at once makes a spiritual attempt to promote ethical understanding and also damns the apparent happiness as the mere hypocrisy Peacham emblematized with the figure of the pilgrim. Shakespeare's unreformed fiction refuses to formulate neat answers. Instead it engages its audience's varying emotional, social, religious, and recreative impulses. It is up to each individual to decide if this has ended well.

Not long after wringing out comedy's ethical difficulties in *All's Well* and *Measure for Measure*, Shakespeare produced one of his bleakest tragic visions in *King Lear*. This grim interrogation of domestic and political structures continues to assess the relationship between self and other that preoccupied Shakespeare in his earlier work. In *King Lear* Catholicism is no longer a visual presence, but in responding to a polemic that equates Catholic ritual with fraudulent illusion, Shakespeare again explores the ideological problems and ethical possibilities of creating fiction.

4

Affecting Possession in *King Lear*

Who is it that can tell me who I am? (*King Lear* 1.4.218)
Take heed o'th'foul fiend (3.4.70).

Counselling both as and against the 'foul fiend', Edgar's Poor Tom stages
the demonic in a manner that is in some senses stolidly untheatrical.
None of the fireworks or fantastic costumes that are familiar from other
early modern devil plays are to be found in *King Lear*.[1] Yet at the same
time the absence of actual devils in the tragedy renders the demonic all
the more theatrical. The audience's awareness of demons is entirely de-
pendent upon what an actor tells them. And the performance of possession is famously sourced from a text that makes an insistent connection
between devilry and staginess: Samuel Harsnett's *Declaration of Egregious
Popish Impostures* (1603). In *King Lear* (1605–6), Shakespeare puts Harsnett's reforming polemic on demonic possession and exorcism in an unreformed light. This chapter reassesses the links between Shakespeare's
and Harsnett's texts by considering the well-established common interest
in theatricality, and moving beyond it to explore the affect produced by
the demonic itself.

Unlike the other plays discussed so far, *King Lear* does not feature
openly 'Catholic' content: gone is the pilgrim's disguise that is put to use
in the earlier *King Leir*. But because Shakespeare here reflects on a purposefully sectarian text, this play affords an instructive opportunity to
explore the variety of his engagements with Catholicism, since he here
works with (or against) full-blooded anti-Catholicism. The fact that
Shakespeare does not 'answer' the *Declaration* with the 'Catholic' devices
found elsewhere in his and other early modern drama is itself telling: *King
Lear* does not Catholicize Harsnett's themes but rather un-reforms them.[2]

---

[1] Alexander Leggatt, *Jacobean Public Theatre* (London: Routledge, 1992), pp. 67–70.
[2] The pre-Christian setting of the play does not necessarily preclude Catholic content,
since Shakespeare and others seem entirely comfortable with anachronism.

Harsnett's narrative is primarily concerned with exorcisms performed by Catholic priests in the 1580s, mostly in the household of Edmund Peckham at Denham in Buckinghamshire. Exorcism had itself been cast out of the Church of England: the second Edwardian Prayer Book removed exorcism from the rite of baptism, and the office of 'Exorcist' was eliminated from the 1550 Ordinal; Canon 72 of the 1604 Church Canons stipulated the need for permission to cast out devils.[3] In specifically denigrating the Jesuit William Weston, the *Declaration* played a part in the Protestant authorities' efforts to increase division within the English Catholic Church, split between the Jesuits and the secular priests during the archpriest controversy.[4] More broadly, the *Declaration*'s explicit anti-Catholicism draws on a key sectarian logic: Catholicism is superstitious, theatrical and hellish. *King Lear* (in its staging of possession and exorcism, and in the use of Harsnettian vocabulary) responds to a particular religious controversy (the exorcisms at Denham) and a wider cultural discourse (anti-Catholic rhetoric).

The textual relationship between Shakespeare and Harsnett is thus illuminating to any consideration of the place of Catholicism in Shakespeare's drama: the playwright draws on material from sectarian propaganda and transforms it into dramatic fiction. Indeed, in recognising the connections between *Lear* and the *Declaration* we gain an insight into Shakespeare's understanding of his theatrical art-form (adapted as a metaphor for vacuous sin by Harsnett). In the late 1980s Stephen Greenblatt put Shakespeare's attitude to theatre in the same band as Harsnett's, suggesting both writers recognized the medium as finally fraudulent.[5] Numerous scholars have since refined and critiqued this argument in various ways, identifying Harsnett's agenda to be dictated by sectarianism rather than rationalism, and detecting a greater acceptance of or even

---

[3] Keith Thomas, *Religion and the Decline of Magic* (New York: Scribner, 1971), pp. 479, 485.

[4] See Frank W. Brownlow, *Shakespeare, Harsnett and the Devils of Denham* (Newark, DE: University of Delaware Press, 1993), p. 70. All references to Harsnett's *Declaration* in the text are to Brownlow's edition. Brownlow argues the *Declaration* is also part of a propaganda campaign by Richard Bancroft (Bishop of London and later Archbishop of Canterbury) and Samuel Harsnett (Bancroft's chaplain) against the puritan John Darrell, whose claims to be able to detect and dispossess devils stirred public interest and threatened to provide an alternative and unorthodox source of authority to the state Protestant Church. Harsnett implicitly damns Darrell and his associates by 'presenting Jesuitry and Puritanism as two varieties of the same fanatical threat to sound religion'; p. 75. For another account of the exorcisms, see John L. Murphy, *Darkness and Devils: Exorcism and King Lear* (Athens, OH: Ohio University Press, 1984).

[5] Stephen Greenblatt, *Shakespearean Negotiations: The Circulation of Social Energy in Renaissance England* (Berkeley, CA: University of California Press, 1988), pp. 94–128.

enthusiasm for the irrational on the part of Shakespeare.[6] This chapter advances on these accounts, not only recognizing the presence of the irrational in Shakespeare, but also assessing its ethical function in the tragedy; it takes heed, in other words, of the foul fiend. Analysing the generic effects of the *Declaration* and *King Lear* reveals how the two writers seek to move their readers and audiences. Both redirect the affect produced by demonism in crucially different ways. In staging a possessed self, Shakespeare addresses the problem of the relationship between the self and the other in still more essential terms than we saw in *Measure for Measure* and *All's Well*.

GENRE

Harsnett's *Declaration* is a work of generic translation. It draws on and denounces William Weston's (no longer extant) manuscript account of Catholic exorcisms known as the 'Book of Miracles', which had been found by the authorities in 1598. This miraculous title is typical of the generic tone of many Catholic writings on exorcism.[7] Miracles (as we saw in chapter 1) were discursively valuable, manifest arguments of the validity and efficacy of the Catholic Church, through which they appeared. Exorcism was part of a rhetorical agenda asserting the singular truth of the old faith. Diego de Yepes' *Historia Particular de la Persecucion de Inglaterra* (1599) celebrates the way in which witnessing exorcisms 'obliged' those present 'to reverence the works of God, and the virtue and power which *Christ* our Lord has bequeathed to the ministers of His Church.'[8] Catholic disputants regarded exorcisms as persuasive. In his autobiography, William Weston speculates that Cecil refused to hear at any length a young Catholic's report of exorcism because 'he was afraid...lest such a striking testimony of the truth should compel him to open his eyes and

---

[6] See, for example, John D. Cox, *The Devil and the Sacred in English Drama, 1350–1642* (Cambridge: Cambridge University Press, 2000), pp. 150–65; Richard Dutton, 'Jonson, Shakespeare and the Exorcists', *SS* 58 (2005), 15–22; Michael Hattaway, 'Possessing Edgar: Aspects of *King Lear* in Performance', in *Shakespeare Performed: Essays in Honor of R. A. Foakes*, ed. Grace Ioppolo (Newark, DE: University of Delaware Press, 2000), pp. 198–215; Hilaire Kallendorf, *Exorcism and Its Texts: Subjectivity in Early Modern Literature of England and Spain* (Toronto: University of Toronto Press, 2003), pp. 12–16.

[7] See also, Jan Frans van Dijkhuizen, *Devil Theatre: Demonic Possession and Exorcism in English Drama, 1558–1642* (Cambridge: D. S. Brewer, 2007), p. 147.

[8] As quoted in, Richard Challoner, rev. John Hungerford Pollen, *Memoirs of Missionary Priests as well Secular as Regular and of other Catholics of Both Sexes, that have Suffered Death in England on Religious Accounts from the Year of Our Lord, 1577 to 1684* (London: Burns, Oates and Washbourne, 1924; repr. Farnborough: Gregg, 1969), p. 118.

assent to it'. Weston goes on to note that during his interrogation by a prison examiner he had expressed a wish that the exorcisms had been seen by the Queen and her council, or that they had taken place in public:

> I had no doubt but that many persons on witnessing and recognizing the power and majesty of the keys of the Church when used against those furies and monsters, and easily discerning the difference of power between the two religions, would yield the palm of victory to the Catholic faith.[9]

Anthony Tyrrell similarly retorted to accusations of having taken part in fraudulent exorcisms: 'they were wonders most true and such apparent miracles as were able to convert the most obstinate heretic in the world'.[10]

Such insistence on the truth of exorcism obscures the rather more ambiguous place of this 'sacramental' within the Catholic Church. The sixteenth century saw the first attempts to standardize the rite of exorcism, which had previously been performed both 'charismatically' by saints and through the ad hoc rituals of priests and ministers.[11] Against this background the Franciscan Girolamo Menghi published numerous works on the subject, which he collected in the anthology *Thesaurus exorcismorum* (1608). Menghi's instructive books proved enormously popular with readers, and Harsnett repeatedly (if sneeringly) quotes him as an example of standard Catholic thinking on the topic. Yet as much as Menghi writes to feed some readers' demands for exorcismal knowledge, he also seeks to convince others of the real need to deal with the demonic at a time when Catholic authorities regarded the practice of exorcism with suspicion and sceptically examined accounts of possession. Reports of demonism, superstitious practice, and sexual abuse tainted the role of the exorcist in the eyes of Counter-Reformation authorities seeking to reform the clergy.[12] As Nicky Hallett remarks, because of its ambiguous status, exorcism had the potential to 'unify *or* divide communities' (my emphasis).[13] Thus behind the enthusiasm of practitioners such as Weston and Menghi remained an institutional caution that reminds us precisely how awkward it was to be seen to deal with the devil. The Catholic Church itself recognized

---

[9] *The Life of Father William Weston*, in *The Troubles of Our Catholic Forefathers*, 2nd series, ed. John Morris (London: Burns and Oates, 1875), p. 103.
[10] *The True and Wonderful Story of the Lamentable Fall of Anthony Tyrrell, Priest, from the Catholic Faith*, in Morris, p. 330.
[11] Moshe Sluhovsky, *Believe Not Every Spirit: Possession, Mysticism, and Discernment in Early Modern Catholicism* (Chicago, IL: University of Chicago Press, 2007), p. 64.
[12] Sluhovsky, pp. 61–93, 49.
[13] Nicky Hallett, *Witchcraft, Exorcism and the Politics of Possession in a Seventeenth-Century Convent: 'How Sister Ursula was Once Bewitched and Sister Margaret Twice'* (Aldershot: Ashgate, 2007), p. 23.

that while exorcism could take the form of miraculous intervention, it might sometimes represent misguided credulity or deliberate fraud.

Nevertheless, the rhetorical appeal of exorcism for an English Catholic cause is obvious. As a dramatic sign of the efficacy of the Catholic faith in a country where that faith has been officially discredited, the supernatural purchase of exorcism (the exorcist has the power to drive out the devil) testifies to Catholic significance. The exorcisms that took place in post-Reformation England were in part a demonstration of the continued significance of the Catholic Church. This is presumably why successful exorcisms appear every year in the records of the Jesuit Mission.[14] Exorcism asserts both a particular Catholic meaning and Catholic meaningfulness more broadly.

Harsnett works hard to dismiss such meaning.[15] The *Declaration* is a massive feat of redefinition: as has been well documented, he entirely transforms the genre of Catholic miracle (an assertion of practical power over real demonic presence) into a piece of theatrical illusion (representational power over feigned presence). Kenneth Muir counts 'some 230 words derived from the theatre' in Harsnett's book.[16] The Catholic reading of exorcism is thereby rejected and its meaningfulness dissolved. This redefinition is achieved through a high degree of generic self-consciousness. The *Declaration* is relentlessly taxonomic, stuffed as it is with generic labels for the Catholic exorcisms. The prevailing metaphor is, of course, theatricality: the exorcists are '*fresh from the Popes tyring house, masked with the vizard of holy burning zeale*' (197) and '*Edmunds*' (i.e. Weston) as the chief exorcist is said to be 'the Author, Actor, and penner of this play' (270). The explanation of the exorcisms as theatrical tricks, rather than real interactions with the supernatural, fits into a broader anti-Catholic theme which sees the religion as pathologically histrionic (as is familiar from descriptions of the mass as theatre). The logic of the exorcisms is, according to Harsnett's mocking exposé, always theatrical, directed by the need to put on a good performance: actions are carefully organized to 'furnish out the play' (281); devils are not driven out too quickly and easily because that would have 'spoiled a good play' (251). Consistently operating at a representational remove from reality, Catholic ministers move still further away from God.

---

[14] Thomas, p. 489.

[15] As a piece of propaganda, Harsnett's *Declaration* is not a reliable account of the exorcisms. In discussing Harsnett's rhetorical strategies and aims I am not endorsing his description as accurate, but rather reflecting the fact that Shakespeare engages with Harsnett's spin on the events.

[16] Kenneth Muir, 'Samuel Harsnett and *King Lear*', *RES* 2 (1951), 11–21 (12).

But the use of more specific theatrical genres is pivotal to Harsnett's project. In deriding Catholic claims to miracles, he occasionally exploits that terminology with sarcastic contempt: 'This play of sacred miracles'; this 'mysticall play' (202). More often, though, he refuses the numinous possibilities of such language by drawing instead on classical genres. The exorcisms are frequently labelled tragic and the exorcists themselves tragic actors: 'our tragedie' (286); 'new tragedie of devils' (208); 'devil-tragaedy' (238, 312, 317); 'holy Tragaedians' (222). This tragic definition is partly an ironic way of puncturing the straight-faced credulity of the Catholics and the high degree of importance they place on the events. Harsnett uses tongue-in-cheek references to tragedy to mock Catholic accounts as over-blown in style and claim:

> The *penner of the miracles*, as if he meant to scare us with the very noyse, reports us the manner of the Hobgoblins in a very tragicall stile. *The whole house* (saith he) *was haunted in very terrible manner, molesting all that were in the same, by locking and unlocking of dores, tinckling amongst the fier-shovels and the tonges, ratling uppon the boards, scraping under their beds, and blowing out the candels, except they were halowed.* (214)

The genre of tragedy pinpoints for Harsnett what he sees as priestly self-importance that is ludicrously wide of the mark. But though the term *tragedy* resonates through derisory incongruity, it is also frequently made to seem grimly appropriate, since it provides a means for Harsnett to condemn the exorcisms as harmful: they represent a 'pestilent tragaedie' (194, 319). When he hints that the abusive nature of the exorcism drove one girl to suicide, he addresses the priests as 'holy gentle devils, the Maisters of this devil-tragedy' (238). Harsnett maintains a satirical tone that laughs at Catholic folly even as it exposes the seriousness of the moral stakes.

Humour is central to Harsnett's rhetorical control over the illicit Catholic content. Laughing at the exorcisms obviously deflates any awe that might, as Weston himself put it, 'compel' people to 'assent' to Catholicism. Rather than simply denying Catholic claims, Harsnett manipulates particular generic effects to direct his readers' intellectual *and* emotional responses. The (supposedly) tragic pretensions of the exorcists are undercut by an equal if not greater number of references to the exorcisms as comedy: 'this comedie' (212, 213); 'holy Comedie' (201); '*Stygian* comedy' (257); 'devil-Comedy' (280). The exorcists perform comic as well as tragic parts: 'devill-comedians' (299); 'disguised comedians' (203); 'fellow Comedians' (257, 274); 'holy Comedians' (310). This designation works to identify the exorcisms as foolish inventions, as outlandish in plot as anything by Plautus (who is referenced at 319).

Clearly, Harsnett was alert to the potency of genre when managing threatening religio-political ideas. It is possible that his employer Richard Bancroft (a Bishop of London and later Archbishop of Canterbury) may have had some influence here: John Whitgift said that back in the 1580s it was 'by [Bancroft's] advice, that Course was taken, w[hi]ch did principally stop Martin and his Fellows' mouths, viz: to have them answered after their own vein in writing'.[17] Just as Bancroft recognized that po-faced rebuttal would not deal with Martin Marprelate, Harsnett felt that something other than theological disputation was needed to counter Catholic exorcisms and Puritan dispossessions. The *Declaration* repeatedly details the reactions produced by the exorcisms in terms of audience response:

> that the whole companie of spectators shal by his false illusions be brought into such commiseration and compassion as they shal all weepe, crie, and exclaime as loude as the counterfet devil; and the end and *plaudite* of the act must be this: *O Catholicam fidem!* (260)

> And thus closed up our worthy Author his woorthy tragedie with the confusion of the great Maister-devils and the consolation of his pittiful possessed captives, and that loude famous acclamation of the spectators, *O Catholicam fidem! O fidem Catholicam!* (317)

Harsnett provides these '*plaudities*' as part of his damning theatricalization of the exorcisms, mere 'false illusions'. But the imagined reactions also isolate his concern that exorcisms might produce conversion to or confirmation of Catholicism through their spectacular effects. Reframing '*Catholicam fidem*' as theatrical applause downplays the meaningfulness of that faith, but also reveals Harsnett's understanding of the way in which genre manages reactions. This recognition underpins the generic structure of the *Declaration*, which is both a piece of reforming literary criticism that re-categorizes the exorcisms as representational tragicomedy rather than presentational miracle, and also a polemical satire, carefully pitched to produce a laughing revulsion in the reader. Harsnett is aware of the riskiness of this strategy, which he necessarily defends in the prefatory letter ostensibly addressed 'TO THE SEDUCED *Catholiques* of England':

> *If the forme and phrase be distasting to some clowdy spirits, as too light and ironicall for one of my profession, let the matter be my Advocat that draweth me thereunto, and the manner my Apologie a little too: trusting I may be excused to*

---

[17] *Tracts Ascribed to Richard Bancroft*, ed. Albert Peel (Cambridge: Cambridge University Press, 1953), p. xvii; as cited by Marion Gibson, *Possession, Puritanism and Print: Darrell, Harsnett, Shakespeare and the Elizabethan Exorcism Controversy* (London: Pickering and Chatto, 2006), p. 13.

jest at their jesting that have made a jest of God and of his blessed Saints in heaven. (199)

Harsnett claims to match style to content, so that the more indecorous his tone, the more damnable the Catholic subject matter.

Early modern religious polemics certainly reached scurrilous extremes, but Harsnett moves a step further. Rather than arguing the theological case against the exorcisms, Harsnett capitalizes on what most disgusts him in order to satirize the ritual as comedy. Dismissing exorcism as foolish invention, he also uses the comic label to identify the priests' physical interactions with the demoniacs as a 'wicked lewd play' (318). In Harsnett's account, the exorcisms become something of a sex farce. Thus instead of adopting the voice of a preacher railing against the physical contact in the exorcisms (the priests allegedly applied relics to female demoniacs' genitalia), Harsnett's satirical tone is closer to a writer like John Marston.[18] Indeed Harsnett was well acquainted with satirical works. As an examiner, working under Bancroft to decide which books could be licensed for publication, Harsnett had direct access to texts from a range of genres, including not only ecclesiastical history and devotional works but also 'tragicke Comedye' (*Celestina*) and 'Comicall Satyre' (*Every Man Out of His Humour*). The Stationers' Register reveals that Harsnett signed off on *The Shadowe of Truthe in Certaine Epigrams and Satyres* and Marston's *Scourge of Vilany* ('beinge *Three bookes of Satires*').[19]

Harsnett thus had some knowledge of a 'new kind of subgenre' which Lynda E. Boose characterizes as combining 'the salaciously erotic with the violent, misogynistic excoriations of the Juvenalian satiric speaker'.[20] There are traces of this mode in the *Declaration* where Harsnett adopts a tone that is both bawdy and nauseated when describing the exorcisms as sexual abuse:

---

[18] One Catholic manuscript account specifies that priests made no such contact during exorcism: 'the preist perceaving that the dyvell was gotten into the bottom of her bellie, gave a relique unto one of the woemen willing her to apply yt unto the belly of the partie'; Bodleian MS Eng. th. B. 1–2 (Summary Catalogue 46533), I.491; as quoted by Gerard Kilroy, *Edmund Campion: Memory and Transcription* (Aldershot: Ashgate, 2005), p. 34.

[19] *A Transcript of the Registers of the Company of Stationers of London. 1554–1640*, vol. 3, ed. Edward Arber (London, 1876), pp. 127, 159, 126, 125. It is unclear whether Harsnett actually read the books he licensed. Attempting to exonerate himself for having passed Hayward's *Henrie IIII* (a book seized and burned for its pro-Essex epistle), Harsnett (perhaps not reliably) claimed that authorizers discussed texts with their authors rather than reading them; see Cyndia Susan Clegg, *Press Censorship in Elizabethan England* (Cambridge: Cambridge University Press, 1997), p. 63.

[20] Lynda E. Boose, 'The 1599 Bishops' Ban, Elizabethan Pornography, and the Sexualisation of the Jacobean Stage', in *Enclosure Acts*, ed. Richard Burt and John Michael Archer (Ithaca: Cornell University Press, 1994), pp. 185–200 (pp. 196–7).

Sara Williams had a little paine in her side (and in an other place beside)[.] (223)

Sometime (she saith) *they lodged the devill in her toe, sometime in her legge, sometime in her knee. Sometime, &c.* Let the devil and his holy charmers make up the rest. (252)

and with your burning hands catched *Sara* by the foot, and so fired the devill along till you made him slip out where no man must name[.] (262)

In repeatedly directing the reader's gaze across Sara's body before omitting the most intimate detail to which he has been leading, Harsnett moralisti-cally refuses to speak Catholic lewdness whilst simultaneously producing a rhetorical striptease. Phrases like '(and in an other place beside)' deco-rously avoid naming the 'namelesse part' (312), but also do the work of a nudge and wink. Rereading the exorcisms as opportunities for lust, Hars-nett draws upon a very familiar anti-Catholic script of clerical lechery. (The Catholic Church itself acknowledged the sexual dangers of the phys-icality of exorcism, as is clear from the stipulation in the 1614 Roman Rite that another woman must be present during the exorcising of female demoniacs.)[21] However, Harsnett's text treads the same dangerous line as the satirist in capitalizing on the energies of what he would condemn. And like other satirical texts, *The Declaration* is angrily topical (though not quite as up-to-the-minute as some of them).

Ironically, the satires of Marston and others were banned and burned by Bancroft in the Bishops' Ban of 1599.[22] Since the wording of the ban does not clarify its motivation, critics disagree about why the authorities suddenly disliked satire. Richard McCabe argues that satires had become regarded as a dangerous 'vehicle for social complaint', whereas Cyndia Susan Clegg contends that the ban responded to the political tensions of Essex's downfall.[23] The two verse satires licensed by Harsnett (*The shadowe of truthe in certaine Epigrammes and Satyres* and *The Scourge of Villainy*) were among those specifically identified in the ban. Given that the in-junction followed on the heels of Harsnett's dangerous faux pas in passing John Hayward's *The first part of the life and raigne of King Henrie IIII* for publication (which saw Hayward imprisoned and Harsnett feebly plead-ing naivety in matters of state), it is somewhat surprising that Harsnett

---

[21] While it was usual for people to support or restrain demoniacs, it was not common practice to bind them, nor were fumigations regularly used; D. P. Walker, *Unclean Spirits: Possession and Exorcism in France and England in the Late Sixteenth and Early Seventeenth Centuries* (London: Scolar Press, 1981), p. 46. Sluhovsky details still more bizarre and disturbing extremes of sexualized exorcisms elsewhere in Renaissance Europe; pp. 47–9.

[22] Arber, pp. 677–8.

[23] Richard A. McCabe, 'Elizabethan Satire and the Bishops' Ban of 1599', *The Yearbook of English Studies* 11 (1981), 188–93 (191); Clegg, pp. 198–217.

should adopt elements of the outlawed sexualized–satirical style in the *Declaration* only a few years later. (Fines were still being issued in 1601 to booksellers ignoring the ban on satires.)[24] But perhaps Harsnett's subsequent use of a satirical voice confirms Clegg's point about the situation rather than the mode itself being the real danger. Furthermore, where the banned verse-satirists posed as alienated outsiders, Harsnett's satirical voice speaks a firmly orthodox message. Just as the anti-Martinists were free to rail in the same genre as the illicit Marprelate writers, Harsnett authorizes satire in the service of the Church of England.

Harsnett explicitly seeks to rescript the response of the audience, using an ambivalent combination of serious moral disgust and humorous amoral distance. He flatly refuses to engage Catholicism in theological terms; it is textual affect rather than intellectual disputation which manages responses to exorcisms. His generic redefinitions of the exorcisms and the satirical tone of the text keep the reader at a mocking and revolted distance. Concluding the *Declaration*, Harsnett finally reconciles tragedy and comedy:

> The end of a Comedie is a *plaudite* to the Authour and Actors, the one for his invention, the other for his good action; of a Tragaedie the end is moving of affection and passion in the spectators. Our *Daemono-poiia*, or devil-fiction, is a *Tragico-comaedia*, a mixture of both, as *Amphitryo* in *Plautus* is; and did by the good invention and cariage obtaine both these ends. First, it had a *plaudite often*: *O Catholicam fidem! and O that all the Protestants in England did see the power of the Catholick Church.* And it mooved affection with expression of teares[.] (319)

Harsnett's sarcastic identification of the exorcists' success in terms of 'invention', 'action', and 'the moving of affection and passion' may well denigrate the events as merely theatrical, but it also highlights his cause for anxiety. Harsnett's generically inflected attack on the exorcisms exposes the workings of the 'invention' and 'good action' and attempts to remove 'affection and passion'.

Shakespeare's decision to deal tragically with material Harsnett so strenuously treats satirically (even when using tragic terms) marks a significant shift from Harsnett's reforming agenda. Indeed this generic transformation represents Shakespeare's main difference from Harsnett's handling of possession. Strikingly, this tragic interpretation also departs from English theatrical tradition. Earlier in his own career, in *The Comedy of Errors* and *Twelfth Night* (which both pre-date Harsnett's *Declaration*), Shakespeare put dispossession in a comic context. Rather than concern

[24] McCabe, 191.

themselves with the numinous possibilities of demonism or the 'passion' of tragedy, these plays focus on (serious) themes of human identity confusion. Later, in *Volpone* and *The Devil is an Ass*, Ben Jonson would share Harsnett's satirical attitude to exorcism as a form of modern (though not necessarily Catholic) trickery that out-devils the devil. When Barnabe Barnes does treat demonic issues tragically, in *The Devil's Charter*, he does so in a manner closer to Harsnett's idea of a 'pestilent tragaedy' rather than one that moves 'affection and passion' (319). Barnes identifies papistry as literally demonic: Pope Alexander VI is an exorcist who conjures up demons to assist his papal tyranny.[25] The implications of Alexander's apparent demonic power are entirely contained, since he proves to have no authority to drive them away again. The Devil jeers: 'Vaine are thy crosses, vaine all exorcismies, | Those be no fruites of faith but mere hypocrisie'.[26] The pre-Christian world of *Lear* lacks the obvious sectarian structure of *The Devil's Charter*, which carefully defines the demonic as a real Catholic threat, if an insubstantial power. *King Lear* conceives of tragedy on a larger scale.[27]

Given Harsnett's satirical exertions at reclassifying exorcism and redirecting his readers' 'affection', Shakespeare's untypically tragic treatment of the topic constitutes a major reformation (or un-reformation) of his source material. At the most basic level, the dissociative mode of Harsnett's satire fosters antipathy, whereas Shakespeare's tragedy fosters sympathy. Of course, the ancient Britain plot does not dramatize the sectarian politics that bedevil Harsnett. Nevertheless, in staging theatricalized demonic possession and exorcism, Shakespeare interrogates Harsnett's contentions about the performance of exorcism and hellish fraud, as well as the polemicist's drive to reject demonized otherness. But within the sympathizing context of tragedy, Shakespeare dramatizes possession and exorcism to question the alterity of the other. In their generic difference, the two texts figure the gap between viewer and demonic subject, self and other, in distinct ways, with Shakespeare forging bonds that Harsnett works hard to sever. I suggest that demonic rhetoric not only registers the depravity of the human condition in *King Lear*, but also opens out new possibilities for social relationships in the midst of that corruption and rethinks the relationship between fiction and ethics. Where Harsnett's

---

[25] The association of Catholicism with demonism was a conventional propagandist manoeuvre in the post-Reformation period; see Nathan Johnstone, *The Devil and Demonism in Early Modern England* (Cambridge: Cambridge University Press, 2006), pp. 27–59.

[26] Barnabe Barnes, *The Devil's Charter: A Critical Edition*, ed. Jim C. Pogue (New York: Garland Publishing, 1980), TLN 3345–6.

[27] For an alternative generic reading of the exorcism in *King Lear*, see Kallendorf, pp. 126–40.

polemical satire aims to keep 'us' (ideal reformed readers) at a revolted distance from 'them' (Catholic exorcists), Shakespeare's tragedy explores revulsion only to show how horror connects character to character, and actor to audience.

TRAGIC SUBJECTIVITY

The title page of the first quarto (1608) twins Lear's tragic experience with that of Edgar: 'True Chronicle Historie of the life and death of King LEAR and his three Daughters. *With the vnfortunate life of* Edgar, *sonne* and heire to the Earle of Gloster, and his sullen and assumed humor of TOM of Bedlam'. In thematic terms, it is the play's other aging father, Gloucester, who most obviously parallels Lear; yet Edgar's is the second longest part in the play and he himself recognizes an affinity with Lear's sufferings: 'He childed as I fathered' (3.6.103, Q). The quarto title embeds the 'historie' of both characters in family relationships. Edgar's role explores tragic subjectivity from a different perspective that reflects back on Lear. In his interactions with Lear, Edgar also affords the solipsistic protagonist an alternative way of looking at the world. Lear may well be 'More sinned against than sinning' (3.2.60), but he helps set the tragedy in motion through an assertion of self that tramples over the anxieties and advice of others (Cordelia is chastised 'Better thou hadst not been born than not to | Have pleased me better' (1.1.223–4); Kent is banished for attempting 'To come between our sentence and our power' (1.1.158)). Even when subsequently moved by Poor Tom's plight, at their 'first' meeting Lear can only comprehend the distress in terms of his own experience: 'Hast thou given all to thy two daughters, | And art thou come to this?' (3.4.42–3); 'What, his daughters brought him to this pass?' (3.4.55); 'Nothing could have subdued nature | To such a lowness but his unkind daughters' (3.4.62–3). However, Lear will eventually arrive not so much at self-knowledge, but at a recognition of the selfhood of others, and a concern for their sufferings. In part this is provoked by the frighteningly open subjectivity represented by the possessed Poor Tom, which at once indicates the damage done to the self and also offers a mode of apprehending the other.

For much of the play Lear is concerned to assert a sense of self, but the character of Edgar comes into being at the moment of his erasure.[28] Little

---

[28] See also Simon Palfrey, *Doing Shakespeare* (London: Arden Shakespeare, 2005), p. 201. The following reading is influenced by Palfrey's account of Edgar's 'radically metamorphic body'; p. 202.

is seen of Edgar before his pragmatic decision to disguise himself as Poor Tom, when he declares: 'Edgar I nothing am' (2.3.21). This statement of theatrical intent—a plan to conceal his identity—also announces an utter loss of self, or at least the form of self that was once 'Edgar'. Similarly, at the end of the play when Edgar fights with his brother as an anonymous knight, he would seem to be paradoxically identifying himself as without identity: 'O, know my name is lost' (5.3.116). Fundamental to Edgar's tragic subjectivity is this sense of loss, of identity without its identifying markers.

Yet while Edgar may be less than what he once was, he is also very much more. Assuming the identity of a possessed beggar enables Edgar to realize the parts of himself that could never be voiced as Edgar. He gets to speak his own torment freed from the conventional restraints that govern the rhetoric of a gentleman, a son, and a subject of a king. Speaking as other allows him to speak himself. The Poor Tom disguise is not about what Edgar puts on but what he puts in. Unlike *Measure for Measure*'s Duke, Edgar is not concealed by a sartorial disguise; instead the part is a vocalization of a weirdly populous interiority. Edgar is bizarrely both outside and inside himself. Poor Tom speaks with the voices of demons and this allows Edgar to relate to otherness, even as he performs his own self-determined role. Where demonic possession is a violation of the demoniac's will and voice, Edgar's assumed possession is also a demonstration of his ability to assert a (damaged) will and voice.[29]

As Poor Tom, Edgar speaks the torment of his current circumstances and the horror of the pursuit: 'Away, the foul fiend follows me' (3.4.39); 'Poor Tom, whom the foul fiend hath led through fire and through ford and whirlpool, o'er bog and quagmire' (3.4.44–6). These statements gesture to the literal situation while also articulating a more profound existential crisis. Now 'nothing', Edgar-as-Poor-Tom articulates suicidal urges: the 'foul fiend' has 'laid knives under his pillow and halters in his pew, set ratsbane by his pottage' (3.4.46–8). This tragic subject is a subject on the edge of annihilation. Poor Tom has been led 'to course his own shadow for a traitor' (3.4.49–50); coursing is a form of hunting. Prior to assuming the disguise, Edgar describes himself as having 'Escaped the hunt' (2.3.3) in which he has been set upon by others, but here he bespeaks

---

[29] Historians of early modern possession likewise note the ambivalence whereby the possessed subject apparently loses his or her own voice, but is thereby liberated to speak outside of strictly defined social parameters. See Armando Maggi, *Satan's Rhetoric: A Study of Renaissance Demonology* (Chicago, IL: University of Chicago Press, 2001), pp. 1–20; Philip C. Almond, *Demonic Possession and Exorcism in Early Modern England* (Cambridge: Cambridge University Press, 2004), pp. 23–6; Gibson, pp. 101–25.

a subjective split in which the self turns on the self. Of course, Edgar is not speaking as 'Edgar' here, but that does not mean that his words lack meaning. Shakespeare devotes too many lines to Poor Tom for them to be disregarded as non-significant; but their significance is self-evidently elusive as well as allusive. The difficulty of this apparently demonic rhetoric is that it refuses the safe analogical order of metaphor, even if it is not exactly literal. On some level Poor Tom hunts himself, but on another Edgar merely says that he does.

The difficulty of identifying who is speaking is also one of the liberating aspects of this demonic discourse, since it opens out different vocal positions for the speaker. In addition to the initial characterological question of where Edgar is located in relation to Poor Tom, the grammar of the speeches complicates the speaking voice still further. Poor Tom frequently speaks in the third person ('Tom's a cold' (3.4.50–1, 3.4.131, 3.4.157); 'Do Poor Tom some charity' (3.4.52)) in the mode of a beggar making a narrative of himself. He also has moments of first-person intensity, which might betoken an address to the self or a different way of speaking about the self to others ('the foul fiend follows me' (3.4.39), 'There could I have him' (3.4.53)). At other times demons speak through Poor Tom ('The foul fiend haunts Poor Tom in the voice of a nightingale' (3.6.26–7, Q only)); but when Tom replies to them it is unclear where one voice ends and another begins ('Beware my follower. Peace, Smulkin; peace, thou fiend!' (3.4.126); 'Croak not, black angel: I have no food for thee' (3.6.28–9)). Selfhood slips between different grammatical and phenomenological possibilities, so that Edgar inhabits different forms of selfhood and otherness at the same time.

The continual sense of dislocation between speaker and voice enables the demonic speech to invoke a range of subjects. For example, when Lear asks Poor Tom the simple question of identification 'What hast thou been?' (3.4.74), the lengthy response looks both inward and outward, and is worth quoting in full:

A servingman, proud in heart and mind, that curled my hair, wore gloves in my cap, served the lust of my mistress' heart, and did the act of darkness with her; swore as many oaths as I spake words, and broke them in the sweet face of heaven; one that slept in the contriving of lust, and waked to do it. Wine loved I deeply, dice dearly, and in woman out-paramoured the Turk. False of heart, light of ear, bloody of hand; hog in sloth, fox in stealth, wolf in greediness, dog in madness, lion in prey. Let not the creaking of shoes nor the rustlings of silks betray thy poor heart to women. Keep thy foot out of brothel, thy hand out of placket, thy pen from lender's book, and defy the foul fiend. Still through hawthorn blows the cold wind. Heigh no nonny. Dolphin my boy, my boy: sessa, let him trot by. (3.4.75–89)

Whose guilt is being detailed here? Poor Tom confesses a fairly comprehensive range of sins (lust, profanity, drinking, gambling, deceit, violence, cunning, greed, sloth) in a manner that does not simply shift blame onto the possessing demons (as a demoniac might typically do). The account might be entirely fictional, or record past behaviour, or express concealed impulses. The meaning of the speech floats uncertainly in relation to its speaker. And although describing his past self gives Poor Tom a more coherent sense of subjectivity than elsewhere, even that 'past self' (which is anyway a kind of fiction) proves unstable: 'False of heart, light of ear, bloody of hand; hog in sloth, fox in stealth, wolf in greediness, dog in madness, lion in prey.' Anatomized as a collection of wicked parts, the human is overtaken by the non-human in a frantic stream of animalistic attributes. Tragic-demonic identity is not only corrupt, but multiple. This is a multiplicity that looks beyond the normal boundaries of the self.

Given the sexual saturation of the speech, Poor Tom could be said to speak simultaneously for the drama's older generation, particularly Edgar's own father, who opened the play telling dirty jokes about the conception of his bastard son, Edmund. A little later, when Gloucester enters the scene, the blurring of identity categories is still more apparent: 'This is the foul fiend Flibbertigibbet' (3.4.102).[30] The deictic conflates Poor Tom with the possessing demon ('*this* inside me') and also with Gloucester ('*this* person here'). (There is also a prescient nod to Gloucester's future plight: 'He gives the web and pin, squinies [F: squints] the eye' (3.4.103–4), the 'web and pin' referring to disease of the eye. The demonic voice thus has a future aspect.) Demonic speech operates as a place to articulate and explore the other as well as the self. And the simultaneity is part of the play's ethical structure. The corrosive nature of sexuality (in this play understood as an 'act of darkness') links the generations not only via the biological ties of procreation, but also through a joint moral preoccupation. Edgar may well speak of his father's sins, but in speaking them he also takes a share in them. The concurrently inside and outside nature of demonic language allows the subject to speak itself in relation both to and as the other. Here the tragedy shrinks the distancing effects achieved by satire.

Indeed the radically open character of possessed dialogue is enlarged to include the audience, to and of whom Poor Tom also speaks. The sins of lust, deceit, pride, gambling, and drinking ring as true in the Jacobean world of the theatre as in the pre-Christian world of the play. Of course, it is not so remarkable for theatrical characters to speak to the human

---

[30] Hattaway, p. 207.

condition. Poor Tom's language does this, but its demonic status makes the meaning uncannily true and false at the same time. After all, the devil was the 'Author of Lies' and not to be trusted. Almond comments that the Christian attitude to the devil was inherently ambivalent: 'For Satan was both divine emissary and divine enemy.'[31] Poor Tom's 'personal' descriptions of his guilty past build to moral exhortation: 'Let not the creaking of shoes nor the rustlings of silks betray thy poor heart to women. Keep thy foot out of brothel, thy hand out of placket, thy pen from lender's book, and defy the foul fiend.' The repeated use of the familiar pronoun ('thy') and the directness of these prescriptions insist on the relevance of the demonic ramblings, which naggingly interpellate all who hear it. But the tone of moral authority is undermined by its demonic quality: why should anyone believe the devil? Furthermore the speech itself quickly recoils from its temporary coherence: 'Still through the hawthorn blows the cold wind. Heigh no nonny. Dolphin my boy, my boy: sessa, let him trot by.' As soon as Poor Tom speaks with something like clarity, he backs away into nonsensically disconnected phrases. Just as demonic rhetoric openly speaks to and about a variety of selves and others, it also resists any ascription. Not knowing who authors the speech makes it difficult, in terms of normal linguistic logic, to know what authority to attribute to it. This is language without a definitely identifiable speaker or addressee; it is a rhetoric in which subjectivity is radically open.

Audiences witness not only Poor Tom bedevilled by the demonic other, but also Edgar wrestling with the sins and torments of his father's generation, the ancient Briton character speaking the vocabulary of a Jacobean controversy and an actor on the post-Reformation stage playing with experiences of Catholic culture. Enacting possession is a means of 'taking in' (in both senses) otherness. This proves an instructive model for the play's tragic subjects, as Edgar, Lear, and Gloucester all become fuller selves through recognizing the selfhood of others.[32]

To Lear, Poor Tom represents the essence of humanity:

> Is man no more but this? Consider him well. Thou owest the worm no silk, the beast no hide, the sheep no wool, the cat no perfume. Here's three on's are sophisticated. Thou art the thing itself. Unaccommodated man is no more but such a poor, bare, forked animal as thou art. (3.4.91–6)

Lear responds to the naked spectacle before him, recognizing in it the fundamental condition of humanity as not the social identity marked by

---

[31] Almond, p. 20.
[32] For a related reading of selfhood, see Nancy Selleck, *The Interpersonal Idiom in Shakespeare, Donne and Early Modern Culture* (Basingstoke: Palgrave Macmillan, 2008).

sartorial coverings (all of which are 'owed' to other species) but rather as a state of exposed deprivation.[33] Lear's epiphany follows directly from Poor Tom's explanation of what he has 'been'. Meaning is located in apparent incoherence. Essence ('the thing itself') would therefore seem to be an identity in flux between performed fiction and reality, self and other, natural and supernatural, human and animal ('unaccommodated *man*' is a 'forked *animal*'). This is an appallingly bleak vision, but also perversely celebratory in its identification of a truth that is both denuded and liberating. Such ambivalence is at the heart of the play's affect. The suffering is almost unbearably grotesque, but profound connections between humans are revealed at the moment they have been reduced to something less than human. Stripped of kingly trappings, Lear may say that humanity is no more than a naked beggar; but it is precisely this recognition of the humanity of the beggar that marks Lear's emotional progression and gives hope for human society. In this tragedy, true kinship will emerge through the wreckage of familial and social relationships. The demonic plays a significant part in the (non-denominational) reformation of subjects and their bonds. Shakespeare's tragedy emphatically rejects the divisive purpose of Harsnett's text, albeit in non-religious terms.

TRAGIC BODIES

The play's meditation on humanity is only partly realized through these rhetorical means; it is also crucially performed at the level of the body. Harsnett's *Declaration* is likewise pervaded by a graphic awareness of the human body, providing a lexicon that Shakespeare translates into his tragedy. But bodily significance varies considerably between the two texts: for Harsnett the body is a vehicle for scoring sectarian points; for Shakespeare, the body is the primary site of human experience. The visceral affect of the bodies staged in *King Lear* sees the impact of the open subjectivity performed by the possessed Poor Tom further extended, as characters and audience members recognize a physical kinship.

In the *Declaration* demoniac flesh is frequently glimpsed as Harsnett mockingly exposes the exorcising priests as lechers more interested in the bodies than the souls of their young charges. Harsnett frequently frames this conventionally anti-clerical narrative with the highly resonant metaphor of hunting. As Brownlow observes, literary critics have 'ignored' the

---

[33] Laurie Shannon, 'Poor, Bare, Forked: Animal Sovereignty, Human Negative Exceptionalism, and the Natural History of *King Lear*', *SQ* 60.2 (2009), 168–96.

'similes from games and hunting' found throughout the *Declaration* in favour of the text's 'theatrical imagery', even though the figures from hunting are 'equally vivid, authentic, and frequent'.[34] Attending to the significance of the hunting tropes clarifies the nature of Harsnett's interest in the body.

In describing the exorcisms as a 'hunt' for the devil, Harsnett re-categorizes the miraculous Catholic ritual into something bathetically worldly. The notion of hunting might seem to capture relevantly the sense of exorcists attempting to drive out devils. But like exorcism-as-theatre, the exorcism-as-hunting analogy describes the practice as material for entertainment rather than as a materially spiritual ritual. Just as those who 'would entertain their friends' with the sight of hunting use 'an Hare-finder, who setting the Hare before doth bring them speedily to their game', Harsnett depicts the Catholic exorcists as 'Hunt-maisters' who have 'a devil ready lodged against any solemne hunting day, that the spectators might not be delayed with tediousnes before they came to their pastime' (253). Spectators gather at Denham to witness the 'coursing of the devill' (253) in the same way that they might gather for the passive recreation of watching hare coursing. The supposedly spiritual exorcism is in reality merely recreational, and far from hunting devils out, devils are 'hunted up into [the demoniac's] body' (249) by the exorcists. Harsnett hereby redefines the 'exorcists' in the term's colloquial meaning: not ministers who sent demons away, but juggling tricksters who brought them into being.

Treating the exorcisms as 'sport' the priests are monstrously sportive. Harsnett exploits the double meaning of *venery* as both the sport of hunting and the pursuit of sexual desire. Hunting tropes describe the exorcists in terms that conflate sex with violence. The hellishness of these priests is largely a very mortal lechery that is part of a revulsion for the female body.[35] Thus Harsnett details them locating the devils in Sara Williams' vagina and directly applying relics to her genitals in an exorcism that takes the form of molestation. The exorcists lust to handle the flesh they identify as literally devilish. Harsnett refers to the 'possessed' girls both as 'haunted' and as 'hunted' by the devil; both spellings are used and the pun yokes together the various connotations of hunting-pursuit-of-the-devil, hunting-as-violence, hunting-as-sex with supernatural haunting-by-the-devil, haunting-by-the-Catholic-devil, and haunting-as-repeated-visit. The demoniac bodies are both the hunting course ('their walke' (262)) and the

[34] Brownlow, p. 12.
[35] The priests tell the teenaged Sara Williams that her first menstruation is the work of the devil (297, 350).

prey ('fallow Deare' (262)) that the priests put to 'hot chase' (261). As if exorcism-as-sexual-hunt were not damning enough, technical vocabulary underlines the disorderliness of the priestly predators who 'hunt ryot' (a term for dogs following the scent of an animal other than the one they were intended to hunt (262)) and 'counter' like 'Curres of an impure sent' (i.e. run along the trail in the opposite direction to that of the animal pursued (261)).

A keen huntsman himself, Harsnett pursues a range of associations that accompanied the hunt in early modern England.[36] R. B. Manning argues that unlawful hunting was 'a symbolic substitute for war'.[37] Game Laws governed which areas of land might be used by hunters, and illicit hunting raids were punishable as 'riots'.[38] Treated as a political misdemeanour, illicit hunting was a way even the most powerful might assert a political point: in 1572 Queen Elizabeth and the Earl of Leicester diverged from the scheduled itinerary of a royal progress and 'havocked' a great number of Lord Berkley's red deer, perhaps as a bloody complaint at Berkley's absence during the progress.[39] Lear's 'riotous' knights (1.3.6) might make a similarly symbolic claim for the old king's authority, since when Goneril complains about the behaviour of her newly 'unburdened' father (1.1.40, F) she mentions that he is 'hunting' (1.3.7). The practice of hunting was also co-opted into real-life denominational strife. Politically marginalized Catholics found themselves the easy victims of poachers who raided their game reserves, but others vented their frustration and signalled their confessional bravado by becoming poachers themselves.[40]

Not surprising then that hunting should prove a useful idiom in polemical literature. Such imagery provided the sectarian organization in numerous anti-Catholic texts: for example, *The Hunting of Antichrist* by Leonard Wright (1589); *The Hunting of the Romish Fox* collected by James Ware (1683); *A Toile for Two-Legged Foxes* by J. Baxter (1600); and *Foot out of the Snare* by John Gee (1624). Often these texts functioned through the associative logic of bigotry, anchored only in the need to denigrate Catholicism. In *A Toile for Two-Legged Foxes* (a text Harsnett himself licensed for publication) we learn that:

---

[36] Sir Gawen Harvey of Marks bequeathed his kennel of beagles to Harsnett. See William Addison, *Epping Forest: Its Literary and Historical Associations* (London: J. M. Dent & Sons, 1945), p. 62; and Brownlow, p. 253 n. 1.

[37] Roger B. Manning, *Hunters and Poachers: A Cultural and Social History of Unlawful Hunting in England, 1485–1640* (Oxford: Clarendon Press, 1993), p. 3.

[38] Manning, p. 55.

[39] Manning, p. 48.

[40] Manning, p. 221.

it is an infallible *maxima*, that yong cubs in time will proue old Foxes, and old Foxes if time serue, will proue cruell Tygres.

But is it true, can the Foxe strip himselfe out of the lambs skin, and play the Lion in his kinde? ca[n] subiects hands acquaint themselues with tempering Italian physicke, and English brests giue harbor vnto Spanish hearts? Yea it is too true.[41]

The frantic movement of the hunt is intensified by Catholic shape-shifting across metaphors and nationalities. While the enumeration of metaphoric items in such texts bespeaks the need to anatomize the slippery Catholic, the imagery is itself fluid in its confessional resonance. Catholics were thought of as both the hunters and the hunted, sometimes even within the same text, so that while John Gee escapes from the Catholic 'snare' and from being turned into 'game', he also offers advice on 'How to kenne or smell a Priest';[42] John Baxter hunts the Catholic 'fox', but also makes reference to the Catholic Church as a 'bloudhound'.[43] Flexible as the terms are, the message is clear: Catholics and Protestants are naturally at war.

Harsnett's *Declaration* thus participates in a broader cultural association of sectarianism and hunting. His use of the metaphor accordingly makes a serious political point. After one of his repeated descriptions of the priests running their hands along Sara's body Harsnett exclaims:

> Fie holy Fathers fie, is this the trailed sent you so greedily pursue with full crie and open mouth? Is this the game you hunt called gayning of soules? Is this the haunt you quest on in Italy, Spain, and England? Is this the foile you sent so hotely that neither Sea nor Land will make you at a fault, but that you call upon it still over hill and dale, through . . . Colledges, Cloysters, Palaces, houses, yea, even into hell it selfe; and thence start the devil, and hunt him a fresh, and lodge him with *Sara Williams* in such muses, conny-beries, and holes as the poore devil but for your hote pursuite would never have come in? (252)

Following on from one of the many 'blazons' of Sara's body, female somatic space and geographical terrain are here rendered equivalent. Again Catholic priests are said to have forced the devil *into* the demoniac (they 'lodge him with *Sara Williams*' where he would otherwise 'never have come'). Harsnett suggests that the priests' claims that Sara is possessed by the devil are false but their handling of her body is a form of possession

---

[41] J. Baxter, *A Toile for Two-Legged Foxes* (London, 1600), sigs. C3r–v. For Harsnett's licensing of the text, see Arber, p. 152.

[42] *John Gee's Foot Out of the Snare (1624)*, ed. T. H. B. M. Harmsen (Nijmegen: Cicero Press, 1992), pp. 138, 127, 143.

[43] Baxter, sig. [B5r].

by Catholic devils. The abuse of this individual girl represents a national political threat. The female body is part of the topography of the Jesuit 'hunt' for 'soules' that encompasses dangerous foreign countries ('Italy, Spain'), the sites which were believed to train traitors or 'seed-men' ('Colledges, Cloysters, Palaces, houses'), and the ultimate source of Catholic nefariousness, 'hell'.[44]

Sara gives a human face to England's vulnerability; she makes the protection of the nation seem urgent. Yet it is also her femininity that weakens England since her body is shown to be a space which renders English national (and theological) boundaries vulnerable. Harsnett's catalogue 'Colledges, Cloysters, Palaces, houses' moves from the institutional to the domestic. The fear that Jesuits received orders in foreign 'Palaces' to wreak havoc in English palaces was coupled with an awareness that they were able to survive in recusant 'houses'. Treason had a domestic base. Accordingly Harsnett frequently euphemizes the vagina in domestic terms (the 'privy parts', a 'gate', and 'the devils port-gate' (312) where the priests are said to 'lodge' the devil), so that by implication national vulnerability is gendered female.[45] The priests' domestic wanderings are intrusions of 'privy parts'. However, this intrusion is possible because of the nature of the female body (gates exclude people and let them in). In particular, the notion of a 'devils port-gate in *Sara*' compounds domestic and national intrusion. The alleged abuse done to Sara is overshadowed by the abuse done to England itself: her body is a piece of landscape (featuring a proliferation of 'muses, conny-berries, and holes') as much as it is an individual, human physique.

Harsnett's interest in the demoniacs' bodies is evidentiary (proof of the priests' 'impostures') and symbolic (representative of political danger). The metaphor of the hunt enables Harsnett to make a string of related points about Catholicism; but it also distances him and his readers from the hunted bodies themselves. *King Lear's* bodily interests are experientially different for the audience. The play utilizes far fewer hunting metaphors than the *Declaration* and is instead overwhelmed by a sense of predation itself: children attack fathers, brother pursues brother, and sister kills sister. *King Lear* borrows the *Declaration's* lexicon of pain but outstrips it in terms of spectacular violence. Shakespeare focuses on bodily suffering in order to explore the suffering of the subject that Harsnett

---

[44] Gordon Williams shows that 'hell' was used as a euphemism for vagina, citing Lear's rant ('there's hell, there's darkness' (4.6.122)) as an example; *A Dictionary of Sexual Language and Imagery in Shakespearean and Stuart Literature*, 3 vols, ii (London: Athlone, 1994), p. 660.

[45] Williams defines both 'gate' and 'port' as euphemisms for vagina; ii, pp. 585, 1073.

ignores. In doing so, he reclaims the tragic 'moving of affection and passion' satirized by Harsnett. *King Lear* functions as a kind of living autopsy
that strips back the flesh to reveal not merely the physical but also the
metaphysical essence of the human.

Bodies in *King Lear* are never allowed to drift away from their literal
significance as bodies (in the way that they do in the *Declaration*), however much imagery is used to convey their plight. In part this is because
bodies are present in theatre in a way that they never can be in written
texts. The staged flesh of Shakespeare's Poor Tom has an immediacy no
written account of the demoniac Sara Williams could achieve. Shakespeare accentuates this theatrical condition: 'Do Poor Tom some charity,
whom the foul fiend vexes. There could I have him, now, and there, and
there again' (3.4.52–4). The urgency of 'now' and the repeated deictic
'there' insist on the significance of Poor Tom's (breached) flesh, even as
that flesh is doubly representational (an actor plays Edgar who plays Poor
Tom). This character (or characters?) cries out for the body's pain. In his
elegant analysis of possession and exorcism in early modern drama, Jan
Frans van Dijkhuizen identifies possession as a phenomenon used in theatre to address cultural anxieties about the stability of selfhood and the
'dangerous energies' perceived to derive from the human body.[46] He reads
the possession in *King Lear* as a statement of utter loss: 'Edgar's possessed
body is here reduced to a mere body, shorn of metaphysical meaning';
similarly 'Lear moves from a mystical physicality to a naked corporeality,
shorn of metaphysical meaning'.[47] While this interpretation captures the
bleakness that is an unquestionable part of the play's spectacle of suffering
flesh, it overstates the extent to which possession removes subjective (i.e.
personal, metaphysical) meaning. Even through an apparent loss of
agency, the importunate demoniac insists on the significance of his mis-
treated body. The possessed beggar speaks for the denuded flesh as bearing
numinous meaning, pointing not only to a violation but also to the existence of something beyond the worldly. As the demoniac suffers the indig-
nity of losing self-control, he simultaneously announces his importance as
a subject. Furthermore, if Poor Tom seems to have lost agency, Edgar apparently has not. As we saw in chapter 1, gestures to the actor's flesh can
weaken the boundary between representation and presentation. Reaching
through representation both Poor Tom and Edgar insist the audience
share the moment of his agony ('now') and confront the real presence of
the actor's flesh ('there'). This body is not stripped of meaning but over-

---

[46] van Dijkhuizen, p. 25.
[47] van Dijkhuizen, pp. 76, 78.

loaded with it: the flesh signifies demons, Poor Tom, Edgar, and the player himself.

Part of the tragic terror in this scene is that selfhood might slip away with the removal of social markers of identity. Shakespeare forces us to contemplate humanity in its 'basest and most poorest shape' (2.3.7), in 'presented nakedness' (2.3.11). But the removal of sartorial meaning is not the same as the shearing of metaphysical meaning. It is through the casting off of 'lendings' (as Lear would have it (3.4.97)) that Edgar protects a more essential (if fluid) self. He uses his body to articulate an ineffable existential pain and insist on its tangible reality. Where suffering is more-or-less anterior to Harsnett's project, in *King Lear* it is suffering that manifests humanity and is the primary principle of kinship within the tragedy.

Poor Tom's is not the only body put into tragic focus in *King Lear*. A different borrowing from Harsnett further exemplifies Shakespeare's concern for the somatic condition of the subject. Throughout the *Declaration*, Harsnett makes much of the way in which the priests bound the demoniacs to chairs, frequently euphemizing the exorcisms as 'chair-work' and thus making this image central to his propagandist depiction. In line with other anti-Catholic polemicists, Harsnett maintained that Catholics were dangerous because they ensnared 'fooles, children, and women' (219). Here was a physical actualization of that threat: a nightmarish and repeated scene of compelled subjugation to the violent rituals of Catholic priests. Harsnett's image is one of complete perversion: adults in positions of moral authority are shown harming the children they should protect, and a mundane item of domestic comfort becomes an instrument of torture. He points out that the exorcisms were illicit even by the Catholic Church's own standards, since Mengus wrote that '*Si mulier sit quae exorcizatur, sit valde senex: We must not exorcize a woman except she be old*' (220). In his list of ironic justifications for the Denham exorcisms of young girls Harsnett suggests:

> there be certain actions, motions, distorsions, dislocations, writhings, tumblings, and turbulent passions fitting a devils part (to make it kindly expressed) not to be performed but by supplenesse of sinewes, pliablenesse of joynts, and nimblenesse of all parts, which an old body is as unapt and unweldie unto, as an old dog to a daunce. It would (I feare mee) pose all the cunning Exorcists that are this day to be found, to teach an old corkie woman to writhe, tumble, curvet [frisk], and fetch her Morice gamboles as *Martha Brossier* [a famously fraudulent demoniac] did. (221)

Harsnett's catalogue of bodily postures collapses bodily torment into sexual titillation. Grotesque as Harsnett defines the exorcists' motivations to be, he also insists that the supposedly miraculous traffic with the super-natural is nothing more remarkable than common lust. Depicting how 'unapt' an 'old corkie woman' would be is a joke that shows the conventional limits of the priests' alleged lechery: who could desire to subject the elderly to such 'distorsions'? Shakespeare explores the horrifying answer to this question.

The scene of Gloucester's blinding reveals its Harsnettian influence in the explicit use of a chair ('To this chair bind him' (3.7.32); 'hold the chair' (3.7.64)) and the reference to Gloucester's 'corkiness' ('Bind fast his corky arms' (3.7.27)). Shakespeare has completely stripped the image of Harsnett's sarcastic humour, and the gouging out of Gloucester's eyes dramatizes the meaning of Harsnett's often merely metaphoric lexicon of agony. Literalizing (with a gender switch) the unseemly situation of Harsnett's joke, Shakespeare goes out of his way to test his character's and his audience's endurance. He enlarges on the violation inherent both in possession and Harsnett's account of exorcism. Elaine Scarry explains that torture, through the use of furniture, 'announces its own nature as an undoing of civilization, acts out the uncreating of the created contents of consciousness'.[48] In this scene Shakespeare peels back various layers of civilized protection: the trappings of domesticity become a trap; the privileged position of host degraded into that of hostage; the vulnerability of old age punished rather than protected. Describing himself as 'tied to the stake' where he 'must stand the course' (3.7.51), Gloucester's torment hints that tragedy is the 'pleasure' of watching hunted prey (in this case a baited bear). Except that the play stages a different spectatorial affect. Offstage audiences wince in visceral sympathy; one of the onstage audience is prompted to sympathetic action as the First Servant bids Cornwall to hold and then fights with him to the death.[49] Gloucester's body is treated as if it had none of the meaning civilization attaches to it, and Shakespeare shows the nightmare that such meaning exists only in a community's agreement. But the play does not share the attitude to the body that Regan and Cornwall demonstrate. The servant's defiance re-establishes a human bond, even as social codes are inverted (fatal disobedience functions as 'better service' (3.7.71)).[50] In the quarto text this fragile fellowship is underlined, as at the end of the scene two more servants tend

[48] Elaine Scarry, *The Body in Pain: The Making and Unmaking of the World* (New York: Oxford University Press, 1985), p. 38.

[49] See also Amy Wolf, 'Shakespeare and Harsnett: "Pregnant to Good Pity?"', *SEL* 38 (1998), 251–64 (256).

[50] See also John D. Staines, 'Radical Pity: Responding to Spectacles of Violence in *King Lear*', in *Staging Pain, 1580–1800: Violence and Trauma in British Theater*, ed. James Allard and Matthew R. Martin (Farnham: Ashgate, 2009), pp. 75–92.

to Gloucester's injury even as they lament the degeneration of humanity (3.7.96–104).

Even as the action of the play seemingly attests to the body's lack of inherent meaning, the tragedy's language identifies bodies as morally meaningful. Characters repeatedly register moral kinship in somatic terms. For example, cursing Goneril, Lear acknowledges:

> But yet thou art my flesh, my blood, my daughter,
> Or rather a disease that lies within my flesh,
> Which I must needs call mine. Thou art a boil,
> A plague-sore, an embossèd carbuncle
> In my corrupted blood. (2.4.191–5)

While he roars insults at his daughter, Lear recognizes her corruption as his own; their biological connection is also a bond of shared moral culpability. Later, having seen the tormented Poor Tom (and imagined daughters at the root of the trouble), Lear reflects: 'Judicious punishment: 'twas this flesh begot | Those pelican daughters' (3.4.66–7). The bleak world of *King Lear* reads bodily meaning as a shared primal guilt. In the previous chapter we saw that the comic problem of *Measure for Measure* was to question how the self relates to the other and how the self could be communal; the tragic understanding of *King Lear* is a bald acceptance of a corruption shared by self and other. *Measure for Measure* frames a problem through plot devices forcing the self to substitute for the other, creating an artificial bond; the tragedy of *King Lear* is that all who suffer are at a deeper level genuinely implicated in the corrosion that has caused this plight, but the price they pay is horrifically out of proportion to their crimes. Thus when confronting his bastard brother, Edgar makes a grim connection between his father's sexual misdemeanours and the violence done to him: 'The dark and vicious place where thee he got | Cost him his eyes' (5.3.166–7). *King Lear* resists the rationalism of Harsnett's text and while the tragedy establishes differences between 'good' and 'bad' characters, it refuses the comfort of a 'them' and 'us' structure (key to Harsnett's polemic), even at the most basic level of physical separation.

FICTION AND BELIEF

The importance of the contrasting representations of the individual and the body is finally determined by the fundamentally different conception of fiction in the *Declaration* and *King Lear*. Harsnett identifies the Denham exorcisms as a performed fiction that is made affectively effective through generic manipulations; his exposure operates on these same (non-theological) terms, by revealing the illusion and deploying different generic tricks to re-affect his readers. Shakespeare seems deeply but improperly affected by Harsnett's language, which reappears in *King Lear* as a lexicon of real agony. Altering Harsnett's genre, the play challenges the *Declaration*'s logic that fictional pretence dissolves meaning. In *King Lear* Shakespeare rehabilitates dramatic fiction as an authentic space to confront existential terror and a moral place to explore the limits of ethics.

Harsnett's antipathy to fiction is partly dictated by the purpose of his polemic. The exorcisms are deprived of any 'real' meaning by their redefinition as a fictive pretence; fiction becomes as sinful as the priestly actors. Of course, Harsnett's depiction of the exorcists as consummate performers is itself an adept performance. His technical understanding of theatre—evident in terms such as 'cue-fellowes' (218)—would seem to imply a less unfavourable attitude to the stage lurking beneath the righteous association of priests, performers, and perfidy. Even if Harsnett presented himself as an anti-illusionist, it was perhaps not unfair of opponents such as John Darrell to cry hypocrisy, describing him as a 'Masker comminge thus to play his part on the stage'.[51] Nevertheless, Harsnett's rhetorical stance in the *Declaration* draws on a body of thought that regarded fiction's remove from reality as not safely amoral but dangerously immoral. Playwrights and other storytellers might have used Catholic aesthetics to set their tales in a benignly fictional realm apart from the real here and now; but for some moralists the association between Catholicism and fiction underwrote the religion's turpitude. Papists drew upon and peddled beguiling fantasies, idolatrously distanced from God's real Word. This is the attitude to fiction that Harsnett strikes in the *Declaration*:

> These Monster-swarmes his *Holinesse* and his helly crue have scraped and raked together out of old doating heathen Historiographers, wisardizing Augurs, imposturizing South-sayers, dreaming Poets, Chimerial conceiters, and coyners of fables, such as puffe up to our young gallants with bigge lookes and bombast phrases, as the booke of *Lancelot du Lake*, *Guy of War-wicke*, *The Mirrour of Knighthoode*, *Amadis de Gaule*, and such like their Legends[.] (307)

This catalogue of 'sources' makes the telling of tales equivalent to superstitious magic: both kinds of illusion are dangerous in their deceptiveness. These airy nothings 'puffe up' readers who forget what is real and true.

---

[51] John Darrell, *A Detection of that Sinnful Shamful, Lying, and Ridiculous Discours, of Samuel Harshnet* (?English secret press, 1600), sig. A3r/p. 5 [both pagination and signatures are disordered and repeated in this text; this quotation is from the recto side of the seventh page].

Laying bare the bankruptcy of Catholic discourse, at another point Harsnett relates, in the mode of anti-papist fabliaux, a 'tale' about a 'daintie peece of flesh' who is 'caught' by a 'holy man', concluding: 'Heere is no morall (gentle Reader), and therefore let us have no application' (223). The Catholic tale even fails on literary terms since it lacks a 'morall' (both message and morality). Mere fiction that is somehow even less than fiction, Catholicism's insubstantiality hellishly threatens to disintegrate the substance of God's created order.

But where Harsnett writes the demonic off as sheer fiction, and identifies this fiction-making as the real demonic threat, Shakespeare variously emphasizes the fictional status of his play. The tragedy is openly shaped by a folkloric structure: an old king subjects his three daughters to a love test that he himself fails (the sincerity of Cordelia's silent love is conventionally obvious).[52] When Lear and his followers exit the storm scene, Poor Tom cries:

> Child Roland to the dark tower come,
> His word was still 'Fie, fo, and fum;
> I smell the blood of a British man.' (3.4.165–7)[53]

As in Harsnett's accusations, the language of possession is here sourced from romance and fairytale. But the words speak Edgar/Poor Tom's fear at being so close to the home which spells death to him; the evocation of a fairytale conveys this 'child's' nightmare in which Edgar is dwarfed by his father into the role of Poor Tom. The refrain does not so much tell us that Edgar is faking as that he inhabits a world governed by fairytale's emotional extremes.

Indeed the Harsnettian vocabulary resonates very differently in *King Lear*'s dramatic fiction than in the *Declaration*'s exposure of pretended fiction. Harsnett reserves particular scorn for the names of the Denham demons, which he highlights as obvious evidence of the exorcisms' emptiness. He stresses the strangeness of these '*strange names*' (239) as a means of identifying Catholic significance as insignificance. Exorcists wrested power back from the possessing demon through the act of naming; the rite was predicated on the assumption that the names carried a particular potency.[54] Harsnett ridicules the notion that the Denham onomastics could bear any real meaning, deriding the novelty of these 'new devil names' and 'new strange names' (an emphasis that keys into familiar

---

[52] See Catherine Belsey, *Why Shakespeare?* (Basingstoke: Palgrave Macmillan, 2007), pp. 42–64.
[53] Folio has: 'Child Roland to the dark tower came' (3.4.169).
[54] Maggi, p. 106.

attacks on Catholic practice as innovation). He reflects on the possible provenance of these names: perhaps the devils copied the Jesuits 'who to dissemble themselves have alwaies three or foure odde conceited names in their budget' (239); or possibly the fumigations administered by the exorcists left the devils 'so giddy-headed that they gave themselves giddy names' (240); or maybe 'there is a confederation between our wandring Exorcists and these walking devils, and they are agreed of certaine uncouth non-significant names which goe currant amongst themselves' (240). These tongue-in-cheek suggestions make the serious point that such inventiveness has Catholic dissimulation at its root. In describing the devilish onomastics as 'non-significant names' Harsnett pinpoints the paradox he finds so offensive: these names are aberrant labels of unmeaning. The 'uncouth' devils' names, like the exorcisms themselves, are mere inventions and thus they idolatrously dissipate God's created Word. It is this dissolution of meaning that Harsnett regards as truly demonic.

The examinations of the demoniacs appended to the *Declaration* proper provide further details about the devilish onomastics. Sara Williams indicates that she called recently exorcized devils by names: 'Hobberdidaunce' and 'Maho'. These were names suggested by characters in a 'merry tale' told by her mistress (343) and 'a booke' read by her uncle (343–4). An even greater number of the names take their provenance from children's graffiti:

> *Lustie Dick, Killico, Hob, Cornercap, Puffe, Purre, Frateretto, Fliberdigibet, Haberdicut, Cocobatto, Maho, Kellicocam, Wilkin, Smolkin, Nur, Lustie Jolly Jenkin, Portericho, Pudding of Thame, Pourdieu, Bonjour, Motubizanto, Bernon, Delicate*, this examinate sayth that there were very strange names written upon the wals at Sir *George Peckhams* house under the hangings, which they said were names of spirits. And addeth that she perceaving stil that when they said it was the devil that spake in her, and that they would needes have her from time to time to give it some name, she to content them did alwayes devise one name or other, and verily thinketh that shee came neere some-times to some of the names which were written upon the wall, because she had often heard them, and saith that they runne then in her head. (344)

Not surprising then that these names should sound comical or folkloric. Stephen Greenblatt may not share Harsnett's Protestant offence, but he agrees that the names 'carry with them a faint but ineradicable odor of spuriousness'.[55] But the priests' credulity suggests that the fantastical quality of the names held a different kind of truth value for them. What

---

[55] Greenblatt, p. 117.

suggests 'spuriousness' to a modern literary critic or dissimulated 'gibridge' to an unsympathetic Protestant minister is afforded validity predicated on a different scale of values in the hidden Catholic community. Two different attitudes to fiction that were certainly not always organized along sectarian lines (compare Philip Sidney and Stephen Gosson) are in this instance worked out as sectarian difference: fiction as productive of a transcendent truth; fiction as reductively untruthful. Of course, many Catholics (not least the Roman hierarchy who strove to regulate the rite of exorcism) had deep objections to the stratification of truth into different degrees. But the covert community in Denham experienced such matters differently. Instead of having a biblical onomastic heritage (a scriptural truth-value) these devils' names come from a more local literary and oral landscape, collectively familiar to the inhabitants of Denham. While dramatists may have sometimes utilized Catholic aesthetics nostalgically to structure a fictive distance, here Catholic priests appropriated names which sounded fictional to give the exorcisms a meaning that could be collectively understood as a folkloric 'truth'. The names have an unspecific familiarity that makes them 'uncanny' and potentially terrifying.

What emerges here is a fluid relationship between truth and fiction, merriness and seriousness. The early modern fictions in which devils do appear are often what Sara Williams calls 'merry tales'. Whereas at Denham 'merry' names take on demonic purchase, elsewhere the overtly fictional and antiquated status of devil tales was a guarantee of their lack of danger.[56] This is precisely the concern Ben Jonson addresses in *The Devil is an Ass* (1616), a play which like *King Lear* draws on the *Declaration*. It opens with Satan warning Pug that his devilry is now outdated by the standards of the seventeenth-century earth. Jonson underlines this point stylistically with the Vice figure Iniquity, whose rhyming couplets (and very status as a Vice) mark him out as an example of textual history. This devil is literally a piece of fiction, outmoded and not to be feared. Jonson's satire, however, insists that the audience recognize the threat of evil, even if the older modes of representing it are now defunct. Thus he lampoons the modern present: seventeenth-century England is more hellish than hell (Pug laments: 'All my days in Hell were holidays to this!' (4.4.223)) and modern citizens more skilled in deceit than demons (Pug feels the meaning of the play's title: 'The devil is an ass! Fooled off and

---

[56] This is not to say that the type of credulity witnessed at Denham was unique; numerous reports of extra devils appearing in performances of *Dr Faustus* indicates the way that, in some quarters, a demonic reality was felt to push through a fictional medium.

beaten!' (2.6.25)).[57] Humanity wreaks its own destruction through a theatrical trickery (à la Harsnett) far worse than anything Satan's minions
can produce. With all the urgency of satire, *The Devil is an Ass* forces its
audience to recognize the hellishness of the present, as the play insists on
its immediacy: Fitzdottrel spends the play attempting to see the new play,
The Devil is an Ass. Furthermore, while seventeenth-century devilry is a
deceitful performance, real hell awaits malefactors, as the literally demonic makes its presence felt through representational effects: the stench
of burning (created by fireworks) that registers the demonic visit to the
characters ('I ha' the sulphur of hell-coal i' my nose' (5.7.10)) would also
have been smelt by the audience. Jonson thus insists on a demonic danger
all too easily distanced in 'merry devil' tales, where supernatural deceit is
safely fictional.

Shakespeare's tragedy likewise refuses the safe distance of merry tales,
but unlike Jonson's comedy it does so through both fictionality and pastness rather than sharpening a contrast with a more 'real' present. The demonic names so derided by Harsnett appear in *King Lear* in the mouth of
Edgar/Poor Tom: 'Five fiends have been in Poor Tom at once, of lust as
Obidicut, Hobbididence, prince of dumbness, Mahu of stealing, Modo
of murder, Flibbertigibbet of moping and mowing, who since possesses
chambermaids and waiting-women' (4.1.56–60, Q). When Jonson alludes to Harsnett and other accounts of contemporary exorcisms his
point is to allude to a famous fraud and establish the deceptive atmos-
phere of present-day reality. Shakespeare's allusion complicates the relationship between performance and reality. Edgar certainly performs Poor
Tom, but this role is not marked out as a deception by any revelation
scene; instead the two parts merge into one another and render distinctions between reality and theatricality impossible if not redundant. Furthermore, in the midst of a story that is overtly fictional, the references to
'Hobbididence', 'Mahu', 'Modo', and 'Flibbertigibbet' introduce reality
(a controversy from the real world) as well as something fictionally familiar (folkloric onomastics). The names ring out uncannily in the ancient
Britain setting, quoting a controversy that will not happen for centuries.
The temporal and empirical crux in the reference to 'chambermaids and
waiting-women' who have '*since*' been possessed by Poor Tom's devils
points to the real-life experiences of Sara, Fid, and Anne from a time in
the future of the ancient Britain story, but strangely concurrent with Poor
Tom's 'performance'. The names puncture the play's chronology and

[57] Ben Jonson, *The Devil is an Ass*, in *The Devil is an Ass and Other Plays*, ed. M. J. Kidnie
(Oxford: Oxford University Press, 2000); all references to *The Devil is an Ass* in the text are
to this edition.

boundaries between fact and fiction. In *The Devil is an Ass* Satan and his demons share the same mortal chronology as the human world; their supernatural essence does not remove them from the linear rationality of earthly time. But *King Lear* threatens us with devils unbound by such schemes. This demonic incursion pierces time so that the audience are brought into an immediate proximity with the staged locus. Jonson's audience are caught in a demonic present, but Shakespeare's feel a horror that collapses past and present. The tragic fiction presents inescapable pain that is always true. The nightmares that take place 'once upon a time' are of all time: then and now simultaneously.

King Lear, then, offers an irreducibly fictive account of authentic pain. It also reclaims fiction and theatre as ethical experiences. The moral possibilities of performance are most clearly raised in the 'Dover Cliff' scene (4.6), where Edgar/Poor Tom frames his attempt to rid his father of suicidal despair as a miraculous escape from a demon. Reading the play in the light of its relationship to the *Declaration*, Stephen Greenblatt notes that 'Shakespeare appropriates for Edgar a documented fraud', and claims therefore that 'the scene at Dover is a disenchanted analysis of both religious and theatrical illusions.'[58] But in revealing the presence of illusion Shakespeare does not necessarily seek to disillusion his audience. The scene opens in a representational hinterland: as the blind man is led on stage, the audience are unclear whether they too are to read apparently 'even' ground as 'Horrible steep' (4.6.3). Clarification comes with a moral explanation: 'Why I do trifle thus with his despair | Is done to cure it' (4.6.33–4). Edgar's theatrical exorcism is an act of compassion that helps re-solder the 'cracked' bond 'between son and father' (1.2.102). Where the *Declaration* characterizes exorcism as mere theatre and therefore sinful, *King Lear* recasts theatre as exorcism that is salvific. Efficacy rather than the pretence at the heart of the miracle is what matters here (compare, for example, *2 Henry VI* where an apparent miracle is unmasked as a theatrical fraud). Edgar does not try to alleviate his father's despair but to provide a situation in which he can fully experience and work through it: it is tragedy in miniature. With extraordinary representational flexibility, Edgar plays himself, a possessed beggar, a dispossessing exorcist, a demon, and a shocked viewer. Yet Edgar hides nothing from the audience (unlike

---

[58] Greenblatt, pp. 117, 118. See also Huston Diehl's richly sensitive account of the Dover Cliff scene in 'Religion and Shakespearean Tragedy', in *The Cambridge Companion to Shakespearean Tragedy*, ed. Claire McEachern (Cambridge: Cambridge University Press, 2002), pp. 86–102 (pp. 95–101). I depart from Diehl in her association of Edgar with the 'rituals and theatricality of Catholicism' and Cordelia and her plain speaking 'with early Protestantism'; this argument imposes too neat a denominational schema on a play stripped of the theological reference points found elsewhere in early modern drama.

All's Well's Helen) and his character's narrative does not arc to a revelation of a 'true' Edgar from out of the disguise of Poor Tom (like other disguised characters in the canon). The very fact that Edgar's eventual revelation to his father takes place offstage indicates that the performance of a role has not been the main point of what the audience has witnessed. Instead they are invited to accept the performance as integral to (rather than a covering of) an identity that is fluid and multifaceted. The theatrical exorcism is an expression of love that affirms faith in humanity: 'Thy life's a miracle' (4.6.55).

In eschewing the central terms of Harsnett's debate (that performance kills truth) Shakespeare's vision is decidedly unreformed. But while he may reject the tenets of Harsnett's criticism, neither does Shakespeare satisfy the claims made by Catholic exorcists. Defenders of exorcism shared Harsnett's contention that for the phenomenon to count it had first to be established that nothing had been feigned.[59] Shakespeare's treatment of both possession and exorcism as fictional performances enacted by a character in disguise hardly does much for any doctrinal cause. Shakespeare reinstates the value of theatrical fiction rather than the veracity of Catholic exorcism. He validates the psychological and emotional changes wrought by fiction. Such affectiveness was, of course, profoundly disturbing to Harsnett, at least as far as the Catholic fiction of exorcism was concerned. He sneers that the consummate performance of exorcism means:

> that the whole companie of spectators shal by his false illusions be brought into such commiseration and compassion, as they shal all weepe, crie, and exclaime as loude as the counterfet devil; and the end and *plaudite* of the act must be this. *O Catholicam fidem! O fidem Catholicam*...That is: *O the Catholique faith, O the faith Catholique, truly faith, holy, pure, powerfull faith*[.] (260–1)

The audience's credulous, Catholic response is associated with the 'counterfet devil' in its volume ('as loude as') and its theatricality.

Harsnett promises that his exposé will reform responses to the exorcisms: 'Now by that time *Sara*, and her play-fellowes be come upon the stage, and have told you how they were burned, and handled likewise, I doubt not but you will helpe their *plaudite* with an O too: *O diabolicam fraudem! O fraudem diabolicam! O diros actores! O ineptos spectatores!* (261). Harsnett isolates the guttural, emotional 'O' as the reaction in need of alteration. Rescripting the Latin confession of Catholic faith as a disavowal, he also crucially reinflects the feeling behind the non-verbal 'O'.

---

[59] Almond, pp. 38–42.

These '*O*'s echo through this passage and the whole text. The demoniac Sara cries '*Oh*' as part of her 'performance'. Harsnett narrates: '*Sara* was content to play the she-devil touching your presence and approach, and to grace you with an *Oh I burne, oh I cannot abide the presence of a Catholique*' (261). Here '*Oh*' means nothing: it is a seemingly involuntary utterance of feeling, voluntarily feigned by an obedient 'play-fellowe'. But it becomes authentic as that which Harsnett views as truly devilish (mortal lechery rather than supernatural possession) enters the action. Harsnett describes the exorcists handling Sara:

> to seize with the same hands upon her toe, slip them up along her legge, her knee, her thigh, and so along all parts of her body till you came neere her neck, and by the way with the same holy hands to handle, pinch, and gripe where the devil in his blacke modesty did forbeare, till you made her crie *oh*[.] (261)

Sara's '*oh*' now pinpoints the ambivalence of Harsnett's tone: it is the cry of shock and pain of one who (it is alleged) is abused, and it also vocalizes a bawdy joke in sounding like an orgasmic climax.[60] Deeply ambiguous as this style is, the satirical oscillation between repulsion and humour carefully directs outraged contempt: '*O diabolicam fraudem!*' And just at the point when '*O*' rings with authenticity, it is quickly evacuated of real meaning: 'you made her crie *oh?* And then you to crie, *O, that* oh *is the devill*' (261). After a disingenuous exclamation ('*O*'), Harsnett's priests swiftly attribute Sara's '*oh*' to the devil, trapping her in a demonic double-bind. By this point '*O*' marks the usurpation of utterance at the very moment when the speaker's sound would seem most essential. When Sara exclaims, the priests hear the devil; but then Harsnett himself dispossesses the Catholic voice, hearing only fraudulent devilry.[61] The multiplication of '*O*'s produces a kind of melodramatic emptiness that cancels out the numinous content of Catholic miracle. As an expression without a referent, '*O*' is used by Harsnett to highlight both emotional reactions and the Catholic dissolution of real feeling and meaning.

In the quarto text Lear's dying howl takes a similarly empty shape: 'O, O, O, O!' (5.3.301, Q). The hellish dissolution of meaning that is specifically a condition of Catholic theatricality in the *Declaration* is here both a more universal and a more personal experience. The point is not that Shakespeare (or the reported actor) quotes Harsnett's '*O*'s, but rather that the textual coincidence helps to pinpoint alternative attitudes to affect,

---

[60] For repeated references to Sara crying '*oh*' see 262, 263, 323.

[61] For an alternative reading of '*O*' in Harsnett, see Steven Connor, *Dumbstruck: A Cultural History of Ventriloquism* (Oxford: Oxford University Press, 2000), pp. 170–5.

and by extension, fiction. Lear groans at a world where all meaning is denuded: political, social, and familial bonds are all violently breached. The play even refuses the security of generic convention, since the happy ending pledged by both the fairytale structure and the story's earlier historical (Geoffrey of Monmouth, Holinshed) and theatrical (*King Leir*) incarnations is ruthlessly snatched away. This most certainly is not 'the promised end' (5.3.256). Nothingness pervades the text, from Cordelia's initial declaration of 'Nothing' (1.1.79 Q; 1.1.86 F; and 1.1.88 F) to the final spectacle of her corpse saying nothing.[62] Entirely appropriate then that Lear—himself identified by the Fool as 'nothing' (1.4.180–2)— should cry 'O'. But what is mocked as affectation in the *Declaration* stands for affect in *King Lear*. Lear's 'O's give authentic voice to ineffable pain. The fiction that is the essence of corruption in the *Declaration* is here a medium for exploring the limits of (the) human being. Through both fiction and tragic deprivation the play discovers something other, and in this a glimmer of redemption.

Lear dies overwhelmed by pity for his daughter. In the quarto text she has met an unequivocally tragic death, the horror of which kills Lear; whereas the Folio's Lear seems to detect life in his dead daughter: 'Do you see this? Look on her, look, her lips, | Look there, look there' (5.3.284–5 F). Both Cordelia's certain death and possible revivification prove equally fatal to Lear; both tragic finality and romantic possibility are too much for the old king. Commentators have long posited the redemptive qualities of one or other ending, but an important aspect of the redemption common to both texts is Lear's complete captivation by his daughter's plight. (In this he differs from both Hamlet and Othello who fantasize a post-mortem existence as the central protagonist in their own tales; even Romeo sends his father a letter explaining his story.) The audience watch Lear's tragedy, but Lear, absorbed by his daughter's tale, experiences a pity so strong as to be fatal. This is an extreme manifestation of the 'moving of affection and passion' that Harsnett describes as the impact of tragedy. This tragedy takes fiction so seriously that generic effects prove fatal. Stressing the fictionality of the scene is not to diminish the reality of the pain it presents. Fiction offers authenticity of a different order.

The scene also marks ethical progress. Where Lear began the play solipsistically driven by a need to see others perform to his script, he ends it desperate to hear his daughter's *own* voice. Overwhelmed by his daughter's suffering, he has been brought to recognize the selfhood of the other. This 'redemption' is not a trite restoration of previous nobility (a quality

---

[62] See also E. W. Tayler, '*King Lear* and Negation', *ELR* 20 (1990), 17–39.

nullified by the action) or a cancelling out of the suffering that has gone before. Rather the intractable tragedy of this play is that the profound kinship it identifies is rooted in agonized deprivation. And the inevitable consequence of sincere and absolute investment in the other's pain is death.[63] The tragedy places ethical demands on its audience. Viewers may not die from the pity of watching Lear die in pity watching Cordelia, but the metatheatrical situation stimulates as well as simulates emotional investment in the other. In the quarto text, Edgar extols the virtue involved in the cross-identification: 'When we our betters see bearing our woes, | We scarcely think our miseries our foes' (3.6.95–6). The vision of this tragedy, even as it meditates on the self, recognizes and restores kinship with the other. The experience of dramatic fiction frames what reality cannot, pushing beyond all normal social, political, and familial codes to deeper bonds.

But in asserting the value of such fiction Shakespeare's play not only un-reforms the critique of illusion found in Harsnett's Protestant polemic, but it also provokes the disapproval of at least one Catholic commentator. The Catholic editor of the martyrology *The Life and Death of Mr. Edmund Geninges Priest* draws on *King Lear* specifically to make a point about the lack of substantial value in fiction. Here fictional affect is mere affectation: those who seek '*Affected wordes*' should '*post to King Liere*' where emotion is the mere deceit of 'feygned passions'. The real-life martyrdom of Edmond Gennings offers a truer experience: '*My authour's playne, nor is his griefe a fiction*'. The artificial catharsis of fiction is replaced by exemplary history: '*learne to suffer by his constancy*'.[64] Not only will readers experience real grief for an actual death ('suffer' in sympathy for his 'constancy'), the narrative will inspire real change ('suffer' martyrdom in imitation of his 'constancy'). Shakespeare's rejection of Harsnett's anti-Catholic account of fiction is thus not itself Catholic. This is not to say that Catholic audiences (less literal-minded than the *Edmund Geninges* editor) couldn't appreciate the tragedy and adapt it to their own experiences: *King Lear* found its way into the repertory of the seventeenth-

---

[63] At the play's conclusion Kent announces: 'I have a journey, sir, shortly to go; | My master calls, and I must not say no' (5.3.313–14). Following Lear into death, he also follows the precedent of exhibiting a fatal tragic pity.

[64] John Gennings and John Wilson [attrib.], *The Life and Death of Mr. Edmund Geninges Priest, Crowned With Martyrdome at London, the 10. day of Nouember, in the yeare M.D.XCI* (St Omer, 1614), sig. A2v. For further discussion of this allusion, see Frank W. Brownlow, 'A Jesuit Allusion to *King Lear*', *Recusant History* 28.3 (2007), 416–23; and Alison Shell, *Shakespeare and Religion* (London: Arden Shakespeare, 2010), pp. 94–103.

century recusant players, the Simpsons.[65] But Shakespeare creates an unreformed rather than a Catholic fiction.

The status of fiction becomes a still more explicit concern in the plays written towards the end of Shakespeare's career. The ethical possibilities of the paradigm are interrogated as reconciliation is entangled with the fantastic action of the denouements, and theatrical fiction becomes more fully recuperative. It is to this world that we now turn, to *The Winter's Tale*, which retrieves the lost daughter and redraws the boundary between life and death.

[65] For an account of the controversy that surrounded the performance of these players at Gowlthwaite Hall in Yorkshire, see Phebe Jensen, 'Recusancy, Festivity and Community', in *Region, Religion and Patronage: Lancastrian Shakespeare*, ed. Richard Dutton, Alison Findlay, and Richard Wilson (Manchester: Manchester University Press, 2003), pp. 101–20.

5

Knowing Fiction in *The Winter's Tale*

The Winter's Tale (1609–10) is the story of the reformation of a bad reader. In the speech that concludes the play, Leontes admits to and begs forgiveness for his critical culpability in generating an intermittently tragic plot through the poor interpretation of the relationship between his wife and his best friend:

> Both your pardons
> That e'er I put between your holy looks
> My ill suspicion. (*The Winter's Tale* 5.3.147–9)

This is a play where bodies are continually placed under scrutiny and characters narrate offstage events in order to provide a gloss on what they have witnessed. But if the play opens with a suspicious reader it concludes with an ideologically suspect sign. As has been noted by a number of critics, the staging of Hermione's 'statue' carries idolatrous potential and Perdita for one is conscious that her attentions to the effigy might be read as 'superstition' (5.3.43). Both suspicion and superstition are concerned with imperfect knowledge, and by assessing character and audience knowledge in *The Winter's Tale* we can better understand its fiction.

As its title makes clear, *The Winter's Tale* is a knowingly fictional text. However, it denies its 'understanders' (as Jonson termed groundlings) the superior knowledge of dramatic irony so crucial to other plays in the contemporary repertory and other texts making use of similar fictional material. Famously, Howard Felperin first pointed out that uncertainty undercuts the assumptions upon which the play's happy ending is founded: we cannot be absolutely sure that Hermione is as chaste as the oracle claims.[1] In fact, there are numerous uncertainties in this play and this chapter focuses on what *The Winter's Tale* does not allow us to know.

---

[1] Howard Felperin, *The Uses of the Canon: Elizabethan Literature and Contemporary Theory* (Oxford: Clarendon Press, 1990), pp. 35–55.

So far I have considered representational disjunctions in different plays: the problematic difference between representation and presentation in *1 Henry VI*; the absence of historical material to match the political onomastics of *Love's Labour's Lost*; the contradictory meanings of Catholic appearance in *Measure for Measure* and *All's Well*; and the uncanny kinship produced by demonic difference in *King Lear*. But it is the disjunctions in the drama's representational logic that are crucial to an understanding of the fiction of *The Winter's Tale*, that is, the gaps in the audience's knowledge of the action. Too often critics elide the awkwardness of the explanation (or rather lack of it) for Hermione's return from the 'grave' (3.2.234), and fail to account for the ways in which the weirdness of this plot device has verbal, structural, and ideological echoes.

So I begin with a desire to speak with the undead. I wish to register and emphasize the ontological ambivalence of Hermione's status in the last scene and the way that rationality and irrationality interact throughout the rest of the play. The conceptual ambiguity fostered in *The Winter's Tale* is related to the nature of the unreformed aesthetics of the text. This play contains no unambiguously Catholic elements (there are no friars or nuns here), but we are presented with rituals, materials, and attitudes whose orthodoxy was under dispute because of the residual Catholicism that haunted them. Characters repeatedly articulate an awareness that a Catholic reading of signs makes for bad semiotic practice (that it is 'superstition') making the audience aware of the semantic and ideological transgressions that help form the dramaturgy. The characters' reformist guilt is anachronistic in their classical world so that Catholic resonance is already ideologically condemned before it has existed. But the unreformed content is not 'dead', 'evacuated' (in New Historicist terms) of all truth value, but rather bears an emotional, literary, and indeed literal vitality: it is undead.

In *The Winter's Tale* Shakespeare probes at the possibilities of dramatic fiction in romantic space, in part through articulating the ideological awkwardness that attends some of its generic features. The revival of Hermione questions logic and a reformed ordering of the world into representation or real life, corpse or living being. I suggest that it is *through* rather than in spite of the logical and ideological aberrance of this revival that *The Winter's Tale* makes great claims for the transcendent value of fiction. In this chapter I analyse those aspects of the dramaturgy that audiences use to orient themselves in the fictional world, in order to show how *The Winter's Tale* is fantastical to a bizarre degree, and thus to get a sense of why its conclusion feels fantastic. I explore (through comparison with contemporary texts) the way the characters themselves read what is going on in their world; the fraught temporal structure of the story; the way the play confuses familiar means of reading representational codes; and its odd narrative logic. Because I wish to stress the importance of the polysemy of the play's paradoxically 'undead' signs I will necessarily double back to focus repeatedly on 5.3. Like Leontes, critics tend to over-determine the suspicious and find sectarian meaning in signs that have theological valence. This would seem to be inappropriate to a tragicomic play that uses paradox not so much to cancel out oppositional meanings as to point to something beyond a reductive binary. Ultimately, the suspiciously superstitious helps us to transcend inevitable denigrations of what is felt to be other.

'ALL'S TRUE THAT IS MISTRUSTED': HOW CHARACTERS INTERPRET THEIR PLAY

The audience is encouraged early on to doubt the state of their knowledge. At the start of the play Leontes is tortured by what he does not know. He realizes sceptically that while he has to read signs in order to make meaning, his interpretations do not yield certain knowledge. He thinks his wife's appearance both deceptively conceals and inadvertently reveals evidence of her infidelity. Trying to convince his lords of this reading of Hermione he exhorts them to 'Look on her, mark her well' (2.1.65) but then warns them that they see only 'her without-door form' (2.1.69). Because certain knowledge is always hidden Leontes assumes that it has something to hide. Emending the folk wisdom that taught that spiders mixed with food or drink rendered those substances poisonous, he claims:

> There may be in the cup
> A spider steeped, and one may drink, depart,
> And yet partake no venom, for his knowledge
> Is not infected; but if one present
> Th'abhorred ingredient to his eye, make known
> How he hath drunk, he cracks his gorge, his sides
> With violent hefts. (2.1.39–45)

Knowledge, in Leontes' understanding, is literally poisonous. Connotations take the force of unequivocal meanings so that he is incredulous at and infuriated by Camillo's alternative interpretative error whereby he refuses to admit any frisson in Hermione's interaction with Polixenes. Leontes expostulates 'Is whispering nothing?' (1.2.281), asking the same question of numerous other signs in an eight-line list before concluding:

> Why then the world and all that's in't is nothing,
> The covering sky is nothing, Bohemia nothing,
> My wife is nothing, nor nothing have these nothings
> If this be nothing. (1.2.290–3)

While this rage may underline Leontes' tyrannical insistence on the validity of his reading to the exclusion of 'everything' else, it also, not entirely
irrationally, warns the audience that to deny the existence of troubling
connotations can produce a void in meaning. This is a text that asks the
audience to acknowledge awkward semantics.

Appropriately, Leontes accuses Hermione with a pun that figures adul-
tery as a form of misreading: 'You have *mistook*, my lady, | Polixenes for
Leontes' (2.1.81–2, my emphasis). The play is populated with bad readers. Antigonus misinterprets his encounter with his dream of Hermione's
ghost as a message from Apollo that Perdita is 'indeed the issue | Of King
Polixenes' (3.3.42–3); while the Shepherd is also mistaken in his interpretative boast about the infant Perdita: 'though I am not bookish, yet I can
read waiting-gentlewoman in the scape. This has been some stair-work,
some trunk-work, some behind-door work; they were warmer that got
this than the poor thing is here' (3.3.70–4). Leontes effectively glosses
such misreadings when he declares: 'All's true that is mistrusted' (2.1.48).
The double logic of this statement resonates throughout the play. Most
obviously it indicates Leontes' wilful conflation of doubt with certainty as
he also unwittingly expounds his misreading (he mistrusts Hermione but
she is true). But the statement also applies to the thematic level of the
drama, whereby what is ideologically mistrusted, what is superstitious,
has a truth value in the play since it is implicated in the plot's progression
to a happy ending.

Antigonus knows better than to trust ghostly apparitions (he has
'heard, but not believed' reports of 'spirits o'th' dead' (3.3.15)) but he
determines 'superstitiously' to 'be squared' by his vision and follow the
ghost's instructions (3.3.39–40). And it is a good thing for the plot that
he does: the encounter with Hermione's ghost provides Perdita with a
name and situates her in a setting where she can meet Florizel and form
a marriage alliance that will reconcile Leontes and Polixenes, Sicily and
Bohemia. But the ideological faultiness of Antigonus's reading supplements his erroneous interpretation of authorial intention: that Apollo
sent him the vision as a message concerned with Hermione's infidelity.
Antigonus describes the ghost as both a classical vision (a dream sent by
Apollo) and a Catholic remnant (a ghost witnessed superstitiously). Furthermore, the ghost seems to precipitate for Antigonus a fate that Alison
Shell characterizes as a sorrow of predestination, since this tragicomedy
follows a Calvinist structure whereby some are saved and some lost,

seemingly at random.[2] Antigonus's plot—which sees him finally eaten by a bear—is structured by strands of competing paradigms: Catholicism, Calvinism, classicism, and nature. The hybridity of the play is not only generic.[3] Such a mixture might be understood to alienate the action of the play from the real world, to advertise its fictionality. The audience can keep at an ironic distance from such goings-on and know the play as 'mere' fiction. Indeed it might seem that Antigonus's credulity is confirmed as risible through his potentially farcical end: '*Exit pursued by a bear*' (3.3.57).

Yet when we compare this scene with the earlier dramatic analogue in *Mucedorus* where the arrival of a bear prompts Segasto's humorously unchivalrous abandoning of his distressed damsel, Amadine, we can see that Shakespeare has here reversed Comedie's brag prior to the bear scene in *Mucedorus*: 'From tragick stuffe' to make 'a pleasant comedie'.[4] The bear in *Mucedorus* facilitates a fantastical, Sidnean plot in which the disguised prince Mucedorus gets to prove his bravery by decapitating the bear (offstage) and saving Amadine. Shakespeare's bear may show proper fictional respect in leaving the royal Perdita unharmed, but Antigonus's grisly death (and the deaths at sea of the 'poor souls' (3.3.87) that the Clown witnesses at the same time) is an all too real affirmation of natural mortality. Antigonus's superstition thus exists in a world that is not just comic *and* tragic, but also fictional *and* real. This context makes it more difficult to dismiss as ideological fiction the role superstitious interpretation plays in the dramaturgy.

Indeed it is crucial that Leontes' redemption and recognition of Hermione's chastity is not predicated on logic or any special access to certain knowledge. Stephen Orgel points out that it is not the unambiguous message of the oracle that corrects Leontes' vision, but rather a reading of the death of Mamillius (that significantly ignores the proffered physiological explanation) as a divine punishment for the misjudgement of his wife: 'The process is no different from that by which he had convinced himself of Hermione's guilt. Being released from one's delusions and restored to one's senses has nothing to do with a return to rationality.'[5]

---

[2] Alison Shell, *Shakespeare and Religion* (London: Arden Shakespeare, 2010), pp. 203–15.

[3] Romance itself is a hybrid genre which combines classical, medieval, Renaissance, Greek, Italian, French, pagan, and Catholic influences. Velma Bourgeois Richmond discusses the medieval, Catholic inheritance of the form, though her insistence on Shakespeare's Catholic habit of mind elides the ambiguity of the drama; *Shakespeare, Catholicism, and Romance* (New York: Continuum, 2000). John Pitcher outlines the tragic and comedic ingredients in romance; 'Introduction', in William Shakespeare, *The Winter's Tale* (London: Arden Shakespeare, 2010), pp. 10–24.

[4] *Mucedorus* (London, 1598; facs. edn, Amersham: Old English Drama, 1913), sig. [A3r].

[5] William Shakespeare, *The Winter's Tale*, ed. Stephen Orgel (Oxford: Oxford University Press, 1996), p. 32.

TIMELY ISSUE: TRYING TO FIND TEMPORAL AND GENEALOGICAL ORDER

The temporal organization of *The Winter's Tale* is both ordered and disordered, and speaks to the way characters attempt to know the universe. The revived Hermione tells Perdita that 'the oracle | Gave hope thou wast in being' and that she 'preserved' herself 'to see the issue' (5.3.126–8). Repeated throughout the play, the word 'issue' is used another six times with the sense of consequence or outcome[6] and a further seven times to refer to an heir (there is also a use of 'issueless' in the same sense).[7] Issue as consequence bespeaks a logical understanding of a temporal process whereby the past explains the present (and fiction as a motivated narrative). Filial issue, especially royal filial issue, expresses time in terms of genealogical order. Hermione yokes these meanings together with a pun that organizes narrative satisfaction in terms of dynastic realization, a doubled sense of order. Leontes' jealousy expresses the fear that Hermione has adulterously disorganized patrilineal order. He obsesses about the meaning of Mamillius's appearance: 'what, hast smutched thy nose? | They say it is a copy out of mine' (1.2.120–1); 'yet they say we are | Almost as like as eggs—women say so, | That will say anything' (1.2.128–30); 'yet were it true | To say this boy were like me' (1.2.133–4). He sceptically understands the somatically legible relationship between himself and his son as mere interpretation: as what people 'say', but what cannot be known as certain. The inscrutable maternal figure that creates this dynastic memory system is also the sexual site of its potential rupture.

But as much as Leontes ostensibly needs to think of his son as his 'reproduction' there is a sense in which it is this same somatic similarity that disturbs him.[8] He explains away what Hermione notices as his 'distraction' (1.2.148) as the shock at finding himself doubled in his son:

> Looking on the lines
> Of my boy's face, methoughts I did recoil
> Twenty-three years, and saw myself unbreeched[.] (1.2.152–4)

In concealing his jealousy Leontes (perhaps consciously) articulates another deep anxiety: the unrolling or reversing of time in his nostalgic recognition of himself in his son is also a process that is frightening or

---

[6] See 1.2.185–8, 1.2.255–9, 2.2.44, 2.3.151–2, 3.1.22, and 5.2.8.

[7] See 2.1.148–50, 2.3.93, 2.3.191–2, 3.3.42–3, 4.2.26–8, 5.1.26–8, 5.1.46–7, and 5.1.173.

[8] For a related argument, see Stanley Cavell, *Disowning Knowledge: In Seven Plays of Shakespeare*, updated edn (Cambridge: Cambridge University Press, 2003), pp. 193–221.

horrifying (he 'recoil[s]'). The existence of his son implies for Leontes an equivalence of past, present, and future: Mamillius now looks like Leontes did in the past ('How like, methought, I then was to this kernel, | This squash, this gentleman' (1.2.158–9)) and will in the future look like Leontes now ('Thou want'st a rough pash, and the shoots that I have | To be full like me' (1.2.127–8)). The genealogical double fractures as it multiplies since children come to substitute for their parents. In act 5 this nearly comes to an incestuous realization when Paulina, nervous of Leontes' appreciation of Perdita's beauty, has to remind him of his old love for Hermione. As Leontes claims that 'I thought of her | Even in these looks I made' (5.1.226–7) the play at once asserts and avoids the incestuous passion that brings tragedy in the source *Pandosto*. Yet in terms of substitution the parent dramaturgically trumps the child in this play since Hermione usurps Perdita's place as the focus of the denouement. As much as the play works to resolve proper 'issue' (establishing that patriarchal order has not been disordered) it also explores 'grammatical tension'.[9] Polixenes looks back fondly to a time when he and Leontes were 'as twinned lambs' (1.2.66):

> Two lads that thought there was no more behind
> But such a day tomorrow as today,
> And to be boy eternal. (1.2.62–4)

Polixenes' fantasy of an eternal present (where the future tense sounds like a residue of the past, 'behind') collapses number and tense, as the 'Two lads' become one 'boy eternal'. Hermione is amused by the clear implication that Leontes and Polixenes 'first sinned' with women (1.2.83). Carnal knowledge of women is associated with an epistemological knowledge, an understanding that simultaneity and unity do not describe the world. One way early modern society managed the uncertainty provided by temporal progression and the separate existence of individuals was through a patriarchal order that celebrated generational continuity. But the appreciation of order entails the possibility of *dis*order; the women who make patrilineal order dynastically possible also threaten to undo it with sexual infidelity.

However, Leontes' initial distrust of the female body shifts to faith in that form as memorial. The play's final scene contains a symbol that acclaims the legitimacy of issue. The construction of 5.3 offers pointed visual and verbal parallels with the tombs that audiences prayed beside

---

[9] This is also structurally evident in the 'untried' growth of the Chorus. See Michael D. Bristol, 'In Search of the Bear: Spatio-Temporal Form and the Heterogeneity of Economies in *The Winter's Tale*', *SQ* 42 (1991), 145–67 (146).

every Sunday. Like other early modern monuments, Hermione's statue is located in a 'chapel' (5.3.86) and is apparently framed by a 'curtain' (5.3.59).[10] It provokes a wonder that causes a statuary stillness in Perdita whom Leontes describes as 'Standing like stone with thee [the statue]' (5.3.42). Perdita thus becomes part of the monumental tableau, just as early modern tombs frequently depicted living children on the tombs of dead parents; like those effigial children, she kneels. When Perdita then expresses a desire to kiss the statue's hand, Paulina exclaims: 'O, patience— | The statue is but newly fixed' (5.3.46–7). 'Patience' operates verbally as an instruction but also nominally as an epithet that links Perdita to the representations of Patience frequently found on contemporary tombs.[11] This monumental image foregrounds the kinds of order that contemporary funerary art celebrated in reaction to the upheaval of death: the presence of children emphasizes the vitality of the state, while the theme of wifely obedience underscores a sense of legitimate lineage that preserves continuity from the ancestral past to the living present.[12]

The symbolic capital of tombs was frequently utilized in early modern theatre.[13] As I mentioned in chapter 2, *The Trial of Chivalry* also features a character who pretends to be his own effigy. In this instance the device helps secure for Ferdinand (the heir of Navarre) the love of Katharina (the daughter of the King of France) that had been inappropriately directed at Pembrooke. Katharina imitates the kneeling Ferdinand saying:

> So to accompany thy shaddow here,
> Ile turne my body to a shaddow too;
> And kneeling thus, confront thy silent lookes,
> With my sad looks: this is the Instrument.
> Now Ferdinand, behold thy Katharine comes. (H2r)[14]

---

[10] Nigel Llewellyn, *Funeral Monuments in Post-Reformation England* (Cambridge: Cambridge University Press, 2000), p. 159; Eric Mercer, *English Art, 1553–1625* (Oxford: Clarendon Press, 1962), p. 251.

[11] Julia Reinhard Lupton also discusses this visual–aural image; *Afterlives of the Saints: Hagiography, Typology, and Renaissance Literature* (Stanford, CA: Stanford University Press, 1996), p. 214. For metaphors of women as monumental Patience, see *Pericles* (21.126–8) and *Twelfth Night* (2.4.110–18); see also *Measure for Measure* (5.1.231–4) for an example of effigial endurance. *The Winter's Tale* also dramatizes another icon found on funeral monuments when Time appears as a chorus. For the funerary depiction of Time, see Brian Kemp, *English Church Monuments* (London: Batsford, 1980), pp. 71, 176.

[12] For a discussion of these themes, see Llewellyn (2000), pp. 272–362.

[13] Michael Neill notes 'no fewer than three tombs among the relatively short list of stage properties in Henslowe's famous inventory'; *Issues of Death: Mortality and Identity in English Renaissance Tragedy* (Oxford: Clarendon Press, 1997), p. 47 n. 99.

[14] *The Trial of Chivalry* (London, 1605; facs. edn, [London]: Tudor Facsimile Texts, 1912); all references to *The Trial of Chivalry* in the text are to this edition.

Her enactment of the pose of the chaste, devoted wife on the family tomb is transformed into marriage as Ferdinand translates her suicidal desperation into bridal passion: within a mere seven lines Katharina is 'A constant wife' (H2r). Both marriage and martial endeavour are essential to the achievement of 'this dayes peace' ([K2r]) that concludes the play. Katharina has learnt her 'proper' place in the play's pattern (like *The Trial of Chivalry*'s other princess, Bellamira, she must love a prince) and a monumentally glorified familial ideology.

By contrast the Duchess of Malfi refuses to be circumscribed by the monumental discourse that her brothers would seek to enforce. Ferdinand, in particular, harbours a carnal fascination for his sister that insists on her sexual abstemiousness. The Duchess uses a monumental lexicon to describe the values of her brother that she wishes to escape. In a wooing scene saturated with images of death the Duchess admonishes Antonio:

> This is flesh and blood, sir,
> 'Tis not the figure cut in alabaster
> Kneels at my husband's tomb. Awake, awake, man[.] (1.1.445–7)[15]

And she later asks of her brother:

> Why should only I
> Of all the other princes of the world
> Be cased up like a holy relic? (3.2.136–8)

The Duchess of Malfi entered the King's Men's repertory about two to three years after *The Winter's Tale* and inverts many aspects of the romance. The confusion of Hermione's living body with a statue becomes in *The Duchess of Malfi* a misreading of effigies as dead bodies. While Leontes invokes 'eating' as a natural process that justifies as vital (in multiple senses) the fantastical nature of the art he encounters and participates in ('If this be magic, let it be an art | Lawful as eating' (5.3.110–11)), Webster's play is suffused with images that equate eating with cannibalism (so that the Duchess instructs her executioner 'Go tell my brothers when I am laid out, | They then may feed in quiet' (4.2.226–7)). The wax figures assist Ferdinand in his wish to have the Duchess 'plagued in art' (4.1.108) perhaps realizing some of the cruelty implicit in the deceit practised on Leontes in the sixteen years of the plot we do not see. But where Ferdinand hopes to bring the Duchess 'to despair' (4.1.113) Paulina's art brings

---

[15] John Webster, *The Duchess of Malfi*, ed. Brian Gibbons (London: A. & C. Black, 2001); all references to *The Duchess of Malfi* in the text are to this edition.

redemption: Hermione comes alive; the corpses of the Duchess's children replace their effigies.[16]

Obviously, Hermione and the Duchess transform their monumental representations in generically opposite ways. The Duchess is emplotted by monumental discourse: she is tortured by Bosola (who claims to be 'a tomb-maker' (4.2.140)) with wax effigies that she is told are the corpses of her husband and children (and also look like a 'piece' of funerary art (4.1.55)). Finally, she is killed on her 'knees' (4.2.224), so that her murder is a literalization of the discourse she had striven to escape. But as Michael Neill argues, the Duchess transforms the kneeling 'image of domestic piety into a martyr's gesture of heroic *singularity*' (my emphasis).[17] In *The Winter's Tale* the monumental image answers in the affirmative Leontes' questioning of the legitimacy of his children and emphasizes the denouement's legitimization of the love between Florizel and Perdita as mutually royal. Webster's tragedy shows such a discourse (where rank must validate romance) to be mortally ossified: the Duchess's morality is exogamous, pushing outside class and familial boundaries. The doubled horror of the '*artificial*' children (4.1.54.1) and the '*strangled*' children (4.2.247.1) renders questions of legitimacy redundant.

However, funeral monuments themselves were not unproblematically 'legitimate'. The genealogical continuity they expressed was complicated by an ideological discontinuity, and perhaps more troublingly, a sometimes inappropriate continuity with a pre-Reformation past. The 'Homilie Agaynst Perill of Idolatry' records that:

> the origine of Images, & worshyppyng of them, as it is recorded in the. 8. Chapter of the booke of wysdome, began of a blynde loue of a fonde father, framyng for his comfort an Image of his sonne beyng dead, and so at the last men fell to the worshippyng of the Image of hym, whom they dyd knowe to be dead.[18]

We might therefore logically expect early modern Protestants—so nervous about the risks of idolatry—to be especially wary of funeral monuments that featured effigies of the dead, but instead these popular tombs served as a properly Protestant alternative to the idolatrous religious images of the Catholic past.[19] As with many 'Protestant' signs, funeral

---

[16] Conversely, while Mamillius remains lost at the end of *The Winter's Tale*, *The Duchess of Malfi*'s concession to a future hope lies with the Duchess's one surviving son.

[17] Neill (1997), p. 344.

[18] *Certaine Sermons appoynted by the Quenes Maiesty* (London, 1563), sigs. Ii(iii)v–Ii(iiii)r.

[19] For the idea of funeral monuments as a substitute for devotional art, see Llewellyn (2000), pp. 340, 353.

monuments are defined by their difference from Catholic signs even as
they perform a similar function. Monuments of the early modern period
were often designed to look like monuments of the medieval past, but
their likeness was confounded by marks of corrective difference. For example, on the Vernon tombs at Tong in the West Midlands the recum-
bent effigy of Sir Edward Stanley (d.1632) duplicates the posture of the
nearby effigy of his ancestor Sir Richard Vernon (d.1451), but the later
tomb chest substitutes allegorical figures for the rows of alternating saints
and angels visible on the Catholic tomb.[20] Perdita articulates the tensions
that underpin the reformed symbolism of funeral monuments when she
requests: 'And do not say 'tis superstition, that | I kneel and then implore
her blessing' (5.3.43–4). Kneeling for parental blessing was an ideologically sound demonstration of filial respect in the post-Reformation period,
yet it also provided a visual pun with behaviour that Perdita acknowledges
as 'superstitious'. Kneeling at communion was a contentious issue;[21] but
when performed before images it was the defining marker of idolatry.
Thus William Perkins defines idolatry as, among other things, an act of
kneeling: he claims that the Roman Catholic Church 'makes the Saints in
heauen Idols. For it teacheth men to kneele downe to them' and defines
Roman Catholic 'religious worship or adoration' of saints and angels as
'the bending of the knee, or the prostrating of the bodie'.[22] The 'Homilie
Agaynst Perill of Idolatry' lists scriptural passages that warn against spiritually dangerous kneeling, and exclaims 'Do not all stories Ecclesiasticall
declare, that our holy martirs, rather then they woulde bowe and kneele,
or offer vp one crumbe of incense before an Image or Idoll, haue suffred
a thousand kindes of most horrible and dreadful death?'[23] As far as Perdita
and first-time audiences of the play are aware, at 5.3.44 Perdita kneels to
a statue, not a parent, and therefore the gesture looks more like idolatry
than filial humility.

---

[20] Maurice Howard and Nigel Llewellyn, 'Painting and Imagery', in *The Cambridge
Guide to the Arts in Britain*, vol. 3: *Renaissance and Reformation*, ed. Boris Ford (Cambridge: Cambridge University Press, 1989), pp. 223–59 (pp. 238–40).

[21] Lori Anne Ferrell, 'Kneeling and the Body Politic', in *Religion, Literature, and Politics
in Post-Reformation England, 1540–1688*, ed. Donna B. Hamilton and Richard Strier
(Cambridge: Cambridge University Press, 1996), pp. 70–92; and Emma Rhatigan, 'Knees
and Elephants: Donne Preaches on Ceremonial Conformity', *John Donne Journal* 23
(2004), 185–213.

[22] William Perkins, *A Warning against the Idolatrie of the Last Times* (Cambridge, 1601),
sigs. [C6r], D2v.

[23] *Certaine Sermons*, sigs. [Cc7r–v], Hh(i)r. This homily capitalizes on the senses of
physicality and disposition of the words 'prone' and 'bent' to illustrate humanity's suscep-
tibility to and performance of idolatry; sigs. [Bb8v], Cc(i)v, [Hh6v], Ii(iii)v, Ii(iiii)r, Ii(iiii)
v, [Ii6v].

Julia Lupton contends that when, after Hermione's animation, Perdita kneels a second time, following Paulina's instruction to 'kneel | And pray your mother's blessing' (5.3.119–20), 'The filial piety of the second bowing corrects and covers over the superstition of the first while continuing to borrow its iconographic charge.'[24] But if the repetition 'remedies' the first action then that previous action is also confirmed as in need of remedy (in spite of Perdita's protestations).[25] To be sure, 'the standard pose signifying Piety on the post-Reformation tomb was the effigial figure kneeling in prayer.'[26] But while medieval tombs commonly featured rows of kneeling bedesmen interceding for the soul of the tomb's subject, post-Reformation kneeling represents the piety of the subject while alive, and reproduces that example in the rows of kneeling children around the tombs.[27] Unlike contemporary tomb subjects and her dramatic analogue in feigned monumentalism, *The Trial of Chivalry*'s Ferdinand (who chooses kneeling as the most obvious posture even though this position is uncomfortable enough to require a cushion [Hv]), Hermione does not kneel. The staged image in *The Winter's Tale* (Perdita kneeling to an erect Hermione) bears a striking resemblance to intercessory kneeling avoided on post-Reformation funeral monuments.[28] Shakespeare ensures the audience is aware of this by having Perdita articulate consciousness of the residual Catholicism that attaches to her action.

Nigel Llewellyn explains that throughout the early modern period 'both patrons and tomb-makers had to deal with periodic bouts of nervousness about monuments.'[29] Indeed, as Margaret Aston notes, 'State portraiture— which included funeral effigies and monumental sculpture—hovered on the borderline of religious imagery',[30] leaving them vulnerable to controversy.

---

[24] Lupton, p. 214.

[25] An earlier reference of Paulina's to kneeling sounds distinctly unreformed. On announcing Hermione's 'death' to Leontes she declares: 'A thousand knees, | Ten thousand years together, naked, fasting, | Upon a barren mountain, and still winter | In storm perpetual could not move the gods | To look that way thou wert' (3.2.208–12). Excluding Leontes from the possibility of heavenly forgiveness, Paulina nevertheless describes a conventional understanding of such redemption in Catholic penitential terms (replete with kneeling) that would earn forgiveness. By the fifth act Cleomenes says that in his 'saint-like sorrow' Leontes has 'paid down | More penitence than done trespass' (5.1.2–4), and thus uses the same mercantile vocabulary that reformers used to castigate Catholic belief in the efficacy of works to insist that Leontes has earned his forgiveness.

[26] Llewellyn (2000), p. 349.

[27] On pre-Reformation monuments as foci for intercessory prayer, see Peter Marshall, *Beliefs and the Dead in Reformation England* (Oxford: Oxford University Press, 2002), p. 21.

[28] Lupton says 'Perdita becomes herself a statue transfixed before and by the statue, kneeling like a donor in an Italian painting of the Virgin'; p. 214.

[29] Llewellyn (2000), p. 7.

[30] Margaret Aston, 'Gods, Saints, and Reformers', in *Albion's Classicism: The Visual Arts in Britain, 1550–1660*, ed. Lucy Gent (New Haven, CT: Yale University Press, 1995), pp. 181–220 (p. 203).

Monuments fell victim to iconoclastic destruction in the years 1547–53, the early years of Elizabeth's reign, and then in the later 1640s.[31] As late as 1596 English soldiers in France had to be reminded not to desecrate monuments under the colour of Protestant righteousness.[32] The wave of iconoclastic violence that had attended the enthusiastic response to Elizabeth's accession to the throne saw the destruction of not just religious but also monumental images in churches. The damage was so severe that Elizabeth issued a proclamation in 1560 insisting on the preservation of secular monuments, and thus officially enshrining their orthodox status while also acknowledging that there were some who regarded them as akin to idolatrous art. *The Winter's Tale* does not first appear at one of these moments of iconoclastic activity, but the minority view never entirely disappeared and Shakespeare explicitly highlights a tension that could easily have been glossed over.

However, *The Winter's Tale* reorganizes the temporal terms on which monuments function. A statue concretizes a memory of a person from the past (perhaps in relation to a series of people from the past) for people living in the present, and looks to endure into the future. It operates in all grammatical tenses even as it is static.[33] In particular, the transi-tomb (which represented the deceased as a corpse) ambivalently acknowledged both the endurance of social memory and the decay of physical presence. *The Winter's Tale* addresses time differently. Where the transi-tomb admits to the present and future reality of the decaying corpse in a manner that marks the subject as passed and past, the statue of the 'wrinkled' Hermione is, as James A. Knapp argues, a 'tantalizing presentation of an inaccessible present';[34] the past is lively. Even prior to the ontological confusion inherent in the moment of animation Hermione's statue concretizes an aberrant memory of a projected future for a life that has ostensibly ended. *The Winter's Tale* remembers the past as living in an astonishingly (and ultimately a-stonish-ly) literal manner. The wonder in 5.3 is primarily human and personal, but ideologically marked anachronisms adumbrate this wonder. The Reformation helps to organize time, to provide ideological coordinates that mark the past as past because Catholic rather than Protestant. Such anachronisms are fairly commonplace on the early

---

[31] Howard and Llewellyn, p. 238.

[32] Llewellyn (2000), p. 271.

[33] Emmanuel Lévinas writes 'In the instant of a statue, in its eternally suspended future, the tragic, simultaneity of necessity and liberty, can come to pass'; 'Reality and Its Shadow', in *The Levinas Reader*, ed. Seán Hand (Oxford: Blackwell, 1989), pp.138–9; as quoted in James A. Knapp, 'Visual and Ethical Truth in *The Winter's Tale*', *SQ* 55 (2004), 253–78 (269). See also Peter Sherlock, *Monuments and Memory in Early Modern England* (Aldershot: Ashgate, 2008), p. 14.

[34] Knapp, 275.

modern stage, and in this instance the anachronism is doubled: the post-Reformation sensibility is out of place in the classical world, but that Protestant sensibility is itself reorganized as denouement relies on an anachronistic logic that allows a woman to come back from the dead.

MATTER 'TWICE DEFINED': WORKING OUT WHAT IS BEING REPRESENTED

Hermione's 'statue' represents not just an impossible compound of tenses but also the interaction of different artistic registers and, more troublingly, of different kinds of matter. We are informed that the statue has been fashioned by 'Giulio Romano' (5.2.95), whose name perpetuates the play's dynamic between the fantastic and the 'real', since as well as referring to a historical person the name also suggests fiction and *roman*ce. Prior to the additional confusions attendant on the animation the statue is both native and continental: it links to a native tradition of funeral monuments in England, but the retrospectively otiose reference to the artist who fashioned it also onomastically insists on the influence of Rome.[35] This Italian allusion emphasizes the tensions that problematize interpretations of the statue. In early modern England 'Rome, ecclesiastical snare as well as an artistic magnet, was an all too roomy metaphorical city'.[36]

As 'ecclesiastical snare', Rome represented an entirely different attitude to images. Where the Church of England condemned the 'worshipping and adoration…of images' as 'repugnant to the word of God', Catholic catechisms taught that 'the first commaundement of God' was broken by those 'that doe not giue due reuerence to God & his Saints, or to their Relickes & Images'.[37]

---

[35] David Kaula notes that in addition to the 'Roman' resonance of the name, 'His first name would also give him "papal" associations, linking him both with Julius Caesar, whom the reformers saw as the progenitor of the popes (see Junius' marginal note to Rev. 7:18 in the Geneva-Tomson Bible), and with one of the more notorious Renaissance popes, Julius II'; 'Autolycus' Trumpery', *SEL* 16 (1976), 287–303 (303 n. 36). Lupton says 'As emblematized by his name, Vasari's Giulio Romano is a pointedly *Roman* artist, a painter of antiquities and an iconographer and servant of the Roman Church, the Catholic patron of classical rebirth'; p. 212. Gary Taylor describes him as 'Italian artist and papal architect'; 'Divine [ ]sences', *SS* 54 (2001), 13–30.

[36] Aston, p. 182.

[37] Article 22 of the 39 Articles (1563), as anthologized in David Cressy and Lori Anne Ferrell (eds), *Religion and Society in Early Modern England* (London: Routledge, 1996), p. 65; Laurence Vaux, *A Catechisme or Christian Doctrine* (n.p., 1599; facs. edn, Menston: Scolar Press, 1969), p. 39. Another Catholic catechism toned down this claim to explain that '*the vse of pictures of Christ and his Saints*' was 'In no wise' contrary to the first commandment; *An Introduction to the Catholick Faith* (n.p., 1633; facs. edn, Menston: Scolar Press, 1973), p. 33.

Idolatry was held to be a sin by Catholic doctrine, but the risk was evaluated differently from in the Church of England. The Catholic controversialist Nicholas Sander elucidated:

> he is bond to the Signe, either who taketh it for the thinge it selfe, or els worshippeth it as a Signe, and yet knoweth not what it signifieth. But we that are made free in Christ, both know our Signes and Images to be Images and signes...and we knowe moreouer, whereof they are the Signes...and we refer to the worship of them, not finally to any Creature...but vnto one God, by Iesus Christ our Lord.[38]

Thus this Catholic image theorist, just as much as Protestant iconoclasts, believed that worshipping signs as the things they represented was sinful; however, Sander argues that Catholics understood and maintained the distinction between signifier and signified. From the Catholic perspective the benefits to be gained from images outweighed any potential harm. Sander seeks to 'proue this danger of Idolatrie to be smale, or not to be such as ought to be esteemed, and the profite of images to be so great, that it ought to be of grand estimation'.[39] Archbishop Matthew Parker produced a very different risk assessment: 'The benefit taken of [images] (if there be any) is very small. The danger ensuing of them, which is the danger of idolatry, is the greatest of all other.'[40] According to Catholic theory, both the profit of images and the avoidance of their danger as idols was achieved internally by the beholder. Sander counselled: 'no man should be offended with the names of *Adoration, worshipping, honouring, reuerencing, bowing, kneeling, kissing,* or any like...The wordes which betoken honour be in maner confounded in all toungs, but the hart whence the honour cometh, knoweth the difference of euery thing.'[41] Sander here comes close to admitting that honouring images looks the same as idolizing them; the difference lay in the individual's 'hart'. How much the heads of ordinary Catholics were muddled by (or even bothered about) such semiotic distinctions is uncertain.

Indeed, as much as Sander insists Catholics recognized an easily understood difference between signifier and signified, his examples reveal a rather more complex relationship: 'as the Sonne of God being naturallie the Image of his Father, is not an other God, but the same one God in an other Person: so the

---

[38] Nicholas Sander, *Treatise of the Images of Christ* (St Omer, 1624), sig. [P7v]. (This text was first published in 1567 and was issued again in 1625.)

[39] Sander, sig. Tr.

[40] *The Correspondence of Matthew Parker*, ed. John Bruce and Thomas Thomason Perowne (Cambridge: Cambridge University Press, 1853), p. 85. This quotation is taken from a letter to Elizabeth; that Parker felt the need to impress upon the monarch the dangers of images indicates their slippery appeal over sectarian boundaries.

[41] Sander, sig. B3v.

Artificial Image of Christ, is not an other Christ, but an other representation of one and the same Christ.'[42] The analogy of the Trinity complicates what could have been a relatively straightforward point about the sign and thing being separate entities: the artificial image of Christ is not a second Christ, but a mere sign of *the* Christ. However, where the representational sign operates through a process of substitution in which the image stands for but is not Christ, the Trinitarian model compounds image and referent. The 'Sonne of God' may be an 'Image of his Father' but he is also God himself. Sander's analogy is out of kilter. To even postulate a comparison between the nature of a holy image and the relationship of the Trinity implies that the image has a significance far in excess of the merely representational: the image of Christ inheres in Christ and is not just a separate mnemonic device for him.

The reverence Catholic doctrine afforded holy images depended on acknowledging the distinction between icon and divine referent, *and* a profound coherence. *The Instruction of the Laudable Ceremonies vsed in the Catholicke Church* (printed with Vaux's Catechism) features an instructional poem on image use.[43] The two stanzas of the poem frame a picture of the crucified Christ, so that contemplation of the image is literally central to the reading of the poem. The opening line invites the reader-viewer to do what iconoclasts most abhorred: 'Christ's picture humbly worship thou'. But the next nine lines carefully parse out a semiotically sound relationship that prevents idolatry: 'Yet Picture worship not, but him | for whome it pictured was.' Yet as much as the poem strives to educate the reader-viewer about a definite distinction between deity and design, its rhetoric also plays on an overlap. The last lines of the first stanza direct: 'Behold this forme, but worship that, | the mind beholds in this.' The repeated use of 'this' draws the reader's eyes to the picture that is positioned immediately beneath these lines. Christ is apprehended in the mind outside of the 'forme', but also '*in* this' picture. The second stanza develops a repentant meditation enabled by the idea generated by the image:

> If thou dost hope with Christ aboue,
> in heauenly blisse to raigne:
> Take vp his Crosse and learne to be,
> pertaker of his paine.

As the rhyme ('raigne'/'paine') guides the reader through the formula of Christian salvation, the reference to 'Christ aboue' links Christ in heaven to Christ pictured above on the page. The poem, like Sander's tract,

---

[42] Sander, sig. V3r.
[43] Vaux, sig. I4v.

strenuously avoids idolatry, but its iconophilic mechanisms depend on a connection between the image and the divine that runs deeper than artificial substitution. It is this that justifies and necessitates not only contemplation of images, but active 'reuerence' and 'honour'. Images do not replace God, but in moving the mind to him they move from representation towards presentation.

But while the Anglican Church rejected outright the Roman Church's pronouncements on image function, Rome's cultural aesthetics held more appeal in England (though the intellectualization of aesthetic appreciation was slower to develop here than in Italy).[44] Indeed, English ambivalence towards Rome could usually be sorted into cultural admiration and theological disapprobation; but at times these attitudes conflicted. Thus even the secular art manual *Trattato dell'Arte* (1585) was subject to denominationally inflected editing when translated from Italian into English in 1598. The translator, Richard Haydock, later given a degree of fame for preaching puritan and anti-Catholic sermons in his (feigned) sleep, undertook the translation of Paolo Lomazzo's text while still a student.[45] Unsurprisingly, Haydock omits Lomazzo's contentions that 'dal principio ed origine della Chiesa Santa cominciò l'uso dell'adorazione delle sacre immagini' (the founding principle and origin of the Holy Church began in the use of the worship of religious images) and that when iconoclasm was attempted God validated the use of images 'con infiniti e stupendi miracoli' (with countless and wonderful miracles).[46] But Haydock also excludes the important claims to which Lomazzo's preamble had been leading: that 'Commuovono le immagini al timor di Dio, che è principio della sapienza' (images move one to the fear of God, which is the beginning of wisdom).[47] The Protestant translator is apparently uncomfortable with the notion that images could generate any redemptive spiritual change.[48] His wariness does not signal absolute difference between English and Italian attitudes to art (after all funeral monuments

[44] Richard L. Williams, 'Collecting and Religion in Late Sixteenth-Century England', in *The Evolution of English Collecting*, ed. Edward Chaney (New Haven and London: Yale University Press, 2003), pp. 159–200.

[45] Sarah Bakewell, 'Haydock, Richard (1569/70–c.1642)', *Oxford Dictionary of National Biography* (Oxford: Oxford University Press, 2004); online edn, May 2010 <http://www.oxforddnb.com/view/article/12746>, accessed 24 August 2012.

[46] Paolo Lomazzo, *Trattato dell'Arte della Pittura ed Architettura*, 3 vols, i (1585, repr. Rome, 1844), pp. 6, 7 (all translations mine).

[47] Lomazzo, pp. 6–8.

[48] Richard Haydock, *A Tracte Containing the Artes of Curious Paintinge Caruinge & Buildinge* (Oxford, 1598). This would seem to be a significantly illicit argument since Haydock leaves much of the work's Catholic credentials intact, including positive references to the 'nobility' of popes. See, for example, sigs. [B6r], Cciiijr.

were thought to perform an exemplary function); rather it is evident that the understanding of the effects of viewing was ideologically fraught, and it is this murkiness of vision that Shakespeare invokes when he has Paulina use verbs like Lomazzo's '*commuovere*' to describe the effect of Hermione's 'image' upon Leontes: 'wrought' (5.3.58), 'transported' (5.3.69), 'stirred' (5.3.74).

Leontes himself declares the sight to be 'piercing to my soul' (5.3.34). But perhaps Haydock would have found it difficult to assess the ideological risks of the 'statue' scene: both Leontes and Perdita want to kiss the statue; Perdita herself looks 'like stone' (5.3.42) and then kneels to the effigy. Haydock uses '*Papistes*' (diverging somewhat from his Catholic source) as a descriptive example of visual signs of 'CREDVLITY':

> [the outward signs] they vse in the presence of the body of *Christ*, the Saints, reliques, Crucifix &c. where they fasten their eies vppon these thinges wherevnto they pray, with divers gesticulations full of humility and devotion: sometimes touching them with their fingers; sometimes kissing them; and sometimes reverently bowing vnto them. Besides, vpon the confidence they haue in the speech of such men, they stande amazed in their presence, not mooving a iot.[49]

So on the one hand Leontes and Perdita both act like typical credulous papists cringing before an image, but then their actions also less damningly signify wonder, which, Haydock records, 'makes a man attentiue, stil, and immooueable like a stone'.[50]

When mentioned, paint was frequently castigated in reformist polemic. Paulina twice tells her guests that the statue has been painted:

> *Perdita* Lady,
> Dear Queen, that ended when I but began,
> Give me that hand of yours to kiss.
> *Paulina* O, patience—
> The statue is but newly fixed; the colour's
> Not dry. (5.3.44–8)

and

> *Leontes* Let no man mock me,
> For I will kiss her.
> *Paulina* Good my lord, forbear.
> The ruddiness upon her lip is wet;
> You'll mar it if you kiss it, stain your own
> With oily painting. (5.3.79–83)

---

[49] Haydock, sigs. Ffjv–Ffijr.
[50] Haydock, sig. [Ff5r].

Robert Cawdrey describes the mass by comparing it to a 'harlot' who 'dooth paint her selfe to all lasciuiousnesse'; and the application of 'paint' to the female body was often understood as a deceptive, sexual entice-ment. Paulina's concern to save both the statue and Leontes from 'mar' and 'stain' carries moral as well as literal meaning.[51] Her pronouns blur the paint on the neuter statue ('it') with face-paint on a woman ('her lip'), and indeed face-painting and 'artistic' paint were related in the early modern period. For example, Haydock inserted into his translation of *Tratatto dell'Arte* a new section entitled 'Of the Painting of *Woemen*' that condemned the use of '*fomentations, waters, ointments, plaisters*', and 'ma-teriall colours' on the skin.[52] Condemnations of female face-painting often insisted that the practice was a physical falsification of the body's truthful testimony of its age:

> I wed, at least I ween, I wed a lasse,
> Young, fresh, and faire: but in a yeere and lesse,
> Or two at most, my louely, liuely bride,
> Is turn'd a hagge, a fury by my side,
> With hollow yellow teeth, or none perhaps,
> With stinking breath, swart cheeks, & hanging chaps,
> With wrinkled neck, and stooping, as she goes,
> With driueling mouth, and with a sniueling nose.[53]

This is the kind of somatic deceit that Bosola mocks when he tells the Old Lady 'To behold thee not painted inclines somewhat near a miracle. These in thy face, here, were deep ruts and foul sloughs the last progress' (2.1.23–5). Similarly, Perdita distrusts both art in general and paint in particular. Unimpressed with 'carnations and streaked gillyvors' (4.4.82) because she has heard it said 'There is an art which in their piedness shares | With great creating nature' (4.4.87–8), Perdita refuses to be swayed by Polixenes' de-fence of them, and sharing the play's concern with legitimate issue, says:

> I'll not put
> The dibble in earth to set one slip of them;
> No more than, were I painted, I would wish
> This youth should say 'twere well, and only therefore
> Desire to breed by me. (4.4.99–103)

---

[51] Robert Cawdrey, *A Treasurie or Store-House of Similies* (1600; facs. edn, Amsterdam: Da Capo, 1971), p. 501.

[52] Haydock, sig. Lliiijr.

[53] Joshua Sylvester's translation of Du Bartas' discussion of Jezebel, as quoted in Thomas Tuke, *A Treatise Against Paint[i]ng and Tincturing of Men and Women* (London, 1616), sig. B3r.

Perdita objects to 'piedness', to the way in which paint brings about a duality that is duplicitous. (Ironically, this is but one point of view in a play that relentlessly doubles: her sibling double, Mamillius—possibly played by the same actor—had earlier seemed rather to enjoy the effects made 'with a pen' on ladies' faces (2.1.11).) So when Shakespeare emphasizes the painted nature of Hermione's statue and has Perdita worry about the superstitious meaning attached to her kneeling, he draws on themes found in theological polemic.

It was reasoned in Thomas Tuke's *A Treatise Against Paint[i]ng and Tincturing of Men and Women* (1616) that, 'A painted face is not much vnlike an Idoll; it is not that, it would be taken for: and they, that make it, are like vnto it, and so are all they that doe delight therein, and worship it',[54] and that if a 'Painted woman' was 'a *Widdow*, shee's but a *connterfet relique*; 'twere too grosse superstition but to kisse or touch her'.[55] The idol–strumpet simile is reversible: in Tuke the painted woman is like the Catholic idol and in 'Homilie Agaynst Perill of Idolatry' the idol is like a strumpet, the axiomatic deceptiveness of either part serving tautologically to enforce that of the other. Lust, paint, women, and idols shared strong connotative links. Funeral monuments were also painted, enabling Everard Guilpin to liken painted faces with the way in which 'old swart bones, | Are grac'd with painted toombs, and plated stones'.[56] Years after Shakespeare's play, John Fletcher used the same network of words found in *The Winter's Tale* to emphasize the illicit nature of Lisander's desire to kiss his friend's wife, Caliste:

> May I not *kisse* ye now in *superstition*?
> For you appear a thing that I would *kneele* to:
> Let me erre that way. *Kisses her.* (3.3.59–61, my emphasis)[57]

Kissing, kneeling, and superstition equate to adulterous idolatry and idolatrous adultery (the verb 'to err' also had theological implications, as made manifest by Spenser's errant Redcrosse Knight who ends up in Error's Den).

However, while Leontes' amorous reaction to Hermione's statue may smack of idolatrous perversion, the statue also functions to keep Leontes on the sexual straight and narrow in marked contrast to his source

---

[54] Tuke, sig. Cv.

[55] Tuke, sig. [K3v].

[56] Everard Guilpin, *Skialetheia* (London, 1598; facs. edn, London: Oxford University Press for the Shakespeare Association, 1931), sig. [C6r].

[57] John Fletcher, *The Lover's Progress*, in *The Dramatic Works in the Beaumont and Fletcher Canon*, ed. Fredson Bowers, 10 vols, x (Cambridge: Cambridge University Press, 1966–96).

counterpart Pandosto, who strays into tragic incest with his daughter. Paulina takes Leontes to see the statue, reminding him that his wife had been 'peerless' (5.3.14), furthering her emphasis of Hermione's greater sexual 'worth' (5.1.225) than Perdita. And the paint on the statue (even before we learn that it might not be paint) functions in a manner contrary to what is polemically castigated. Where the Whore of Babylon conventionally concealed wrinkles with paint, in *The Winter's Tale* it is the work of the Romish artist that produces them: 'So much the more our carver's excellence, | Which lets go by some sixteen years, and makes her | As she lived now' (5.3.30–2). Even as they attempt to dissuade women from painting over their wrinkles, writers like Tuke assume that aging skin is ugly, something that women would inevitably seek to conceal. More logical in his cynicism, Bosola's contemplation of the painted face of an Old Woman prompts his exclamation: 'I do wonder you do not loathe yourselves' (2.1.43–4), and the conviction that 'continually we bear about us | A rotten and dead body' (2.1.57–8). For Bosola time is a process of putrefaction and wrinkles mark this corruption. But where life is a living death or living corpse for Bosola, in *The Winter's Tale* death turns out to be a living body. The past that could not be fully revived in *1 Henry VI* is here vital. Hermione's 'painted' wrinkles are a celebration of a passage of time even as that passage has been syncopated in the drama.

The policing of boundaries between life and death were crucial to a Protestant iconoclastic agenda. As Susan Zimmerman attests:

> The mantra repeated most often throughout ['Homilie Agaynst Perill of Idolatry']—'dead as stocks and stones', or as 'blocks and stocks'—initially identifies insentient materiality as 'dead', so that the chief danger of anthropomorphic images made from 'stocks and stones' is, as Tyndale argued, their pretence at vitality, or sentience...In complete opposition to the idol, the 'incomprehensible majesty' of the Protestant God is *im*material, *dis*embodied and *in*visible[.][58]

The appearance of life through dead materials and the application of dead materials to a living woman's face created a semiotic disorder intolerable to Protestant orthodoxy. Tuke describes the figure of the painted lady in riddling language that defers apprehension of a 'creature' he wants to defame, even as it exposes her flaws:

---

[58] Susan Zimmerman, *The Early Modern Corpse and Shakespeare's Theatre* (Edinburgh: Edinburgh University Press, 2005), pp. 52–6. See also Scott Dudley, 'Conferring with the Dead: Necrophilia and Nostalgia in the Seventeenth Century', *ELH* 66.2 (1999), 277–94.

> She is a creature, that had need to be *twice defined*; for she is not that she seemes. And though shee bee the *creature* of God, as she is a *woman*, yet is she her owne *creatrisse*, as a *picture*. Indeed a plaine woman is but halfe a painted woman, who is both a substantiue and an adiectiue, and yet not of the neuter gender: but a feminine as well consorting with a masculi[n]e, as *Iuie* with an Ash.[59]

The lady's semiotic integrity is fractured by the superfluous paint which introduces doubleness and paradox to her being. Just as the painted woman is 'her owne *creatrisse*, as a *picture*' we also come to be told that the Shakespearean statue is actually a signified (or 'substantiue') posing as a signifier ('adiectiue'): the character Hermione pretending to be a statue. 'Twice defined' in the denouement as statue and then as Hermione, the painted icon–woman reverses the rhetoric of iconoclastic discourse by exposing a living, chaste woman rather than a mortified strumpet. *The Winter's Tale* thus actualizes and extends the semiotic confusion polemicists associated with paint; dead and living matter are mixed and reversed. Critics have tended to read this scene as favouring one denominational paradigm.[60] However, *The Winter's Tale* celebrates the doubleness, the 'consorting' of seemingly opposed meanings that horrifies polemicists like Tuke. As the animated statue/Hermione descends, Paulina warns Leontes:

> Do not shun her
> Until you see her die again, for then
> You kill her double. (5.3.105–7)

The *OED* does not record the sense of 'double' as 'A counterpart; an image or exact copy (of a thing or person)' as being in use until the eighteenth century. However, it was, perhaps, incipient in the idea of a double as a 'duplicate, copy, transcript (*of* writing)', as seen in Florio's definition: 'Doppia, *a doubling, a foulding, a double, a copie*'.[61] The word 'double' was also used with reference to people in such definitions as: 'Gemellus, a, um, Ovid. *Double: a twinne*' and 'Gemelier: m. ere: f. *Double, or twinne-like*'.[62] Thus in Paulina's line the word 'double' has an uncannily double

---

[59] Tuke, sig. Kr.

[60] Compare, for example, Phebe Jensen, *Religion and Revelry in Shakespeare's Festive World* (Cambridge: Cambridge University Press, 2008), pp. 194–233; Lupton, esp. p. 216; and Huston Diehl, "'Does not the Stone Rebuke Me?'": The Pauline Rebuke and Paulina's Lawful Magic in *The Winter's Tale*', in *Shakespeare and the Cultures of Performance*, ed. Paul Yachnin and Patricia Badir (Aldershot: Ashgate, 2008), pp. 69–82.

[61] John Florio, *A Worlde of Wordes* (London, 1598), p. 112.

[62] Thomas Thomas, *Dictionarium Linguae Latinae et Anglicanae* (London, 1587), sig. Bbiiir; Randle Cotgrave, *A Dictionarie of the French and English Tongues* (London, 1611), sig. Ssiiiv.

meaning: Leontes might kill Hermione a second time (this in itself repeating the impossibility of 'die again', of a person dying twice); or, Leontes might kill Hermione's double.

Most, but not all, critics assume that the double status of the statue/Hermione is resolved by details that allow us to piece together a rational story of Hermione's sixteen-year hidden survival (and for some that the potentially controversial resonance of the painted statue is reformed).[63] Hermione tells Perdita:

> For thou shalt hear that I,
> Knowing by Paulina that the oracle
> Gave hope thou wast in being, have preserved
> Myself to see the issue. (5.3.125–8)

Most obviously this suggests that Hermione, after hearing about the oracle, kept herself alive presumably at 'that removed house' to which we know Paulina has been making regular visits (5.2.103–5). This is to read 'preserved' in the same sense as Hermione uses when she asks Perdita 'Where hast thou been preserved' (5.3.124): preservation as being kept alive. But 'preservation' also had the alternative sense: 'To keep (organic bodies) from decomposition, by chemical treatment, freezing, etc.'[64] In his definition of 'Alabaster' John Bullokar used the term with reference to monuments: 'A kinde of marble white and very cleare, which by reason of the naturall coldnes therof doth preserue things long from corruption; and therefore they vsed to make boxes of it to keepe sweete ointments, and toombes to

---

[63] Discussions of the importance of 'a double-reading, one in which Hermione is both dead and alive, and the statue scene is both mythic animation and theatrical performance', include Scott F. Crider, 'Weeping in the Upper World: The Orphic Frame in 5.3 of *The Winter's Tale* and the Archive of Poetry', *Studies in the Literary Imagination* 32 (1999), 153–72 (154); Leonard Barkan, '"Living Sculptures": Ovid, Michelangelo, and *The Winter's Tale*', *ELH* 48 (1981), 639–67; Catherine Belsey, *Shakespeare and the Loss of Eden: The Construction of Family Values in Early Modern Culture* (Basingstoke: Palgrave Macmillan, 2001), pp. 85–127; Stanley Cavell, *The Claim of Reason: Wittgenstein, Skepticism, Morality, and Tragedy* (New York: Oxford University Press, 1979), pp. 481–2; and Michael O'Connell, *The Idolatrous Eye: Iconoclasm and Theater in Early-Modern England* (New York: Oxford University Press, 2000), pp. 138–42. David N. Beauregard shies away from a miraculous reading of the 'resurrection' scene; *Catholic Theology in Shakespeare's Plays* (Newark, DE: University of Delaware Press, 2008), p. 121.

[64] *OED* s.v. 'preserve', 3.b. The earliest citation the *OED* provides for this sense dates from 1613, but the definition falls under the broader meaning of sense 3 ('To keep from physical or chemical change') and the related sense 3.a ('To prepare (fruit, meat, etc.) by boiling with sugar, salting, or pickling, so as to prevent its decomposition or fermentation') dates from 1579.

bury Princes and great Personages in.'[65] Haydock, relating his interest in art to his work 'as a Physician', metaphorically discusses the way in which art is '*a kind of preservatiue against Death and Mortality: by a perpetuall preserving of their shapes, whose substances Physicke could not prolong, no not for a season*'.[66] Hermione is reintroduced to the play, is revivified, from a statuary form that memorializes and preserves. And at least one other early modern text links the *preservation* of the body with the practice of idolatry. In discussing the idolatry of 'Indians' (in his translation of José de Acosta) Edward Grimeston says that 'they came to the height of Idolatry by the same meanes the Scripture maketh mention of:...they had a care to keepe the bodies of their Kings and Noblemen whole, from any ill scent or corruption above two hundred yeares', that is, 'a wonderfull care...to *preserve* the bodies which they honoured after death' (my emphasis).[67] The mode of Hermione's 'preservation' is obscured. Her wrinkles would seem to offer organic proof of her continued survival rather than a return from death or sculptural animation, but this very aspect of her physicality was what was earlier offered as proof of Romano's artistic genius with inorganic matter. It is not my contention that we should substitute a fantastical reading for a rationalized one, but rather that we should pay attention to an ambivalence that is so recurrent in the text as to seem deliberate.

When Paulina announces Hermione's 'death' she declares:

> I say she's dead—I'll swear't. If word nor oath
> Prevail not, go and see; if you can bring
> Tincture or lustre in her lip, her eye,
> Heat outwardly or breath within, I'll serve you
> As I would do the gods. (3.2.201–5)

Her defensive emphasis on the truth of her statement rather than on lament for the alleged death has the effect of creating the possibility of doubt where there was no reason to suspect fraudulence. In 5.3 Hermione does indeed have 'tincture' and 'lustre', then 'breath'; the very proclamation of her death contains within it the representational (if not literal) manner of her return from it. At the end of 3.2 Leontes is taken to see the corpses of his wife and son, providing for the audience, in Orgel's terms, 'our guarantee that the two deaths are real'.[68] For Orgel the inconsistency

---

[65] John Bullokar, *An English Expositor* (London, 1616), sigs. B4r–v.

[66] Haydock, sig. ¶iijr.

[67] José de Acosta, *The Naturall and Morall Historie of the East and West Indies*, trans. Edward Grimeston (London, 1604), pp. 344–6. (Like the 'Homilie agaynst Perill of Idolatry' Grimeston cites 'the booke of Wisedome' as recording the origin of idolatry as attention to dead bodies and images of the dead.)

[68] Orgel, p. 36.

between this 'guarantee' and the marvellous conclusion simply registers the flexibility of Shakespeare's fictional world that 'continually adjusts its reality according to the demands of its developing argument'.[69] But the characters themselves do not all adjust so easily to this new 'reality'. Polixenes asks for it to be made 'manifest where she has lived, | Or how stol'n from the dead' (5.3.114–15), imagining both a fraudulent death and a resurrection from death as possibilities. In a speech that concludes the play Leontes tells Paulina:

> 'Thou hast found mine [my spouse]—
> But how is to be questioned, for I saw her,
> As I thought, dead, and have in vain said many
> A prayer upon her grave. (5.3.138–41)

Hermione has been 'found', not 'kept', and there are questions that are articulated but not resolved. If such uncertainty may be explained away in the verisimilar terms of the characters' shock it is notable that Paulina is deliberately equivocal. Prior to Perdita's arrival she tells Leontes he must not take a wife:

> Unless another
> As like Hermione as is her picture
> Affront his eye. (5.1.73–5)

As in her later warning to Leontes not to kill Hermione('s) 'double' (5.3.107) this dialogue hints at a representational rather than an organic survival.[70] Furthermore, she is ambiguous in response to Polixenes' query about whether Hermione has survived or been resurrected:

> That she is living,
> Were it but told you, should be hooted at
> Like an old tale; but it appears she lives[.] (5.3.115–17)

Focusing on what 'appears' rather than what has happened, Paulina skirts the issue. The conclusion is not simply, as Orgel suggests, a different reality state, but rather a concatenation of different kinds of realities and fictions.

The troubled nature of the distinctions between living body, corpse, and icon inhere not just in the role of Hermione but also in that of the Lady in *The Lady's Tragedy*, which was in the King's Men's repertory at the

---

[69] Orgel, p. 36.
[70] A similar suggestion is present in the Third Gentleman's appreciation of the reunion scene: 'Who was most marble there changed colour' (5.2.88).

same time as *The Winter's Tale*.[71] Although it is not certain that the same boy played both these parts, the performance of each play haunts the other.[72] Like Shakespeare's play, *The Lady's Tragedy* is preoccupied with superstitious viewing. Govianus is instructed by the Ghost of his betrothed Lady to thwart the idolatrous and necrophiliac intentions of the Tyrant who has stolen her corpse from its tomb. Thus the plotting is equivalent to a Protestant reordering of papist confusion: in this play the doubling of the Lady as Ghost and corpse posits a division between spirit and body that *The Winter's Tale* blurs. However, the effect of the play is pointedly at odds with this structural organization.[73] The character charged with the task of averting idolatrous disaster is far from ideal. In the opening scene Govianus lacks faith in the Lady's fidelity, assuming that she desires 'advancement' (1.1.64) and will readily submit to the Tyrant's insistent courtship; when in act 3 the Lady determines to avoid being raped by the Tyrant and keep herself chaste in death for Govianus, he fails to meet her request to kill her because, somewhat comically, he faints mid sword-thrust.[74] The Tyrant's death by poisoned-paint as he kisses the Lady's corpse would seem to actualize the play's condemnation of his idolatry, but his kiss also doubles one bestowed by Govianus, who earlier tells the corpse 'I will kiss thee | After death's marble lip' (3.1.236–7). In fact the two supposed antagonists are kept in an ideologically awkward pattern of doubling, so that in the scene after the Tyrant has apostrophized and broken into the tomb, Govianus 'salute[s]' (4.4.4) and enters it; and even after the apparent iconoclastic closure of the Tyrant's death Govianus, like the Tyrant before him, decorates the Lady's corpse and is aware of the Ghost's 'mistrust' (5.2.158) of his determination to return it to the tomb.

At the very moments when the play might seem to be moving towards a reformation of papist error ideological distinctions are weakened by residually Catholic imagery. For example, if we had seen Govianus's ap-

---

[71] This play is also known as *The Second Maiden's Tragedy*, a non-authorial title attributed by Master of the Revels, George Buc, who had recently licensed *A Maid's Tragedy*. For another discussion of the connection between these two plays, see Sarah Beckwith, *Shakespeare and the Grammar of Forgiveness* (Ithaca, NY: Cornell University Press, 2011), pp. 138–40.

[72] See Marvin Carlson, 'Invisible Presences—Performance Intertextuality', *Theatre Research International* 19 (1994), 111–17 (114).

[73] For an alternative view which regards the ideological ambiguity of this play as a lack of artistic control, see Zimmerman, p. 105.

[74] Thomas Middleton, *The Lady's Tragedy*, ed. Julia Briggs, in *Thomas Middleton: The Collected Works*, ed. Gary Taylor and John Lavagnino (Oxford: Oxford University Press, 2007); all references to *The Lady's Tragedy* in the text are to the B-text (representing the performance script) of this parallel edition.

proach to the Lady's tomb as a reverent correction of the Tyrant's violent breaking-and-entry (instead of a doubling), this 'reformation' is confounded by his expression of grief via metaphoric rosary beads:

> in my grief's devotion
> At every rest mine eye lets fall a bead
> To keep the number perfect. (4.4.11–13)

Most significantly the neat Protestant division of the Lady into material corpse and '*Spirit*' is itself undone by the doubling that paradoxically attends bifurcation. The first words the Ghost utters at the tomb—'I am not here' (4.4.40)—admit to a doubling of the 'I': the 'I' who speaks here and the 'I' who is elsewhere. Indeed to associate the 'I' with the corpse is to partake in the 'overvaluation of her corpse [that] evokes the Catholic fixation with materiality so inimical to reformists'.[75] The dramatists make this point visibly and physically evident as not just the corpse but also the Lady's Ghost is decorated with a '*crucifix*' (4.4.42.5; 5.2.13.4).

In doubling some of the issues found in *The Winter's Tale, The Lady's Tragedy* also seems to literalize their negative ideological inflection: we are confronted with a corpse rather than a statue, decorated with poison rather than paint.[76] However, ideological slippage functions rather differently in the tragedy. The political consensus that the characters of *The Lady's Tragedy* celebrate at the tragedy's close (Govianus rightfully takes his throne) depends on their being blind to the lack of difference between Govianus and his double the Tyrant; the audience, however, may remain at an ironic distance. By contrast, at the end of *The Winter's Tale*, Leontes' faults are often mentioned. In this and in many other aspects, the audience might be said to share the same knowledge as most of the characters on stage, and this is crucial to the play's ethical impact.

---

[75] Zimmerman, p. 100.

[76] In its subplot *The Lady's Tragedy* actualizes the adultery between a Wife and her husband's best friend that Leontes suspects in his play. Furthermore, where reanimation marks an emotional climax in *The Winter's Tale, The Lady's Tragedy* features multiple reanimations or false deaths: Govianus shoots at Helviutus who falls to the ground, only to be told 'Up...I missed thee purposely' (2.1.103–4); as Govianus runs to stab the Lady he falls down dead (as both the Lady and the audience think) only to start up after she has killed herself (3.1.148–64); Anselmus apparently dies at 5.1.142 but is awoken 'e'en from death' (5.1.166) at the news of his Wife's infidelity, breathing long enough to condemn her corpse as a 'whore' (5.1.170).

IRONY AND THE 'LIVING CORSE': THE SIGNIFICANCE OF AUDIENCE KNOWLEDGE OR LACK OF KNOWLEDGE

However, the knowledge the audience shares with the characters (excluding Hermione and Paulina) in *The Winter's Tale* is significantly limited. If we reverse the Chorus's request and skip back 'sixteen years' (4.1.6) previous to the staging of Hermione's undead statue, we find Shakespeare's company dramatizing another 'living corpse' (5.2.29) in *Romeo and Juliet*. The audience know far more about Juliet's circumstances than they do about Hermione's. The denouement of the earlier play literalizes both Catholic and anti-Catholic rhetoric as the onomastic 'pilgrim' Romeo thinks he finds his idol Juliet (the woman he first addresses as a 'shrine' and a 'saint' able to 'grant' prayers (1.5.93–103)) dead in the Capulet tomb; the audience meanwhile are painfully aware that Juliet is alive. Like Hermione at 5.3.61–70, Juliet looks like a corpse who bears tantalizing signs of life. Both Juliet and Hermione turn out to be alive, but the audience's experience is reversed: we know that Juliet is alive, but she dies by the end of the play; we think that Hermione is dead, but she is alive by the end of the play.[77] Our omniscience is crucial to the dramatic irony that emphasizes the tragedy in *Romeo and Juliet*. The scene is frustrating because of our overwhelming sense of our knowledge and Romeo's ignorance. But in *The Winter's Tale* our false knowledge of Hermione's death is further confounded by our potential confusion when faced with the statue (ostensibly created by Giulio Romano, whose name happens to be haunted homophonically by the tragic lovers). When first confronted with the 'statue', viewers new to the play might be unclear as to how they are 'supposed' to decode the body of the actor playing Hermione: is one 'meant to think' this is an actor playing a statue, or an actor playing a character playing a statue? At the most basic representational level the distinctions between life and death (so frustratingly evident in *Romeo and Juliet*) are blurred.

In this respect *The Winter's Tale* is also significantly different to *The Trial of Chivalry*. As mentioned earlier, Paulina evades Polixenes' request for narrative clarity remarking:

> That she is living,
> Were it but told you, should be hooted at
> Like an old tale; but it appears she lives[.] (5.3.115–17)

---

[77] When women return from a reported death in *Much Ado About Nothing* and *All's Well that Ends Well* the audience is in on the surprise. In *Pericles* Thaisa's revival is more of a marvel, though the audience have believed in her death for only a short time.

Indeed other 'old tales', or rather old-fashioned tales like *The Trial of Chivalry*, would seem to maintain a humorous detachment from the fantastical mechanisms of their plots. This play advertises the symmetry of its plotting (convenient for royal succession) through parallel family situations, doubled lines, and patterned entrances and exits, and is thus somewhat self-conscious about its fictional status. The audience are privy to Ferdinand's dramatic preparations to act the effigy, involving method acting and the deployment of props:

> *Pem.* Soft, there's a cushe[n]: nay, you must be bare,
> And hold your hands vp, as the maner is.
> *Fer.* What if I held a booke, as if I prayed?
> *Pem.* 'Twere best of all; and now I think vpon't,
> Here is a booke: so, keepe your countenance,
> You must imagine now you are transform'd.
> Yonder she comes, in any case stir not. (Hv)

What is surprising and obfuscated in *The Winter's Tale* is prepared for in full detail in *The Trial of Chivalry*. The audience of the earlier play experience no confusion about representational meaning. Instead their ideological superiority to Katharina (whose iconophilia borders on the idolatrous) is augmented by their omniscience. Katharina is also denied the space to express much wonder at Ferdinand's survival: a mere eight lines after the revelation of the ruse Pembrooke insists that he and Ferdinand need to go and fight. The scene thus revolves through grief and revivification, marital and martial activity, at a near-farcical pace. But when watching *The Winter's Tale* audiences share the characters' wonder because they share their uncertainty. Meta-fictional remarks such as Paulina's bring realism to the fantastical plot as they speak the audience's incredulity.[78]

Shakespeare creates wonder from material that was more frequently used in deflationary terms. The animation of a statue has obvious associations with the Pygmalion myth, a tale which was ripe for ironic exploitation.[79] For example, when George Pettie retells the Pygmalion myth as a Petrarchan fable set in modern Italy, he offers a long list of explanations

---

[78] A. D. Nuttall, *William Shakespeare:* The Winter's Tale, Studies in English Literature 26 (London: Edward Arnold, 1966), p. 58. See also his comments on meta-fiction in '*The Winter's Tale*: Ovid Transformed', in *Shakespeare's Ovid: The Metamorphoses in the Plays and Poems*, ed. A. B. Taylor (Cambridge: Cambridge University Press, 2000), pp. 135–49 (pp. 146–7); though as will become clear I differ from Nuttall in some crucial aspects of my argument.

[79] In *The Trial of Chivalry* Katharina also makes reference to 'the Image of Pigmalion' (H2r).

for his Pigmalion's perverse agalmatophilia, including the possibility of papist idolatry:

> Or whether his Religion were to loue Images, I know not: neither is it any more to be maruailed at in him, then in an infinite number that liue at this day, which loue Images right well, and verily perswade themselues that Images haue power to pray for them, and helpe them to heauen.[80]

This ideological error undercuts the moment of animation itself. We learn that Venus:

> seeing how idolatrously he was addicted to his Image,...put life into it, & made it a perfect Woman. The like miracles wee haue had many wrought within this few yeares, when Images haue bin made to bow their heads, to hould out their hands, to weep, to speak. &c.[81]

The mocking of papist credulity is juxtaposed with the most fantastic moment of the plot, where the reader's suspension of disbelief is most critical. In making ideological and literary fiction equivalent in this way Pettie offers the reader textual enjoyment by fostering a sense that author and reader collude in 'knowing better'.

However, in *The Winter's Tale* the audience is not allowed to know fully the explanation behind Hermione's return. Directing the animation Paulina articulates a bizarre potential back-story:

> I'll fill your grave up. Stir—nay, come away,
> Bequeath to Death your numbness, for from him
> Dear life redeems you. (5.3.101–3)

These lines have been read as Paulina's indulging in theatrical hype, like a ringmaster.[82] But when Paulina is first heard, the rational explanation behind her illusionism is not available. In fact, once the logical story of Hermione's preservation has been provided the denouement does not

---

[80] George Pettie, *A Petite Palace* (London, 1613), sig. Y2r–v. (This text was first published in 1576.) The association of the Pygmalion myth, Petrarchanism, paint, and papism was not infrequently made in the early modern period. John Marston makes a comparison between his Pigmalion and Catholic practice: 'Looke how the peeuish Papists crouch, and kneele | To some dum Idoll with their offering, | As if a senceles carued stone could feele | The ardor of his bootles chattering, | So fond he was, and earnest in his sute | To his remorsles Image, dum and mute'; *The Metamorphosis of Pigmalions Image* (London, 1598), stanza 14, sig. Br. And in his satirical complaint against painted faces Guilpin remarks, 'Then how is man turnd all *Pygmalion*, | That knowing these pictures, yet we doate vpon | The painted statues, or what fooles are we | So grosly to commit idolatry?'; sig. [C6v]. Haydock also warns that painted faces turn women into 'Pigmalions creatures'; sig. Lliiijv.

[81] Pettie, sig. Y2v.

[82] Nuttall (1966), p. 54; and (2000), p. 143.

offer complete explication, but rather emphasizes the play's internal inconsistency. Leontes points out that 'I saw her, | As I thought, dead' (5.3.139–40). This fantastical awkwardness haunts the dialogue. Preparing her guests to see the statue Paulina claims that 'her dead likeness I do well believe | Excels whatever yet you looked upon' (5.3.15–16). Referring to both a perfect likeness and likeness to a corpse, the phrase 'dead likeness' highlights the marvel of the accuracy of representation, as well as the peculiarity of its resemblance to a corpse that has wrinkled rather than rotted.[83] Indeed at various points the text dwells not just on a Lazarus-style resurrection from death to life, but on images of life in a corpse. Both Leontes and Paulina conceive of the animated corpse of a wronged wife. Leontes declares:

> One worse [than Hermione],
> And better used, would make her sainted spirit
> Again possess her corpse, and on this stage,
> Where we offenders now appear, soul-vexed,
> And begin, 'Why to me?' (5.1.56–60)

And imagining supernatural fury at remarriage Paulina warns:

> Were I the ghost that walked, I'd bid you mark
> Her eye, and tell me for what dull part in't
> You chose her; then I'd shriek, that even your ears
> Should rift to hear me, and the words that followed
> Should be, 'Remember mine.' (5.1.63–7)

Earlier in the same scene Paulina remarks on the freakish nature of such images and provides an anticipatory critical commentary on the nature of the play's conclusion:

> Is't not the tenor of [Apollo's] oracle,
> That King Leontes shall not have an heir
> Till his lost child be found? Which that it shall
> Is all as monstrous to our human reason
> As my Antigonus to break his grave
> And come again to me, who, on my life,
> Did perish with the infant. (5.1.38–44)

Yet the lost child herself finds romance in the notion of an animated corpse: she wishes to strew Florizel's body with flowers 'Not like a corpse; or if, not to be buried, | But quick, and in mine arms' (4.4.131–2). Even in the Shepherd's colloquial idiom we find a bizarrely articulate corpse: 'If

---

[83] In glossing 'dead' Orgel notes 'The word also meant perfect, exact (*OED* 31); compare the modern "dead ringer".'

thou'lt see a thing to talk on when thou art dead and rotten, come hither' (3.3.77–8).

Just as the 'statue' carries with it the tensions of denominational dispute, these images of life inhering in corpses raise problems that had a sectarian dimension: what was the significance of the dead body? Both the Church of England and the Roman Catholic Church broadly agreed that at the moment of death the soul departed from the body to be judged immediately. Thus the Catholic *Dialogue of Dying Wel* explained: 'ordinarlie without delay after the Soule be separated from the bodie it receyueth his particuler iudgment'; 'the holy Catholike Churche holdeth and firmly beleeueth, that our soules beeing departed out of our bodies; do after their particular iudgeme[n]ts ordinarily passe vnto the place of euerlasting ioy or paine'.[84] In his *Synopsis* clarifying the differences between reformed religion and 'papistry', Andrew Willet agreed 'that euery soule is iudged presently after death', a point which he saw as repudiating the 'pause' Catholics allowed in purgatory.[85] However, a difference emerged not only in the purgatorial interval Catholicism claimed for souls, but also in the possibilities available for the corpse left behind. As the *Dialogue of Dying Wel* qualified, '*ordinarilie*' the soul departed the body leaving the corpse to rot until its resurrection on judgment day. But in the continuingly miraculous world of Catholicism, corpses could sometimes speak (even literally) God's will in the mortal realm. The writer of the *Dialogue* recounts how a funeral for a seemingly good Parisian was delayed as over the course of three days his corpse pronounced the trial of his soul: 'I am called to iudgement'; 'I am iudged'; 'I am condemned'.[86] This spectacular negative example inspired onlookers to establish a pious way of life that would become the order of the Carthusians. Other corpses attested to divine pleasure rather than wrath. For example, the corpse of Saint Francis, many years after his death, was reported as:

> standing vpright on his feet without any stay, his face turned towards the east, his eyes lifted vp to heauen looking very attentiuely as he was accustomed in his life time, his handes ioyned . . . in all parts his body is as entire & free from corruptio[n] as at the first day of his death: nothing being lacking vnto him but speech and motion: his woundes and the bloud of them are exceeding fresh[.][87]

---

[84] Pietro da Lucca, *A Dialgue of Dying Wel*, trans. Richard Verstegan (Antwerp, 1603), sigs. G3v, G4v.

[85] Andrew Willet, *Synopsis Papismi* (London, 1592), pp. 311–12.

[86] Lucca, sig. G4r.

[87] Luke Wadding, rev. Francis Hendricq, *The History of the Angelicall Virgin Glorious S. Clare*, trans. Magdalen Augustine (Douai, 1635; facs. edn, Scolar Press: Menston, 1973), sigs. [X4r–v].

Such stories of corpses manifesting spiritual meaning long after their souls' departure stand in direct opposition to Protestant theology concerning the body and the distinction between life and death. As we saw in chapter 1, Protestant orthodoxy regarded the mortal body as separated from God's physical presence; as a body lacking a soul, the corpse was definitively severed from spiritual function. Zimmerman identifies ' "Killing" the corpse' as 'a major desideratum of English religious reformist' who sought to close down any transformative possibilities attendant on more liminal readings of cadavers.[88]

This is not to say that Protestants recognized the finality of death where Catholics clung to a porous relationship between life and death. A seventeenth-century Catholic translation of Augustine's *Care fore the Dead* maintains that death is natural and normal, and miraculous corpses an exception: 'Nether bicause ded *Lazarus* rize again, therefore euerie one ded, rises when he will . . . one thing is the limits of humane matters, & an other the signes of diuine power, those things which ar naturally effected, are one, & those which miraculously, an other.'[89] Death and the miracles that sometimes occurred through dead bodies are to be understood as entirely different phenomena. God's special favour and personal intervention was evident when corpses resisted the natural corrosion of death: for example, the medieval Saint Clare's corpse was said not to have rotted; in the seventeenth century the head of the executed Henry Garnet (a priest alleged to have conspired in the Gunpowder Plot) was reported as retaining its 'lively colour'.[90] These events spoke not to an understanding of what happened at death, but rather as an affirmation of the sanctity of saints or denominational righteousness of martyrs. But they also register the sense of miraculous possibility in the Catholic world.

The Winter's Tale brings a corpse back to life and admits an unreformed acceptance of possibility. The rational reading of the living Hermione pretending to be a statue is founded on a (Protestant) division between life and death, organic and inorganic, signifier and signified; but it is entangled with a fantastical reading predicated on the (unreformed and classical) confusion of those epistemological distinctions. On the one hand some characters are irretrievably lost, but on the other the play fudges the axiomatic knowledge of the binary distinction between life and death. In a genre that Jonson ridicules as 'mouldy'

---

[88] Zimmerman, p. 9.

[89] *Saint Austins Care fore the Dead*, trans. Anon. (n.p., 1636), pp. 52–3.

[90] Wadding, sigs. Q2v–Q3r; Arthur F. Marotti, *Religious Ideology and Cultural Fantasy: Catholic and Anti-Catholic Discourses in Early Modern England* (Notre Dame, IN: University of Notre Dame Press, 2005), pp. 18–19.

Shakespeare makes what is past (the genre, the wrinkled skin, the dead body, superstition) startlingly lively.

PLOTTING THE UNDEAD: THE DIFFERENCE BETWEEN NARRATIVE EXPLANATION AND OBFUSCATION

A peculiarly lively female corpse also features in *Cymbeline* (1610), a play in the King's Men's repertory at around the same time as *The Winter's Tale*, and which insists on somatic legibility *and* the propensity of characters to misconstrue what they read.[91] The audience know more about the working of the narrative than they do when they watch *The Winter's Tale*. We know that Cornelius has duped the Queen by substituting for poison a potion in which he believes there is (apparently not having seen *Romeo and Juliet*):

> No danger in what show of death it makes
> More than the locking up the spirits a time,
> To be more fresh, reviving. (1.5.40–2)

Undeterred by the further confusions that the Queen gives the substance to Pisanio as a 'restorative' in the hope that it will eventually poison Innogen, the attentive viewer or reader knows that Innogen does not die when she swallows Pisanio's drug. Yet the text, in both stage direction and dialogue, registers a similar uncanniness to that found in *The Winter's Tale*. When we are first confronted with Innogen's dead-seeming body the stage direction in the Folio reads '*Enter Aruiragus, with Imogen dead, bearing her in his Armes*'.[92] Both reader and viewer experience the moment as revealing Innogen's death rather than as a feigned death. The audience's 'misreading' may be swiftly corrected but in the play's final scene Innogen herself asserts 'I was dead' (5.6.259), emphasizing the trauma of her experience. Belarius is incredulous at the sight of Innogen: 'Is not this boy

---

[91] Belarius repeatedly remarks on how Arviragus's and Guiderius's royalty is physically manifest though they themselves are unaware of their origins, for example, 'princely blood flows in [Guiderius's] cheek' (3.3.93). Ultimately it is the somatic 'mark of wonder' of a mole on Guiderius's neck that confirms the revelation of their true status (5.6.366). However, misreadings are endemic in the text. Innogen famously misinterprets Cloten's corpse as Posthumus's (4.2.310–12), and compounds her error by incorrectly detecting a plot enacted by 'damned Pisanio' (4.2.319, 320); Giacomo turns the details of Innogen's body into a story of her infidelity that Posthumus readily believes.

[92] The Folio stage direction at the head of the last scene of *The Winter's Tale* reveals parenthetically that Hermione is standing '*like*' a statue (5.3.0.2), creating a different experience for newcomers who read the play and those that view it.

revived from death?' (5.6.120) but Guiderius registers his astonishment in terms of an epistemological conundrum: Innogen is 'The same dead thing alive' (5.6.123) and he contends 'But we see him dead' (5.6.126). Leaving the past tense unspoken ('But we see him *who we had thought* dead') gives space in the utterance to the bizarre. Such declarations might seem to place the irrational at the centre of the denouement more insistently than in *The Winter's Tale*. In the later play it seems possible that Hermione has risen from death (Leontes is unlike Guiderius in his tentativeness and use of the past tense when he utters the previously discussed words, 'I saw her, | As I thought, dead' (5.3.139–40)),[93] and the living corpse is present in puns and daydreams rather than interpretations of the staged reality.

However, in *Cymbeline* the audience is in possession of the single (if lengthy) explanation that will clear Guiderius's confusion, whereas in *The Winter's Tale* the exposition of which of the alternative possible plots it was that enabled the unlooked-for denouement is postponed to after the play's end.[94] Guiderius's articulation of epistemological paradox underlines and celebrates the dramatist's skill in knotting the strands of his plot together so tightly. Wonder is a product of and is reserved for the plot. It is narrative that saves in *Cymbeline*: only by getting together and telling their stories can the characters avert the tragedy to which their misreadings take them. In *The Winter's Tale* Paulina dismisses the importance of the need for narrative explanation in the denouement ('There's time enough for that' (5.3.128)) and while Leontes may look forward to a time and place 'where we may leisurely | Each one demand and answer to his part | Performed in this wide gap of time since first | We were disseuered' (5.3.152–5), the denouement of *The Winter's Tale* features a revelation without an unequivocal explanation, even as the theatrical vocabulary ('part', 'Performed') emphasizes the fictionality of the scene. Audience wonder is reserved for something other than a plot (and the chronological and motivational logic that usually attends it).

The juxtaposition of 5.2 and 5.3 structurally enacts the alternative attitudes to knowledge that are explored in *The Winter's Tale*. In 5.2 the Second Gentleman suggests that the news of Leontes' discovery of an heir 'is so like an old tale that the verity of it is in strong suspicion' (5.2.28–9). In this sense Shakespeare strips this 'conclusion' (as it appears to first-time

---

[93] The Oxford edition keeps Guiderius's present tense found in the Folio; Riverside prosaically emends Guiderius's confusion to the more rational past tense.

[94] Ros King counts 'some thirty denouements [at the end of *Cymbeline*] except that they are not revelations to the audience, who know all but one of them already'; *Cymbeline: Constructions of Britain* (Aldershot: Ashgate, 2005), p. 1.

viewers) of the conventional trappings of such an old tale, transforming the emotional reunion of characters into a report about veracity discussed by a frustrated Autolycus and unknown gentlemen interested in the 'news' (5.2.27):

> Most true, if ever truth were pregnant by circumstance. That which you hear you'll swear you see, there is such unity in the proofs. The mantle of Queen Hermione's; her jewel about the neck of it; the letters of Antigonus found with it, which they know to be his character; the majesty of the creature in resemblance of the mother; the affection of nobleness which nature shows above her breeding; and many other evidences proclaim her with all certainty to be the King's daughter. (5.2.30–9)

The Third Gentleman enjoys the forensic process ('circumstance', 'proofs', 'evidence') that confirms the happy ending of a well-plotted tale. But his contention that 'That which you hear you'll swear you see' perhaps seems overly optimistic to an audience who may feel that all this 'certainty', this absolute knowledge that it all ends happily, is somehow lacking. He says that those (on and off stage) who missed out on witnessing the reunion 'lost a sight which was to be seen, cannot be spoken of' (5.2.42–3). This assertion does not prevent him from continuing to speak about this 'sight' for some fifteen lines (his reports account for sixty-four of the lines in this scene), but his ironic remark registers the way in which the described awe of the reunited characters is not shared by the distanced audience. In the next scene they are confronted with an entirely different kind of 'knowledge' in which they 'see' a great spectacle but narrative explanation is sparse. It is a conclusion wholly anterior to the expectations formed by their knowledge of the plot.

The return of Hermione provides a conclusion, which, as Leonard Barkan nicely puts it, 'knit[s] up strands of the plot which had not appeared to be loose';[95] the anticipated reunion is dismissed in reported speech in the scene previous. The statue scene is oddly appended both to the source material and the audience's expectations. Structural oddness is related to the play's disregard for the unities of time and place. The King's Men also staged Jonson's *The Alchemist* at the same time as *The Winter's Tale*. As Ian Donaldson has shown, through a plot that rigorously observes temporal and spatial unities Jonson's play reveals (if also revels in) the fact that fiction is illusion. The locus of the plot, Lovewit's house, is neatly equivalent to Blackfriars' playhouse where it is likely that it was first staged, so that the audience's experience (paying money for illusion at a house in Blackfriars) is coterminous with the gulls they watch on

---

[95] Barkan, 640.

stage.[96] Furthermore, the play's careful observance of temporal unity means that it embodies a 'regular, orderly, faithful view of the operation of human affairs, depicting a world amenable to explanation, in which events move more or less rationally through various stages of crisis and denouncement to a given end; a world aptly realized in the great figure of a clock.'[97]

The fiction of *The Winter's Tale* is more absolute that that of *The Alchemist*, since in breaking the unities of time and place (and supplementing this with the geographical oddity of providing Bohemia with a seacoast) Shakespeare creates a fiction that is in some ways anterior to, rather than alternative to, reality. We have seen how years earlier, in another oddly concluded play, *Love's Labour's Lost*, the outcome of the lords' one-year trial remains unknown because one year is 'too long for a play' (5.2.866). *The Winter's Tale* fast-forwards sixteen times this duration and then snatches back a character ostensibly left behind.

FICTIONAL FAITH

Yet if the structure of *The Winter's Tale* allows for a lively past, the dead past is not forgotten. Warning Leontes against remarriage Paulina imagines the ghost of his wronged wife shrieking "'Remember mine'" (5.1.67) and the oracle insists that at least one lost child must be recalled for political as well as narrative satisfaction.[98] Both Perdita and Hermione return, but the losses of Antigonus (5.1.42–4; 5.2.58–65; 5.2.73–4; 5.3.132–5), Mamillius (5.1.115–22; 5.1.130–4; 5.1.175–7), and even Antigonus's fellow travellers (5.2.66–71) are recorded in the final act. The forgiveness celebrated in this play depends on remembering, not forgetting. It has been argued that revenge tragedy speaks to the anxieties of a culture still trying to find reformed ways to remember the dead, as remembrance gets actualized as revenge.[99] *The Winter's Tale* offers a different mode of

---

[96] See Ian Donaldson, *Jonson's Magic Houses: Essays in Interpretation* (Oxford: Clarendon Press, 1997), pp. 82–3.

[97] Donaldson, p. 105.

[98] Frances Dolan sees in this hypothetical ghost the more 'alarming' aspects of a punitive Catholicism that vengefully seeks remembrance rather than passive nostalgia. This reading usefully illuminates the darker aspects of the play, though I read the return of the 'wrinkled mother' as a more positive challenge to rational structure than the 'defanged' picture Dolan detects. See 'Hermione's Ghost: Catholicism, the Feminine, and the Undead', in *The Impact of Feminism in English Renaissance Studies*, ed. Dympna Callaghan (Basingstoke: Palgrave Macmillan, 2007), pp. 213–37 (pp. 216, 229).

[99] See, for example, Neill (1997), esp. pp. 216–61.

remembrance. With a plot that is finally fantastical as well as forensic, it shows that giving space to the absolutely fictional (that is, to something that exceeds the internal logic of a plotted narrative) can bring about a forgiveness that is literally vital.

While *The Winter's Tale* is, in so many aspects of its dramaturgy, concerned with the fantastic, it is simultaneously intensely realistic. A. D. Nuttall has shown how it breaks Aristotle's rule that in art 'a probable impossibility is to be preferred to an improbable possibility',[100] that is, that the events in a work of fiction must always seem likely even if they are impossible. As noted before, the characters themselves articulate the unlikeliness of Hermione's sixteen-year 'preservation' thus allowing the play to address the question: '"I see that it is very unlikely that this would happen, but, if it did, what would it *really* be like?"'[101] In focusing on the way the play is able to speak realistically of the unlikely (or 'improbable possibility') Nuttall assumes that the play does not feature 'impossibility'.[102] However, the paradox of the animated statue (which is alive and dead, organic and inorganic) is present at the very level of plot. Audiences are confronted with an improbable possibility and an improbable *im*possibility. As we have seen, Hermione's statue provokes a fundamental confusion in the audience about how they are meant to interpret the actor's body. It is at this point that Paulina tells Leontes 'It is required | You do awake your faith' (5.3.94–5). Knapp suggests that Leontes' decision 'to affirm the unknown constitutes a risk that is the guarantor of an ethics freed from the restrictions of prescriptive thought (prescriptions, for example, of conventional epistemology or institutional religion).'[103] The audience are asked to make a similar leap of faith at the very moment that they are trying to work out which conventions govern the representational logic before them. But the play's consciousness of Knapp's parenthetical 'institutional religion' is pivotal to the ethical decision facing the audience.

Walter S. H. Lim, who shows that the play interrogates the meaning of faith, suggests that the presence of residual Catholicism finally undermines

---

[100] Aristotle, *Poetics* 1461b, as quoted in Nuttall (1966), p. 57.

[101] Nuttall (1966), p. 57.

[102] Commenting on Paulina's description of the animated statue, Nuttall says that it would be 'disastrous' to give credence to a version of the plot in which Hermione really died: 'The marvellous dramatic irony of Paulina's lines (the conjuror transcended by his trick) would be reduced to sub-dramatic vulgarity'; (1966), p. 55. However, at the moment Paulina utters those words the audience do not know how to interpret them; there is *no* irony.

[103] Knapp, 254.

the moral transcendence associated with a positive understanding of faith:

> The exercise of Leontes' faith, we recall, takes place at a narrative moment redolent of the superstition embedding Roman Catholic practice and thought. If we, like Leontes, must exercise our faith in relating to the play, and this faith cannot be extricated from superstition, then it may be that the foundation of our sure knowledge is perhaps nothing more than ignorant or fond credulity—the acceptance of events that the play suggests are even more ridiculous than a tale told in the winter.[104]

But at the end of *The Winter's Tale* the ridiculous is not ridiculed. Ironic detachment rarely forms a part of the theatrical experience of this play in the way that it might for, say, *The Trial of Chivalry* or other old tales to be 'hooted at'. Lim is right to associate Catholic credulity with a credulous response to fiction. Superstition is defined as 'Unreasoning awe or fear of something known, mysterious, or imaginary' and is thought etymologically to mean 'standing over a thing in amazement or awe': standing (or sitting) around the stage wondering at but not knowing how Hermione has returned, audiences experience 5.3 superstitiously.[105]

Making superstition integral to the play's climactic moment, in Leontes' leap of faith, is the ideological equivalent of exploding the unities of time and place. For Lim the paradox between faith as positive and superstition as negative means that their association undercuts the climax. However, these paradoxical attitudes and the paradox that underpins the denouement (the rational and irrational explanations for Hermione's 'preservation') are meaningfully related to Leontes' ability to move beyond a profoundly damaging scepticism.[106] Michael Neill explains that paradox provides a way for sceptics to access the truth.[107] He cites art historian Arnold Hauser: '[Since] nothing in this world exists absolutely, the opposite of every reality is also real and true. Everything is expressed in extremes opposed to other extremes, and it is only by the paradoxical pairing of opposites that meaningful statement is possible... truth inherently has

---

[104] Walter S. H. Lim, 'Knowledge and Belief in *The Winter's Tale*', *SEL* 41 (2001), 317–34 (331).

[105] *OED*, s.v. 'superstition'.

[106] In the final scene Leontes celebrates what he initially fears: when Perdita kneels before her mother (or her mother's statue) the image is a gendered reversal of Leontes' earlier enraged incredulity, 'Shall I live on to see this bastard kneel | And call me Father?' (2.3.154–5), and in the match between Perdita and Florizel Polixenes' issue does indeed become his heir.

[107] Michael Neill, 'The Defence of Contraries: Skeptical Paradox in *A King and No King*', *SEL* 21 (1981), 319–32 (320).

two sides.'[108] The structure of *The Winter's Tale* provides Leontes and his audience with paradox at a conceptual level: the play maintains a sense of the absolutely fictional on the one hand and the logically explainable on the other. Like faith, paradox is concerned with transcendence; it 'is a way of accessing knowledge that is inaccessible to other kinds of epistemological structure.'[109] It is through the conceptual paradox that underpins the plot that *The Winter's Tale* celebrates fictional transcendence, celebrates the way that fiction can remove us from ourselves and show us something entirely other. This is the 'ethical' movement that enables the reconciliation of the final scene.[110] Forgiveness, like the emergence of a living woman from the shape of a statue, is wonderful and in some sense irrational (in contrast to the eye-for-an-eye logic of revenge). *The Winter's Tale* thus audaciously embraces the emotional reach of unreformed representation that in other plays serves to engage the audience in intellectual problems.

Shakespeare shows that fiction can help train people to make the leaps of faith or ethical decisions necessary to enable them to forgive and to love. Here he deploys unreformed fiction to stretch the bounds of what his dramatic fiction can do. We might, as twenty-first-century critics, expect overt fictionality and the articulation of superstition to bring post-Reformation audiences to a semiotic impasse in which self-referentiality and ideological aberrance finally short-circuit the broader significance of the play. But *The Winter's Tale* is a knowing fiction not because it works by a sly irony that insists that the dramatist and audience know better, but because it celebrates fiction's ability to negotiate and extend the limits of knowledge in a meaningful way and helps audiences to transcend the inevitably negative understanding of the other (Catholic, woman, pagan, or whatever). In this way, the play finally urges: 'awake your faith'.

---

[108] Arnold Hauser, *Mannerism* (London: Routledge, 1966), p. 13; as quoted by Neill (1981), 320.

[109] Georgia Brown, *Redefining Elizabethan Literature* (Cambridge: Cambridge University Press, 2004), p. 28.

[110] Hermione's forgiveness of Leontes is humanly limited: it is predicated on Perdita's return. However, although it is performed in silence, I think it is a mistake to dismiss, as critics sometimes do, the moment of spousal forgiveness. Hermione may not say anything to Leontes but the dialogue emphasizes (as it does not for the speechless Isabella or Sylvia elsewhere in the canon) that she is physically demonstrative. The dialogue specifies: 'She embraces him' and 'She hangs about his neck' (5.3.111, 112). If the silence is awkward it is also realistic and understandable, and stresses the value of forgiveness which does not come easily.

Bibliography

PRIMARY SOURCES

Abbot, George, *The Reasons which Doctour Hill hath Brought, for the Upholding of Papistry, which is Falselie Termed the Catholike Religion, Unmasked and Shewed to be Very Weake, and Upon Examination Most Insufficient for that Purpose* (Oxford, 1604).

Abbot, John, *Iesus Praefigured* ([Antwerp], 1623).

Acosta, José de, *The Naturall and Morall Historie of the East and West Indies*, trans. Edward Grimeston (London, 1604).

Allen, William, *A True, Sincere and Modest Defence, of English Catholiques that Suffer for their Faith both at Home and Abrode* ([Rouen], 1584).

Anon., *Certaine Sermons Appoynted by the Quenes Maiesty* (London, 1563).

——*A Comparison of the English and Spanish Nation*, trans. R[obert] A[shley] (London, 1589).

—— *A Skeltonicall Salutation* (London, 1589).

—— *A Briefe Declaration of the Yeelding vp of Saint Denis to the French King the 29. of Iune, 1590* (London, 1590).

—— *The Coppie of a Letter Sent into England* (London, 1590).

——*A Discourse of All Such Fights* (London, [1590]).

—— *The Discouerer of France to the Parisians, and all other the French Nation*, trans. E[dward] A[ggas] ([London], 1590).

——*An Excellent Ditty made vpon the Great Victory, which the French King Obtayned against the Duke de Maine, and the Romish Rebels in his Kingdome* (London, 1590).

—— *The Oration and Declaration of the French King, Henrie the Fourth of that Name and by the Grace of God, King of Nauarre* (London, 1590).

——*An Answeare to the Supplication Against Him, Who Seeming to Giue the King Counsel to Become a Catholike,* trans. Edward Aggas (London, 1591).

——*A Discourse Vppon a Question of the Estate of this Time*, trans. Edward Aggas (London, 1591).

—— *The Troublesome Raigne of Iohn King of England* (London, 1591).

—— *The True Tragedie of Richard the Third* (London, 1594).

—— *The Mutable and Wauering Estate of France* (London, 1597).

—— *Le Franc Discours*, trans. William Watson ([London], 1602).

—— *The Hellish and Horribble Council* (London, 1610).

—— *The True Chronicle History of King Leir* (London: Oxford University Press for the Malone Society, 1907).

—— *The Trial of Chivalry* (London, 1605; facs. edn, [London]: Tudor Facsimile Texts, 1912).

—— *The Weakest Goeth to the Wall*, ed. W. W. Greg (London: Oxford University Press for the Malone Society, 1912).

Anon,. *Mucedorus* (London, 1598; facs. edn, Amersham: Old English Drama, 1913).

——*S. Ignatius his Triumph*, printed with *The Theater of Iaponia's Constancy*, trans. William Lee ([St Omer, 1624]; facs. edn, Menston: Scolar Press, 1972).

——*An Introduction to the Catholick Faith* (n.p., 1633; facs. edn, Menston: Scolar Press, 1973).

—— *The Rule of the Holy Virgin S. Clare* (n.p., 1621; facs. ed, Menston: Scolar Press, 1975).

Arber, Edward (ed.), *A Transcript of the Registers of the Company of Stationers of London. 1554–1640*, vol. 3 (London, 1876).

Arnauld, Antoine, *The Arrainment of the Whole Society Of Iesuits in France* (London, 1594).

——and Michel Hurault, *The Coppie of the Anti-Spaniard*, trans. Anthony Munday (London, 1590).

Ascham, Roger, *The Scholemaster* (London, 1570).

Augustine, *Saint Austins Care fore the Dead*, trans. Anon. (n.p., 1636).

—— *The City of God against the Pagans*, ed. R. W. Dyson (Cambridge: Cambridge University Press, 1998).

Bale, John, *The Complete Plays of John Bale*, ed. Peter Happé, 2 vols (Cambridge: D. S. Brewer, 1985).

Bancroft, Richard, *Tracts Ascribed to Richard Bancroft*, ed. Albert Peel (Cambridge: Cambridge University Press, 1953).

Barnes, Barnabe, *The Devil's Charter: A Critical Edition*, ed. Jim C. Pogue (New York: Garland Publishing, 1980).

Baxter, J., *A Toile for Two-Legged Foxes* (London, 1600).

Bell, Thomas, *The Suruey of Popery* (London, 1596).

Bernard, St, *A Rule of Good Life*, trans. Antonie Batt (Douai, 1633; facs. edn, Menston: Scolar Press, 1971).

Berry, Lloyd (ed.), *The Geneva Bible: A Facsimile of the 1560 Edition* (Madison, WI: University of Wisconsin Press, 1969).

Bilson, Thomas, *The True Difference betweene Christian Subiection and Vnchristian Rebellion* (Oxford, 1585).

Boys, John, *An Exposition of al the Principal Scriptures Vsed in our English Liturgie* (London, 1610).

Breton, Nicholas, *The Passion of a Discontented Minde* (London, 1601).

Bruce, Robert, *Sermons vpon the Sacrament of the Lords Supper* (Edinburgh, [1591]).

Bullokar, John, *An English Expositor* (London, 1616).

Bullough, Geoffrey (ed.), *Narrative and Dramatic Sources of Shakespeare*, 8 vols, (London: Routledge, 1957–75).

Bunny, Francis, *A Suruey of the Popes Supremacie* (London, 1595).

Byfield, Nicholas, *An Exposition Vpon the Epistle to the Colossians* (London, 1615).

Calendar of State Papers, Domestic, 1575–1625, 12 vols, ed. M. A. E. Green et al. (London: Longman, Brown, Green, Longmans & Roberts, 1856–72).

Calendar of State Papers, Venetian, 39 vols, ed. Rawdon Brown et al. (London: Longman, Green, Longman, Roberts & Green, 1864–1947).

Calvin, John *Institutes of Christian Religion*, trans. Thomas Norton (London, 1562).

Canisius, Peter, *A Summe of Christian Doctrine*, trans. Henry Garnet ([London?, *c.*1592]).

Cawdrey, Robert, *A Table Alphabeticall* (London, 1604).

——*A Treasurie or Store-House of Similies* (1600; facs. edn, Amsterdam: Da Capo, 1971).

Cecil, William, *The Execution of Justice in England* (London, 1583).

Chapman, George, *May Day*, ed. R. F. Welsh, in *The Plays of George Chapman*, gen. ed. A. Holaday (Urbana, IL: University of Illinois Press, 1970).

Clapham, Henoch, *A Tract of Prayer* (London, 1602).

Clay, W. K. (ed.), *Liturgical Services of the Reign of Queen Elizabeth* (Cambridge: Cambridge University Press, 1847).

Cockeram, Henry, *The English Dictionarie* (London, 1623).

Colette, St, *The Declarations and Ordinances made vpon the Rule of our Holy Mother, S. Clare* (n.p., 1622; facs. edn, Menston: Scolar Press, 1975).

Colynet, A., *The True History of the Ciuill Warres of France* (London, [1591]).

Constable, Henry, *A Discouerye of a Counterfecte Conference* (Paris, 1600).

Coote, Edmund, *The English Schoole-Maister* (London, 1596).

Cotgrave, Randle, *A Dictionarie of the French and English Tongues* (London, 1611).

Coton, Pierre, *The Hellish and Horribble Councell*, trans. Anon. (London, 1610).

Cressy, David, and Lori Anne Ferrell (eds), *Religion and Society in Early Modern England* (London: Routledge, 1996).

Daniel, Samuel, *The Civil Wars* (London, 1595).

Darrell, John, *A Detection of that Sinnful Shamful, Lying, and Ridiculous Discours, of Samuel Harshnet* (?English secret press, 1600).

Davenport, Robert, *A Critical Edition of Robert Davenport's The City-Night-Cap*, ed. Willis J. Monie (New York: Garland Publishing, 1979).

Daza, Antonio, *The Historie, Life and Miracles, Extasies and Revelations of the Blessed Virgin, Sister Ioane, of the Crosse*, trans. James Bell (St Omer, 1625).

Dekker, Thomas, *The Dramatic Works of Thomas Dekker*, ed. Fredson Bowers, 4 vols (Cambridge: Cambridge University Press, 1953–61).

——*The Ravens Almanacke* (London, 1609).

Dent, Arthur, *The Plaine Mans Path-way to Heauen* (London, 1607).

Drayton, Michael, *Mortimeriados* (London, 1596).

Du Bartas, Guillaume de Salluste, *A Canticle of the Victorie Obteined by the French King, Henrie the Fourth*, trans. Joshua Sylvester (London, 1590).

Earle, John, *Micro-cosmographie* (London, 1628).

Elizabeth I, *Collected Works*, ed. Leah S. Marcus, Janel Mueller, and Mary-Beth Rose (Chicago, IL: University of Chicago Press, 2000).

Estienne, Henri, *The Stage of Popish Toyes* ([London], 1581).

Fennor, William, *Pluto his Trauailes* (London, 1612).

Fletcher, John, *The Lover's Progress*, in *The Dramatic Works in the Beaumont and Fletcher Canon*, ed. Fredson Bowers, 10 vols (Cambridge: Cambridge University Press, 1966–96).

Florio, John, *A Worlde of Wordes* (London, 1598).

Fulbecke, William, *An Historicall Collection of the Continuall Factions [...] of the Romans and Italians* (London, 1601).

Garnet, Henry, *An Apology Against the Defence of Schisme* (?1593; facs. edn, Menston: Scolar Press, 1973).

Gee, John, *John Gee's Foot Out of the Snare 1624*, ed. T. H. B. M. Harmsen (Nijmegen: Cicero Press, 1992).

Gennings, John, and John Wilson [attrib.], *The Life and Death of Mr. Edmund Geninges Priest, Crowned With Martyrdome at London, the 10. day of Nouember, in the yeare M.D.XCI* (St Omer, 1614).

Gerard, John, *The Autobiography of an Elizabethan*, trans. Philip Caraman (London: Longmans, Green, 1951).

Granada, Luis de, *A Memoriall of a Christian Life*, trans. R. Hopkins (Rouen, 1586).

Greene, Robert *The Spanish Masquerado* (London, 1589).

—— *The Comicall Historie of Alphonsus, King of Aragon* (London, 1599).

—— *Friar Bacon and Friar Bungay*, ed. J. A. Lavin (London: Benn, 1969).

Guilpin, Everard, *Skialetheia* (London, 1598; facs. edn, London: Oxford University Press for the Shakespeare Association, 1931).

Harington, John, *The Most Elegant and Witty Epigrams* (London, 1618).

Harvey, Gabriel, *A New Letter of Notable Contents with A Straunge Sonet, Intituled Gorgon, or The Wonderfull Yeare* (London, 1593).

Haydock, Richard, *A Tracte Containing the Artes of Curious Painting Caruinge & Buildinge* (Oxford, 1598).

Hayward, John, *An Answer to the First Part of a Certaine Conference* (London, 1603).

Heywood, Thomas, *The Second Part of Queene Elizabeths Troubles* (London, 1606).

—— *The Rape of Lucrece* (London, 1608).

Holmes, Peter, Ginerva Crosignani, Thomas M. McCoog, and Michael Questier (eds), *Recusancy and Conformity in Early Modern England: Manuscript and Printed Sources in Translation* (Rome: Institutum Historicum Societatis Iesu, 2010).

Hughes, Paul L., and James F. Larkin (eds), *Tudor Royal Proclamations*, 3 vols (New Haven, CT: Yale University Press, 1964–9).

Jerome, Stephen, *Seauen Helpes to Heauen* (London, 1614).

Jonson, Ben, *The Devil is an Ass and Other Plays*, ed. M. J. Kidnie (Oxford: Oxford University Press, 2000).

Lloyd, Lodowick, *Certaine Englishe Verses* (London, 1586).

Loarte, Gaspare, *Instructions and Advertisements How to Meditate vpon the Misteries of the Rosarie of the most Holy Virgin Mary* (Rouen, 1613; facs. edn, Menston: Scolar Press, 1970).

Lodge, Thomas, *The Wounds of Ciuill War* (London, 1594).

Lomazzo, Paolo, *Trattato dell'Arte della Pittura ed Architettura*, 3 vols (1585, repr. Rome, 1844).

Lucca, Pietro da, *A Dialgue of Dying Wel*, trans. Richard Verstegan (Antwerp, 1603).

Marlowe, Christopher, *The Complete Plays and Poems*, ed. E. D. Pendry (London: Everyman, 1976).

Marston, John, *The Metamorphosis of Pigmalions Image* (London, 1598).

Martin, Gregory, *A Treatise of Schisme* (Duaci [i.e. London], 1578).

Massinger, Philip, *The Maid of Honour* (London, 1632).

Middleton, Thomas, *The Lady's Tragedy*, ed. Julia Briggs, in *Thomas Middleton: The Collected Works*, ed. Gary Taylor and John Lavagnino (Oxford: Oxford University Press, 2007).

Miola, Robert S. (ed.), *Early Modern Catholicism: An Anthology of Primary Sources* (Oxford: Oxford University Press, 2007).

More, Thomas, *The Co[n]futacyon of Tyndales Answer* (London, 1532).

——*A Dialogue Concerning Heresies*, in *Early Modern Catholicism: An Anthology of Primary Sources*, ed. Robert S. Miola (Oxford: Oxford University Press, 2007).

Morton, Thomas, *A Full Satisfaction Concerning a Double Romish Iniquitie* (London, 1606).

Munday, Anthony, *The Death of Robert, Earle of Huntington* (London: Oxford University Press for the Malone Society, 1965).

Nashe, Thomas, *Pierce Penilesse his Supplication to the Diuell* (London, 1592).

——*Christs Teares Over Ierusalem* (London, 1594).

Numan, Philippe, *Miracles Lately Wrought by the Intercession of the Glorious Virgin Marie*, trans. Robert Chambers (Antwerp, 1606; facs. edn, Menston: Scolar Press, 1975).

P., R., *The Iesuits Miracles* (London, 1607).

Parker, Matthew, *The Correspondence of Matthew Parker*, ed. John Bruce and Thomas Thomason Perowne (Cambridge: Cambridge University Press, 1853).

Peacham, Henry, *Minerva Britanna* (London, 1612).

Perkins, William, *The Foundation of Christian Religion Gathered into Six Principles* ([London?], 1591).

——*A Warning against the Idolatrie of the Last Times* (Cambridge, 1601).

Persons, Robert, *A Brief Discours Contayning Certayne Reasons Why Catholiques Refuse to goe to Church* (Douai, 1580).

——*A Treatise Tending to Mitigation towardes Catholicke-Subiectes in England* ([St Omer], 1607).

——[under R. Doleman], *A Conference About the Next Succession to the Crowne of Ingland* (1594; facs. edn, Menston: Scolar Press, 1972).

——*Letters and Memorials of Father Robert Persons*, ed. L. Hicks (London: J. Whitehead & Son, 1942).

Pettie, George, *A Petite Palace* (London, 1613).

R., L., *A Subtill Practise* (London, 1590).

Reynoldes, William, *A Treatise Conteyning the True Catholike and Apostolike Faith of the Holy Sacrifice and Sacrament Ordeyned by Christ at his Last Supper* (Antwerp, [1593]).

Rich, Barnabe, *The True Report of a Late Practise Enterprised by a Papist* (London, 1582).

Richeome, Louis, *The Pilgrime of Loreto*, trans. E. W. (Paris [i.e. St Omer], 1629; facs. edn, Menston: Scolar Press, 1976).

Robinson, Thomas, *The Anatomy of the English Nunnery at Lisbon in Portugall* (London, 1622).

Rogers, Thomas, *An Historical Dialogue Touching Antichrist and Poperie* (London, 1589).

Sander, Nicholas, *Treatise of the Images of Christ* (St Omer, 1624).

Shakespeare, William, *The Works of Mr. William Shakespear*, ed. Nicholas Rowe, 6 vols (London, 1709).

—— *The Plays and Poems*, ed. Edmund Malone, 10 vols (London, 1790).

—— *All's Well that Ends Well*, ed. Russell Fraser (Cambridge: Cambridge University Press, 1985).

—— *The First Part of King Henry VI*, ed. Michael Hattaway (Cambridge: Cambridge University Press, 1990).

—— *All's Well that Ends Well*, ed. Susan Snyder (Oxford: Oxford University Press, 1993).

—— *The Winter's Tale*, ed. Stephen Orgel (Oxford: Oxford University Press, 1996).

—— *The Riverside Shakespeare*, 2nd edn, ed. G. Blakemore Evans and J. J. M. Tobin (Boston, MA: Houghton Mifflin Company, 1997).

—— *Love's Labour's Lost*, ed. H. R. Woudhuysen (London: Arden Shakespeare, 1998).

—— *Measure for Measure*, ed. N. W. Bawcutt (Oxford: Oxford University Press, 1998).

—— *King Henry VI Part 1*, ed. Edward Burns (London: Arden Shakespeare, 2000).

—— *Henry VI: Part One*, ed. Michael Taylor (Oxford: Oxford University Press, 2003).

—— *The Oxford Shakespeare: The Complete Works*, 2nd edn, ed. John Jowett, William Montgomery, Gary Taylor, and Stanley Wells (Oxford: Oxford University Press, 2005).

—— *King Lear: A Parallel Text Edition*, 2nd edn, ed. René Weis (Edinburgh: Pearson Education Ltd, 2010).

—— *The Winter's Tale*, ed. John Pitcher (London: Arden Shakespeare, 2010).

Sheldon, Richard, *A Survey of the Miracles of the Church of Rome* (London, 1616).

Sidney, Philip *The Countesse of Pembrokes Arcadia*, ed. Albert Feuillerat (Cambridge: Cambridge University Press, 1912).

—— *The Defence of Poesy*, in *Sir Philip Sidney: The Major Works*, ed. Katherine Duncan-Jones (Oxford: Oxford University Press, 2008).

Smith, Richard, *The Prudentiall Ballance of Religion* (n.p., 1609; facs. edn, Menston: Scolar Press, 1975).

Southwell, Robert, *Collected Poems*, ed. Peter Davidson and Anne Sweeney (Manchester: Fyfield Books, 2007).

Spenser, Edmund, *The Faerie Queene*, ed. A. C. Hamilton, Hiroshi Yamashita, and Toshiyuki Suzuki (London: Longman, 2001).

Stanney, William, *A Treatise of Penance* (Douai, 1617; facs. edn, Menston: Scolar Press, 1972).

Stubbes, Philip *The Pope's Monarchy* (London, 1585).

—— *The Anatomie of Abuses*, ed. M. J. Kidnie (Tempe, AZ: Arizona Center for Medieval and Renaissance Studies in conjunction with Renaissance English Text Society, 2002).

Texeda, Fernando, *Miracles Vnmasked* (London, 1625).

Thomas, Thomas, *Dictionarium Linguae Latinae et Anglicanae* (London, 1587).

Tuke, Thomas, *A Treatise Against Paint[i]ng and Tincturing of Men and Women* (London, 1616).

Tyndale, William, *An Answere vnto Sir Thomas Mores Dialogue*, ed. Anne M. O'Donnell and Jared Wicks (Washington, DC: The Catholic University of America Press, 2000).

Vaughan, William, *The Arraignment of Slander Periury Blasphemy, and Other Malicious Sinnes, Shewing Sundry Examples of Gods Iudgements Against the Ofenders* (London, 1630).

Vaux, Laurence, *A Catechisme or Christian Doctrine* (n.p., 1599; facs. edn, Menston: Scolar Press, 1969).

Vignolle, *Abridgement of the Life of Henry the Great, the Fourth of that Name*, trans. Anon. (London, 1637).

W., R., *Martine Mar-Sixtus* (London, 1591).

Wadding, Luke, rev. Francis Hendricq, *The History of the Angelicall Virgin Glorious S. Clare*, trans. Magdalen Augustine (Douai, 1635; facs. edn, Menston: Scolar Press, 1973).

Ware, James (ed.), *The Hunting of the Romish Fox* (Dublin, 1683).

Webster, John, *The Duchess of Malfi*, ed. Brian Gibbons (London: A. & C. Black, 2001).

Willet, Andrew, *A Fruitfull and Godly Sermon, Preached at Paules Crosse Before the Honourable Audience and Assemblie there, this Present Yeare 1592. Vpon the 5. Chapter of the Prophesie of Zacharie, 1, 2, 3, 4 Verses* (London, 1592).

—— *Synopsis Papismi* (London, 1592).

Wright, Leonard, *The Hunting of Antichrist* (London, 1589).

Yepes, Diego de, *Historia Particular de la Persecucion de Inglaterra, y de los martirios mas insignes que en ella ha auido, desde el año del Señor. 1570* (Madrid, 1599).

SECONDARY SOURCES

Addison, William, *Epping Forest: Its Literary and Historical Associations* (London: J. M. Dent & Sons, 1945).

Allard, James, and Matthew R. Martin (eds), *Staging Pain, 1580–1800: Violence and Trauma in British Theater* (Farnham: Ashgate, 2009).

Allison, Antony, and D. M. Rogers, *The Contemporary Printed Literature of the English Counter-Reformation Between 1558 and 1640*, 2 vols (Aldershot: Scolar Press, 1989–94).

Almond, Philip C., *Demonic Possession and Exorcism in Early Modern England* (Cambridge: Cambridge University Press, 2004).

Archer, John Michael, and Richard Burt (eds), *Enclosure Acts* (Ithaca, NY: Cornell University Press, 1994).

Asquith, Clare, 'Oxford University and *Love's Labour's Lost*', in Dennis Taylor and David Beauregard (eds), *Shakespeare and the Culture of Christianity* (New York: Fordham University Press, 2003), 80–102.

——*Shadowplay: The Hidden Beliefs and Coded Politics of William Shakespeare* (New York: PublicAffairs, 2005).

Aston, Margaret, 'Gods, Saints, and Reformers', in *Albion's Classicism: The Visual Arts in Britain, 1550–1660*, ed. Lucy Gent (New Haven, CT: Yale University Press, 1995), pp. 181–220.

Aveling, J. C. H., *The Handle and the Axe: The Catholic Recusants in England from Reformation to Emancipation* (London: Blond and Briggs, 1976).

Baines, Barbara J., 'Assaying the Power of Chastity in *Measure for Measure*', *SEL* 30 (1990), 283–301.

Bakewell, Sarah, 'Haydock, Richard (1569/70–c.1642)', *Oxford Dictionary of National Biography* (Oxford: Oxford University Press, 2004); online edn, May 2010 <http://www.oxforddnb.com/view/article/12746>, accessed 24 August 2012.

Barasch, Frances K., 'Folk Magic in *Henry VI, Parts 1* and *2*: Two Scenes of Embedding', in *Henry VI: Critical Essays*, ed. Thomas A. Pendelton (London: Routledge, 2001), pp. 113–25.

Barkan, Leonard, '"Living Sculptures": Ovid, Michelangelo, and *The Winter's Tale*', *ELH* 48 (1981), 639–67.

Barnard, John, and D. F. McKenzie (eds), *The Cambridge History of the Book in Britain*, vol. IV *1557–1695* (Cambridge: Cambridge University Press, 2002).

Barton, Anne, *The Names of Comedy* (Oxford: Clarendon Press, 1990).

——'The One and Only', *New York Review of Books*, vol. 53, no. 8, 11 May 2006.

Baskervill, C. R., 'Sidney's "Arcadia" and "The Tryall of Chevalry"', *Modern Philology* 10 (1912), 197–201.

Beal, Peter, and Jeremy Griffiths (eds), *English Manuscript Studies 1100–1700* (Oxford: Blackwell, 1989).

Bearman, Robert '"Was William Shakespeare William Shakeshafte?" Revisited', *SQ* 53.1 (2002), 83–94.

——'John Shakespeare's "Spiritual Testament": A Reappraisal', *SS* 56 (2003), 184–202.

——'John Shakespeare: A Papist or Just Penniless?', *SQ* 56.4 (2005), 411–33.

Beauregard, David N., *Catholic Theology in Shakespeare's Plays* (Newark, DE: University of Delaware Press, 2008).

Beckwith, Sarah, 'Medieval Penance, Reformation Repentance and *Measure for Measure*', in *Reading the Medieval in Early Modern England*, ed. Gordon McMullan and David Matthews (Cambridge: Cambridge University Press, 2007), pp. 193–204.

—— *Shakespeare and the Grammar of Forgiveness* (Ithaca, NY: Cornell University Press, 2011).

Belsey, Catherine, *Shakespeare and the Loss of Eden: The Construction of Family Values in Early Modern Culture* (Basingstoke: Palgrave Macmillan, 2001).

—— *Why Shakespeare?* (Basingstoke: Palgrave Macmillan, 2007).

Berger, Thomas L., William C. Bradford, and Sidney L. Sondergard (eds), *An Index of Characters in Early Modern English Drama: Printed Plays, 1500–1660* (Cambridge: Cambridge University Press, 1998).

Bevington, David, 'The Domineering Female in *1 Henry VI*', *SSt* 2 (1966), 51–8.

—— *Shakespeare and Biography* (Oxford: Oxford University Press, 2010).

Billings, Wayne L., 'Ironic Lapses: Plotting in *Henry VI*', *Studies in the Literary Imagination* 5 (1972), 27–49.

Bindoff, S. T., J. Hurstfield, and C. H. Williams (eds), *Elizabethan Government and Society* (London: Athlone Press, 1961).

Bireley, Robert, *The Refashioning of Catholicism, 1450–1700* (Washington, DC: The Catholic University of America Press, 1999).

Birrell, T. A., 'English Counter-Reformation Book Culture', *Recusant History* 22 (1994), 113–22.

Blanpied, John W., '"Art and Baleful Sorcery": The Counterconsciousness of *Henry VI, Part 1*', *SEL* 15 (1975), 213–27.

Boose, Lynda E., 'The 1599 Bishops' Ban, Elizabethan Pornography, and the Sexualisation of the Jacobean Stage', in *Enclosure Acts*, ed. Richard Burt and John Michael Archer (Ithaca: Cornell University Press, 1994), pp. 185–200.

Bossy, John, 'The Character of Elizabethan Catholicism', *Past and Present* 21 (1962), 39–59.

—— *The English Catholic Community, 1570–1850* (London: Darton, Longman and Todd, 1975).

—— 'The Social History of Confession in the Age of Reformation', *Transactions of the Royal Historical Society* 25 (1975), 21–38.

Bristol, Michael D., 'In Search of the Bear: Spatio-Temporal Form and the Heterogeneity of Economies in *The Winter's Tale*', *SQ* 42 (1991), 145–67.

Brown, Carolyn E., 'Erotic Flagellation and Shakespeare's *Measure for Measure*', *ELR* 16 (1986), 139–65.

Brown, Georgia, *Redefining Elizabethan Literature* (Cambridge: Cambridge University Press, 2004).

Brown, Nancy Pollard, 'Paperchase: The Dissemination of Catholic Texts in Elizabethan England', in *English Manuscript Studies 1100–1700*, ed., Peter Beal and Jeremy Griffiths (Oxford: Blackwell, 1989), pp. 120–43.

—— 'Robert Southwell: The Mission of the Written Word', in *The Reckoned Expense: Edmund Campion and the Early English Jesuits: Essays in Celebration of the First Centenary of Campion Hall, Oxford (1896–1996)*, 2nd edn, ed. Thomas McCoog (Rome: Institutum Historicum Societatis Iesu, 2007), pp. 251–75.

Brownlow, Frank W., *Shakespeare, Harsnett and the Devils of Denham* (Newark, DE: University of Delaware Press, 1993).

——'A Jesuit Allusion to *King Lear*', *Recusant History* 28.3 (2007), 416–23.

Brydon, Anne, and Sandra Niessen (eds), *Consuming Fashion: Adorning the Transnational Body* (Oxford: Berg, 1998).

Buccola, Regina, and Lisa Hopkins (eds), *Marian Moments in Early Modern British Drama* (Aldershot: Ashgate, 2007).

Burnett, Mark Thornton, 'Giving and Receiving: *Love's Labour's Lost* and the Politics of Exchange', *ELR* 23 (1993), 287–313.

Bynum, Caroline Walker, *Holy Feast and Holy Fast: The Religious Significance of Food to Medieval Women* (Berkeley, CA: University of California Press, 1987).

Callaghan, Dympna 'Shakespeare and Religion', *Textual Practice* 15.1 (2001), 1–4.

——(ed.), *The Impact of Feminism in English Renaissance Studies* (Basingstoke: Palgrave Macmillan, 2007).

Carlson, Marvin, 'Invisible Presences—Performance Intertextuality', *Theatre Research International* 19 (1994), 111–17.

Cavell, Stanley, *The Claim of Reason: Wittgenstein, Skepticism, Morality, and Tragedy* (New York: Oxford University Press, 1979).

——*Disowning Knowledge: In Seven Plays of Shakespeare*, updated edn (Cambridge: Cambridge University Press, 2003).

Challoner, Richard, rev. John Hungerford Pollen, *Memoirs of Missionary Priests as well Secular as Regular and of other Catholics of Both Sexes, that have Suffered Death in England on Religious Accounts from the Year of Our Lord, 1577 to 1684* (London: Burns, Oates and Washbourne, 1924; repr. Farnborough: Gregg, 1969).

Chambers, E. K., *The Elizabethan Stage*, 4 vols, i (Oxford: Clarendon Press, 1923).

Chambers, Mary Catherine E., *The Life of Mary Ward (1585–1645)*, 2 vols (London: Burns and Oates, 1882–5).

Chaney, Edward (ed.), *The Evolution of English Collecting: Receptions of Italian Art in the Tudor and Stuart Periods* (New Haven, CT: Yale University Press, 2003).

Clancy, Thomas H., *Papist Pamphleteers: The Allen–Persons Party and the Political Thought of the Counter-Reformation in England, 1572–1615* (Chicago, IL: Loyola University Press, 1964).

——'Papist–Protestant–Puritan: English Religious Taxonomy 1565–1665', *Recusant History* 13 (1975–6), 227–53.

Clayton, Frederick W., and Margaret Tudeau-Clayton, 'Mercury, Boy Yet and the "Harsh" Words of *Love's Labour's Lost*', *SS* 57 (2004), 209–24.

Clegg, Cyndia Susan, *Press Censorship in Elizabethan England* (Cambridge: Cambridge University Press, 1997).

Coakley, Sarah (ed.), *Religion and the Body* (Cambridge: Cambridge University Press, 1997).

Coffey, John, *Persecution and Toleration in Protestant England, 1558–1689* (Harlow: Longman, 2000).

Coleman, Simon, and John Elsner, *Pilgrimage: Past and Present in the World Religions* (London: British Museum Press, 1995).

Collinson, Patrick, Arnold Hunt, and Alexander Walsham, 'Religious Publishing in England 1557–1640', in *The Cambridge History of the Book in Britain*, vol. IV: *1557–1695*, ed. John Barnard and D. F. McKenzie (Cambridge: Cambridge University Press, 2002), pp. 29–66.

Connelly, Roland, *The Women of the Catholic Resistance in England: 1540–1680* (Edinburgh: Pentland Press, 1997).

Connor, Steven, *Dumbstruck: A Cultural History of Ventriloquism* (Oxford: Oxford University Press, 2000).

Corthell, Ronald J., '"The Secrecy of Man": Recusant Discourse and the Elizabethan Subject', *ELR* 19 (1989), 272–90.

Corthell, Ronald, Frances E. Dolan, Christopher Highley, and Arthur F. Marotti (eds), *Catholic Culture in Early Modern England* (Notre Dame, IN: University of Notre Dame Press, 2007).

Corum, Richard, '"The Catastrophe Is a Nuptial": *Love's Labor's Lost*, Tactics, Everyday Life', in *Renaissance Culture and the Everyday*, ed. Patricia Fumerton and Simon Hunt (Philadelphia, PA: University of Pennsylvania Press, 1999), pp. 271–98.

Cotterill, Rowland, 'The Structural Role of France in Shakespeare's First and Second Historical Tetralogies', *Renaissance Studies* 9 (1995), 460–76.

Cox, John D., 'Devils and Power in Marlowe and Shakespeare', *Yearbook of English Studies* 23 (1993), 46–64.

—— *The Devil and the Sacred in English Drama, 1350–1642* (Cambridge: Cambridge University Press, 2000).

Craik, Katharine A., *Reading Sensations in Early Modern England* (Basingstoke: Palgrave Macmillan, 2007).

Crawford, Katherine B., 'The Politics of Promiscuity: Masculinity and Heroic Representation at the Court of Henry IV', *French Historical Studies* 26 (2003), 225–52.

Crider, Scott F., 'Weeping in the Upper World: The Orphic Frame in 5.3 of *The Winter's Tale* and the Archive of Poetry', *Studies in the Literary Imagination* 32 (1999), 153–72.

Cummings, Brian, *The Literary Culture of the Reformation: Grammar and Grace* (Oxford: Oxford University Press, 2002).

Cust, Richard, and Ann Hughes (eds), *Conflict in Early Stuart England: Studies in Religion and Politics, 1603–1642* (London: Longman, 1989).

Daniell, David, Review of Velma B. Richmond, *Shakespeare, Catholicism, and Romance*, *Modern Language Review* 97.2 (2002), 387–8.

Davies, Michael, 'On this Side Bardolatry: The Canonisation of the Catholic Shakespeare', *Cahiers Elisabéthains* 58 (2000), 31–47.

Davis, Alex, *Chivalry and Romance in the English Renaissance* (Cambridge: D. S. Brewer, 2003).

Davis, Lloyd, *Guise and Disguise: Rhetoric and Characterization in the English Renaissance* (Toronto: University of Toronto Press, 1993).

Dawson, Anthony B., *Indirections: Shakespeare and the Art of Illusion* (Toronto: University of Toronto Press, 1978).

Dean, Paul, 'Shakespeare's *Henry VI* Trilogy and Elizabethan "Romance" Histories: The Origins of a Genre', *SQ* 33 (1982), 34–48.

Dessen, Alan C., and Leslie Thomson, *A Dictionary of Stage Directions in English Drama, 1580–1642* (Cambridge: Cambridge University Press, 1999).

Dickson, Lisa, 'No Rainbow Without the Sun: Visibility and Embodiment in *1 Henry VI*', *Modern Language Studies* 30 (2000), 137–56.

Diehl, Huston *Staging Reform, Reforming the Stage: Protestantism and Popular Theater in Early Modern England* (Ithaca, NY: Cornell University Press, 1997).

—— '"Infinite Space": Representation and Reformation in *Measure for Measure*', *SQ* 49 (1998), 393–410.

—— 'Religion and Shakespearean Tragedy', in *The Cambridge Companion to Shakespearean Tragedy*, ed. Claire McEachern (Cambridge: Cambridge University Press, 2002), pp. 86–102.

—— '"Does not the Stone Rebuke Me?": The Pauline Rebuke and Paulina's Lawful Magic in *The Winter's Tale*', in *Shakespeare and the Cultures of Performance*, ed. Paul Yachnin and Patricia Badir (Aldershot: Ashgate, 2008), pp. 69–82.

Dijkhuizen, Jan Frans van, *Devil Theatre: Demonic Possession and Exorcism in English Drama, 1558–1642* (Cambridge: D. S. Brewer, 2007).

Dolan, Frances E., *Whores of Babylon: Catholicism, Gender, and Seventeenth-Century Print Culture* (Ithaca, NY: Cornell University Press, 1999).

—— 'Hermione's Ghost: Catholicism, the Feminine, and the Undead', in *The Impact of Feminism in English Renaissance Studies*, ed. Dympna Callaghan (Basingstoke: Palgrave Macmillan, 2007), pp. 213–37.

Donaldson, Ian, *Jonson's Magic Houses: Essays in Interpretation* (Oxford: Clarendon Press, 1997).

Dudley, Scott, 'Conferring with the Dead: Necrophilia and Nostalgia in the Seventeenth Century', *ELH* 66.2 (1999), 277–94.

Duffy, Eamon, *The Stripping of the Altars: Traditional Religion in England, c.1400–c.1580* (New Haven, CT: Yale University Press, 1992).

—— 'Was Shakespeare a Catholic?', *The Tablet*, 27 April 1996, pp. 536–8.

Dutton, Richard, 'Jonson, Shakespeare and the Exorcists', *SS* 58 (2005), 15–22.

Dutton, Richard, Alison Findlay, and Richard Wilson (eds), *Region, Religion and Patronage: Lancastrian Shakespeare* (Manchester: Manchester University Press, 2003).

—— *Theatre and Religion: Lancastrian Shakespeare* (Manchester: Manchester University Press, 2003).

Edelman, Charles, *Brawl Ridiculous: Swordfighting in Shakespeare's Plays* (Manchester: Manchester University Press, 1992).

Elam, Keir, '"In What Chapter of His Bosom?": Reading Shakespeare's Bodies', in *Alternative Shakespeares Vol. 2*, Terence Hawkes (London: Routledge, 1996), pp.140–63.

Ellis, David, 'Biographical Uncertainty and Shakespeare', *Essays in Criticism* 55 (2005), 193–208.

—— *That Man Shakespeare* (Hastings: Helm Information, 2005).

Felperin, Howard, *The Uses of the Canon: Elizabethan Literature and Contemporary Theory* (Oxford: Clarendon Press, 1990).

Fernie, Ewan (ed.), *Spiritual Shakespeares* (London: Routledge: 2005).

Ferrell, Lori Anne, 'Kneeling and the Body Politic', in *Religion, Literature, and Politics in Post-Reformation England, 1540–1688*, ed. Donna B. Hamilton and Richard Strier (Cambridge: Cambridge University Press, 1996), pp. 70–92.

Findlay, Alison, *A Feminist Perspective on Renaissance Drama* (Oxford: Blackwell, 1999).

—— '"One that's Dead is Quick": Virgin Re-Birth in *All's Well that Ends Well*', in *Marian Moments in Early Modern British Drama*, ed. Regina Buccola and Lisa Hopkins (Aldershot: Ashgate, 2007), pp. 35–46.

Fleming, Juliet, 'Whitewash and the Scene of Writing', *SSt* 28 (2000), 133–8.

Ford, Boris (ed.), *The Cambridge Guide to the Arts in Britain: Vol. 3 Renaissance and Reformation* (Cambridge: Cambridge University Press, 1989).

Fowler, Alastair, 'Enter Speed', *TLS*, 4 February 2005, pp. 3–5.

Freeman, Arthur, and Paul Grinke, 'Four New Shakespeare Quartos', *TLS*, 5 April 2002, pp. 17–18.

Fumerton, Patricia, and Simon Hunt (eds), *Renaissance Culture and the Everyday* (Philadelphia, PA: University of Pennsylvania Press, 1999).

Gallagher, Lowell, *Medusa's Gaze: Casuistry and Conscience in the Renaissance* (Stanford, CA: Stanford University Press, 1991).

Gent, Lucy (ed.), *Albion's Classicism: The Visual Arts in Britain, 1550–1660* (New Haven, CT: Yale University Press, 1995).

Gerrish, B. A., *Grace and Gratitude: The Eucharistic Theology of John Calvin* (Edinburgh: T&T Clark, 1993).

Gibson, Marion, *Possession, Puritanism and Print: Darrell, Harsnett, Shakespeare and the Elizabethan Exorcism Controversy* (London: Pickering and Chatto, 2006).

Gless, Darryl J., *Measure for Measure, the Law, and the Convent* (Princeton, NJ: Princeton University Press, 1979).

Goy-Blanquet, Dominique, *Shakespeare's Early History Plays: From Chronicle to Stage* (Oxford: Oxford University Press, 2003).

Greenblatt, Stephen, *Shakespearean Negotiations: The Circulation of Social Energy in Renaissance England* (Berkeley, CA: University of California Press, 1988).

—— *Hamlet in Purgatory* (Princeton, NJ: Princeton University Press, 2001).

—— *Will in the World: How Shakespeare became Shakespeare* (London: Jonathan Cape, 2004).

Gregerson, Linda, *The Reformation of the Subject: Spenser, Milton, and the English Protestant Epic* (Cambridge: Cambridge University Press, 1995).

Gregory, Tobias, 'Shadowing Intervention: On the Politics of *The Faerie Queene* Book 5 Cantos 10–12', *ELH* 67 (2000), 365–97.

Griffin, Benjamin, 'The Birth of the History Play: Saint, Sacrifice and Reformation', *SEL* 39 (1999), 217–37.

Groves, Beatrice, *Texts and Traditions: Religion in Shakespeare, 1592–1604* (Oxford: Clarendon Press, 2007).

Gutierrez, Nancy A., 'Gender and Value in "1 Henry VI": The Role of Joan de Pucelle', *Theatre Journal* 42 (1990), 183–93.

Haigh, Christopher (ed.), *The English Reformation Revised* (Cambridge: Cambridge University Press, 1987).

Haigh, Christopher, *English Reformations: Religion, Politics, and Society Under the Tudors* (Oxford: Clarendon Press, 1993).

Hallett, Nicky, *Witchcraft, Exorcism and the Politics of Possession in a Seventeenth-Century Convent: 'How Sister Ursula was Once Bewitched and Sister Margaret Twice'* (Aldershot: Ashgate, 2007).

Hamilton, Donna B., and Richard Strier (eds), *Religion, Literature, and Politics in Post-Reformation England, 1540–1688* (Cambridge: Cambridge University Press, 1996).

Hamlin, Hannibal, Review of David Beauregard, *Catholic Theology in Shakespeare's Plays*, *SQ* 59.4 (2008), 506–8.

Harbage, Alfred, '*Love's Labour's Lost* and the Early Shakespeare', *PQ* 41 (1962), 18–36.

Hardin, Richard F., 'Chronicles and Mythmaking in Shakespeare's Joan of Arc', *SS* 42 (1990), 25–35.

Harrawood, Michael, 'High-Stomached Lords: Imagination, Force and the Body in Shakespeare's *Henry VI* Plays', *Journal for Early Modern Cultural Studies* 7 (2007), 78–95.

Harris, Max, *Theatre and Incarnation* (London: Macmillan, 1990).

Hass, Andrew, David Jasper, and Elisabeth Jay (eds), *The Oxford Handbook of English Literature and Theology* (Oxford: Oxford University Press, 2007).

Hassel, R. Chris, *Shakespeare's Religious Language: A Dictionary* (London: Continuum, 2005).

Hattaway, Michael, 'Possessing Edgar: Aspects of *King Lear* in Performance', in *Shakespeare Performed: Essays in Honor of R. A. Foakes*, ed. Grace Ioppolo (Newark, DE: University of Delaware Press, 2000), pp. 198–215.

Hattaway, Michael (ed.), *A Companion to English Renaissance Literature and Culture* (Oxford: Blackwell, 2000).

Hauser, Arnold, *Mannerism* (London: Routledge, 1966).

Hawkes, Terence, (ed.), *Alternative Shakespeares Vol. 2* (London: Routledge, 1996).

Healy, Thomas, 'Selves, States, and Sectarianism in Early Modern England', *English* 44 (1995), 193–213.

Hibbard, Caroline M., 'Early Stuart Catholicism: Revisions and Re-revisions', *Journal of Modern History* 52 (1980), 1–34.

Hillman, David, and Carlo Mazzio (eds), *The Body in Parts: Fantasies of Corporeality in Early Modern Europe* (New York: Routledge, 1997).

Hillman, Richard, *Shakespeare, Marlowe and the Politics of France* (Basingstoke: Palgrave Macmillan, 2002).

Holden, Anthony, *William Shakespeare* (London: Abacus, 2000).

Holland, Peter, 'Theseus' Shadows in *A Midsummer Night's Dream*', *SS* 47 (1994), 139–52.

Holmes, Peter, 'The Authorship and Early Reception of a *Conference about the Next Succession to the Crown of England*', *The Historical Journal* 23 (1980), 415–29.

—— *Resistance and Compromise: The Political Thought of the Elizabethan Catholics* (Cambridge: Cambridge University Press, 1982).

Honan, Park, *Shakespeare: A Life* (Oxford: Oxford University Press, 1998).

Honigmann, E. A. J., *Shakespeare: The 'Lost Years'*, 2nd edn (Manchester: Manchester University Press, 1998).

Howard, Clare M., *English Travellers of the Renaissance* (London: John Lane, 1914).

Howard, Maurice, and Nigel Llewellyn, 'Painting and Imagery', in *The Cambridge Guide to the Arts in Britain: Vol. 3 Renaissance and Reformation*, ed. Boris Ford (Cambridge: Cambridge University Press, 1989), pp. 223–59.

Hunt, Maurice, *Shakespeare's Religious Allusiveness* (Aldershot: Ashgate, 2004).

Hurstfield, Joel, 'The Succession Struggle in Late Elizabethan England', in *Elizabethan Government and Society*, ed. S. T. Bindoff, Joel Hurstfield, and C. H. Williams (London: Athlone Press, 1961), pp. 369–96.

Hutson, Lorna, 'From Penitent to Suspect: Law, Purgatory, and Renaissance Drama', *HLQ* 65 (2002), 295–319.

Ioppolo, Grace (ed.), *Shakespeare Performed: Essays in Honor of R. A. Foakes* (Newark, DE: University of Delaware Press, 2000).

Jackson, Gabriele Bernhard, 'Topical Ideology: Witches, Amazons, and Shakespeare's Joan of Arc', *ELR* 18 (1988), 40–65.

Jardine, Lisa, *Still Harping on Daughters: Women and Drama in the Age of Shakespeare* (Brighton: Harvester, 1983).

Jasper, Alison, 'Body and Word', in *The Oxford Handbook of English Literature and Theology*, ed. Andrew Hass, David Jasper, and Elisabeth Jay (Oxford: Oxford University Press, 2007), pp. 776–92.

Jensen, Phebe, 'Recusancy, Festivity and Community', in *Region, Religion and Patronage: Lancastrian Shakespeare*, ed. Richard Dutton, Alison Findlay, and Richard Wilson (Manchester: Manchester University Press, 2003), pp. 101–20.

—— *Religion and Revelry in Shakespeare's Festive World* (Cambridge: Cambridge University Press, 2008).

Johnstone, Nathan, *The Devil and Demonism in Early Modern England* (Cambridge: Cambridge University Press, 2006).

Jones, Ann Rosalind, and Peter Stallybrass, *Renaissance Clothing and the Materials of Memory* (Cambridge: Cambridge University Press, 2000).

Jones, Emrys, *The Origins of Shakespeare* (Oxford: Clarendon Press, 1977).

Jones, Malcolm, 'The English Print, *c*.1550–*c*.1650', in *A Companion to English Renaissance Literature and Culture*, ed. Michael Hattaway (Oxford: Blackwell, 2000), pp. 352–66.

Kallendorf, Hilaire, *Exorcism and Its Texts: Subjectivity in Early Modern Literature of England and Spain* (Toronto: University of Toronto Press, 2003).

Kamaralli, Anna, 'Writing About Motive: Isabella, the Duke and Moral Authority', *SS* 58 (2005), 48–59.

Kamps, Ivo (ed.), *Shakespeare Left and Right* (New York: Routledge, 1991).

Kastan, David Scott (ed.), *A Companion to Shakespeare* (Oxford: Blackwell, 1999).

Kaula, David, 'Autolycus' Trumpery', *SEL* 16 (1976), 287–303.

Kelly, Faye L., 'Oaths in Shakespeare's *Henry VI* Plays', *SQ* 24 (1973), 357–71.

Kemp, Brian, *English Church Monuments* (London: Batsford, 1980).

Kilroy, Gerard, *Edmund Campion: Memory and Transcription* (Aldershot: Ashgate, 2005).

King, Ros, *Cymbeline: Constructions of Britain* (Aldershot: Ashgate, 2005).

Kirk, Andrew M., 'Marlowe and the Disordered Face of French History', *SEL* 35.2 (1995), 193–213.

Kirsch, Arthur, *Shakespeare and the Experience of Love* (Cambridge: Cambridge University Press, 1981).

Knapp, James A., 'Visual and Ethical Truth in *The Winter's Tale*', *SQ* 55 (2004), 253–78.

Knapp, Jeffrey, *Shakespeare's Tribe: Church, Nation, and Theater in Renaissance England* (Chicago, IL: University of Chicago Press, 2002).

Knight, G. Wilson, *The Wheel of Fire* (London: Oxford University Press, 1930).

Kozuka, Takashi, and J. R. Mulryne (eds), *Shakespeare, Marlowe, Jonson: New Directions in Biography* (Aldershot: Ashgate, 2006).

Lake, Peter, 'Anti-Popery: The Structure of a Prejudice', in *Conflict in Early Stuart England: Studies in Religion and Politics, 1603–1642*, ed. Richard Cust and Ann Hughes (London: Longman, 1989), pp. 72–106.

——'Religious Identities in Shakespeare's England', in *A Companion to Shakespeare*, ed. David Scott Kastan (Oxford: Blackwell, 1999), pp. 57–84.

Lake, Peter, with Michael Questier, *The Antichrist's Lewd Hat: Protestants, Papists and Players in Post-Reformation England* (New Haven, CT: Yale University Press, 2002).

Lamb, Mary Ellen, 'The Nature of Topicality in "Love's Labour's Lost"', *SS* 38 (1985), 49–59.

Laven, Mary, *Virgins of Venice: Enclosed Lives and Broken Vows in the Renaissance Convent* (London: Viking, 2002).

Leggatt, Alexander, 'Substitution in *Measure for Measure*', *SQ* 39 (1988), 342–59.

——*Jacobean Public Theatre* (London: Routledge, 1992).

Lévinas, Emmanuel, *The Levinas Reader*, ed. Seán Hand (Oxford: Blackwell, 1989).

Levine, Nina, *Women's Matters: Politics, Gender, and Nation in Shakespeare's Early History Plays* (Newark, DE: University of Delaware Press, 1998).

Lewis, Cynthia, '"Derived Honesty and Achieved Goodness": Doctrines of Grace in *All's Well that Ends Well*', *Renaissance and Reformation* 14 (1990), 147–70.

Lim, Walter S. H., 'Knowledge and Belief in *The Winter's Tale*', *SEL* 41 (2001), 317–34.

Llewellyn, Nigel, *Funeral Monuments in Post-Reformation England* (Cambridge: Cambridge University Press, 2000).

Low, Anthony, Review of Maurice Hunt, *Shakespeare's Religious Allusiveness*, *SQ* 57.3 (2006), 359–61.

Lupton, Julia Reinhard, *Afterlives of the Saints: Hagiography, Typology, and Renaissance Literature* (Stanford, CA: Stanford University Press, 1996).

MacIntyre, Jean, *Costumes and Scripts in the Elizabethan Theatres* (Edmonton: University of Alberta Press, 1992).

Magedanz, Stacy, 'Public Justice and Private Mercy in *Measure for Measure*', *SEL* 44.2 (2004), 317–32.

Maggi, Armando, *Satan's Rhetoric: A Study of Renaissance Demonology* (Chicago, IL: University of Chicago Press, 2001).

Magnussen, Lynne, 'Scoff Power in *Love's Labour's Lost* and the Inns of Court: Language in Context', *SS* 57 (2004), 196–208.

——'To "Gase So Much at the Fine Stranger": Armado and the Politics of English in *Love's Labour's Lost*', in *Shakespeare and the Cultures of Performance*, ed. Paul Yachnin and Patricia Badir (Aldershot: Ashgate, 2008), pp. 53–68.

Maguire, Laurie, *Shakespeare's Names* (Oxford: Oxford University Press, 2007).

——(ed.), *How to Do Things with Shakespeare* (Blackwell: Oxford, 2008).

Malone, Edmund, *An Inquiry into the Authenticity of Certain Miscellaneous Papers and Legal Instruments* (London, 1796).

Manning, Roger B., *Hunters and Poachers: A Cultural and Social History of Unlawful Hunting in England, 1485–1640* (Oxford: Clarendon Press, 1993).

Marcus, Leah S., *Puzzling Shakespeare: Local Reading and Its Discontents* (Berkeley, CA: University of California Press, 1988).

Marotti, Arthur F., *Religious Ideology and Cultural Fantasy: Catholic and Anti-Catholic Discourses in Early Modern England* (Notre Dame, IN: University of Notre Dame Press, 2005).

Marshall, Peter, *Beliefs and the Dead in Reformation England* (Oxford: Oxford University Press, 2002).

Maus, Katharine Eisaman, 'Transfer of Title in *Love's Labor's Lost*: Language, Individualism, Gender', in *Shakespeare Left and Right*, ed. Ivo Kamps (New York: Routledge, 1991), 205–23.

——*Inwardness and Theater in the English Renaissance* (Chicago, IL: University of Chicago Press, 1995).

Mayer, Jean-Christophe, *Shakespeare's Hybrid Faith: History, Religion, and the Stage* (Basingstoke: Palgrave Macmillan, 2006).

Mazzaro, Jerome, 'Shakespeare's "Books of Memory": *1* and *2 Henry VI*', *Comparative Drama* 35 (2001–2), 393–414.

Mazzola, Elizabeth, *The Pathology of the English Renaissance: Sacred Remains and Holy Ghosts* (Leiden: Brill, 1998).

McCabe, Richard A., 'Elizabethan Satire and the Bishops' Ban of 1599', *The Yearbook of English Studies* 11 (1981), 188–93.

McClain, Lisa, *Lest We Be Damned: Practical Innovation and Lived Experience Among Catholics in Protestant England, 1559–1642* (New York: Routledge, 2004).

McCoog, Thomas (ed.), *The Reckoned Expense: Edmund Campion and the Early English Jesuits: Essays in Celebration of the First Centenary of Campion Hall, Oxford (1896–1996)*, 2nd edn (Rome: Institutum Historicum Societatis Iesu, 2007).

McCoog, Thomas, and Peter Davidson, 'Unreconciled: What Evidence Links Shakespeare and the Jesuits?', *TLS*, 16 March 2007, p. 12.

—— 'Edmund Campion and William Shakespeare: *Much Ado About Nothing?*', in *The Reckoned Expense: Edmund Campion and the Early English Jesuits: Essays in Celebration of the First Centenary of Campion Hall, Oxford (1896–1996)*, 2nd edn, ed. Thomas McCoog (Rome: Institutum Historicum Societatis Iesu, 2007), pp.165–85.

McCullough, Peter E., *Sermons at Court: Politics and Religion in Elizabethan and Jacobean Preaching* (Cambridge: Cambridge University Press, 1998).

McEachern, Claire (ed.), *The Cambridge Companion to Shakespearean Tragedy* (Cambridge: Cambridge University Press, 2002).

McGrath, Patrick, and Joy Rowe, 'The Elizabethan Priests: Their Harbourers and Helpers', *Recusant History* 19 (1989), 209–33.

McMullan, Gordon, and David Matthews (eds), *Reading the Medieval in Early Modern England* (Cambridge: Cambridge University Press, 2007).

Mercer, Eric, *English Art, 1553–1625* (Oxford: Clarendon Press, 1962).

Milton, Anthony, *Catholic and Reformed: The Roman and Protestant Churches in English Protestant Thought, 1600–1640* (Cambridge: Cambridge University Press, 1995).

Milward, Peter, *Shakespeare's Religious Background* (London: Sidgwick & Jackson, 1973).

—— *Religious Controversies of the Elizabethan Age: A Survey of Printed Sources* (London: Scolar Press, 1977).

—— *Religious Controversies of the Jacobean Age: A Survey of Printed Sources* (London: Scolar Press, 1978).

—— Letter, *TLS*, 28 March 2007.

Mincoff, M., 'The Composition of *Henry VI, Part I*', *SQ* 16 (1965), 279–87.

Morris, John (ed.), *The Troubles of Our Catholic Forefathers*, 2nd series (London: Burns and Oates, 1875).

Muir, Kenneth, 'Samuel Harsnett and *King Lear*', *RES* 2 (1951), 11–21.

Murphy, John L., *Darkness and Devils: Exorcism and King Lear* (Athens, OH: Ohio University Press, 1984).

Murray, Molly, *The Poetics of Conversion in Early Modern English Literature: Verse and Change from Donne to Dryden* (Cambridge: Cambridge University Press, 2009).

Myers, Anne M., 'Father John Gerard's Object Lessons: Relics and Devotional Objects in *Autobiography of a Hunted Priest*', in *Catholic Culture in Early Modern England*, ed. Ronald Corthell, Frances E. Dolan, Christopher Highley, and Arthur F. Marotti (Notre Dame, IN: University of Notre Dame Press, 2007), pp. 216–35.

Neill, Michael, *Issues of Death: Mortality and Identity in English Renaissance Tragedy* (Oxford: Clarendon Press, 1997).

—— 'The Defence of Contraries: Skeptical Paradox in *A King and No King*', SEL 21 (1981), 319–32.

Nuttall, A. D., *William Shakespeare: The Winter's Tale*', Studies in English Literature 26 (London: Edward Arnold, 1966).

—— '*The Winter's Tale*: Ovid Transformed', in *Shakespeare's Ovid: The Metamorphoses in the Plays and Poems*, ed. A. B. Taylor (Cambridge: Cambridge University Press, 2000), pp. 135–49.

O'Connell, Michael, *The Idolatrous Eye: Iconoclasm and Theater in Early-Modern England* (New York: Oxford University Press, 2000).

Owens, Margaret E., *Stages of Dismemberment: The Fragmented Body in Late Medieval and Early Modern Drama* (Newark, DE: University of Delaware Press, 2005).

Palfrey, Simon, *Doing Shakespeare* (London: Arden Shakespeare, 2005).

Parker, Patricia, 'Preposterous Reversals: *Love's Labor's Lost*', MLQ 54 (1993), 435–82.

Parmelee, Lisa Ferraro, *Good Newes From Fraunce: French Anti-League Propaganda in Late Elizabethan England* (Rochester, NY: University of Rochester Press, 1996).

Paster, Gail Kern, *The Body Embarrassed: Drama and the Disciplines of Shame in Early Modern England* (Ithaca, NY: Cornell University Press, 1993).

Pelikan, Jaroslav, *The Christian Tradition: A History of the Development of Doctrine*, 5 vols, iv (Chicago, IL: University of Chicago Press, 1984).

Pendleton, Thomas A. (ed.), *Henry VI: Critical Essays* (London: Routledge, 2001).

Poole, Kristen Elizabeth, 'Garbled Martyrdom in Christopher Marlowe's *The Massacre at Paris*', Comparative Drama 32.1 (1998), 1–25.

Potter, Ursula, 'The Naming of Holofernes in *Love's Labour's Lost*', ELN 38.2 (2000), 11–24.

Prescott, Anne Lake, 'Foreign Policy in Fairyland: Henri IV and Spenser's Burbon', *Spenser Studies* 14 (2001), 189–214.

Preston, Claire, 'Sidney's Arcadian Poetics: A Medicine of Cherries and the Philosophy of Cavaliers', in *English Renaissance Prose: History, Language, and Politics*, ed. Neil Rhodes (Tempe, AZ: Medieval and Renaissance Texts and Studies, 1997), pp. 91–108.

Prior, Mary (ed.), *Women in English Society, 1500–1800* (London: Methuen, 1985).

Questier, Michael C., *Conversion, Politics and Religion in England, 1580–1625* (Cambridge: Cambridge University Press, 1996).

Questier, Michael C., *Catholicism and Community in Early Modern England: Politics, Aristocratic Patronage, and Religion, c.1550–1640* (Cambridge: Cambridge University Press, 2006).

Rackin, Phyllis, 'Anti-Historians: Women's Roles in Shakespeare's Histories', *Theatre Journal* 37 (1985), 329–44.

Relle, Eleanor, 'Some New Marginalia and Poems of Gabriel Harvey', *RES* 23 (1972), 401–16.

Rhatigan, Emma, 'Knees and Elephants: Donne Preaches on Ceremonial Conformity', *John Donne Journal* 23 (2004), 185–213.

Rhodes, Neil (ed.), *English Renaissance Prose: History, Language, and Politics* (Tempe, Arizona: Medieval and Renaissance Texts and Studies, 1997).

Richmond, Hugh, 'Shakespeare's Navarre', *HLQ* 42 (1978–9), 193–216.

Richmond, Velma Bourgeois, *Shakespeare, Catholicism, and Romance* (New York: Continuum, 2000).

Riggs, David, *Shakespeare's Heroical Histories: Henry VI and Its Literary Tradition* (Cambridge, MA: Harvard University Press, 1971).

Rowlands, Marie B., 'Recusant Women, 1560–1640', in *Women in English Society, 1500–1800*, ed. Mary Prior (London: Methuen, 1985), pp. 149–80.

Rutter, Carol Chillington, *Enter the Body: Women and Representation on Shakespeare's Stage* (London: Routledge, 2001).

Ryan, Kiernan, '"Where Hope is Coldest": *All's Well That Ends Well*', in *Spiritual Shakespeares*, ed. Ewan Fernie (London: Routledge, 2005), pp. 28–49.

Ryan, Patrick, 'Shakespeare's Joan and the Great Whore of Babylon', *Renaissance and Reformation* 28 (2004), 55–82.

Sawday, Jonathan, *The Body Emblazoned: Dissection and the Human Body in Renaissance Culture* (London: Routledge, 1995).

Scarisbrick, J. J., *The Reformation and the English People* (Oxford: Blackwell, 1984).

Scarry, Elaine, *The Body in Pain: The Making and Unmaking of the World* (New York: Oxford University Press, 1985).

Scholz, Susanne, *Body Narratives: Writing the Nation and Fashioning the Subject* (Basingstoke: Palgrave Macmillan, 2000).

Schwarz, Kathryn, 'Fearful Simile: Stealing the Breech in Shakespeare's Chronicle Plays', *SQ* 49 (1998), 140–67.

—— '"My Intents are Fix'd": Constant Will in *All's Well that Ends Well*', *SQ* 58 (2007), 200–27.

Scott, Charlotte, *Shakespeare and the Idea of the Book* (Oxford: Oxford University Press, 2007).

Scott, Sarah, 'The Empress of Babylon's "Carbuncles and Rich Stones"', *Early Theatre* 7 (2004), 67–95.

Scott-Warren, Jason, 'Harington, Sir John (*bap.* 1560, *d.* 1612)', *Oxford Dictionary of National Biography* (Oxford: Oxford University Press, 2004), online edn, May 2010 <http://www.oxforddnb.com.eresources.shef.ac.uk/view/article/12326?docPos = 4, accessed 24 August 2012>.

Sell, Roger D., and Anthony W. Johnson (eds), *Writing and Religion in England, 1558–1689: Studies in Community-Making and Cultural Memory* (Aldershot: Ashgate, 2009).

Selleck, Nancy, *The Interpersonal Idiom in Shakespeare, Donne and Early Modern Culture* (Basingstoke: Palgrave Macmillan, 2008).

Shagan, Ethan (ed.), *Catholics and the 'Protestant Nation': Religious Politics and Identity in Early Modern England* (Manchester: Manchester University Press, 2005).

Shaheen, Naseeb, *Biblical References in Shakespeare's Plays* (Newark, DE: University of Delaware Press, 1999).

Shannon, Laurie, 'Poor, Bare, Forked: Animal Sovereignty, Human Negative Exceptionalism, and the Natural History of *King Lear*', *SQ* 60.2 (2009), 168–96.

Shapiro, James, *1599: A Year in the Life of William Shakespeare* (London: Faber and Faber, 2005).

Shell, Alison, *Catholicism, Controversy and the English Literary Imagination, 1558–1660* (Cambridge: Cambridge University Press, 1999).

—— 'Why Didn't Shakespeare Write Religious Verse?', in *Shakespeare, Marlowe, Jonson: New Directions in Biography*, ed. Takashi Kozuka and J. R. Mulryne (Aldershot: Ashgate, 2006), pp. 85–112.

—— 'Divine Muses, Catholic Poets and Pilgrims to St Winifred's Well: Literary Communities in Francis Chetwinde's "New Hellicon" (1642)', in *Writing and Religion in England, 1558–1689: Studies in Community-Making and Cultural Memory*, ed. Roger D. Sell and Anthony W. Johnson (Aldershot: Ashgate, 2009), pp. 273–88.

—— *Shakespeare and Religion* (London: Arden Shakespeare, 2010).

Sherlock, Peter, *Monuments and Memory in Early Modern England* (Aldershot: Ashgate, 2008).

Shorney, David, *Protestant Nonconformity and Roman Catholicism: A Guide to Sources in the Public Record Office* (London: PRO Publications, 1996).

Shuger, Debora K., *Habits of Thought in the English Renaissance: Religion, Politics, and the Dominant Culture* (Berkeley, CA: University of California Press, 1990).

—— *The Renaissance Bible: Scholarship, Sacrifice and Subjectivity* (Berkeley, CA: University of California Press, 1994).

—— *Political Theologies in Shakespeare's England: The Sacred and the State in Measure for Measure* (Basingstoke: Palgrave, 2001).

Simpson, Lynne M., 'The Failure to Mourn in *All's Well that Ends Well*', *SSt* 22 (1994), 172–88.

Slights, Jessica, and Michael Morgan Holmes, 'Isabella's Order: Religious Acts and Personal Desires in *Measure for Measure*', *Studies in Philology*, 95 (1998), 263–92.

Sluhovsky, Moshe, *Believe Not Every Spirit: Possession, Mysticism, and Discernment in Early Modern Catholicism* (Chicago, IL: University of Chicago Press, 2007).

Smith, Bruce R. (ed.), *Shakespeare Studies: Body Work* (2001).

Snyder, Susan, *Shakespeare: A Wayward Journey* (Newark, DE: University of Delaware Press, 2002).

Southern, A. C., *English Recusant Prose 1559–1582* (London: Sands, 1950).

Staines, John D., 'Radical Pity: Responding to Spectacles of Violence in *King Lear*', in *Staging Pain, 1580–1800: Violence and Trauma in British Theater*, ed. James Allard and Matthew R. Martin (Farnham: Ashgate, 2009), pp. 75–92.

Stapleton M. L., '"Shine it like a Comet of Revenge": Seneca, John Studley, and Shakespeare's Joan la Pucelle', *Comparative Literature Studies* 31 (1994), 229–50.

Streete, Adrian, 'Charity and Law in *Love's Labour's Lost*: A Calvinist Analogue?', *Notes and Queries* 49 (2002), 224–5.

—— 'Reforming Signs: Semiotics, Calvinism and Clothing in Sixteenth-Century England', *Literature and History* 12 (2003), 1–18.

—— *Protestantism and Drama in Early Modern England* (Cambridge: Cambridge University Press, 2009).

Sullivan, Ceri, *Dismembered Rhetoric: English Recusant Writing, 1580–1603* (London: Associated University Presses, 1995).

Sullivan, Rebecca, 'Breaking Habits: Gender, Class, and the Sacred in the Dress of Women Religious', in *Consuming Fashion: Adorning the Transnational Body*, ed. Anne Brydon and Sandra Niessen (Oxford: Berg, 1998).

Sutherland, N. M., *Henry IV of France and the Politics of Religion, 1572–1596*, 2 vols (Bristol: Elm Bank, 2002).

Tayler, E. W., '*King Lear* and Negation', *ELR* 20 (1990), 17–39.

Taylor, A. B. (ed.), *Shakespeare's Ovid: The Metamorphoses in the Plays and Poems* (Cambridge: Cambridge University Press, 2000).

Taylor, Dennis, and David Beauregard (eds), *Shakespeare and the Culture of Christianity in Early Modern England* (New York: Fordham University Press, 2003).

Taylor, Gary "Swounds Revisited: Theatrical, Editorial, and Literary Expurgation', in *Shakespeare Reshaped, 1606–1623*, ed. Gary Taylor and John Jowett (Oxford: Clarendon Press, 1993), pp. 51–106.

—— 'Forms of Opposition: Shakespeare and Middleton', *ELR* 24 (1994), 283–314.

—— 'Shakespeare and Others: The Authorship of *Henry the Sixth, Part One*', *Medieval and Renaissance Drama in England* 7 (1995), 145–205.

—— 'Divine [ ]sences', *Shakespeare Survey* 54 (2001), 13–30.

—— 'The Cultural Politics of Maybe', in *Theatre and Religion: Lancastrian Shakespeare*, ed. Richard Dutton, Alison Findlay, and Richard Wilson (Manchester: Manchester University Press, 2003), pp. 242–58.

Taylor, Gary, and John Jowett (eds), *Shakespeare Reshaped, 1606–1623* (New York: Oxford University Press, 1993).

Tentler, Thomas N., *Sin and Confession on the Eve of the Reformation* (Princeton, NJ: Princeton University Press, 1977).

Thomas, Keith, *Religion and the Decline of Magic* (New York: Scribner, 1971).

Bibliography   231

Thomas, Vivian, *The Moral Universe of Shakespeare's Problem Plays* (London: Croom Helm, 1987).
Tiffany, Grace, *Love's Pilgrimage: The Holy Journey in English Renaissance Literature* (Cranbury, NJ: University of Delaware Press, 2006).
Tricomi, Albert H., 'The Witty Idealization of the French Court in *Love's Labor's Lost*', SSt 12 (1979), 25–33.
Tripp, David, 'The Image of the Body in the Formative Phases of the Protestant Reformation', in *Religion and the Body*, ed. Sarah Coakley (Cambridge: Cambridge University Press, 1997), pp. 131–52.
Vickers, Brian, 'Incomplete Shakespeare: or, Denying Coauthorship in *1 Henry VI*', SQ 58 (2007), 311–52.
Voss, Paul, 'The Antifraternal Tradition in English Renaissance Drama', *Cithara* 33 (1993), 3–16.
—— *Elizabethan News Pamphlets: Shakespeare, Spenser, Marlowe and the Birth of Journalism* (Pittsburgh, PA: Duquesne University Press, 2001).
Walker, D. P., *Unclean Spirits: Possession and Exorcism in France and England in the Late Sixteenth and Early Seventeenth Centuries* (London: Scolar Press, 1981).
Walsh, Brian, '"Unkind Division": The Double Absence of Performing History in *1 Henry VI*', SQ 55 (2004), 119–47.
Walsham, Alexandra, *Church Papists: Catholicism, Conformity and Confessional Polemic in Early Modern England* (Woodbridge: Boydell Press for the Royal Historical Society, 1993).
—— '"Domme Preachers"?: Post-Reformation Catholicism and the Culture of Print', *Past and Present* 168 (2000), 72–123.
Warren, Roger, '"Contrarieties Agree": An Aspect of Dramatic Technique in "Henry VI"', SS 37 (1984), 75–83.
Waterfield, John, *The Heart of his Mystery: Shakespeare and the Catholic Faith in England Under Elizabeth and James* (Bloomington, IN: iUniverse, 2009).
Watson, Robert N., 'False Immortality in *Measure for Measure*: Comic Means, Tragic Ends', SQ 41.4 (1990), 411–32.
Weimann, Robert, and Douglas Bruster, *Shakespeare and the Power of Performance* (Cambridge: Cambridge University Press, 2008).
Williams, Gordon, *A Dictionary of Sexual Language and Imagery in Shakespearean and Stuart Literature*, 3 vols (London: Athlone, 1994).
Williams, Richard L., 'Collecting and Religion in Late Sixteenth-Century England', in *The Evolution of English Collecting: Receptions of Italian Art in the Tudor and Stuart Periods*, ed. Edward Chaney (New Haven, CT: Yale University Press, 2003), pp. 159–200.
Williamson, Elizabeth, *The Materiality of Early Modern English Drama* (Farnham: Ashgate, 2009).
Willis, Deborah, 'Shakespeare and the English Witch-Hunts: Enclosing the Maternal Body', in *Enclosure Acts*, ed. John Michael Archer and Richard Burt (Ithaca, NY: Cornell University Press, 1994), pp. 96–120.

Wilson, Ian, *Shakespeare: The Evidence: Unlocking the Mysteries of the Man and His Work* (London: Headline, 1993).

Wilson, Richard, *Secret Shakespeare* (Manchester: Manchester University Press, 2004).

——Letter, *TLS*, 18 February 2005.

Wolf, Amy, 'Shakespeare and Harsnett: "Pregnant to Good Pity?"', *SEL* 38 (1998), 251–64.

Wolfe, Michael, *The Conversion of Henri IV: Politics, Power and Religious Belief in Early Modern France* (Cambridge, MA: Harvard University Press, 1993).

Wood, Michael, *In Search of Shakespeare* (London: BBC, 2003).

Woods, Gillian, 'The Contexts of *The Trial of Chivalry*', *Notes and Queries* 252.3 (2007), 313–18.

——'Catholicism and Conversion in *Love's Labour's Lost*', in *How to Do Things with Shakespeare*', ed. Laurie Maguire (Oxford: Blackwell, 2008), pp. 101–30.

——'The Confessional Identities of *'Tis Pity She's a Whore*', in *'Tis Pity She's a Whore: A Critical Guide*, ed. Lisa Hopkins (London: Continuum, 2009), pp. 114–35.

——' "Strange Discourse": The Controversial Subject of *Sir Thomas More*', *Renaissance Drama* 39 (2011), 3–35.

Worden, Blair, *The Sound of Virtue: Philip Sidney's 'Arcadia' and Elizabethan Politics* (New Haven, CT: Yale University Press, 1996).

Yachnin, Paul, and Patricia Badir (eds), *Shakespeare and the Cultures of Performance* (Aldershot: Ashgate, 2008).

Zimmerman, Susan, *The Early Modern Corpse and Shakespeare's Theatre* (Edinburgh: Edinburgh University Press, 2005).

Index